BLACK IDENTITIES

Mary C. Waters

BLACK IDENTITIES

WEST INDIAN

IMMIGRANT

DREAMS

AND AMERICAN

REALITIES

RUSSELL SAGE FOUNDATION

New York

HARVARD UNIVERSITY PRESS

Cambridge, Massachusetts & London, England

First Harvard University Press paperback edition, 2001

Library of Congress Cataloging-in-Publication Data

Waters, Mary C.
Black identities : West Indian immigrant dreams and
American realities / Mary C. Waters.
p. cm.
Includes bibliographical references and index.
ISBN 0-674-00067-6 (cloth)
ISBN: 0-674-00724-7 (pbk.)
1. West Indian Americans—Ethnic identity.
2. West Indian Americans—Race identity.
3. West Indian Americans—Cultural assimilation.
4. Immigrants—United States—Social conditions.
5. United States—Ethnic relations.
6. United States—Race relations.   I. Title.
E184.W54W38   1999
305.896'9729073—dc21   99-33813

For Ric

ACKNOWLEDGMENTS

I find that when I try to write I am productive and enjoy the process about 5 percent of the time. The other 95 percent is pretty miserable. I am either producing bad drafts that are better destroyed, going down false alleys, worrying that I have nothing new to say, worrying that what I do have to say is wrong, or just plain wishing I was doing something else. Something easier. As a result I would never have produced this book without a lot of help. I needed encouragement that it was worth doing, money to do the actual work, support in the field, time to write, experts to help me get the facts right, friends to help me decide which drafts to keep and which ones to destroy, and, above all, a life apart from the book to help me keep the whole thing in perspective.

I was lucky to find encouragement and money, although I could have used more time. A fellowship from the John Simon Guggenheim Foundation allowed me to analyze my data and begin the process of writing. A small grant from the Milton Fund at Harvard gave me the opportunity to get started and a sabbatical at Harvard years later permitted me to finish the writing. The bulk of the project was supported by the Russell Sage Foundation. The Foundation's president, Eric Wanner, saw the potential in this project from the beginning. He funded the project and gave me a year at the Foundation to work on it. He asked intelligent and informed questions that enriched my thinking and the work, and was extraordinarily patient in waiting for the finished product. The staff at Russell Sage were spectacular and made it a pleasure to come to work every day. Thanks especially to Lisa Nachtigall and Eileen Ferrer. Though I was supposed to be writing while at Russell Sage, I was actually doing research in the field that year. All of the scholars who were there listened to my tales from the field over lunch and helped me to think through issues I needed to ask about. Robert Merton was very enthusiastic about the project and gave me enormously helpful feedback on an early draft of a chapter. Larry Aber's knowledge of adolescent and child development opened up a new field for me to consider. Eroll Rickets was a gracious "native informant" who shared his scholarly insights and his own experiences as a Jamaican immigrant with me. Christopher Jencks and Jane Mansbridge not only listened to me at lunch, they often cooked me dinner and, together with Nathaniel, helped me to make sense of everything I was learning during the day.

Many other scholars encouraged, corrected, and inspired me. Herb Gans was enlisted by Eric to review my grant proposal, and his enthusiasm and guidance at an early stage greatly improved the study design. I owe a special debt of gratitude to the late William Alonso. He always thought this was a terrific project, gave me wonderful feedback on my ideas and my writing, and was a good friend. As a beginner in the field of Caribbean studies I was very lucky to meet Nancy Foner—she shared her work and expertise with me, kept me from making several errors, and, most important, became a good friend. I also got to know Phil Kasinitz because of our shared interest in West Indian immigrants. Little did we know that we would become experts on certain aspects of China as well! Phil shared his expertise on both parts of the world with his characteristic good humor. Phil and John Mollenkopf and I started another project together long before this one was done. As a result they both became cheerleaders for me to finish, and our discussions about the second generation in general shaped many of my ideas about second-generation West Indians in particular. Thanks especially to John for some last-minute computing.

Many other scholars provided advice and feedback on parts of the manuscript, gave me encouragement and support, shared their published and unpublished work, and greatly enriched my ideas. Thanks to Richard Alba, Frank Bean, Roy S. Bryce-Laporte, Steve Cornell, Jennifer Eberhardt, Karl Eschbach, Gary Gerstle, Nathan Glazer, Joyce Hamilton, Nazli Kibria, Micheline Labelle, Michele Lamont, Bonnie Leadbeater, Stan Lieberson, David Lowenthal, Peter Marsden, David Mittelberg, Sue Model, Kathy Newman, Orlando Patterson, Joel Perlmann, Alex Portes, Reuel Rogers, Ruben Rumbaut, Theda Skocpol, Yasemin Soysal, Niobe Way, John Western, Franklin Wilson, William Julius Wilson, Flore Zephir, and Ari Zolberg. Several people gave detailed comments on the entire manuscript. Thanks especially to Roger Waldinger, Marilyn Halter, Doug Massey, Peggy Levitt, Monica McDermott, and Naomi Schneider. Of course, all of these great minds did not always agree with me. I learned a lot from our disagreements, and I am responsible for the mistakes that remain.

I gave talks based on this research at the University of Texas at Austin, the University of Toronto, the University of Pennsylvania, the University of California at San Diego, Columbia University, McGill University, the University of Montreal, Tufts University, the Massachusetts Institute of Technology, Yale University, the University of Washington at Seattle, Northwestern University, the New School for Social Research, Brooklyn College, the City University of New York Graduate Center, Williams College, the Jerome Levy Institute at Bard College, Massachusetts General Hospital, and Cambridge City Hospital. At Harvard I also spoke at the Du Bois Institute, the Center for International Affairs, the Medical Anthropology Program, the Center for Kibbutz Studies, the Murray Research Center, and the Center for Population Studies. I am sure I would have finished much sooner had I stopped talking so much and spent the time writing, but I am also sure that the dialogue with all of the scholars and students I met at these talks, too numerous to mention here, greatly improved my thinking and my writing.

A project of this scope and time frame also includes many other people who worked on it. I owe a special debt of gratitude to my research assistants who conducted interviews, ran data, went to the library, and challenged and enriched my thinking. They include Kayode Owens, Jimmy Phillipe, Diana Davis, Lisa Walke, Crystal Byndloss, Mendis Brown, Cheryl Ault, Maxine Robertson, David Porter, Patricia Blackburn, Laurie Dance, Joe Swingle, Faustina Haynes, Nancy Lopez, Amy Chin, Sarah Song, and Monica McDermott. Several Caribbean-American students at Harvard did their senior theses on one or another aspect of this topic and greatly influenced my thinking on the subject. Thank you to Maggi Apollon, Rhonda Edwards, and Charissa Latabaudiere. The preparation of the manuscript and early drafts and chapters was greatly aided by Lynne Farnum, Suzanne Washington, Mary Quigley, and Liz Gardner. Suzanne Washington also helped me by ferrying all of the tapes to the transcribers whom she found—Brian and Carmen Berenty.

Michael Aronson at Harvard University Press gave me useful feedback on the manuscript. He and David Haproff at the Russell Sage Foundation worked very hard on the many details of copublication. Richard Audet did a terrific job copyediting the manuscript.

Portions of Chapter 4 appeared as "West Indians and African Americans at Work: Structural Differences and Cultural Stereotypes" in Frank Bean and Stephanie Bell Rose, eds., *Immigration and Opportunity: Race, Ethnicity, and Employment in the United States* (New York: Russell Sage Foundation Press, 1999). Portions of Chapter 5 appeared originally as "Explaining the Comfort Factor: West Indian Immigrants Confront American Race Relations" in Michele Lamont, ed., *The Cultural Territories of Race: Black and White Boundaries,* copyright © 1999, The University of Chicago Press and Russell Sage Foundation. All rights reserved. Parts of Chapter 6 contain material that is a substantially revised version of "Immigrant Families at Risk: Factors That Undermine Chances for Success" in Alan Booth, Ann C. Crouter, and Nancy Landale, eds., *Immigration and the Family: Research and Policy on U.S. Immigrants* (Mahwah, N.J.: Lawrence Erlbaum Publishers, 1997). Portions of Chapter 8 appeared originally as "The Intersection of Gender, Race, and Ethnicity in Identity Development of Caribbean American Teens" in Bonnie J. Ross Leadbeater and Niobe Way, eds., *Urban Girls: Resisting Stereotypes, Creating Identities* (New York: New York University Press, 1996). Other parts of Chapter 8 appeared as "Ethnic and Racial Identities of Second Generation Black Immigrants in New York City" in Alejandro Portes, ed., *The New Second Generation* (New York: Russell Sage Foundation Press, 1996).

I am always amazed when I begin interviewing at how open, trusting, and honest people can be. I hope I have done justice to the people I interviewed for this book by presenting their views honestly and fairly. I am extremely grateful for the time and energy these strangers invested in this project. I owe a very special debt to Mrs. Owens and to Kusil Moorley for their help and guidance in the field.

There were times when my writing was in its infancy that only very close friends were allowed to see it. Carolyn Boyes Watson helped me sketch out the structure of the book on a napkin at the Au Bon Pain and endured years of almost daily phone calls about the book's progress. Chris

Williams read early drafts and told me not to throw them out and shared her amazing secret to getting work done, "just do it." Jim Jasper read the whole book and gave me detailed and insightful comments that greatly improved the book and moved it forward when it was stalled.

Many other friends were there to give me encouragement and diversion. Thanks to Mark Boyes Watson, Bahaa Fam, Carol Nowacki, Sandy Waxman, Lucia Benaquisto, Steve Rytina, Martin Button, Judy Auerbach, Helen Schwartz, Robert Halliday, Kwok Kian Woon, Steve Cornell, Deb Umberson, Rose Frisch, Francois Ramaroson, and Luna Razafinary.

My family as usual provides a healthy diversion to matters academic as well as unusual amounts of support and aid. My brother Michael first sparked my interest in this subject when he was teaching in Brooklyn and getting to know his West Indian students. My mother, Margaret Waters, offered a ton of help—contacts in the New York City schools, advice on how to approach the Board of Ed, comments on drafts of chapters, and advice about what to wear at all times. I took all of her advice except the latter. My father, Michael F. X. Waters, was an active observer of the research and writing process, and always showed his belief in my abilities to do just about anything. My mother-in-law, Kay Bayly, was always supportive and interested. My sister Margaret bore the brunt of local support duties as she lives nearby and is a world-class editor and negotiator. My sisters Liz, Anne, and Joan were pressed into sibling-in-service roles on the project more than once. In addition, my brothers and sisters, my in-laws, and my nieces and nephews clipped articles from newspapers that might have been related to the project, put me up when I came through town, lent moral support, and, most of all, helped to divert me throughout the years from anything approaching a single-minded approach to this project. Thanks to Mary Kay Bauer, Tom and Sheila Waters, Joel Robbins, Thomas Battle, John Waters, Pat Cusanelli, Steve Bayly, Linda James, Joan Higbee, Cathy Higbee, Matthew Higbee, Brendan Waters, Savannah James Bayly, Cecelia Waters, Nora Cusanelli, and Sullivan Waters.

My daughter Katie's arrival came long after we expected her. Yet in retrospect her timing, like everything else about her, is perfect. Her imminent arrival forced me to work hard on finishing the book, and her delayed arrival allowed me to actually finish it, since everything always takes longer than one thinks. Her presence in our lives brings us enormous joy and renews my passion for the work contained in this book. Ending racial discrimination and celebrating our common humanity are the goals that led me to this work in the first place. My love for my daughter makes these lofty goals all the more personal and urgent.

I could fill several books with all of the ways I should acknowledge the contributions of my husband, Ric Bayly. Suffice it to say he played a crucial role in making the book happen, he plays the central role in my life, and he is a very good man. I dedicate this book to him.

CONTENTS

TABLES AND MAP

BLACK IDENTITIES

INTRODUCTION

1

I grew up in Brooklyn, New York, in the 1960s and '70s. From 1971 to 1975 I took the subway from my parents' home in Flatbush to my high school in the neighborhood of Park Slope. The neighborhoods of Brooklyn were changing rapidly during those years. Social scientists would describe these changes as white flight, rising immigration, and the growth of black neighborhoods through blockbusting and panic real-estate selling by whites. My own experiences of these changes were less complicated. As a teenager I saw the neighborhood "becoming black." While my liberal parents welcomed the diversity and I felt no fear about this change, I watched with some sadness as my friends and their families quickly bought houses in Long Island or New Jersey, and as the white immigrant neighborhoods of Jews, Italians, and Irish became Puerto Rican and black neighborhoods.

The daily subway trip to high school gave me direct experience of these changes for four years. The subway stops along the IRT were literally changing color, and with each year the complexion of the people boarding the cars would change. I would board at the all-white end of the line at Flatbush Avenue. The next stops—Newkirk, Beverly, Church, Winthrop, Sterling, Park Plaza, Brooklyn Museum, and Grand Army Plaza—changed swiftly during those years. By the time I graduated, only Flatbush Avenue riders were white and the riders boarding at the rest of the stops through Flatbush were black, until one reached the gentrified neighborhood of Park Slope at Grand Army Plaza.

What I did not understand at the time was that, for the most part, it was not black Americans who were moving into these neighborhoods but black immigrants from the Caribbean. The fact that they were immigrants was invisible to me because the only characteristic I noticed about them was their race. It was only years later as the Caribbean presence grew in New York that white New Yorkers began to notice the immigrant backgrounds of the newest black New Yorkers. By 1990 foreign-born blacks made up 4.8% of the entire U.S. black population, but in New York City, where black immigrants are highly concentrated, the immigrants numbered 23% of the city's 1,847,049 non-Hispanic blacks.

One of the ways in which New Yorkers came to recognize the West Indian immigrants in their midst was through their tragic involvement in some of the worst incidents of racial violence in New York in the 1980s and '90s, including the Howard Beach killing, the Korean grocery store boycott in Flatbush, and the Crown Heights riots. In 1987 the Queens neighborhood of Howard Beach became notorious overnight when 23-year-old Michael Griffith, who had immigrated from Trinidad when he was 5 years old, was chased to his death by a white mob. In 1990 a much publicized boycott of a Korean grocery in the Flatbush section of Brooklyn came about because a black customer claimed she had been treated disrespectfully and then attacked by the Korean grocery-store owner. The woman, 46-year-old Jiselaine Felissaint, was a Haitian immigrant. In August 1991 in the Crown Heights neighborhood, a 7-year-old child, Gavin Cato, who had immigrated earlier that year from Guyana with his family, was struck and killed by a car driven by a Hasidic Jew who was part of a motorcade escorting the leader of the Lubavitcher Hasidic sect. A crowd of people gathered, many of whom believed that the black boy had been ignored by the first emergency vehicle—owned by a Jewish ambulance service—that responded to the accident. The crowd became enraged, and as the evening went on demonstrations and riots and looting began. As a result 163 people were arrested, 66 civilians and 173 police officers were injured, and 28 police cars were damaged. A 29-year-old Australian rabbinical student named Yankel Rosenbaum was stabbed to death.

In all three cases the national press reported the racial angle—blacks vs. whites, blacks vs. Koreans, and blacks vs. Jews. The fact that each incident involved an immigrant was sometimes reported in the local New York press, which heightened New Yorkers' awareness of the transformation in the demographics of blacks in the city. But, outside of the city, the immigrants were "invisible" in press accounts. The Crown Heights riots were reported in the press and perceived by many residents as growing out of black and Jewish relations. However, Crown Heights is an unusual neighborhood composed of about 90,000 Caribbean immigrants as well as 35,000 African Americans.[1] While press reports at the time went to great lengths to identify the Hasidic sect of Judaism as the ethnicity of the Jewish people involved, the West Indian immigrants involved were usually referred to as "blacks."[2]

The invisibility of the Caribbean immigrants as immigrants and their visibility as blacks are part of the story I want to tell here.[3] The questions and ambitions that motivated this study come out of my experiences, both personal and academic. I wanted to tell the stories of people who have been invisible to white America and who now live where I grew up. I wanted to understand the experience of immigration—one that is very strongly a part of my family's history and a part of the fabric of the neighborhoods I remember from my childhood and for those who live there now. I originally framed the study around two basic theoretical questions aimed at understanding the experience of the immigrants in light of what I knew about the experiences of earlier waves of white immigrants and their children.

I begin by describing these early framing questions because I think they reflect assumptions and approaches I shared with most Americans who have thought at all about the experiences of black immigrants, and because as I conducted my study, I learned that the assumptions I first held were misguided in many ways and were based on incorrect notions of what the terms immigration, race, ethnicity, and identity meant for Caribbean immigrants.

Initially I had wanted to ask how similar or different is it to be a black immigrant or descendant of immigrants in Brooklyn in the late twentieth century from what it was like to be an Irish, Italian, or Jewish immigrant in the earlier part of the century? How useful are the old social psychological theories of immigrant assimilation for understanding the non-Europeans who make up the newest Americans?

I had wanted to "test" the theories sociologists had for understanding the assimilation process for white immigrants to see which parts fit the experiences of black immigrants. But that question assumed that race was the key defining difference between what happened to earlier waves of Irish, Italian, and Jewish immigrants and what was happening to Jamaican, Barbadian, Trinidadian, and Guyanese immigrants. There were some similarities between the two waves of immigrants—the earlier European immigrants and the current Caribbean immigrants came to make a better life for themselves in the United States, both waves of immigrants came with optimistic hopes and beliefs about becoming American, and both waves came primarily as economic migrants, not refugees. Yet many other factors have changed the process of immigration between these two periods.

The changed technology that links sending and receiving societies, the proximity of the Caribbean to the United States, and the interpenetration of the economies and societies of the West Indies and the United States all transform the process of migration itself. The recent immigrants do not make the abrupt change from one society to another that early models of assimilation (often erroneously) ascribed to European immigrants.[4] In fact, some authors have suggested abandoning the ideas of immigration and assimilation altogether, adopting instead the notions of transnationalism and diaspora culture to explain the experiences of recent migrants.[5] While I believe that some who describe immigrants as "transnational" actors are exaggerating the extent to which current immigrants maintain ties across national boundaries and the extent to which earlier waves of immigrants did not, I discuss in Chapter 3 the ways in which a simple dichotomy between "before" immigration and "after" immigration does not fit the experiences of the people I studied.

The consequences of "becoming American" have also changed. As I worked on this study during the last decade, a number of new models for understanding the experiences of post-1965 immigrants have been developed. The standard models of assimilation that were used to explain the incorporation of European immigrants described a process where becoming American was coupled with economic incorporation into the society. The more "assimilated" people became, the more economically successful they were. The generational march of assimilation meant that poor immigrants became working-class ethnics and then over time successful ethnic Americans.

A key proposition of the new models of immigrant incorporation studies how the social capital immigrants bring with them, and the racial and ethnic definitions of nonwhite immigrants as minorities, combine to create a situation where becoming American in terms of culture and identity and achieving economic success are decoupled. Some immigrants and their children do better economically by maintaining a strong ethnic identity and culture and by resisting American cultural and identity influences. In fact, many authors now suggest that remaining immigrant- or ethnic-identified eases economic and social incorporation into the United States. These new assumptions turn models of identity change on their head—now those who resist becoming American do well and those who lose their immigrant ethnic distinctiveness become downwardly mobile. West Indians, it turns out, fit this model very well because when West Indians lose their distinctiveness as immigrants or ethnics they become not just Americans, but black Americans. Given the ongoing prejudice and discrimination in American society, this represents downward mobility for the immigrants and their children. The overwhelming importance of race, as well as the changed theoretical notions of assimilation and economic mobility, meant that this could not be an immigrant study alone—it was also to be a study of American race relations and the ways in which immigrant and American blacks were similar or different, and the ways in which they interacted with each other.

The second question that originally motivated the study was how the immigrants and their children formed identities in the United States when they could choose from both a racial identity as black and an ethnic identity as Jamaican or West Indian. I knew that in the past black ethnics had been defined in terms of the *master status* of their race. I refer here to sociologist Robert Merton's insight that while people can have a number of different aspects to their identity, often one aspect of themselves will be used by society to define them. In this case the fact that a person might be male or female, educated or uneducated, immigrant or native, is not noticed. Race serves as a master status defining the person to others.[6] I knew that Americans tend to see race and ethnicity as interchangeable for black Americans—failing to recognize any ethnic heterogeneity within the racial category of black. I was interested in the macro question of whether that recognition was changing with the large volume of Caribbean immigrants arriving since the revision of the U.S. immigration laws in 1965. I was also interested in the more mundane but fascinating question of how the immigrants and their children handled their day-to-day presentation of self. West Indian immigrants who wanted to identify ethnically seemed to have to struggle to form and maintain their identities in a society that defined them racially. If, for instance, a family of Jamaicans wanted to be known as Jamaican and not black Americans, how would they signal their island identity to other Americans as they encountered them? I wondered how they coped with what I perceived to be a contradiction between their self-identity (as Jamaican) and the identity imposed upon them by outsiders (as black).

But this way of phrasing the question assumed identity was a zero-sum process. I viewed the immigrants as having to choose between a racial and an ethnic identity. This assumption arose out of a very American sense that black racial identity and the solidarity that it entails involve not having other identities. This is nonsense, of course. As I began talking with immigrants about their identities, I soon realized that identity was a much more fluid, malleable, and layered phenomenon that did not require people to choose between race and ethnicity. The immigrants were from complex multiracial and multiethnic societies. Their "ethnic" as well as their "racial" identities reflect the history of those societies and the political and social meanings attached to those identities in American society.

The findings of the study touch on the issues raised by the original framing questions I describe here, but the crux of the story about the experiences of the West Indian immigrants and their children revolves around the interaction between the specific culture and identities of the immigrants and their children and how that culture and those identities are shaped and changed by conditions in America—especially the American racial structure.

The main argument of this book is that black immigrants from the Caribbean come to the United States with a particular identity/culture/worldview that reflects their unique history and experiences. This culture and identity are different from the immigrant identity and culture of previous waves of European immigrants because of the unique history of the origin countries and because of the changed contexts of reception the immigrants face in the United States. This culture and identity are also different from the culture and identity of African Americans.

At first, two main aspects of the culture of West Indians help them to be successful in America. First, because they are immigrants they have a different attitude toward employment, work, and American society than native-born Americans. Employers value this highly. Their background characteristics, including human capital and social network ties, ease their entry into the U.S. labor force. Middle-class immigrants come with qualifications and training that are needed in the U.S. economy (nurses, for example). Because English is their native language, they are able to transfer their foreign qualifications (teaching credentials, nursing degrees) into American credentials. In addition, working-class immigrants have extensive networks of contacts that facilitate their entry into low-level jobs.

Second, the immigrants' unique understanding and expectations of race relations allow them to interact with American racial structures in a successful way. Specifically, their low anticipation of sour race relations allows them to have better interpersonal interactions with white Americans than many native African Americans. Because they come from a society with a majority of blacks and with many blacks in high positions, the immigrants have high ambitions and expectations. Yet their experience with blocked economic mobility due to race and their strong racial identities lead them to challenge blocked mobility in a very militant fashion when they encounter it. This combination of high ambitions, friendly relations with whites on an interpersonal level, and strong militance in encountering any perceived discrimination leads to some better outcomes in the labor market for West Indians than for black Americans.

Ultimately, however, the structural realities of American race relations begin to swamp the culture of the West Indians. Persistent and obvious racial discrimination undermines the openness toward whites the immigrants have when they first arrive. Low wages and poor working conditions are no longer attractive to the children of the immigrants, who use American, not Caribbean, yardsticks to measure how good a job is. Racial discrimination in housing channels the immigrants into neighborhoods with inadequate city services and high crime rates. Inadequate public schools undermine their hopes for their children's future. Over time the distinct elements of West Indian culture the immigrants are most proud of—a willingness to work hard, a lack of attention to racialism, a high value on education, and strong interests in saving for the future—are undermined by the realities of life in the United States.[7]

These changes are particularly concentrated among the working-class and poor immigrants. Middle-class immigrants are able to pass along aspects of their culture and worldview to their children, but the majority of the working-class immigrants are not. Race as a master status in the United States soon overwhelms the identities of the immigrants and their children, and they are seen as black Americans. Many of the children of the immigrants develop "oppositional identities" to deal with that status. These identities stress that doing well in school is "acting white." The cultural behaviors associated with these oppositional identities further erode the life chances of the children of the West Indian immigrants.

While many white conservatives blame the culture of African Americans for their failures in the economy, the experiences of the West Indians show that even "good culture" is no match for racial discrimination. Over the course of one generation the structural realities of American race relations and the American economy undermine the cultures of the West Indian immigrants and create responses among the immigrants, and especially their children, that resemble the cultural responses of African Americans to long histories of exclusion and discrimination.

Much previous writing on the experience of West Indians in the United States uses their experiences to criticize African-American "culture," to demonstrate that it is a dysfunctional culture among African Americans that explains their problems in American society, not racial discrimination. Yet this in-depth study of two generations of West Indian Americans reaches a very different conclusion. Rather than criticize the culture of African Americans and praise the culture of West Indians, as many conservative writers do, this study finds that the real solution to the problems of racial disadvantage in American life involves changing the racist structures and behaviors that deny equal opportunities to people identified in our society as black.

DESCRIPTION OF THE RESEARCH

I set out to answer my original research questions by interviewing immigrants to New York City from the English-speaking islands of the West Indies. Because I was interested in the social process of identity construction among the immigrants and their children, I wanted to interview people in a context in which they interacted with others. So, among the first-generation immigrants, I interviewed white and black American coworkers of the immigrants. I did this to include both the self-definitions and identifications of the immigrants and the definitions and identifications others in the United States made about who they were and what their culture entailed. Because of the strong patterns of residential segregation in U.S. society, I believed that the workplace was the best site to capture the most diverse interactions the immigrants would have. Recognizing that social-class differences among the immigrants could make a difference in the outcomes, I interviewed a sample of middle-class teachers and working-class food-service workers. In all, I conducted fifty-nine interviews with West Indian immigrants, twenty-seven interviews with black Americans, twenty-five interviews with white Americans, and six interviews with coworkers of different racial and ethnic backgrounds. In addition to the formal interviews I spent a great deal of time doing participant observation in the worksites, the public schools, and the cafeteria.

Since generation is one of the key variables in explaining what happens to immigrant groups over time, I also interviewed a sample of eighty-three adolescent and young-adult children of immigrants,[8] half of whom were immigrants themselves but had been in the United States over three years, and half of whom were American-born children of immigrants. These interviews also included young people from a range of class backgrounds, including middle-class students, students enrolled in two public high schools located in West Indian neighborhoods in Brooklyn, and some students who were dropping out of school. I also spent a great deal of time doing participant observation in the two public high schools, where I conducted surveys of all second-generation West Indian students.[9] I also interviewed teachers, some of whom were West Indians, in both of these schools. The teacher interviews in effect did double duty—I asked the teachers about their own lives and their relations with one another, but I also asked them about the experiences of the immigrant and second-generation youth they taught.

In the end the project included 202 formal life history interviews, 140 of which I conducted myself; the rest were conducted by a team of research assistants, including African Americans, West Indians, and whites. The interviews lasted between one and three hours and covered the respondents' life histories, experiences of immigration, attitudes toward other racial and ethnic groups, and their own racial and ethnic identities. Tables 1.1, 1.2, and 1.3 provide an overview of the general characteristics of the sample. Since this was not a randomly chosen sample, it cannot be generalized to the wider population with any degree of statistical confidence. Rather, the sample was designed to establish an in-depth look at the experiences and interpretations of as wide a range of immigrants as possible, and to study at close range their racial and ethnic identities and their experiences with American race relations. The inclusion of white and black American coworkers also furnishes the context in which immigrants experience U.S. society and some insights into how institutions and individual Americans are changed by the presence of growing numbers of

Table 1.1   Adult sample characteristics

Race	Gender	Teachers	Food-service employees	Total
White	Male	6	3	9
	Female	10	6	16
American black	Male	4	6	10
	Female	10	9	19
West Indian	Male	7	11	18
	Female	18	23	41
Other[a]	Male		3	3
	Female		3	3
Total		55	64	119

a. Includes Bangladeshi and Puerto Rican workers who were interviewed as part of the food-service workplace sample.

Table 1.2 National origin distribution of adult immigrant sample

National origin	Food service	Teachers	Total
Jamaica	6	10	16
Trinidad	9	4	13
Guyana	10	9	19
Barbados	1	1	2
Grenada	1	1	2
Other West Indies	7	0	7
Total	34	25	59

West Indians. The interviews with the white and black managers at the food-service company, American Food, also offer insights into how Americans interpret the behaviors and identities of the immigrants. Placing all of the interviews within specific institutional contexts also provided ethnographic opportunities. In many cases I was able to study not only what people said about their lives, but also their actions and their relationships with other immigrants and native-born black and white Americans. (Details of all of the methodological decisions and issues I faced in actually conducting the study and advice to other researchers contemplating similar studies are provided in the Appendix.)

Table 1.3   1.5- and second-generation youth national origin distribution

Country of origin	Number
Jamaica	26
Trinidad	17
Guyana	13
Barbados	8
Grenada	4
Haiti	8
Other West Indies	7
Total	83

Note: "Country of origin" refers either to the birthplace of the parents of the adolescents we interviewed or, if the teenagers were born abroad, to the respondents' birthplace. In the ten cases where respondents had parents who were from different islands, they were counted according to the island they most identified with.

PLAN OF THE BOOK

Chapters 2 and 3 examine the identities and culture of West Indians before and after immigration. Chapter 2 shows how the history of the islands creates the repertoire of cultures and identities people bring to New York. I argue that our assumption that national identities are fixed, salient, and predominant in the identity of immigrants before immigration is incorrect. I show how the national identities of West Indians reflect their colonial history, and the multilayered identities available to them from that history. I also explore how the meaning and definition of the racial category "black" reflect different histories and cultures in the Caribbean and the United States. This means that the self-definitions and understandings of being black for immigrants are different from the definitions and understandings of Americans, both black and white.

Chapter 3 discusses the subjective identification of the immigrants, including the ethnic and racial boundaries they find most salient, the expectations they have of life in the United States, and the methods they develop to present their self-identities to others. West Indian immigrants to New York demonstrate a typically immigrant attitude toward work and employment, a militance about racial discrimination combined with a belief that racial barriers will not affect them personally, a belief in the United States as both a land of opportunity and a land of racism, and a sense of themselves as very different from black Americans. I argue that the assumption that higher social status is achieved by becoming American rather than by remaining an immigrant is not true for this population. In fact, the opposite is so. Remaining an immigrant means higher status because becoming American for West Indians entails becoming black American—something that they perceive as downward mobility.

Chapters 4 and 5 show how the culture and identity of the immigrants interact with American society by examining the relative success of West Indians in the American economy. Chapter 4 reviews the debate in the literature about this success, concluding that while West Indians are not as successful as the cultural stereotypes and some analysts would lead us to believe, they do have certain advantages in the economy relative to African Americans, most especially the much higher labor force participation rates among foreign-born unskilled and uneducated workers. This is done through a case study of food-service workers at a company I call American Food. I show how the white employers prefer West Indians to American workers because the immigrants value these extremely low-level jobs much higher than any native-born American would. Yet these white managers explain the lack of interest by African Americans in these low-level jobs by using racial stereotypes. Through interviews with black Americans and West Indians I document the tensions and stereotypes that exist between these groups and analyze the reasons for their development and perpetuation.

Chapter 5 examines the experiences of the immigrants with race and discrimination in the United States. The immigrants come to the United States expecting that there will be structural racism blocking their access to the highest rungs of the hierarchy in jobs, in politics, and in the community. Because they all have heard that the United States is a racist society and because they understand racism to mean blocked access to the highest positions in the social hierarchy, they come prepared to challenge blocked mobility when it occurs. This makes sense to these immigrants because in the Caribbean there is a strong correlation between color and the highest reaches of the social hierarchy.

The immigrants are most shocked and least prepared for the degree of interpersonal racism they encounter with whites, and for the overwhelming presence of race in all facets of American life. The difference between the high level of immigrant expectation of structural racism and the low level of expectation of interpersonal racism explains some of the contradictory writing on West Indian racial politics in the United States and the contradictory responses of my white respondents.[10] Because West Indians have experience with everyday hierarchies in which race is not a factor, such as in completely black-owned-and-operated businesses, and because they have less expectation of racism in chance encounters with whites, employers, and customers, the whites who have interpersonal encounters with West Indians find them to be friendly and easier to deal with on an interpersonal level. At the same time, because West Indians are very sensitive to American racial ceilings, they are perceived as more militant and angry in organizational interactions in which they try to break through barriers to upward mobility. Thus food-service employers report that West Indians are nicer to give orders to and more friendly on an interpersonal level, and yet file more grievances and question promotions and perks more often. This chapter describes the everyday, and the occasionally violent, racial discrimination the immigrants face in New York and the ways in which this changes their understanding of race relations in the United States.

Chapters 6 through 8 examine the future of West Indian culture and identity as these factors interact with American social structure. What happens to the children of the immigrants? In Chapter 6 I examine some of the main sources of intergenerational conflict in Caribbean families. They include the separations between parents and children that result from the immigration process itself, the clash between American rules against physical discipline of children and traditional West Indian parenting practices, and the ways in which materialism and the strains of long work hours take their toll on family functioning.

Chapter 7 describes the neighborhoods and schools that poor and working-class immigrants must deal with. I show that residential segregation and de facto educational segregation are key factors in the experiences and future trajectory of a good proportion of the second generation.[11] The crumbling schools of New York dash many of the dreams the immigrants have for their children.

Chapter 8 looks at the opinions, aspirations, and identities of working-class and middle-class Caribbean immigrant children. I suggest that those students who do well in school and appear to be on an upward socioeconomic trajectory will be the most likely to maintain a strong ethnic identity and the cultural values and outlooks that have contributed to their parents' success. For the majority of students, however, American society imposes severe disadvantages on the second generation at every level. Working-class and poor students in segregated neighborhoods identify as African Americans, rejecting their parents' ethnic distancing from black Americans. This identity is also associated with a pessimism about their own life chances as well as with a heightened awareness of racial discrimination and limits to opportunities for black people in America.

Chapter 9 concludes by examining the implications of these findings for public policy and for the future of American race relations in general. The policy implications lie in the ways in which the economic and cultural disinvestment in American cities erodes the social capital of immigrant families. The families need recognition of their inherent strengths and the supports necessary to maintain their ambitions. Instead, they greet a society in which a materialist and often racist culture undermines their abilities to provide for their children.

I also reflect on the possible impact of current immigration on the future of the American color line, arguing that while West Indians may not be successful in the long term by distancing themselves from American blacks, this may be the strategy adopted by other non-European immigrants. If this is the case and new immigrants from a variety of countries around the world position themselves as "non-blacks" in order to be accepted in American society, then both later-generation West Indians and American blacks will continue to be stigmatized and excluded because of their race.

HISTORICAL

LEGACIES

Most Americans have an image of the "Caribbean islands" as either island paradises with crystal blue waters, white sandy beaches, and cool rum drinks by the pool, or as poor Third World nations filled with shanty towns and the homes of the Haitian or Cuban boat people who are desperately trying to reach the United States. These disparate associations reflect media images of the region that originate either in news reports of poverty and political upheaval or in advertisements of inviting vacation destinations paid for or inspired by the tourist industry. As a result Americans are more familiar with some islands than others, and mostly ignorant about the complex world and sometimes savage history of the Caribbean islands. While most Americans know about Jamaica and Aruba as vacation spots, and know of Haiti's desperately poor people and political strife, they know little about the island of Trinidad beyond the existence of calypso, and probably have not even heard of the island of Montserrat because of its small size, absence of political upheaval, and, most important for the tourist industry, lack of sandy beaches for development.[1]

Even the definition of the Caribbean or the West Indies is a fuzzy one—with most popular definitions not matching the academic ones. Popular definitions would include the Bahamas and perhaps Bermuda as "Caribbean islands" but would exclude Surinam and Guyana because they are countries in South America. Yet historians tend to define these South American countries as West Indian because their history and social structure are so similar to those of the islands, and they generally do not include Bermuda and the Bahamas. The Caribbean islands stretch from

The Caribbean Islands

the tip of Florida to the coast of South America in the body of water called the Caribbean Sea (see map). The northernmost islands, called the Greater Antilles, are the largest ones, including Cuba, Hispaniola (the island that is half Dominican Republic and half Haiti), Jamaica, and Puerto Rico. The smaller, more eastern islands are called the Lesser Antilles and include Saint Kitts (Saint Christopher), Nevis, Antigua, Guadeloupe, Dominica, Martinique, Saint Lucia, Barbados, Saint Vincent, Grenada, and Trinidad and Tobago.[2]

Distinctions based on language—English, Spanish, or French—are most often used to characterize the different islands. But these current linguistic differences are not clear-cut reflections of colonial histories. In the five centuries since Columbus arrived on the island of Hispaniola in 1492, the individual islands have been controlled by various European powers, with many of them trading hands among a number of different powers at different times. The Spanish, French, Dutch, Danish, English, and later the United States all controlled and colonized various islands, often relinquishing control back and forth over time. While Spain laid claim to the whole of the Caribbean after Columbus "discovered" the land, it concentrated its attention on the larger islands of the Greater Antilles. The other European powers—the Netherlands, England, and France—laid claim to the smaller islands of the Lesser Antilles. These islands changed hands many times, and the specific European heritage of particular islands is sometimes difficult to pin down. For instance, the island of Tobago was controlled by the Dutch from 1658 to 1667, variously held by the British and French from 1667 to 1763, held by the British from 1763 to 1781, by the French again from 1781 to 1793, back to the British from 1793 to 1802, by the French again from 1802 to 1803, and finally back to the British from 1803 to independence in 1962. Trinidad, which combined with Tobago is now a sovereign state, was held by the Spanish from 1532 to 1797 and by the British from 1797 to independence in 1962.[3]

Only Barbados was held by a sole power—Britain—throughout its history. The other islands changed hands at least once and sometimes much more often. Even Jamaica, often thought by Americans to be a quintessentially British former colony, was controlled and colonized by Spain from its first European discovery in 1494 until it was ceded to England in 1670. Jamaica gained independence from Britain in 1962.

The Caribbean region as a whole contained 32.5 million people at the beginning of the 1990s. Of those, 61% lived in Spanish-speaking societies—Cuba, Puerto Rico, and the Dominican Republic. Another 20% lived in societies that were officially French-speaking, 17% lived in societies where English was the official language, and 2% were in Dutch-speaking areas.[4]

Those islands that remained Spanish property for a long period of time and developed into the Spanish Caribbean are different in some fundamental ways, most especially in the types of race relations and racial categories that developed. While all of these countries had large numbers of African slaves, in the Hispanic Caribbean the distinction between white

and black was not as sharply denoted as in the English and French countries. (This is discussed in depth later in this chapter.)

This book examines immigrants who have come from the countries
defined as constituting the "West Indies"—that is, the current English-
speaking islands and the country of Guyana (formerly British Guiana).[5]
The immigrants we spoke to primarily came from Jamaica, Guyana, Trinidad, Barbados, and Grenada, with a few each from the smaller islands of
Montserrat, Saint Thomas, Anguilla, Saint Kitts, Saint Lucia, Dominica,
and Nevis, and the Central American country of Panama. In addition I
included second-generation respondents from the French Creole-speak-
ing country of Haiti. (See the Appendix for the reasons for this decision.)
There are about 2 million people from these islands living in the United
States.[6] Table 2.1 gives the distribution of West Indians that I and my
research assistants interviewed and the demographic background of the
countries they came from.

While the islands that make up the Caribbean vary in size, cultural
background, demographics, geography, and the specifics of their history,
I focus here on three commonalities in Caribbean history that influence
the societies and their people today: the legacies of European colonialism,
the legacies of slavery, and the domination of the island economies and
cultures in recent times by the United States. These commonalities together shape a particular West Indian identity and culture that the immigrants bring with them to New York.

Table 2.1   National origin and background of West Indian respondents

Country	Respondents in current sample	Foreign-born in U.S. in 1990	Ancestry in U.S. in 1990	Immigrants admitted in 1991
Jamaica	42	334,140	435,024	23,828
Guyana	32	120,698	81,665	11,666
Trinidad	30	115,710	76,270	8,407
Barbados	10	43,015	35,455	1,460
Haiti	8	225,393	289,521	47,527

Sources: For foreign-born: United States Census Bureau, Ethnic and Hispanic Branch,
Population Divison, The Foreign Born Population in the United States: 1990, Publication
CPH-L-98. For ancestry: United States Census Bureau, Ancestry of the Population: 1990. For
immigrants admitted: Immigration and Naturalization Service, Statistical Yearbook 1991.

THE LEGACIES OF EUROPEAN COLONIALISM

The societies created on the Caribbean islands have been described as "artificial" societies or "manufactured" ones.[7] The Caribbean islands were Europe's first colonies, and they were unique in terms of the colonial experience. Since the indigenous population of Indians was decimated quite early by disease and warfare, the Europeans faced land that was virtually unpopulated. The Europeans used the colonies to create enormous profits, combining European capital, Caribbean land, and imported coerced labor. For the first four hundred years this coerced labor took the form of enslavement of black Africans and then, after emancipation, indentured servitude of East Indians and Chinese. In the early Spanish colony of Hispaniola, slaves were imported as early as 1505, just thirteen years after Columbus first arrived, in order to work in enormous mining ventures aimed at finding gold. In the smaller Leeward Islands, early attempts to colonize the islands with European settlers on small farms soon were abandoned when large-scale production of sugarcane became a possibility. In historian Franklin Knight's words, a "settler" society was replaced with an "exploitation" society.[8] In 1640 sugarcane was introduced into Barbados, and by the 1650s sugarcane production spread to the other Lesser Antilles. The introduction of sugarcane led to the development of the specific social organization of the plantation, which included regimented work and large-scale production. The production of sugar on extensive plantations with imported African slaves, from which European planters reaped enormous profits, dominated the region for centuries and left its mark on the land, the peoples, the culture, and the very form of Caribbean society.

The key to understanding this history is that the European planters developed societies that were transplanted and designed for profit. The anthropologist Sidney Mintz has pointed out that these societies included plantation production so massive in scale that it created the common features of the industrialized West, including imported foods, time-conscious work regimes, factory production, and impersonal work relations long before such "modern" features of life ever appeared in Europe.[9] He goes on to argue that the distinctive social history of the Caribbean "gave to its peoples a life style adapted to the anonymity, depersonalization, and individualization of modern life, but did so when such phenomena were by no means yet recognized for what they are."[10]

The artificiality or manufactured nature of Caribbean society is evident in the mixing of multiracial and multiethnic populations on the islands, none of whom felt that they were "from there." David Lowenthal points out that the planter class was always oriented toward their European homeland, sending profits back to the sending country and never developing the close tie to place usual in settler colonies.[11] The culture of the Caribbean peoples that evolved from this mix was a transplanted and syncretic one—a Creole culture in that no particular parts were indigenous, and the parts of Africa, Europe, and Asia that survived were combined and passed on from generation to generation. The environment itself was transformed, and though the slaves working on the plantation raised some food, most food was imported and the slaves were dependent on supplies coming from far away.[12]

These profitable societies rested squarely on the backs of the imported slaves. In the 400 years of slavery in the West Indies, an estimated 4.6 million slaves were brought to the region.[13] The Africans taken from their native lands through the horror of the Middle Passage were themselves from a polyglot of societies, language groups, villages, and ethnic groups. The mixing of these separate African cultures created a Creole culture of its own, as human beings struggled to continue to make sense of their transformed lives and common destiny. Sugar "homogenized" the different islands as well, the common structure of the plantation causing similar social structures on the different islands. European rivalries, warfare, and economic wheeling and dealing also mixed cultures in an unprecedented way.

This mix of Africans and Europeans was further augmented after the emancipation of the slaves in the nineteenth century when planters, complaining of labor shortages, instituted a new importation of workers, principally in the form of indentured laborers on five-year contracts from India. From 1838 to 1917 over 400,000 Asian Indians came to the Caribbean, with 240,000 going to British Guiana, 135,000 to Trinidad, and 33,000 to Jamaica. The French and Dutch also imported approximately 100,000 Asian Indians to their colonies from 1852 to 1885.[14] In addition, about 135,000 Chinese and more than 33,000 Javanese were brought to the Caribbean in numbers large enough to create minority communities in many of the islands.[15]

Migration became a way of life in the islands of the Caribbean as emigration emerged as a way of coping with limited resources, the small size of the islands, and limited economic opportunities. During slavery there was a practice of "seasoning" slaves in the harsh environment of the West Indies and then transferring them to the United States.[16] Following emancipation in the 1830s, there was a great deal of interterritorial migration as the former slaves sought to leave the plantations they had been tied to. In the larger territories like Jamaica people were able to find land to till as peasants, and villages were formed. In the smaller islands such as Barbados, Grenada, Saint John, and Saint Thomas, the only option for the emancipated people who wanted a better life was often migration because all available land was owned by large plantations. Movements from these smaller islands to the newer colonies of Guyana and Trinidad dominated the mid-to-late nineteenth century.[17] These movements were often the result of solicited contract labor and were often seen as temporary. So Grenadians, for instance, moved to Guyana for work but maintained ties to their home island—possibly returning there after working and living in Guyana for decades.

After 1880 people from the English-speaking Caribbean began moving to the sugar plantations on the Spanish-speaking islands of Cuba and the Dominican Republic, while others moved on to the United Fruit Company plantations of Central America as well as to Panama to work on the Canal. These two flows combined had enormous effects. There was a net population loss in the 1880s of 130,000 British West Indians, the majority from Barbados and Jamaica.[18] The West Indians who took part in these migrations created villages and towns in the Central American countries they lived in, many of which survive to this day as separate English-speaking areas. Many of them moved back and forth between their home islands and their place of employment.

Huge numbers of workers were imported to the Panama Canal Zone between 1880 and 1914 to work on that giant project. This massive undertaking coincided with a drop in sugar prices and production that led to large increases in unemployment on the islands. These Panama Canal workers often then moved to the United States after their work on the

Canal, and this became a common route for early West Indian immigrants to the United States.[19] They were joined during the early twentieth century by a wave of West Indian immigrants coming directly from the islands who formed a large West Indian community in New York City.[20] Many of these immigrants settled in Harlem, where they were an active and vibrant part of the Harlem community; others settled in Miami and Boston.[21]

In the 1940s and 1950s interisland migration continued as workers from the smaller islands took work in the oil refineries of Trinidad, Curacao, and Aruba. However, the big change in the post–World War II period was the shift to Europe as a destination. A large number of migrants in the postwar period moved to Great Britain, with migration peaking in the two years prior to the restrictive Commonwealth Immigration Act of 1962, which all but curtailed immigrants from the former colonies. The 1965 liberalization of American immigration laws, which had been restrictive toward the islands, along with the reduced cost and ease of travel between the United States and the islands, led to the migration pressure shifting toward the United States. Since 1965 the volume of immigration to the United States has grown enormously. (The characteristics of this wave of immigrants are discussed later in this chapter.)

Thus two features we think of as modern or in fact postmodern in their effects on identity—the mixing of cultures and peoples from different continents, and migration and restlessness as a way of life—have been a feature of the peoples of the Caribbean for hundreds of years.[22] With a culture described as "almost entirely transplanted [which] has only recently been synthesized,"[23] Caribbean peoples who come to the United States seem particularly prepared to be immigrants in a multicultural society such as our own where pressure is not put on immigrants to give up their premigration identities, and where celebrations of distinctive national cultures are commonplace. Yet the premigration identity these immigrants bring with them is not a fixed, stable national identity like the ones we imagine Europeans brought from England or Ireland or Sweden.[24] Indeed, it is not as strong or developed a sense of national identity as seen in such other immigrants as those from the Dominican Republic, China, or Russia. This is not to say that West Indians do not feel a very strong sense of attachment to place. They often strongly identify with their village or town or their island. Yet very often if you scratch the identity of a Trinidadian, you find roots in Grenada or Jamaica.

In the Caribbean only Haiti and the Dominican Republic achieved independence before the twentieth century. Jamaica and Trinidad and Tobago achieved independence from England only as recently as 1962, Barbados in 1966, Guyana in 1966, and smaller islands even more recently—Grenada in 1974 and Saint Kitts and Nevis in 1983.[25] The complex process in the United States by which a national identity becomes an ethnic identity as immigrants arrive and find much in common with their compatriots is in part shaped by the recency of Caribbean nationhood and by the intermixing and migration history of its peoples.

These immigrants should be understood as coming from societies where cultures of Europeans and non-Europeans have mixed in numbers more similar to their actual distribution in the world than has ever been the case in the United States (though this is becoming the case in the late twentieth century), and from societies that have been artificially created and oriented toward profit. Such an individual faces the global cities of New York and Miami with a more malleable and multilayered identity than one might imagine if just thinking of an agricultural migrant from the Third World moving to a First World city.

The multilayered identities of most of these migrants include a specific national origin identity as, say, Trinidadian or Guyanese, a subnational racial identity as black, and a supranational regional identity as West Indian or Caribbean. The legacies of European colonialism laid the foundation for similar experiences across the different islands—creating a West Indian culture that Guyanese, Jamaicans, and Trinidadians share. Central to that culture is the legacy of slavery, which created racial hierarchies and meanings attached to race.

LEGACIES OF SLAVERY

The Caribbean shares with the United States the ugly fact that slavery is a key element of both of our histories. Slavery was central to the plantation system, and thus to the societies of the Caribbean islands and the American South, from the beginning of the seventeenth to the mid-nineteenth centuries. There are some similarities and some important differences in the ways that slavery affected the development of the two societies.

In both the United States and the Caribbean, slavery fed economic development and created huge profits and wealth for whites. Tied together in a world economic system, many whites in the United States profited directly from the Caribbean slave trade. Others profited indirectly by producing food for the islands and by consuming the sugar and other cash crops that fed the system. The people of African origin in both the Caribbean and the United States are the descendants of slaves, and the cultures of whites and blacks in both regions are suffused with the residues of the images, ideas, and rationalizations such a system must engender.

However, there are a number of key differences between the United States and the West Indies. These differences shape current ideas about race, the relations between socially defined races, and the degree to which issues of slavery and race permeate day-to-day interactions in the United States and the Caribbean. They include

1. the relative numbers of Europeans and Africans in the two societies;
2. the rules and practices surrounding mixed-race people, manumission, and determination of racial status;
3. the harshness of the slave system and the resulting death rates, and therefore the ratio of African slaves to slaves born in the new world; and
4. the conditions of emancipation in both societies, including the independence of the United States and the continued control of the Caribbean by European powers.

Each of these differences will be examined below.

Relative Numbers

Blacks far outnumber whites in the Caribbean and have done so since soon after slavery was instituted. The planter class was never very large in the islands; there were many absentee landlords, and many white Europeans who came to the islands to make their fortune left their families behind in Europe. It is important not to make the mistake of North Americans who do not describe the native whites of the Caribbean in their discussions of race relations there.[26] However, the non-Hispanic Caribbean blacks outnumber whites by a vast amount, and whites are usually under 5% of the population.[27]

This has been true throughout the colonial and postcolonial history of the islands. It has affected the political and economic decisions made by Europeans who, though having economic, political, and military power, were always aware that they were vastly outnumbered. Some scholars argue that the shortage of white working-class people prompted more toleration of free blacks on the part of the white planters, and those free blacks had better fortunes in West Indian societies than in the American South; "the West Indians needed colored men in occupational niches that whites pre-empted in the United States."[28]

This balance of numbers affected the accommodations made after slavery ended. At that time a small white elite controlled the economy and the government, yet they were greatly outnumbered by their former slaves. This situation was too dangerous and precarious for the white planters, who decided to cede control back to the mother country in order to retain their racial and economic privileges. Most colonies then gave up whatever local control they held in return for direct imperial rule. "During the last third of the nineteenth century," writes David Lowenthal, "every British Caribbean territory except Barbados (which had a white population large enough to assert authority) regressed from self-government to Colonial Office rule."[29]

When independence was finally established (mostly in the 1950s and 1960s), however, the demographic preponderance of people of African origin allowed them to begin to seize some degree of political and economic power. Although there is still a very high correlation between color and economic power in the Caribbean, the blacks in the West Indies enjoy a degree of self-government and control over their own internal affairs that black Americans have never enjoyed. Even in segregated towns and areas in the United States where blacks have some degree of control of the local government, they are always subject to white majorities at the state and national level. That is not true in the Caribbean, and the demographics there favor more black political and economic power.

Many authors have noted that West Indian immigrants who come to the United States have a strong sense of personal efficacy and ambition because of growing up in a society in which blacks are the majority.[30] This was often noted by the respondents in this study when they contrasted themselves with black Americans. In addition to the obvious consequence of a black-majority society—that a child will see blacks occupying a wide variety of occupations and positions of power within the society and therefore grow up believing all of those positions could be his or hers—there are a number of other cultural differences that stem from the relative numbers of blacks and whites in the two societies. These differences can be summed up as a different sense of how class and race intersect. In a society such as the modern Caribbean, hierarchy is divorced from race yet still tied to color.[31] The oppressors of black people are all other black or brown people. Thus Lowenthal notes that even when Caribbean and black American political leaders spoke of "black power," the political programs they pursued were in a major sense different:

> West Indian black power demonstrations and threats of violence are not racial conflicts in the American or British senses. The American civil rights movement, black power movement and white backlash are racial in programme, in focus and in purpose . . . But Caribbean conflicts are chiefly socioeconomic in nature, and racial mainly in name. To be sure, these problems have their roots in slavery and in colonialism, both of which were racially organized. But these antecedents are not operationally significant today. Race and color are rallying points for protest, not their essential ingredients or their major determinants.[32]

In Caribbean society the culture of the white European is still seen as superior by many, especially middle-class people, but there are few whites who represent that culture. Instead, the middle-class blacks who run these independent societies have a great deal of political and economic power, and many of them have adopted European culture, or a creolized version of it, as their own. Orlando Patterson describes the pervasiveness of white culture in the Caribbean without the pervasiveness of whites:

> Most West Indians pass their childhoods in communities where they never once come in contact with a white person, or where all the "significant others" of their social universe are black or brown people. Teacher, preacher, lawyer, policeman, judge, civil servant,

politician—these are now almost all black or at least non-white . . .
This is not to say that one grows up in the West Indies without an
awareness of Whites. The white presence in the society, however, is
mediated almost entirely through the cultural system: It is through
such agencies as the school, the church, and the mass media, as well
as through the value system acquired from one's parents, that one
learns the status and meaning of being white. Thus, in the process
of his socialization the West Indian acquires both an extraordinary
amount of knowledge about white or European customs and a deep
sense of the superiority of these patterns of behavior and of the
status of those who share them. But there are few, if any, white role
models. European values are reinforced not by the crushing presence of the carriers of the alien "superior" culture, but mainly by
fellow black and brown role models who have mastered the art of
performing in accordance with the "superior" cultural patterns.[33]

So, as Lowenthal points out, "[i]n the West Indies anyone in power is
expected to be culturally white. Whereas blacks who succeed in white
America alienate other blacks, colored and black West Indians who
achieve prominence are praised as exemplars, no matter how remote their
way of life and tenor of thought from that of the masses."[34] Because of this
expectation, success does not challenge the racial identity of upwardly
mobile West Indians, though it might challenge their cultural identity.
The contrast with upwardly mobile African Americans is sharp:

> In white America blacks can gain prestige but little power; and the
> greater their success the more they tend to be lost to the black
> community, which remains a world apart. In America as in the West
> Indies the upwardly mobile leave families and humble origins be-
> hind, but the black man who makes good in the United States is
> more déraciné than the West Indian. And he is ultimately less suc-
> cessful because America remains white; the black West Indian in-
> creasingly inherits his own society.[35]

Determination of Color

The social construction of race in the Caribbean has historically been
different than in the United States. Nowhere in the Caribbean is race a

simple bipolar distinction between white and black. Race is more of a continuum in which shade and other physical characteristics, as well as social characteristics such as class position, are taken into account in the social process of categorization. The determination of race is quite variable; different local codes predominate in different islands or in different parts of the same island, and this leads to subtle differences in categorization. However, the contrast between the overall West Indian system and the United States is stark. In the Caribbean an intermediate category of colored mixed-race people was recognized in a way that only occurred in the United States in Louisiana and parts of South Carolina prior to the Civil War.[36]

The Hispanic Caribbean and the English Caribbean are alike in that both sets of societies recognize shades of color between black and white. While the United States developed a system where "one drop of black blood," defined as any black ancestor, made a person black, in the Hispanic and English Caribbean there developed an elaborate racial terminology for shades of color between black and white.[37]

But the Hispanic and English Caribbean differ in more subtle aspects of race relations and race classifications. H. Hoetink argues that historically the sharp line dividing white from black in the United States meant that there could be no mobility between the blacks at the bottom and the whites at the top of the society. The English-speaking Caribbean allowed mobility between the blacks at the bottom of society and the middle category of light-skinned people, but not all the way to the top category of whites. The intermediate group of "coloreds," Hoetink argues, is more of social bridge in the Iberian model, where social mobility from the bottom group to the very top group is possible in stages.[38] He goes on to argue that there is less of a sharp division between the white ruling class in the Hispanic societies of the Caribbean and the lower classes, noting that in the English, French, and Dutch Caribbean a Creole language is spoken by the vast majority of the common people, and in the Hispanic Caribbean all of the people speak Spanish.

This recognition of gradations of color between white and black is also bound up with class divisions in the islands. The common phrase "money whitens" refers to the fact that education, language use, and other markers of class can change the social designation of a person in the Caribbean, and two people with the exact same skin coloring can be seen as different degrees of white or black if one is middle class and the other poor. The categorization of race and the determination of a particular person's race are thus very complex. For instance, Jack Alexander notes that middle-class Jamaicans in Kingston use a five-category system of categorization, including the designations white, fair, brown, dark, and black.[39] These categories, Alexander argues, "refer not to physical facts in themselves but to physical facts as an expression of the consequences of an original historical Jamaican mixture of 'white' and 'black.'"[40] Mintz cautions the North American that West Indian society will often be erroneously interpreted if North American categories are used to understand it.[41]

The reasons for these historically produced differences in the two societies have been explored and debated in a number of different studies. The absence of a large white population on the islands, the higher ratio of white males to females, and the practice by some planters of freeing the offspring that resulted from their matings with black slaves all contributed to a different social understanding of race. Recent changes in Caribbean society also have made this a dynamic process—in the decades following independence more social mobility for the lower classes has led to less of a correlation between actual color and socioeconomic status.

One consequence of the variability and lack of a one-drop rule in determining racial identity in the Caribbean is that census figures on the racial distribution in each island are only rough guides and are indeed quite changeable. For instance:

> Dominica reported a "coloured" population of 30 percent in 1921, 75 percent in 1946, and 33 percent in 1960—variations explicable only as shifts of evaluation, not of population. Jamaica exhibits similar anomalies: between 1943 and 1960 the "coloured" proportion of Kingston declined from 33 to 14 percent. The explanation lies in nomenclature as well as in-migration; dark-skinned Kingstonians were less content to be labeled black in 1943 than "African" in 1960.[42]

This difference between North America and the Caribbean has confused and led astray many social commentators who look at the Caribbean though the lens of North American racial categories and thus conclude that racism either does not exist or is a tiny problem. As we shall see in Chapter 5, this difference also affects the understandings that the immigrants in this study hold of racial identity, of race relations in the United States, and of their memories of race relations back in the islands. Accustomed to subtle and more fluid race relations and to intermediate categories between blacks and whites, West Indian immigrants faced with the stark and blatant race relations of the United States tend to minimize or erase their own memories of racism at home.

Harshness of Slavery

Another key historical difference between the United States and the Caribbean is that because of the much higher death rate of slaves on the islands compared to slaves in the American South, the Caribbean always had a much higher ratio of slaves born in Africa to slaves born in captivity. Lowenthal concludes that "conditions of work, nourishment, confinement and punishment [in the Caribbean] were probably the worst in the New World."[43] West Indian slaveholders found it more economically efficient to work slaves literally to death and import new ones, than to treat slaves well enough that they would survive in sufficient numbers to reproduce. Bonham Richardson attributes this abhorrent economic calculation to the immense profits that could be made growing sugar.[44] Owners in the Caribbean were preoccupied with sugarcane and thus relied on imported foodstuffs to a great degree. When these supplies of food were interrupted due to weather or other events, slaves were malnourished or starved, thus making them highly susceptible to disease and leading to a particularly high infant mortality rate.

Lowenthal also cites the higher incidence of West Indian slave revolts and the songs of West Indian slaves, which stressed rebellion rather than obedience, as further proof of the severity of Caribbean as opposed to North American slave conditions. Of course, slave revolts could have occurred more frequently in the islands because of the demographic ratio and the greater possibility of escape. However, demographic studies show a much higher death rate for Caribbean slaves than for North American slaves. "When the slaves were emancipated, the Caribbean contained scarcely one-third the number imported; the United States had eleven times the number brought in."[45] Richardson notes that despite academic debates about which national characteristics made whites kinder or crueler masters, "the high slave death rates seem to have characterized all Caribbean slavery with little distinction between islands or colonial powers."[46]

As noted above, one lasting consequence of this difference in slave mortality is that the Caribbean always had a higher number of newly arrived African people at any one time. This has led scholars to expect, and to find, more African cultural carryovers surviving in present-day Caribbean societies than in American black culture. Melville Herskovitz in his pioneering study of African culture among African Americans identified many elements of West African culture in the Creole languages of the West Indies and in the foods, family forms, and other daily practices of blacks in the Caribbean.[47] Ironically, those people with the closest ties to their African ancestry in the new world, who could perhaps make the best claim of an "African culture," are actually much less likely than American blacks to do so.[48]

Emancipation of Slaves

A final key difference between the Caribbean and the United States has to do with the conditions surrounding emancipation and the political developments that followed. The slaves in the United States were emancipated after a Civil War in which the planter class and the plantation system in the South were defeated. While blacks were granted de jure civil rights, in effect an organized political and social system was enforced for 100 years following the Civil War that effectively denied those rights to blacks in the South. Blacks were systematically disenfranchised and were kept from most skilled occupations through a system of organized terror and exclusion.

In the Caribbean emancipation was decreed by the colonial powers of England and France. Planters were compensated a set sum for the loss of their slaves, and the social system continued as before, although the freed blacks were allowed freedom of movement. The plantation system stayed intact, and free blacks continued to work the land for the planters, augmented by indentured laborers, primarily from India, who were imported to alleviate perceived labor shortages. The growth of peasantries in the Caribbean following emancipation and the success of many West

Indians in acquiring land and occupational skills have been identified as key points of divergence between Caribbean and American black experiences. While the period following emancipation in West Indian societies was not characterized by complete rights and fair treatment of the former slaves, Sidney Mintz writes that there may have been more freedom for the development of individuals "to become persons, to define themselves in terms of what they knew and could do." Mintz contrasts this with the ways in which American blacks in the century following the Civil War were systematically prevented from defining themselves economically as persons.[49]

One important consequence of these historical developments is that when black Americans have contested their inferior position in society and the assaults on their personhood, they have struggled against their white fellow citizens, who are the perpetrators. When black West Indians fought against the injustices that had led to their inferior positions, their white fellow citizens, though directly implicated and surely responsible, were at the same time the agents of a colonial power that had the ultimate responsibility and reaped the ultimate profits. Thus antiracist struggles in the United States are direct personal struggles against an oppressor who is present and implicated in one's very own society. In the Caribbean the struggle against injustice has often been perceived as a struggle against colonial exploitation. Anticolonialism and antiracism are very much intertwined for Caribbean people. Racial domination and the struggle for racial equality in the United States had more immediate and personal targets.[50]

The consequences of these historical differences are that race and the meaning of being black are overall similar in the Caribbean and the United States since both societies were founded with a similar plantation slavery system at their core. But key differences remain that are acutely felt by the black immigrants in New York. First, the demographic reality means that being black is not tied to being minority in the Caribbean in the way that it is in the United States. There are more arenas of life that are racially homogeneous in the Caribbean, and more areas of culture, especially among the peasantry, that are less involved with whites and white culture. The immigrants interviewed for this study describe this demographic difference as central to their own experiences, arguing that race and the problems of race relations are more present in day-to-day life in the United States because of the amount of interpersonal interactions blacks have with whites.

Second, the very definition of being black is sometimes different because of the more complex classification schemes in the Caribbean that take into account color and class. Especially for light-skinned, middle-class immigrants, it can literally be true that they only "became black" when they arrived on American soil.

Finally, the struggle against racism in the Caribbean is less personal and more tied to nationalism and anticolonialism, while in the United States it is a struggle that takes place between coworkers, neighbors, and school-mates. This permeation of race in everyday culture in the United States is also hard for the immigrants to cope with.

RECENT HISTORY

The Americanization of the Caribbean

In the middle of the twentieth century many of the Caribbean islands finally achieved independence. However, the United States came to dominate the islands in a neocolonial relationship that has itself altered these societies. In fact, the very migration experience this book seeks to understand and explain is fundamentally changing the sending islands. Also, in addition to migration, direct American military intervention, American media penetration, and the tourist and drug industries are all leaving their marks on Caribbean life and race relations.

While the European countries controlled most of the Caribbean islands, the proximity of the islands to the United States and its growing economic and political power in the twentieth century made the United States a natural destination for Caribbean people seeking a better life. Immigration laws regulated the flow of people coming from the Caribbean, and changes in the laws over time created distinct waves of West Indian immigrants. The United States had allowed unlimited immigration from the Western Hemisphere until the enactment of immigration restriction laws in 1924. The first immigrant wave of West Indians started circa 1900 and peaked in the late 1910s and early 1920s, with approximately 85,000 West Indians entering between 1900 and 1930.[51] This wave of immigrants settled throughout the East Coast, but they were highly concentrated in New York City, settling in the black neighborhoods of Harlem and Central Brooklyn.[52] West Indians in this wave were on the whole a highly selected group (immigrant laws selected for literacy), and by all accounts these early West Indian immigrants "were over-represented in the professions. They thus played prominent roles in the intellectual, political, and economic leadership of the community."[53]

The immigration laws passed in the 1920s attempted to restrict immigration, but West Indians were able to enter the United States under Great Britain's quota until the Depression.[54] During the Depression pressure to immigrate to the United States dissipated, and in fact some immigrants returned home during this period. Immigration resumed again following World War II, but the McCarran-Walter Act of 1952 prohibited colonial subjects from using the home country quotas and reduced the colonies to quotas of 100 per year, thus cutting off the option of legal immigration for all but a handful of West Indians.[55] It was after this law that the volume of immigration shifted toward Great Britain. During the period of 1952–1965 only relatives of earlier immigrants and a small number of middle-class students or professionals were allowed entry to the United States.[56]

In 1965 the Hart-Celler Act transformed American immigration law by removing racial quotas and substituting a visa preference system with a 170,000 annual limit for the Eastern Hemisphere and a quota of 20,000 legal immigrants per nation.[57] A 120,000 annual quota was put in place for the Western Hemisphere, but there was not a per country limit. While the Western Hemisphere was not subject to the preference system, which set up categories for immigration of either family reunification or occupation, immigrants from the Western Hemisphere who were not immediate family members of U.S. citizens or of permanent resident aliens were subject to labor certification. At that time many Caribbean islands were winning their independence from Great Britain and were poised to take advantage of the slots available. The newly independent West Indian nations were not subject to the small number of slots available for dependencies of European powers and could take advantage of the large Western Hemisphere total of 120,000. Quotas of 20,000 immigrants per country were added in 1976, and the preference system was extended to the

Western Hemisphere. In addition, England severely restricted West Indian migration beginning in 1964, thus creating increased pressure on the United States.

As Philip Kasinitz points out, the numbers of immigrants grew notably after 1965: "In the ten years following the Hart-Celler reforms, West Indian immigration exceeded that of the previous seventy years, and the numbers continued to grow after that. By the early 1980's, fifty thousand legal immigrants from the anglophobe Caribbean and another six thousand to ten thousand from Haiti were arriving in the U.S. each year; approximately half settled in New York City."[58]

According to the 1990 census there were 1,455,294 foreign-born blacks living in the United States, or 4.8% of blacks nationwide. The vast majority of foreign-born blacks were from the Caribbean. The volume of this immigration has affected both the sending and receiving areas. For instance, during the 1980s small islands such as Saint Kitts, Nevis, and Grenada were sending 1 to 2% of their citizens to the United States every year. In the 1980s alone, Jamaica sent 213,805 people to the United States—a full 9% of its total population of 2.5 million people. Guyana too was sending a large proportion of its population, counted in 1984 at 775,000. The New York City Department of Urban Planning estimated that approximately 8% of Guyana's population in the early 1980s was resident in New York City by the end of the decade.[59]

New York City is one of the gateway cities in the United States. In the last few decades it has absorbed a large number of immigrants from around the world and a very high percentage of the nation's Caribbean immigrants. New York is a popular destination for immigrants from both the Hispanic and non-Hispanic Caribbean and draws a disproportionately large share of those immigrants. For instance, among immigrants arriving in the 1980s, 45% of all Jamaican immigrants live in New York, as do 37% of all Haitians, 49% of all Trinidadians, 61% of all Barbadians, and 70% of all Guyanese.[60] While the total population of New York declined from 1970 to 1990, the foreign-born population grew substantially so that 28.2% of the city's population was foreign-born by 1990, with 46% of those immigrants arriving in the previous ten years.[61] By 1996 the number of foreign-born in the city had grown to 2.4 million or 33.9% of the city's total population. In 1990 there were 417,506 non-Hispanic foreign-born blacks in New York City, 23% of the city's non-Hispanic black population. The West Indian ancestry population in the city grew by a very large rate, from 172,192 in 1980 to 391,744 in 1990, an increase of 127.5%. By 1996 it was estimated that 35.1% of the city's black households was headed by a foreign-born person—the vast majority from the Caribbean.

There are a few important reasons why New York is such a popular destination for Caribbean immigrants. A migration flow to New York had already been established by earlier immigrants during the first few decades of the twentieth century. These earlier immigrants chose New York for much the same reasons that black Southerners did at the time. They were enticed both by the jobs available during World War I and its aftermath and by the existence of a thriving black community, especially in Harlem.

The structure of the New York economy also played a large part in the recent immigration. The restructuring of the economy in New York away from manufacturing and toward service made available a number of jobs that could be filled by Caribbean immigrants.[62] Some workers, especially nurses and other health care professionals as well as teachers, were actually recruited during the last few decades.

This migration has been for the most part one way, but there have been considerable permanent return migration and circular migration. The islands have grown dependent on economic remittances from workers abroad for economic survival. The migrants also return with social remittances—notions of race from the United States and Europe and what the West Indians describe as a "concern with racialism."[63] The returning immigrants and the letters and telephone calls home from settled migrants in the United States foster new ideas about categorizing race back home, which are indeed changing conditions on the island.

The growing availability of American television, radio, and music in the islands exports American ideas about race and the tensions between the races in ways that Caribbean people had not experienced or thought about before. West Indians therefore are much more likely to become familiar with American racial categories and etiquette before ever leaving their homes, either through media discussions, experiences with tourists, or the stories of former migrants who have returned home for good or only for a visit.

The interpenetration of the cultures and economies of the Caribbean with the United States means that media images of the beating of Rodney King are shown constantly on Jamaican television. Whites from suburban New York make comments about black laziness as they wait for their bags at the Kingston airport, and little children called niggers on playgrounds in Queens tell their grannies in Trinidad about it on the phone that night.

"Racialism"—the concern with race and the perception of race differences as responsible for other inequalities in society—is growing and becoming widespread in the Caribbean. Lowenthal quotes a Trinidadian in the 1960s: "The Caribbean is a part of the world where racialism is growing. Each act of racial discrimination in England or the United States shakes the foundations of racial harmony in the West Indies."[64]

Economic development in the islands is also having a significant effect on conditions there. The changes in the agricultural world market have undermined the ability of peasants to stay afloat. Many former peasants who cannot make it on the land anymore crowd the slums in the cities of Kingston and Port of Spain looking for work in the cities and mostly not finding it. In all Caribbean states, unemployment grew absolutely and the standard of living declined in the 1970s. At the end of the 1980s unemployment ranged from 10 to 40%.[65] The growth of the drug supply economy in which the Caribbean is a link between the demand of the United States and the supply of South America has also created opportunities for certain sectors of island economies but has undermined traditional workers. As Richardson notes, the production of drugs for the North American economy is part of a long tradition: "In producing and transporting narcotics for metropolitan consumption, Caribbean peoples simply are providing tropical staples for external sources, just as they have for the past five centuries."[66]

Perhaps, however, the growth of tourism has had some of the greatest effects. As Richardson notes, "Roughly 11 million people, including cruise passengers and 'stopovers,' visit the region each year. Tourism is the only activity of note in some smaller islands and, in good years, the leading earner of foreign exchange even in Jamaica."[67] Tourism creates contact between rich, almost always white, North Americans and Europeans and poor, overwhelmingly black, islanders. The resentment of this racial and socioeconomic gulf is growing, as is the daily experience of racial prejudice and unease, which most West Indians had not experienced in as direct and frequent a fashion as black Americans because they lived in societies in which blacks were the majority.

Direct military involvement by the United States in the Caribbean has occurred in many different countries. Haiti, of course, is the most well-known. The U.S. military occupied Haiti from 1915 to 1934 and again in 1994. Mintz has argued that the early occupation exposed the Haitian people to white American racism and prejudice, helped to create a Haitian nationalism, developed a sense of national identity, and reinforced a pride in Haitians for their African origins, in distinction to the ways in which Americans denigrated them for being black.[68] During World War II the United States gave Britain fifty ships in exchange for leases for ninety-nine years for naval bases in Antigua, the Bahamas, British Guiana, Jamaica, Saint Lucia, Trinidad, Bermuda, and Newfoundland. The American base in Trinidad was a major employer of people from Trinidad and the surrounding islands and exposed a great number of them to American conceptions of race relations.

The American invasion of Grenada in 1983 also changed that country dramatically. The U.S. military intervened after a leftist government installed itself after a bloody coup and began building an airstrip to accommodate Soviet jets. After the U.S. military left, the United States granted large amounts of financial aid, leading to improvements in the airport to accommodate bigger jets bringing more tourists and improvements overall in agriculture and the local economy.[69]

The Caribbeanization of the United States

While conditions in the Caribbean and ideas about race and class relations have come to resemble those in the United States, the United States is in some ways also moving closer to the Caribbean model. The effects go both ways, and part of what this study describes is the effect of West Indian immigrants on race relations and concepts of race in New York and in American society more generally.

This chapter has outlined certain key differences between race relations in the Caribbean and the United States—blacks are the majority in the Caribbean and not in the United States; class and race are intertwined in ways that are subtle and fluid in the Caribbean, whereas race has been an overriding status in the United States; blacks have political, if not economic, power in the Caribbean because of their numerical majority. In the United States the "one-drop rule" has defined anyone with any black ancestors as black. An intermediate category for mixed-race people or colored people is socially recognized in the West Indies but not in the United States. Finally, conflict in the Caribbean that is seemingly about race is often one where race is better understood as a marker of socioeconomic inequality; fights about race are more about the gulf between rich and poor.

On each of these points the changes in American race relations and race classifications since the civil rights movement are moving American ideas and practices closer to Caribbean ones. The changes since the civil rights movement in the United States have created a wider gulf between middle-class and poor blacks.[70] As in the Caribbean the differences in behaviors between middle-class and working-class blacks in such areas as school completion, illegitimacy, and so on are quite strong.

While class might not yet determine race classification in the United States, class determines how race is seen. For instance, while Joe Feagin argues that his research with middle-class blacks shows the continuing significance of race for the middle class in terms of prejudice and discrimination, one can also find evidence in his book for the great lengths to which middle-class blacks go to telegraph their class identity to whites in order to prevent such discrimination.[71] In fact, it is in impersonal public places where class status is ambiguous and not proven that much of this discrimination takes place. Sociologist Elijah Anderson's work on presentation of self among blacks in Philadelphia similarly shows that blacks there try to showcase their identities as middle class to differentiate themselves from underclass blacks.[72]

Far from a system that assigns people to one race and then treats all of them alike because of their racial classification, the American race relations of the post–civil rights era are becoming much more subtle and intertwined with class in ways that bring this system closer to the race classification system of the Caribbean. In the United States black-white intermarriage, while still representing a small percentage of marriages overall, is also very much on the rise. While there were 150,00 interracial couples in the United States in 1960, the number had grown to more than

1 million in 1990.[73] Although black-white marriages are still the least prevalent form of intermarriage, among younger people there is evidence of dramatic change. Among black men between ages 25 to 34, 10% have intermarried, most with white women.[74] And as intermarriage grows, the one-drop rule and the lack of an intermediate category for multiracial people are very much under scrutiny and attack from many quarters. The Census Bureau, for instance, will allow multiple responses to the race question for the year 2000 census. A number of groups have pressed for the federal government to create a new "multiracial" category in its statistical system.

In addition, it should be noted that shade and color differences in the United States have always mattered more than either blacks or whites were willing to acknowledge. Recent research by Michael Hughes and Bradley Hertel[75] has shown a strong correlation between shade and socioeconomic position for blacks in the United States. This correlation probably derives from similar forces that gave rise to the correlation in the Caribbean. Black Americans have always been very much aware of color prejudice within the community and of white preferences for lighter-skinned blacks. However, there has long been a taboo about talking about such things outside of the black community. Perhaps there was more official recognition of these divisions in the Caribbean because blacks were the majority.

While it is also true that blacks are the majority in the Caribbean and a minority in the United States, and that they have political control in many countries in the Caribbean as a result of this demographic predominance, conditions in American cities are mimicking to some extent the demographic balance in the Caribbean. In large cities in the United States racial and ethnic minorities are now majorities as whites have abandoned central cities for the surrounding suburbs. Thus in many American cities such as Washington, D.C., Baltimore, New York, Chicago, Detroit, and Los Angeles, blacks have been elected mayor and hold local political power. But just as in the Caribbean situation, those with local political power find that the economic decisions that affect the livelihood of people in their cities are made by absentee whites and a remote national government.

When the black mayor of Washington, Marion Barry, asked the federal government to call in troops to stem the violence in the city's poor neighborhoods that even the local police force, made up overwhelmingly of black officers, was helpless to stop, blacks in Washington, had the experience of what it is like to be in the majority but without the overall power to change conditions they find unacceptable. So too middle-class blacks in the suburbs may not feel that "money whitens," but they think their American Express card changes the ways in which white people respond to them. And mostly it does.

In the thirty years following the civil rights movement the American race-relations scene has changed from a caste system to a system based more on a subtle intersection of past economic discrimination, class and race interactions, and the increasing separation of local political power from ultimate economic power. These factors, along with a growing ac- knowledgment of categories of race between black and white, indicate that the experiences and understandings of blacks in the Caribbean are indeed models for what is happening to blacks in the United States.

However, there are two ways in which race relations are still starkly different between the Caribbean and the United States. Both are clearly a major influence on the experiences of the immigrants from the Caribbean and not likely to change in the United States. First, while the local demo- graphics might be changing in some cities, the United States is still a white-majority society, and this has important everyday implications for blacks. The degree of interracial contact in the United States is quite high, especially for people in the workforce and most especially for middle-class blacks. The dominance of whites in positions of authority is also a crucial factor affecting all aspects of race relations.

Second, American society is a fundamentally racist society. The Carib- bean is a society where there is racism.[76] The difference has to do with the development by the large white-majority population in the United States of a culture and rationale surrounding slavery and its aftermath of subju- gation of blacks; this involved the white majority defining itself as opposed to and not including black people.[77] Despite the formal rights and privi- leges accorded to black people in the United States, the culture of white Americans is exclusionary in certain fundamental ways toward blacks.[78] Many people are working toward changing the attitudes and behaviors that follow from this, but at its core the United States is still a racist society.

The Caribbean, on the other hand, never had a large enough white population, nor a developed enough national culture based on that population, to develop the deep structures necessary to ingrain racism within the national consciousness. While white planters most clearly developed ideas of black inferiority, the combination of fluid boundaries and demographic majorities of blacks meant that while racism was endemic, it was not defining.

It is important to understand the very distinctive social history of the Caribbean in order to understand the immense subtleties and layers of meaning attached to race and color among present-day immigrants. The fragile and recent sense of "nationality" the immigrants inherit means that simple analogies to the sense of ethnic identity brought to the United States by earlier European immigrants are not accurate. Indeed, the sense of nationality that Jamaicans or Barbadians hold may also be less meaningful to them than the nationality that Chinese or Dominican or Haitian immigrants bring with them. This is because a regional identity as West Indian is a meaningful category of identity for people who have long migration histories in their backgrounds, and because of the recency of the nation-states in the Caribbean. Migration is nothing new to Caribbean islanders; it has been a way of coping with economic and political troubles for generations. Simple before-and-after migration dichotomies are likely to be less useful with such a mobile population than they may have been with other immigrant groups to the United States. The differences between sending and receiving societies are also very dynamic in nature, so in addition to asking how moving from one society to another changes the migrant, it is also important to study how the links of migration and of the economy are changing both societies. The next chapter examines how the immigrants fashion their own identities and cultures in New York out of the raw materials history has given them.

RACIAL AND ETHNIC
IDENTITY CHOICES

3

The question of identity has always been particularly salient for the immigrant. Arriving as
a stranger in a new society, the immigrant
must decide how he or she self-identifies, and
the people in the host society must decide how
they will categorize or identify the immigrant.
This is a dynamic and ongoing process as the
newcomers fit into their new environment and as the environment itself
is changed by their arrival. The social identities the immigrants adopt or
are assigned can have enormous consequences for individuals. This chapter examines the racial and ethnic identities of black Caribbean immigrants. Given the historical baggage described in the previous chapter that
the immigrants bring with them, how do they define themselves once they
get to the United States?

Ethnic or racial identities are social identities. As Virginia Dominguez
notes, they can only be understood in context as people relate to one another:

> Social identities are unlike material objects. Whereas material ob-
> jects have a concrete existence whether or not people recognize their
> existence, social identities do not. An identity is a conception of the
> self, a selection of physical, psychological, emotional or social attrib-
> utes of particular individuals; it is not an individual as a concrete
> thing. It is only in the act of naming an identity, defining an identity
> or stereotyping an identity that identity emerges as a concrete real-
> ity. Not only does that identity have no social relevance when it is
> not named; it simply does not exist when it has not been conceived
> and elevated to public consciousness.[1]

Psychologists have shown in controlled experiments that humans have an in-group preference. The desire to feel good about themselves leads individuals to also want to feel good about their group.[2] Even something as simple as an experiment dividing people according to an arbitrary distinction, such as eye color or whether they overestimate or underestimate the length of a line, can lead to an accentuation of group boundaries and to a desire to make oneself look better by making the out-group look worse. Though a desire that one's own group be better than the "other" group seems to be hardwired into humans, the question of the boundaries that are salient to any one individual at any one time is an open one. Individuals have a range of possible groups they can feel attachments to—groups based on interests, shared histories, shared futures, achievements, or ascribed characteristics. The in-group that contributes to social identity could be a community when one roots for the home baseball team, gender when one decides whom to vote for, ethnicity when one decides how to celebrate family holidays, or, as numerous science fiction movies point out, humanness if one were faced with the possibility of alien invaders from outer space.

The word "ethnic" has generally referred to groups defined by cultural attributes, while "racial" groups have been defined by physical attributes. In the folk usage of these terms in present-day America, whites and blacks are racial groups distinct from one another based on skin color, hair texture, and facial features—physical characteristics that define a person as socially white or black. Ethnic groups refer to groups that share practices, languages, behaviors, or ancestral origins. Italians and Poles are ethnic groups, as are Cape Verdeans, Jamaicans, and Ethiopians. Yet Americans have generally paid a great deal of attention to ethnic differences within the white race, while treating black Americans as if they were both a racial and an ethnic group with no intraracial differences. Thus Census Bureau reports will contrast the incomes of Irish Americans, Japanese Americans, and African Americans—yet the category of African Americans glosses over subgroups defined ethnically, such as West Indians or Haitians.

Even if we limit the possible sources of social identity to race and ethnicity, individuals logically have a multitude of possible ways of identifying. For instance, I can think of myself as a white person and see all whites as my in-group, or I can claim an Irish-American identity and regard many other non-Irish whites as outsiders to my group, or I can identify as an American and define all other Americans, regardless of race, as my ethnic group. Often Americans only come to think of themselves as an ethnic group when they are traveling or living abroad because at home we are more focused on what divides us. Yet for all of these possibilities, it is clear that several forces affect and shape the social identities people adopt—the definitions and meanings attached to different groups by the individual and the definitions and meanings attached to groups by society.

Recent writing in the humanities as well as in the social sciences on the concept of social identities has built upon a foundation laid by the nineteenth-century German social theorist George Simmel. In an essay entitled "The Stranger," Simmel argues that a stranger serves a very important function for the group that he or she encounters. The stranger helps the group to define what its members have in common and who they are because the stranger provides an example of what they are not. The characteristics, beliefs, or behaviors of the stranger are defined as "the Other," which then makes clear who the "we" of the group are.[3] Much recent writing, especially in the humanities, has focused on the use of an "Other" to create social identities. Kian Woon Kwok describes the importance of "the Other" to the construction of social identities:

> Identity is a relational concept; it implies a relationship between one group and an Other or Others, whether real or imagined, whether clearly specified or not. Thus, part of the process of identifying "us" is to make the Other out to be different. In some instances, the Other is clearly specified and the relation is that of "us" vs. "them." Thus "us" is identified by how "they" perceive "us" as "their Other," and a more conscious position is taken to counter *their* perception of us if it is negative and to confirm it if it is positive. In either case, when this is done, the group consciously or unconsciously builds its self-image through the perception of others.[4]

The construction and adoption of a racial and ethnic social identity represent an ongoing negotiation between self and other identification, which reflects the meanings attached to possible identities and boundaries. Alejandro Portes and Dag MacLeod describe the process as a symbolic interaction between ethnic minorities and the host society that in-volves a dizzying loop: "what they think your ethnicity is influences what you think your ethnicity is, to say nothing of what they think you think your ethnicity is."[5]

But racial and ethnic identities are not zero-sum entities; it is possible to hold several at any one time, and they are very clearly situational. In one situation a person can feel very American, at another time Irish, and at yet another time white—or one could hold all identities simultane-ously. But the recognition of the multiplicity and situationality of social identities does not mean that people are free to choose any identity they want or to attach any meaning they want to any particular identity. History and current power relations create and shape the opportunities people face in their day-to-day lives, giving some people "ethnic options" and others "racial labels." There are also shared or contested meanings attached to different groups that affect individuals' ways of thinking about themselves.

An incident recounted by one of the respondents in the study shows in a concrete way many of these meanings as they shape the identities of black Caribbean immigrants. Shelley was a 25-year-old woman from Barbados, who had been in the United States three years. She was a poor woman who came as a domestic worker, and after a while left the family she came to work for and got a job as a cashier in a 7-Eleven convenience store. On one of her first nights on duty, a black American woman attempted to steal some food. Shelley pointed out to the woman that this was wrong, and that she had to put the food back. Shelley also threatened to call the police. The woman replied, "Come on, you are my sister, you are from down South, from Georgia too." Shelley responded, "No, I am Caribbean." She remem-bers this as the first time she used this word to describe herself. Later, she told the manager of the store, who was Jamaican, what had happened, and the manager told her, "No, you are a West Indian, not a Caribbean." He told her that "Caribbean" included Spanish people, whereas "West In-dian" did not. And so from then on Shelley knew she was a West Indian, and that is how she answered people when they inquired.

The participants in this incident were invoking various layers of boundaries separating groups in our society. In other words, there were various "Others" being held up to Shelley as possible contrasts to help her define herself. When the would-be thief invoked a sisterhood based in part on race and on a common origin in the South, she was saying to Shelley: we are both black and not white. The blacks are the "us" and the whites are the "them." When Shelley responded that she was Caribbean, she was including her Jamaican boss as part of her group and encompassing within the line that separated "us" and "them" all foreign-born people of whatever race from a particular part of the world—the Caribbean. It did not occur to her in that situation to draw the line based on her particular island, although one could imagine a situation where that could happen. When her Jamaican boss told Shelley that she was not Caribbean but, rather, West Indian, he was once again invoking race and ethnicity to draw the lines—redefining the "we" to mean foreign-born blacks and distancing Hispanics as "the Other."

Myths and stereotypes as well as personal experience play a part in the definitions used by all of these players. While Shelley came to her identity in the very act of denying sisterhood to a black American, the circumstances under which she did so highlight the views many West Indian immigrants hold of black Americans. The sisterhood she was denying was not one of challenging white racial privilege or working together for positive goals for the black community, but instead it was a sisterhood of poverty and theft. The bonds she shared with her Jamaican boss were hard work and strong moral values. Of course, most black Americans would also deny an ethnic or racial link that was invoked to deter them from asserting their strong values against criminality. Yet for Shelley and many other immigrants, the image they hold of black Americans often does not include good hard-working black Americans, who are often invisible in their neighborhoods and in the mass media. Rather their image of American blacks most often includes the images of the underclass, including drugs, broken families, and criminality.

As Chapter 2 has shown, history and circumstance have conspired to give West Indian immigrants in New York a variety of choices and possibilities in terms of describing their racial and ethnic identities. There are layers of ethnic and racial appellations available to them, and there is a great deal of variation in how individuals choose to deal with those layers. These individuals could describe themselves as blacks, as Caribbean people, as West Indians, or as different specific ethnic or national origin groups such as Trinidadians, Grenadians, or Jamaicans, or they could adopt an American identity—either hyphenated or unhyphenated. While certain variations in individual taste play a part in how respondents in the study described themselves, certain patterns did emerge. For all the respondents identity was socially constructed and situational: it mattered who they were with, what the circumstances were, and who was doing the asking and defining of identities and labels. After a brief review of the difficulties of capturing all of the different identities and subidentities of West Indian immigrants using American census categories, this chapter will describe the various ways these immigrants come to define themselves in New York and the various "Others" they use to create those identities.

STATISTICAL DATA ON WEST INDIAN IMMIGRANTS

Most research conducted on the experiences of West Indians in the United States, particularly research focused on their socioeconomic incorporation, utilizes quantitative data collected by the U.S. government.[6] But the ambiguities of race, ethnicity, and nationality described in Chapter 2 ensure that there is a clash between the identities of the immigrants and American record-keeping systems. The main sources of data on black immigrants are the U.S. decennial census questions on race, ancestry, and birthplace and the data provided by the Immigration and Naturalization Service (INS). The INS data on immigrants entering the country each year are categorized by birthplace and by place of last residence. As we have seen, however, the countries of the Caribbean are multiracial and multiethnic, and the INS does not ask an immigrant's race. Knowing that someone is from Trinidad or Guyana does not indicate whether that person is East Indian or black.[7] INS data are also limited to legal immigrants. Since some proportion of immigrants from these countries enter illegally, this is another source of bias.

The decennial census asks a separate birthplace, race, and ancestry question, along with a question on year of immigration. These are the data that are most often used to ascertain the racial and ethnic mix of immigrants. Table 3.1 provides data on birthplace by race for New York State immigrants and data on the percentage of black or African in the home countries of the immigrants. Table 3.1 shows that immigrants coming from

Table 3.1   Race of foreign-born, New York State, 1990

Place of birth	Foreign-born population, New York	Percent black on U.S. race question	Percent black in country of origin
Jamaica	150,924	97.1	97.5
Guyana	82,232	68.3	30.5
Trinidad	63,813	88.2	41.1
Barbados	27,760	97.1	94.0
Haiti	88,266	97.9	95.0
Grenada	12,702	98.5	100.0

Sources: For foreign-born: United States Census Bureau, Ethnic and Hispanic Branch, Population Divison, *The Foreign Born Population in the United States: 1990,* Publication CPH-L-98. For U.S. race question: Calculated from United States Census Bureau, Public Use Microdata Sample Tapes (PUMS), Sample C. New York State (1990). For black in country of origin: Gale Research, Inc., *Countries of the World and Their Leaders Yearbook* (1994).

countries such as Jamaica, Barbados, Haiti, and Grenada, who are from more homogeneously black societies, overwhelmingly identify as black on the U.S. census. Guyanese and Trinidadians are more diverse in their immigrant streams, as they are in their native countries. But note that while 68.3% of Guyanese in New York State say they are black, only 30.5% of those in Guyana say they are. And while 88.2% of Trinidadian New Yorkers say they are black, only 41.1% of people in Trinidad say they are.

The immigrants enter the United States with experience of a different racial and ethnic categorization system—one that recognizes a variety of categories between black and white. The race question on the U.S. census thus causes difficulties for many respondents. Often the immigrants will not answer a race question or will not answer it in the way the census takers want them to. In fact, the 1990 census results included about 370,000 persons out of the entire black population of 30,000,000 who did not mark the "black" category in their responses. About 50% of these people had checked the "other" race category on the race question. The Census Bureau reported that although it had "anticipated that most of the write-ins would be African-American, most, about three-quarters, were ethnic subgroups such as Jamaican and Haitian within the Black population."[8]

An examination of the patterns of answers to the census ancestry question shows some of the variations across national origin groups that reflect the demographics and histories of the different islands. Table 3.2

Table 3.2   Ancestry distribution of foreign-born blacks, New York State, 1990

Place of birth	Place of birth	West Indian	Afro-American	None	Other
			Ancestry		
Jamaica	80.5	3.0	5.2	9.2	2.1
Guyana	60.3	6.4	10.6	8.8	13.9
Trinidad	51.9	17.8	11.0	11.1	8.2
Barbados	55.9	17.0	10.6	10.6	5.9
Haiti	84.7	1.0	1.6	11.1	1.6
Grenada	49.2	18.3	12.7	12.7	7.1

Source: Calculated from United States Census Bureau, Public Use Microdata Sample Tapes (PUMS), Sample C (1990).

Note: Ancestry is first ancestry reported.

provides a cross-tabulation of ancestry by birthplace for immigrants who said they were black on the race question. This table shows that there is not a one-to-one correspondence between birthplace and ancestry for immigrants. For instance, among black immigrants who report their birthplace as Barbados, 55.9% report their ancestry as Barbadian (either as single or multiple ancestry), 17% report their ancestry as the pan-ethnic "West Indian," 10.6% report that they are Afro-American, and 10.6% give no response. People born in Jamaica and Haiti are far more likely to give Jamaican or Haitian as their ancestry than those born in other West Indian countries, reflecting Haiti's more established national identity and Jamaica's greater "presence" as an identity in New York. Still, only 80.5% of black people reporting Jamaica as their birthplace say they are Jamaican on the ancestry question; 9% give no response, 5% say they are Afro-American, and 3% say they are West Indian.

Those born in Trinidad and Barbados are likely to give West Indian as a response and are also far more likely than other immigrants to say they are Afro-American. Guyanese are also likely to say they are Afro-American. This is understandable because Guyanese and Trinidadians come from societies that are more diverse ethnically and racially than the other countries, and Barbados has had the largest and most continuous white presence in the islands.[9] Immigrants from these three countries are probably used to identifying themselves via their African heritage or black race to differentiate themselves from other ethnic and racial groups in their country.[10] The Guyanese and Trinidadians were also more likely to give a double ancestry response than immigrants from other islands, reflecting the heterogeneity of their sending societies.

There are problems of bias in all of the methods available to estimate black immigrants from the Caribbean. Take, for instance, Jamaican immigrants. If we use the INS data on people immigrating from Jamaica to estimate the population of first-generation black Jamaican Americans, we would overestimate the number because nonblack Jamaicans would be included. But we would also be underestimating the number because we would miss illegal immigrants who do not show up in INS statistics. If we used the census birthplace question, we would still include some non-blacks. If we used the ancestry question, we would miss some people who identify as Afro-American or West Indian. (Only 80.5% of New York State people who were born in Jamaica say they are Jamaican on the ancestry question.) Likewise, if we used the ancestry question alone, we would include people who do not identify as black racially. In New York State 5% of those born in the United States who say they are of Jamaican ancestry do not choose "black" on the race question.[11] If we used the race question together with the birthplace question, we would have a reasonable approximation, but we would still miss those people who describe themselves as "other" on the race question, but who would probably be labeled as black in American society.

While these difficulties in clearly defining the groups using census data may seem esoteric, they actually can have important implications for research and policy debates. The birthplace question provides a "hard" piece of data that allows us to identify the first generation. But once we start using "softer" data such as the ancestry question, we lose some people. In the case of Trinidadians in New York State, for instance, the ancestry "Trinidadian" only identifies 52% of people born in Trinidad. Among the second generation—children of immigrants—we have no "hard" piece of data to reclassify those of West Indian ancestry. So if second-generation Trinidadians or Guyanese say they are African American on the ancestry question, there is no way of using the census data to differentiate them from African Americans whose families have been in this country for hundreds of years. (This problem of identifying the second generation using subjective data is explored more fully in Chapter 8.)

Table 3.3   Ancestry response by years in the United States by foreign-born blacks,
             New York State, 1990

Place of birth	Year of immigration				
	1985–90	1980–84	1970s	1960s	Pre-1960
Jamaica	75.0	80.4	82.1	84.5	83.6
Guyana	61.0	58.2	60.2	64.9	61.1
Trinidad	49.6	47.7	54.3	52.8	55.6
Haiti	76.4	84.8	86.2	92.0	82.4

Source: Calculated from United States Census Bureau, Public Use Microdata Sample Tapes
(PUMS), Sample C (1990).
   Note: Ancestry is first ancestry reported.

It appears that the identities adopted by the first generation are in part
a learned response to American categories and ways of defining people.
There are some shifts in reporting the longer people are here. Table 3.3
provides the pattern of responding to the ancestry question by number of
years in the United States for people born in Jamaica, Guyana, Trinidad,
and Haiti. Among all the groups, the most recent immigrants are most
likely not to answer the ancestry question, and the percentage reporting
an ancestry that matches their place of birth rises with more time spent in
the United States. The percentage of people answering West Indian and
Afro-American remains relatively constant over time, although it varies by
group in the ways just described above.

EXPLAINING THE PATTERNS

The immigrants in this study provide further details to explain these
patterns of identification. The very act of having to answer these questions
bothered many respondents, and they commented on the constant questioning about race on forms for employment, educational institutions,
and the government as one of the most surprising and troubling aspects
of life in the United States. Learning that they were black according to
American racial schemes and learning how to fill out the various questions
on race, ethnicity, and nationality were important parts of the immigrant
adjustment experience. We took advantage of these experiences when I
and the other interviewers asked all of the immigrants a series of questions
about their race and ethnicity. The question we posed was "When forms

or surveys ask about your race, what do you usually put down?" Then we
followed up with "When forms or surveys ask about your ethnicity, what
do you usually say?" Like people nationwide answering the census, our
respondents were much more apt to have problems with the ancestry or
ethnicity question than the race question.[12] When they requested
clarification, we said something like "ethnic group, as when you are asked
if you are Italian or Irish or Haitian or the like."[13]

While most people did understand the questions and answered with
appropriate labels and then went on to discuss them with us, some people
had more difficulty. One teacher responded to the question "What is your
race?" with the reply "What races do you have?," as if she were ordering a
type of sandwich. When told the possibilities were up to her, she chose
"Negro" as the answer, and then explained that there had been interbreed-
ing in her past and she knew she had some Irish blood in her. Another
man responded directly that he did not understand the question: "Ethnicity? I didn't bring my dictionary, so break it down into so many words."
When told the standard definition of ethnicity, he replied, "I'm Jamaican,
right?," as if this were a school test he could pass or fail. One individual
responded to a question about race by saying, "You mean skin color, don't
you?" Some people told us the question was strange or used the occasion
to launch into a discussion of the difficulties they had understanding
questions on race and ethnicity. Others asked whether nationality was the
same as ethnicity because they knew from their own experiences that
nationality and ethnicity are not the same.

A few people volunteered that they were very skeptical of people asking
about their racial identities and that whenever possible they did not answer the question. These individuals thought people were gathering information about their race in order to possibly discriminate against them:

> I always want to know why they want to know that. You know? I
> understand it's for the census takers—but the sooner we stop that,
> I think this demanding to know if it is white or black, and these
> census forms, the sooner we will get rid of this bias in attitudes.
> (Trinidadian female teacher, age 63, in United States ten years)

The different systems of race classification especially confused middle-
class light-skinned or mixed-ancestry people. Many of these respondents

would have had their mixed ancestry and their higher social status recognized back home where "money whitens." Some people dealt with this dilemma by accepting the United States racial categories and the fact that in America one is seen by others as black. This Guyanese food-service worker has a black mother and an Indian father and answered the question as follows:

> I still put black because in America you are either black, Spanish, or you're white. So if I put mixed, then they would want to know mixed with what? So I just put black, because I am a black woman. (Guyanese female worker, age 48, in United States twelve years)

Others dealt with the starkly different categories of American race relations by developing a "raceless" persona; that is, they denied that they ever had thought of themselves as black or that being black made a difference in their lives. Interestingly, all of the individuals who chose this path were middle class, and most were light-skinned (although they would be classified as black by most Americans). For instance, this Jamaican teacher describes how race does not matter to her either here or in Jamaica:

> I always think of myself as Jamaican. I really never think of color. It's something that is the furthest thing from me. I've got to see it on TV to remember that I'm black. I'm sorry, but I grew up with a lot of white people, a lot of Chinese. I went to school with a lot of white people and I was just another student, another person. I went to their house. I never felt any different and these were all strangers. That black business is not in my book . . . I never knew I was black until I left Jamaica. I left Jamaica when I was 22 years old. It's difficult at that time to start learning anything and I refused to learn that. (Jamaican female teacher, age 51, in United States eighteen years)[14]

As we shall see in Chapter 5, coming to terms with the meaning of being black in America is particularly hard for middle-class people with this particular coping strategy.

Using the Term "West Indian"

For most people the decision to call themselves West Indian or a more specific nationality is situation-specific, and the identities are more or less interchangeable. When they are with a large number of non-West Indians, they tend to identify themselves as West Indian or as "island people" and to feel an affinity with any other immigrant from the islands. When there is a critical mass of people of their own ethnic group, or when they are among only or predominantly island people, they tend to identify with their particular island and to make distinctions and draw social boundaries between different islands.

We found some exceptions to this general pattern. Two middle-class respondents preferred the term "Caribbean" to "West Indian." One took issue with Columbus's original use of the term "Indian" and saw "West Indian" as continuing to embody colonialist views of the region. He preferred "Caribbean" because the root of the word, "Carib," came from the indigenous people of the islands. The other person who preferred "Caribbean" related the choice to the political attempts in the 1960s to form a federation of the new republics in the Caribbean. He was opposed to the nationalistic tendencies that had undermined that federation and did not want to identify with his native Jamaica because it fed into that sense of disunity.

People from Guyana had some special considerations in making the decision to call themselves West Indians. Some of the food-service workers from Guyana stressed that their country was not an island and was not part of the West Indies; rather, it was part of South America, and they preferred to be called South American. They were tired of Americans who had no idea where Guyana was and usually assumed it was in Africa. Interestingly, a few food-service workers and all of the middle-class teachers from Guyana argued exactly the opposite, lecturing me on how people did not usually understand that Guyana was West Indian, how it shared the culture and history of the islands, and how it had joined a federation with the islands of the region. They believed they had every right to call themselves West Indian.[15]

Yet for most respondents "West Indian" was a natural identity that reflected situational concerns. Some of the immigrants explained that they had thought of themselves as West Indians before immigrating because they had attended the University of the West Indies where there were people from many different islands, and they had seen how similar they were. Some immigrants had come to New York after living in another country as a migrant. For example, some Grenadians and Bajans[16] had lived in Trinidad or Panama before arriving in the United States. Though their island nationality was heightened while they resided in the island they had migrated to, their sense that they were West Indian similarly heightened when they moved to New York because they had a background that included more than one island. In addition, individuals from small islands such as Grenada, Saint Kitts, Nevis, and Montserrat were likely to encounter Americans who had never heard of their islands. Sometimes people from the smaller islands found it easier to tell Americans that they were West Indians:

> I say I'm from the West Indies. I'm from Saint Kitts, the West Indies, because some of them they don't know about Saint Kitts. They say, what's that? Jamaican? I say, don't you know? They say, no I never heard about Saint Kitts. If they don't know where you are from and you have an accent, as long as you're black, they say you are from Jamaica. But West Indians we come from the same background. No matter if it is Jamaican or Saint Kitts, you know, you still a West Indian. (Saint Kitts female worker, age 37, in United States sixteen years)

Other immigrants from the larger islands of Jamaica or Trinidad, which had more of a sense of developed nationhood, did not think of themselves as West Indians until they arrived in New York:

> Before I came here I used to be Jamaican. But now I'm West Indian. I think West Indian places you in a position with other people. We share a lot of the same culture, climate, whatever. So I think it's easier to say I'm West Indian. If you want to know more, I'll say, well, I'm from Jamaica. (Jamaican female teacher, age 38, in United States seven years)

Like immigrants from villages in Poland and Italy who did not discover they were Polish or Italian until they came to the United States at the end of the last century, these newcomers discover that the milieu of New York tends to reinforce a West Indian identity. People from the different islands tend to live and work together; while they continue to see differences in behaviors and personalities among those from different islands, they primarily see more similarities than differences and thus call themselves West Indians.

Images of Different Islands

Even though people slip easily between a wider West Indian identity and a more specific national origin identity, the immigrants have definite images of what people from different islands are like. What is striking in the patterns of responses is that respondents could describe various cultural differences across the islands, but these perceived differences did not seem to affect the respondents' willingness to be grouped together as West Indians or to affect their attitudes toward very close interactions such as intermarriage. People smiled when we asked whether different islands had different personalities or characteristics, and most answered, "Of course." And, surprisingly, people were as likely to describe the negative images of their own island as well as the positive images they and others held. For instance, the response of this Jamaican immigrant was typical:

> Trinidadians don't save—they spend, they are consumer-driven. On the other hand, Barbadians plan, even younger ones, for the future. Jamaicans are more self-confident to some extent and therefore will tend to be more boastful and show off and will tend to look down on other Caribbean people. (Jamaican male teacher, age 41, in United States five years)

Barbadians were seen as very British in their identities, often cheap, and uptight. The men were described as sexist. Trinidadians were described primarily as party-loving people:

> You just love to be Trinidadian because the Trinidadian people love to have fun. They just love to party . . . All the Trinidadians are into having fun and a good time and partying and eating and dressing well. You know the men dress, they look good, and they smell good. (Trinidadian female supervisor, age 38, in United States twenty-one years)

Negative images associated with this happy-go-lucky reputation included being lazy and not working as hard and not saving money as much as other West Indians. But another Trinidadian woman, though agreeing that Trinidadians are easy-going people who like to enjoy themselves, went on to say that the Trinidadian people who fit this description are those, like herself, who are from the countryside; in New York, however, she has met some Trinidadians from Port of Spain who are mean fighters and will "stab you for something in a minute."

The Guyanese are also described as easy-going and laid-back. Several Guyanese people stressed that they are exceptionally respectful to the elderly, courteous, and honest. Several of the women interviewed stated that Guyanese men were very sexist and macho, and they did not understand how Guyanese women could put up with them. (This was a complaint heard in general about West Indian men, especially from African American women and some African American men.)

People had the most to say about Jamaicans. Perhaps because they are the most numerous group in New York, Jamaicans similarly had the largest "presence" in terms of recognition of a specific Jamaican identity by immigrants and nonimmigrants alike. Positive characteristics of Jamaicans included their ambition, their business sense, and their fearlessness. They were also seen to be more liberal than some of the other groups. The most common negative images centered on their supposed violence. They were described as short-tempered, feisty, evil, and prone to aggressive and violent behavior. This Guyanese teacher describes the images she has of Jamaicans:

> You go into these schools and the West Indians are the best behaved except for the Jamaicans. And I don't know what it is in them that they're so feisty; they got like this evil type of thing. They could just like shoot you off in a minute without even thinking. You know they have no regard for life. Even their own people are scared of them sometimes. You know, 'cause my Jamaican friend he was saying, "Boy, I don't go near to no Jamaican person." 'Cause he said they have no regard for life. (Guyanese female teacher, age 33, in United States eight years)

Jamaicans were the only group that were consistently described as having a criminal element, and many of the respondents, Jamaican and non-Jamaican alike, talked about Jamaican posses and the drug trade as distinguishing Jamaicans from other West Indian groups. Most people who did speak about these differences did make a distinction between law-abiding, middle-class Jamaicans, whom they described as maybe a little arrogant but hard-working and with good family values, and the lower-class, more recently arrived Jamaican immigrants, who were involved in violence and drugs:

> Jamaica is a place where we have many different people. Our motto says it best—"Out of many, one people"—and I have seen many people here who are very negative, who I really wish didn't leave Jamaica, because they come here and I too see them in a negative light. They cuss, they're loud, they play the music loud, they really behave in a way that puts Jamaica in a bad light. But they are not the typical Jamaican. The typical Jamaican is a person like me, nice, good, qualified. (Jamaican female teacher, age 47, in United States twelve years)

While Jamaicans are described in both negative and positive terms, the Haitians are described by all of the different groups in the most negative terms possible. Haitians definitely have a bad reputation. Everyone we spoke with shared many negative stereotypes about Haitians,[17] many of which originate in Haiti being a very poor country and the source of the poorest immigrants in New York. The Haitians were described as noisy, not dressing well, not bathing enough, smelling bad, and living like savages in dirt and squalor, with many people to one room. They were also described as aggressive, selfish, and pushy people who would cheat anyone if they had the chance. Voodoo practices were mentioned by many as another threat posed by Haitians. The teachers described a great deal of tension in the schools with all of the various West Indian children looking down on the Haitian children. These conflicts are exacerbated because few Haitians speak English, and the language divide makes close friendships or alliances unlikely among the first generation. The implications of these negative images of Haitians for the second generation will be explored in detail in Chapter 8.

Intermarriage

Sociologists have long used intermarriage as the ultimate test of assimilation. Attitudes toward intermarriage and the actual likelihood of inter-

marriage across ethnic, religious, or racial lines signify psychological acceptance and the close day-to-day contact that is necessary for romance to
develop. In a previous study I conducted of later-generation white ethnics
in the United States, racial boundaries were still paramount in how my
respondents thought of intermarriage.[18] Religious boundaries were of
some limited importance, and ethnic boundaries were routinely crossed.
Yet even though the white ethnics I talked to were just as likely to marry
someone from another white ethnic group as they were to marry someone
from their own, there was still attention paid to the boundary. For instance, in discussions of Italians marrying Irish, no respondents in that
study expected their families would disown them (as some families still
would for an interracial marriage, and as was common in white in-
terethnic marriages only a generation or two ago). But there were still
discussions of the adjustments that would have to be made—that Italian
spouses might expect different foods or levels of emotional expressiveness
than Irish spouses would be accustomed to.

It was surprising therefore to find that the respondents in this study did
not make parallel distinctions in talking about intermarriage between
people from different islands, despite the fact that these respondents
differentiate among the islands and ascribe different personalities to people from these separate societies.

We asked a series of questions about intermarriage and found that
none of the respondents defined a marriage between West Indians from
different islands as an intermarriage. They thought the cultural and social
differences between these two groups were so slight that they would not
cause any problems in any families. Hardly anyone saw any problems with
intermarrying with American blacks. This was true however the question
was asked—whether the respondents themselves could ever have married
someone from a different island or the United States, whether their parents would have been upset if they had intermarried, or whether the
respondents would have any reactions to their children intermarrying.
Although some people said the differences between the groups were stark,
everyone knew of individuals who did not fit their negative stereotypes of
the other groups. Most people saw no problems.

Though most respondents noted that interracial marriages could pose
problems for the couple and the children, they were open to such mar-

riages both for themselves and for their relatives. A small minority reported that they would be upset by such marriages. Immigrants from Guyana and Trinidad stressed the pluralist nature of their homelands and pointed out that there was a great deal of intermarriage occurring there already and they were used to it.

The question of intermarriage provoked much less discussion and emotion than similar questions I asked of white ethnics in my earlier study, *Ethnic Options.* I got the impression that boundaries around marriage were just not as important to these immigrants. Many pointed out that with so few people actually marrying these days, they were grateful whenever a marriage took place and took joy in it rather than second-guessing whether ethnic or racial characteristics should play a part.

The one boundary that was important to a significant number of respondents was religion. People who were born-again Christians or who were extremely active in their church did not believe in marriages across religious lines, and they said they would be very disappointed if their children were to marry people of a different religion. They were mostly referring to marrying nonbelievers or Jews, Moslems, or Hindus. Protestants and Catholics did not see much difference between their two religions, and different Protestant denominations or sects did not seem to proscribe intermarriage with other denominations or sects.[19]

I did not ask a question about marriage across class lines, reflecting no doubt my American bias to emphasize race, ethnicity, and religion but not class. It is possible that some of the emotional valence surrounding marriage I picked up in my study of whites would have appeared with these respondents if I had thought to ask the intermarriage question in terms of light-skinned people marrying dark-skinned people, or middle-class people marrying lower-class people. What is clear from the questions I did ask is that the immigrants were either truly not making group distinctions when it came to evaluating their own or their relatives' marriage choices, or the categories I was asking about did not match the categories that would trigger their reactions. In retrospect I think it was the latter.

Racial Identities

The situation determines the identity chosen by most people, and there is a great deal of ease in moving back and forth between different identities.

This interchangeability of identity labels also extends to many people for whom their racial identity as black is foremost in their consciousness. Many respondents stated that they thought of themselves as black when they felt threatened by whites. This Guyanese immigrant describes how racial threats call forth his racial identity:

> When I am in the situation in which blacks are threatened as such by whites generally, I assume a position of a black man. Whenever you have general problems at work, for example, it may not be against Guyanese or a West Indian, it may be against a black American, and in that context therefore I assume a black posture. And whenever the conflict relates mainly to Guyana, or if I am discussing an issue in the Caribbean of which there is a particular feature of Guyana which would play an important part in the discussion, then in those circumstances, I am Guyanese. (Guyanese male teacher, age 36, in United States two years)

Finding oneself in the minority also calls forth a racial identity. One 38-year-old Jamaican teacher described how she looks for black faces whenever she enters a neighborhood she has never been in before. It does not matter whether the faces are Jamaican or not; in order to feel at home she wants to see a black face: "It's good to identify a face that's you know, looks like yours, but black is black, it's not Jamaican."

This Jamaican teacher describes how his racial and ethnic identities coexist for different purposes:

> I think of myself as a black person when it comes to fighting some of the structures. A West Indian among blacks and whites when it comes to being different and distinct, full of pride, having a solid history and solid background, educationally and socially and everything else, achievements in school, in politics, in government, in economics, and breakthroughs. Some of the West Indians who have come here and done very well here, I identify with that. (Jamaican male teacher, age 41, in United States five years)

But this does not mean that people are equally comfortable with all of the different groups. Most people claimed to be far more comfortable with foreign-born blacks than American-born. One Jamaican teacher explains why:

> I am much more comfortable with Jamaicans. That's home. When you are with Jamaicans you are with people that you understand, people that you know, who eat the same food you eat, people when you say something that is not English they understand . . . I can laugh and chat and feel at home. I know their likes and dislikes. I know how not to offend them. With the others you have be on your p's and q's all the time just in case you may say something they don't understand or you may say something that may offend them because people are so touchy. (Jamaican female teacher, age 50, in United States eighteen years)

The fact that the situation determined whether their race or national identity was most salient at any one time did not mean that people were choosing *between* race and ethnicity. Most respondents were very proud and identified as black or Negro people (with the exception of the light-skinned middle class, mentioned previously), and there was no contradiction in their mind between being a proud and strongly identified black person and a proud and strongly identified Jamaican or West Indian. This did not mean that strongly identified West Indians did not distance themselves from American blacks and believe strongly that they did not want to be identified with American blacks or confused with them. From an American point of view this distinction is sometimes hard to understand. Used to seeing racial solidarity among black people, and accustomed to talking about people who "betray their race" or pass as not black, both American whites and American blacks sometimes misunderstand the strong regional, national, or ethnic identities of West Indians as a denial of racial identity. The two are not at all conflated for the immigrants, however. They simply do not understand their pride as black persons as entailing solidarity or identity with black Americans.

Distancing from Black Americans

For most of the respondents their self-identification as West Indians, Jamaicans, or as immigrants, along with their identity as black, entailed their coming to terms with how they were different from black Americans.

Indeed, African Americans played the role of "the Other" in the construction of a West Indian identity in New York. The immigrants did not
regard having a strong racial identity as meaning that they identified with
black Americans. In fact, most immigrants distanced themselves from
black Americans and wanted other people to know that they were not the
same. They saw themselves as superior to black Americans, and they were
disappointed and dismayed at the behaviors and characteristics they associated with black Americans. Although some adopted the term "American" as part of their identity, referring to themselves as Jamaican
American or West Indian American, they did not want to be seen as
simply "black American" because for most of them assimilation to black
America was downward mobility. This reason was cited by the many
respondents who disliked the term "African American" because, unlike
the term "black," it did not leave room for ethnic distinctiveness within
the racial umbrella. (Others objected to "African American" because they
did not come from Africa and resented the association.)

Over and over the immigrants said they did not want to be confused
with black Americans because they did not share the same culture. When
asked to define what she meant by that, one woman replied that the
two groups were "looking in different directions, having different mo-
tivations." Both the middle-class and the working-class immigrants argued that West Indians were much harder-working than black
Americans and that they were less likely than black Americans to engage
in all kinds of wrongdoing, from being discourteous to using drugs and
murdering people. The immigrants see many differences in the home
life of black Americans and West Indians, arguing that West Indians
have stronger, more intact, families and stricter upbringing of children.
There was definitely a great deal of blame piled on black Americans for
the negative circumstances they found themselves in and for their sense
of entitlement:

The blacks here should have more of life—they don't try to promote
themselves. They in too much drugs, on the streets, doing wrong
things. Getting into trouble. We West Indians do things a lot different from their self. We try hard to work. But I feel that the majority
of them they depend on someone to give them a hand out all the

time. You just have to get up and work for your own. But they figure
that, OK, I was born here, and because I was born here, I supposed
to get this. (Saint Kitts female worker, age 37, in United States
sixteen years)

The immigrants knew that black Americans thought they had come to
take their jobs and were angry with them for it, but they felt this was
unfair:

> Most Americans feel that when the West Indians come here, they
> come to actually take their jobs, but you come and you want to
> work, and you work. If Americans don't want to work, too tough for
> them. A lot of Americans do not want to work. They want money
> but they do not want to work. American blacks have the opportunity
> to go to school, to elevate themselves, and they just sit and allow
> things to go idle by. People coming from the outside just using the
> system and trying to get up as much as possible and that makes them
> angry in some respect. (Guyanese female teacher, age 43, in United
> States four years)

The idea that black Americans do not take advantage of opportunities
available to them is contrasted with the immigrants who have risked and
sacrificed a great deal to come to the United States for those opportunities.
Education in particular divides the groups. Many of the immigrants set a
great store on education for both themselves and their children, and they
quickly come to believe that black Americans do not value education the
same way:

> The general trend for American blacks is that you look after your
> emotional life first and then you go to school, while we are different,
> most of us were brought up that you go to school and then you get
> married. West Indians are always pushing ahead, trying to get to
> school and finish, while Americans, maybe because they are Ameri-
> cans, feel that they have it forever, so why the rush. (Jamaican female
> teacher, age 36, in United States ten years)

There are a number of reasons for these stereotypical beliefs. The image
of African Americans as "preferring welfare" and prone to criminality and

violence is widespread in the United States.[20] This stems from long-standing cultures of racism, as well as biased reports in the media that stress negative news about blacks and fail to portray the existence of hard-working black people.[21]

But many of the West Indian immigrants come to these images of black Americans through personal experience as well. Class differences are often conflated with ethnic differences in the minds of the immigrants. Given the racial segregation in New York City, the new immigrants very quickly perceive that the black areas where they live are not in as good shape as the white residential areas, and once again they blame black Americans for "not taking care of themselves." Both middle-class and working-class immigrants settle in West Indian neighborhoods in central Brooklyn, and many poorer African Americans are their neighbors. Often the immigrants generalize from the behaviors of lower-class African Americans in these neighborhoods to all African Americans, further lowering their overall impressions of native-born blacks.

These gross generalizations are factually wrong about black Americans as a group, although they may stem from the immigrants' individual experiences or encounters. For example, the widespread belief among the immigrants that African Americans do not value education is not statistically true. Between 1940 and 1990 African Americans narrowed the gap for years of schooling between whites and blacks from three years to one year. The decline in high school drop-outs has been much steeper among blacks than whites in recent years.[22] Jennifer Hochschild points out that blacks not only believe in education, but they act on that belief: "Controlling for sex and socioeconomic status, African Americans are no more likely to drop out of school than whites, are more likely to choose an academic than a vocational curriculum, and are more likely to choose a four-year than a two-year college."[23]

Yet the immigrants believed that these perceived differences between the groups were real, and they had various theories about why there were such stark differences between the two groups. Some people spoke about the different histories of the groups. They argued that black Americans had lower self-esteem and that this explained their not trying to get ahead. Many of the middle-class teachers, while noting the same differences as the working-class food-service workers, pointed to class differences as a root cause of these perceptions. For instance, one teacher argued:

> They [West Indians] think black Americans are lazy, they don't want to work, they want to be on welfare, and it's just a basic lazy stereotype and the reason why many of us have this stereotype is because a lot of times we probably didn't see Americans—well there are Americans out there, black Americans that are in good positions, you know that have the nice family, mother, father working. Most of the time when most West Indians come here they got to the lower, you know, area, in the lower economic area where the houses are not so large. And in those neighborhoods we get to meet the worst people and then we build our stereotypes on that. We see these people, you know, just sitting around, drinking, hanging out on the street, and from there we build out stereotypes. (Guyanese female teacher, age 48, in United States twenty years)

Both the working-class and the middle-class immigrants thought black Americans were disadvantaged by living in a society in which they were the minority. Black Americans were often described as "behind" the West Indians because only since the civil rights movement of the 1960s have they experienced the basic rights that the West Indians have enjoyed since emancipation:

> They are just now striving to overcome many of the discriminations and what the whites have been doing to them over the period. You see, we West Indians came here with the idea that nobody was better than we are. It was not a matter of color in the Caribbean, it was a matter of haves and have-nots. You came here, it was definitely a matter of black and white. We really haven't ever been discriminated against in Jamaica. (Jamaican female teacher, age 47, in United States twelve years)

Another teacher mentioned that there were also class differences among the immigrants, and not all of them lived up to the image of successful West Indians that she had just described. A few respondents described their own family practices when pressed about West Indian culture and were not aware of how much what they were describing was particular to their own family and how much to West Indians in general. Middle-class immigrants often described West Indians as more likely than Americans to enjoy an intact husband-wife family. While their own families might be of this form, they ignore that households headed by single parents are prevalent throughout the Caribbean.[24]

Many of the responses from working-class and middle-class West Indians about the distinctive values of their own groups toward family, hard work, and education echoed the themes I uncovered among white third-generation symbolic ethnics in California and Pennsylvania.[25] These whites also thought that the Irish or the Italians or the Poles were superior because of their belief in the American dream and their strong commitment to family and to education. Indeed, many of the African Americans we interviewed described their group as being characterized by two values above all else—a love of family and a love of education:

Q: What are the traits of African Americans?

A: Families. The family is very important. I just think about like when the slaves were emancipated, how the first thing they did was open up schools. Which just amazes me. Like wow, how did you do that? And there's always an optimism. (Black American female teacher, age 23)

In fact, the very traits that many West Indians said differentiated themselves from black Americans were cited by one teacher as proof that there were no differences between foreign-born and American-born blacks:

Q: Do you perceive any differences between West Indians and American blacks?

A: Well, there are differences among all of us, even within a particular culture. But with me I find that a lot of the rearing and perceptions are the same, in terms of hard working and going to school and furthering your education and doing the best that you can. I find that to be the same. (Black American female teacher, age 32)

But the African Americans we spoke to were not as free as my earlier white respondents or as the West Indian respondents in citing education and family for their group without qualification. Many felt the need to explain that they knew these values were the opposite of the stereotypes many people held of African Americans:

> I think that Afro-American family feelings are stronger than most other group family feelings. I know that it doesn't appear that way because what you see on the news is fathers abandoning children in the street homeless, but having been brought up in the South through some hard times myself I know how everybody helps out—aunts and uncles—help out everybody in the family and it's just one big family. It's not on Dan Rather or Walter Cronkite. They don't want to talk about the good things, about a lot of mothers wanting their children. I think that's the biggest misconception that everybody has about the black family is that they don't realize how much love there is among us. (Black American male teacher, age 41)

Yet the negative stereotypes of African Americans and the stark differences the immigrants paint between themselves and the "other" black Americans resonate very deeply with American cultural images of the "defective" culture of poor African Americans. The present-time orientation that one teacher criticized in black Americans echoes decades-long debates about the "culture of poverty" of poor black Americans:

> The average American, when he has money, what he goes to do? Buy the most expensive clothes, sneakers, and stuff, look how they dress. A West Indian person, like my aunt, she would come here and she would work, save her money, and buy a house. And then a black person who was born here would look at her and say, how did you do that? You see, because I figure that most blacks in this country try to live like what they see on TV. The West Indian coming here would wear his sneakers, would wear his jeans even if it was [unfashionable], and try to save his money and buy a house or something like that . . . He's not dressing contemporary with the fancy stuff and partying every night like the blacks here. (Guyanese male teacher, age 40, in United States ten years)

Social-identity theory helps to explain the tenacity of some of the negative images that the West Indians hold of African Americans, even as the immigrants encounter many upstanding African Americans whom they recognize as good people. Because West Indians define themselves as the in-group and African Americans as the out-group, the attributions they attach to individuals' behaviors follow psychological rules that have been discovered in many social psychology experiments. Individual West Indians who do not work or who engage in criminal activity are defined as exceptions to the general rule that West Indians are good people. Their behavior is attributed to situational or environmental factors. Individual African Americans who exhibit the same behavior are regarded as reflecting deep character flaws. Out-group members are often given dispositional attributions for the same behavior that is granted situational attributions for in-group members. These psychological decisions about the behaviors of individuals and groups help people to maintain stereotypes, both good and bad, in the face of disconfirming evidence.[26]

Even those who had warm feelings toward black Americans and felt sorry for them saw them as crippled by their experiences with American race relations in a way that made them very different from West Indians:

> I love American blacks, most of them. But I find that, I guess because of their slavery experience and the problems after that, there is a total difference with American blacks as against West Indians. For example, I grew up seeing blacks in charge; that was my experience so I expect to be in charge. That's my frame of reference. American blacks because of what was done to them, they don't see it quite like that. Something was done to them that they just don't think that they are, it's as if something is lacking in them, they don't see themselves as human beings. They see themselves as inferior, and I've heard black Americans say, "OK, you think that I am a nigger, so I'm going to be a nigger." And that bothers me. That's how they see themselves. (Jamaican female teacher, age 37, in United States ten years)

While distancing from black Americans was the norm, the immigrants did not see black Americans as an undifferentiated whole. A few middle-class immigrants argued that West Indians were very similar to middle-class black Americans. (One woman accounted for this by explaining that middle-class black Americans are all second-, third-, or fourth-generation West Indians, an idea many whites also hold.)[27] But almost all of the working-class immigrants, and most of the middle-class immigrants, did strive to differentiate American blacks from the South from those from the North. Southern blacks were seen as much more like West Indians in their ability to work hard, their "traditional family values" of respect for elders, and strict child raising. Southern blacks were described as making better coworkers and neighbors, and many respondents said that an intermarriage between a southern American black and a West Indian was a good one. Because southern blacks are more likely to have grown up in the countryside, some respondents noted, they were better people for not having been "worn down" by the problems of living in a city ghetto. One respondent noted that he saw southern blacks treated badly by northern blacks much in the way that West Indians are treated badly—the northern blacks were aggressive toward them, regarded them as a threat, and accused them of coming to steal their jobs. Interestingly, the American blacks from the South interviewed in this study stressed that they were like the West Indians—they had stronger, more traditional, values than the northerners, and that they were more likely to get along with West Indians than native New Yorkers. It is not surprising that the immigrants would single out southern blacks as more like them. The important characteristic that the West Indians and the southern blacks share is that both groups are migrants and therefore selected populations. Any group of self-selected migrants is likely to be a group with greater ambition, capacity for work, and the like. This is discussed further in Chapter 4.

As if the negative images of American blacks that the immigrants hold are not enough, the immigrants report that they are aware of the negative images that American blacks hold of them. When asked what she believed American blacks thought of West Indians, this Guyanese teacher responded:

> I think they think we are these funny-speaking people, they are coming here to take our jobs, they're here to take our jobs, to rob them or whatever. I think that's how they see any stranger, foreigner, as a robber or a threat . . . It starts with the lower class. They have no ambition and they might see a West Indian coming over and doing so much better than they are, working hard while they're

laying around sleeping or drinking or hanging out or whatever. I think it starts there and it just develops. (Guyanese female teacher, age 34, in United States nine years)

The immigrants receive a hostile reception from black Americans in the streets of the city. In addition to the problems at work, the immigrants describe black Americans yelling at them "to go home" in encounters on the subway, in the supermarket, at school meetings, and on the street. While some immigrants had been forewarned about strained relations between American blacks and the West Indians, many immigrants were nonetheless surprised at the hostile reception they received from black Americans:

I was going on train and [someone said] something, he hate West Indians. I just look at him and thought, "But he's a black person just like us too, just that we're from a different country but we're all black." So I figure, what's this black fighting this fuss about? (Trinidadian female worker, age 26, in United States three years)

The immigrants tried to sharpen the boundary between themselves and black Americans and tried to use the image of black Americans to construct a West Indian identity by saying what they were not; the African-American respondents were, for the most part, much more likely to minimize differences between the two groups. While resentful that West Indians try to distance themselves, this black American reacts by denying the distance:

They [West Indians] honestly think they are better than American blacks. I have heard a few of them even say so. And as far as I'm concerned, we are all the same. We have two strikes against us. We are blacks and we are women. I have two strikes against me. I'm black and I'm a woman. Now them, they are black, they are women, and they are foreign. (Black American female worker, age 27)

Other African Americans were particularly upset that West Indians were distancing themselves from black Americans in order to avoid white prejudice and discrimination. As one African-American worker pointed out, this might not work:

West Indians like to say that they are West Indian blacks, but I have a feeling that the white man says it's all black, straight across the board. (Black American female worker, age 51)

While working-class African Americans often were resentful that West Indians were coming to take jobs from Americans, middle-class African Americans recognized further tensions and some of the distancing behaviors of West Indians:

> Q: What about West Indians, are there any images of them that come to mind?
> A: I think of arrogance, somewhat abrupt, loud. It certainly does not pertain to all of them, but those that I have been around. They do tend to think that they know a little more than we do. And I don't know how they can feel that when most of them come here to seek an education. But they are ready to put us down as Americans. (Black American female teacher, age 42)

But racial solidarity was a strong value for many of the black Americans we spoke with, and the Americans were much more likely than the immigrants to see the two groups as very close:

> Q: What about West Indians, any characteristics that come to mind?
> A: I think of West Indians as black people. And I feel that same way towards them. Obviously, if I had never met them, I would not even know that they are West Indian until I hear them speak. When I see them, to me they are just black. When they speak to me, then I know they are West Indian, but I don't see that as a major difference between us. That camaraderie is still there, if there's two of us in the room, we know we better watch each other's backs. (Black American male teacher, age 41)

While the working-class African Americans were generally hostile toward the West Indian immigrants and felt very competitive, the middle-class African Americans were much less likely to see the West Indians as a job threat. The middle-class African Americans were more likely to see West Indians as potential allies and as people who basically had experiences very similar to theirs based on race. Many of the teachers stressed that when there was race-based discrimination or conflict, all black people had to come together to fight it, regardless of their class or ethnic backgrounds. For instance, this teacher assumed that even if West Indians came from black-majority societies, they had still experienced the same kind of racism African Americans have to face:

> Tourists go to the island; there are tourists from all different backgrounds. I don't care where you live, even if you lived in the islands most of your life, with people of the same background and color, you have experienced at some point and time, someone doing something to you that had been a negative experience for you. (Black American male teacher, age 50)

The middle-class respondents were generally quite aware of the ways in which West Indians thought about African Americans. Yet, unlike the working-class respondents, they were less upset about it and more likely to think the West Indians would change over time:

> West Indians feel very strongly that the American blacks have been brainwashed—and that they are the superior group. Basically because they come from a culture that is predominantly run by Jamaican blacks or West Indian blacks. So they feel that they are in control, whereas we have never been in control of anything, and that we are very wasteful as far as education is concerned. Which is true in some cases, but I get a little upset because they all feel that way, and it's not always true with all of the American blacks. It's not necessarily true with all of us. But they have taken on that attitude and that tends to separate us as a group of people instead of meshing together as a race . . . I find the people who have been here longer much easier to deal with, to work with, to associate with, as opposed to the ones who have just gotten here. That come here already with an attitude. (Black American female teacher, age 42)

In fact, one teacher noted with sympathy the problems middle-class West Indian immigrants faced:

> Q: Do you think that the West Indians that you know understand the race relations situation in the United States?

A: If they've been over here for a while, yes. If they have not, no. No.
I've had friends who really didn't understand what was going on
because usually the West Indians that I meet, they come from a
system that is more class-oriented rather than your color. So for
them to switch over to this system really is a real culture shock
for them. (Black American female teacher, age 32)

A number of people who told us of vast differences in the values of
American blacks and West Indians went on to describe close friendships
and admiration for specific individuals from the other group. And, in fact,
while most people could describe the differences they saw between black
Americans and West Indians and labeled these differences as ethnic, many
also saw change in the relations between the two groups. More than a few
immigrants described the "Caribbeanization" of New York's black Americans. These people described American blacks who tried to dress or talk
like West Indians. They stressed the high degree of intermixing and intermarriage between the two groups. Instead of describing the immigrants
assimilating to an undifferentiated American core culture, these immigrants described a situation in which the black Americans were becoming
indistinguishable from the West Indians.

Language and Accent

In the immigrants' minds the distinction between American blacks and
West Indians was more important than the distinctions among the various West Indian groups. Accent and language were important to both
distinctions, however. This may seem surprising since West Indians are
from English-speaking islands, and so language is not usually regarded as
a key factor in their adjustment or identity. But the accent and the type of
patois or Creole slang or language spoken by the immigrants were important markers of identity for them.

The immigrants said that their accent was a topic that came up again
and again in their interactions with each other and with both black and
white Americans. Americans knew they were immigrants once they heard
the Caribbean accent. The immigrants used each others' accents to pinpoint which island they were from, with varying degrees of success. Many
immigrants said the longer they stayed in the United States, the less ability

they had to distinguish island accents. Also, many immigrants had spent time in other islands, aside from the ones they were raised in, before coming to the United States. Their accents were then "jumbled up" and difficult for another person to pinpoint.

Many of the working-class immigrants were proud of their island patois language and talked about how they would use it to speak to each other on the job, so outsiders could not understand them. The middle-class immigrants were more conflicted about the use of the patois. They all said they could speak it, and often did speak it at home, but they also described how their parents had tried to discourage their use of it, and how they in turn did not want their children speaking it outside of the home. The middle-class immigrants tended to call the patios a separate language. They were very proud of their use of standard English, and they saw the use of the patios in any public situation as a lower-class thing to do. This woman describes the code-switching she performs as a food-service worker:

> When I'm with my people from Trinidad, you know, we speak English but you know, we just have the, you call it the twang. And you just get down when you just say, you know, "tell she," and nobody is there to tell you, "What, what did you say?" But when I'm with my American friends, you know, I speak properly because I don't like people asking me "What you say?" You know, I feel funny. (Trinidadian female worker, age 29, in United States thirteen years)

Some people claimed that a Trinidadian could not understand a Jamaican speaking his island's patois and vice versa, but others claimed that there were only slight variations. While speaking patois was sometimes looked down on because of its association with the lower class, the West Indian accent was universally admired. Because the accent was such an important badge of identity, people were very proud of the accent and critical of those who tried to lose it or suggested they try to lose it. It was often a source of tension between immigrants and American blacks who criticized the accent because it made it harder for them to understand the immigrants.

Most respondents claimed that the accent was the only surefire way of knowing that a person was West Indian. Some claimed they could identify other West Indians through body language and the way they carried themselves. Others thought that there were distinctive styles of dress. Some who were very concerned that they be recognized as West Indian placed flag decals on their cars or wore ornaments, such as this Guyanese woman:

> I prefer to be recognized as Guyanese. I wear a pin that has the flag. And then they would say, "Oh, she's Guyanese." Because constantly, you can't keep telling everybody, "I'm from Guyana," you know. (Guyanese female worker, age 26, in United States ten years)

The reality for these immigrants, however, was that until they spoke the only thing other people usually noticed about them was the color of their skin; beforehand most Americans assumed that the immigrants were in fact black Americans. one Guyanese teacher described this phenomenon:

> I figure once I'm in America, and anywhere in America, anybody will look at you and figure, well you're black American. But then until you open your mouth, then they will know that you're not from America, you're from somewhere else. (Guyanese female teacher, age 33, in United States six years)

Immigrants who had been in the United States a long time could take advantage of accent and language to code-switch back and forth between American and foreign identities. This Grenadian teacher describes this phenomenon eloquently:

> I can say "hey mon," you know, I can slip and slide and I can go back into that, you know, and people laugh and I laugh too. But I can go into that dialect and with that accent walk into a West Indian club and be West Indian. I can also walk into a bar and be American. You know? But I can never stop being black. (Grenadian male teacher, age 46, in United States twenty-six years)

Because West Indians were generally identified by other Americans, both white and black, as "black" first, this identification was often at odds with their self-identification as West Indians. Their accent played a large role in ensuring that they be seen as different from black Americans. As the chief way they could "manage" their presentation of self, the West

Indian accent was a very clear marker of identity, and thus it is not surprising that some autobiographies and historical studies of West Indians mention deliberate cultivation and maintenance of the accent.[28]

Meaning of Being American

Once the immigrants arrive and settle in the United States, a new identity label becomes available to them—they are now eligible to call themselves Americans. But America is a contradictory place for the immigrants—a land of greater opportunities than their homelands but simultaneously a land of racial stigma and discrimination.

In this interconnected world with frequent travel back and forth between the islands and the United States, and with television and radio broadcasts on the islands that mostly originate in America, the immigrants possess information about the United States before they immigrate. At the very least even individuals with neither friends nor family members in the United States report that they absorbed images of America from movies, television, and radio. But most people have more direct communications as well; most respondents were part of a migrant network—they had ended up in New York because they already had friends or family members there who had written, visited, or called back home with information about life in the United States. In addition, many respondents reported that they had visited before moving permanently to the United States.

Most commonly respondents had heard two things about the United States—that it was a land of educational and job opportunities that rewarded hard work, and that it was a place where race was very important and where whites discriminated against blacks. No one commented that these pieces of information could be seen as contradictory.

While a few people spontaneously mentioned race relations and the negative reactions they got from American blacks as their biggest shocks, it was the more everyday, immediate things that most noticed and were surprised about when they first arrived—the size, scale, and colors of the houses, the number of abandoned houses, the degree of poverty, homelessness, and despair they saw on the streets, the garbage in the streets, and the filth and graffiti they found in their apartment buildings. It took awhile before American race relations became truly apparent to the immigrants:

> When you first come, basic things, the buildings are different because when you walk down the streets and all the buildings look the same, like a military camp or something. Whereas back there people design their own homes, they have different colors they use, they make their homes attractive, each one is unique, not everyone having the same style, the same size, the same color. It was like monotonous and drab. Also things like foods, fresh foods. Back home you have a kitchen garden, you grow your vegetables, or you have to go to the market to buy stuff. The fisherman would come in, and you would see the fish jumping, you know, alive. You know you are getting fresh stuff. Over here, no you don't. Everything is in cans . . . And I think most people that go back that's one thing they welcome—fresh foods, fresh fish, fresh air. (Jamaican female teacher, age 26, in United States eight years)

One of the immigrant workers contrasted the freedom she had back home to visit back and forth with neighbors and work in her garden to the trapped feelings she had in her housing project in Brownsville where she had to stay inside at night, not daring to leave the apartment because of the fear of crime.

Yet there were also positive impressions. People were impressed by American superhighways, which were much larger and faster than anything they had seen in the islands. Several young people who arrived as children recall the size and bustle of the airport and their first ride on an escalator with a mixture of fascination and horror. People were pleasantly surprised by the low cost of, and the ease of shopping for, electronic goods and high-quality clothing. The excitement of being in a big city was particularly impressive for immigrants from the countryside who had not experienced the city's wonders:

> When I first came and I came out of the airplane and I come out, it was like a different place, a different world. Like I was just born over. It was totally different. You see so many cars. So many things on the street. It was so exciting. You come out and you look and it was like,

like a new creation, you know? Like you know how they have the spaceships? Like you be at that different world. (Guyanese female worker, in United States ten years, age 26)

One might assume that a visit to New York at some point before immigrating would have provided clues that it was not a land of milk and honey; however, even people who had visited this country before deciding to immigrate reported that they believed that the United States would be a much better place, and that their expectations were contradicted once they arrived to live rather than to visit:

Q: What had you heard about the United States before you arrived?

A: The United States was this place where you got everything so eas- ily. You could become wealthy; it had all you could want. You got schools, people came here to study so you knew that it had good universities. Housing, everybody lived in nice houses and they wore nice clothes, you drove a car, you could have six cars if you wanted to. You know, life was fun, there was more to life in the United States than there was in Jamaica. Life does seem easy when you're just here for three weeks on vacation. Because every- body stops what they're doing and entertains you and takes you out. You get money to buy things and you didn't go work for it or anything. So it really did seem like it was easy. But when you got here and you were thrown out on your own and you have to find a job and you had to pay the bills and, even though you might work, a little more money does not meet all the living costs. It's just such a different life, a great disappointment I must say . . . I've always thought about going back. It's very difficult though to really decide to go back. It's easier to think about it and to say you're going back than to really go back. But I've thought about it over and over but I know I'm not going to go back right now. One day surely when I get older and I can retire and when the children are grown and finished school. (Jamaican female teacher, age 42, in United States seven years)

This is the classic immigrant dream—to make enough money to return home in style, to buy a house where one can be comfortable, and to be in a place where an American dollar goes a much longer way. But one teacher who has been in this country for six years eloquently explains why the dreams so many immigrants have of making money in the United States and returning home to live well will probably not come true:

> When I was thinking of coming here, people were talking about how best you can make some money and go back to the Caribbean and build a big house. It wasn't ever coming over to stay. But I think people really got trapped when they come, 'cause their family really don't tell them exactly what it is over here. And even though it is very hard here now, a lot of people still think, "Oh yeah, I can come and make it and they tell me [the negative things about the United States] because they don't want me to come" and when they come, what happens? They can't go back because it's difficult. Because of the money. They realize they can't make it overnight, you know, and then once you come here, there are things you have to do to make yourself happy. You gotta make yourself comfortable. It's just like setting yourself all up again. That takes money. By the time you finished doing that, then you can start saving. By then, if you got kids, you know, they're getting demanding in terms of school things, school clothes, or whatever. And then no sooner than you think you're ready to go back, the kids are ready for college. (Guyanese female teacher, age 33, in United States six years)

The United States spoils people—it changes their expectations about material comforts and about ways of behaving:

> People come here with the intent to come here to work, get the money, and then go back home. But it just doesn't happen. When you get here, you realize that it's different. The longer one remains, the more difficult it is to go back. 'Cause after a while you get used to it. You get used to the lifestyle. Things are cheaper. When I go back home, I find things are expensive. I find life is different. Because the style of life in the United States is much higher. I mean back home, it's very simple. You know, after you've lived in the United States for quite a while, then you get used to it. You like the city, the good roads . . . You see, if one is ambitious there are a lot

of opportunities, although it could be difficult and frustrating to be here. (Grenadian male manager, age 42, in United States nine years)

Many individuals were shocked at the level of poverty they encountered when they first arrived. Most expected to see a nation that was, as one respondent called it, 90% middle class. When they saw the large numbers of poor people, most of them black, they were dismayed. While both the teachers and the food-service workers were shocked at the degree of poverty and decay in inner-city neighborhoods, the teachers were also concerned about the downward mobility they faced. Many of the teachers decided to emigrate because they were having trouble maintaining a decent standard of living in the islands on a teacher's salary, and because they learned that even domestic workers in the United States were earning more than they were as teachers in the West Indies. And once they arrived here, they did have greater buying power for consumer goods and the like. However, they also faced the reality that housing and labor costs were much higher in the United States. So even though they were making more money and consumer goods were relatively cheaper, they were paying a much higher percentage of their salary for housing, and they could no longer afford household help and other perks of the middle-class lifestyle back home. This Jamaican teacher describes the pluses and minuses for her:

> You don't earn enough here to get some of the luxuries you would be entitled to in Jamaica. Because if you are earning a reasonable salary in Jamaica, which is like a teacher or a nurse or someone like that, they would put you in the middle class in Jamaica. Right? And for a middle-class person you can afford to pay for a housekeeper. You could not do that here. I could not even pay someone for day's work to have some work done. So no matter how you work here, you still have to come home to all this stuff. Because I had a full-time housekeeper. I had someone who took care of my children. I came here, it's different. When I first came here, I did not bring my children, and I saw these girls pushing the strollers with the kids and closing them up on the bus and they have the bags—I said, God, I couldn't do that. You know, they always looked so tired. When I came here with my children, I thought this is hard work. This is too

much work. And you have your own house there. You come here, you have to rent. Your kids have to share a room. (Jamaican female teacher, age 38, in United States seven years)

In terms of their identities as Americans, some immigrants chose to focus on the opportunities and freedoms America provided for them, while some stressed the dangers in America awaiting people with dark skin. This Trinidadian food-service worker holds both views simultaneously, as do many other immigrants:

> In this country it's a white world. Yes, it has a lot to do with your foreparents. I guess the white people have the money. And they could afford better living, whereas the blacks didn't have anything. So the white people take advantage of it.
>
> Q: So do you think there are too many immigrants coming to the United States?
>
> A: No, I don't think so. Because this is a place that was made up for everyone to come. It's not owned by, let's say, one set of people. It's a melting pot. It's a place where everyone has opportunity. (Trinidadian female worker, age 34, in United States twelve years)

For those who saw America in a positive light, becoming American meant having access to all of the opportunities the country offered:

> To be an American means to be able to grasp all the opportunities that are here and that I need to be in a position to achieve, to be in a position to walk into any place and apply for a job for which I am qualified. I love this country. It has, after all the heartaches and the meanness and the struggles of this land, I love this place. To be an American, to be loyal. (Jamaican female teacher, age 47, in United States twelve years)

It also meant freedom to become someone new, someone they would not be if they had stayed behind. For many of the poor and working-class people the opportunities in the United States to live at a higher standard of living instilled a great deal of gratitude toward the country:

> Back home the food stuff is so expensive, you can't afford it. 'Cause imagine, can you imagine paying forty dollars for one pound of

sugar? Some days you have to eat like plain rice. It's nothing to do, you know. So, as the opportunity came along, I come to New York for betterment . . . Everybody [in my family] is here in this country. Everybody. This is the only place we could have come to be better. Because there are so many people home that died. Died from hunger. People that worked in the field. So everybody is here and we're proud of it and we thank Uncle Sam for it, truly. From my heart, I really do. Because I don't know what would have become of us if we were back there. (Guyanese female worker, age 26, in United States ten years)

Respondents were likely to regard "American" as an identity that applied to people who were born in the United States and more often saw themselves as Jamaican or Jamaican American. Some thought the question of whether they considered themselves American referred to citizenship. Yet most of those who had become citizens did not volunteer that they were American—they tended to use that word to describe their American-born children:

I wouldn't even consider my son to be Jamaican American. I would consider him to be American. Because I think where the person is born, that's where you should consider him to be. Like I'm born in Jamaica and I'm Jamaican. You know, I don't even consider myself Jamaican something else. Just Jamaican. (Jamaican female teacher, age 48, in United States twenty years)

A few people thought of the trade-off between a national identity and an American identity in purely practical terms, mistakenly assuming that if they took American citizenship, they would have to give up their island citizenship.[29] This woman envisions a situation in which she could get into trouble for being an American:

There could be times when it could be trouble. Possibly in a conversation with Jamaicans with some who would think that now I am not loyal to Jamaica, I've switched loyalties and am now loyal to America. Or maybe if I went on a plane that was hijacked by some Palestinians and they ask me if I am American, I might say that I was

Jamaican with an American passport. (Jamaican female teacher, age
37, in United States ten years)

The only second-generation teacher interviewed was also the only person
who answered questions about claiming an American identity by referring
to cultural differences between the islands and the United States and his
divided cultural loyalties and tastes:

Q: Do you consider yourself American?
A: Well, I'm born here. But I like my West Indian food and I like
   jazz. So I guess I consider myself both. I would like to go back to
   Barbados when I retire and I would like to live in Barbados, you
   see. But maybe if I saw more of this country, I might change my
   mind about it. But you know I feel West Indian. But I find calypso so boring. And I like jazz. I like John Coltrane and Miles
   Davis and those kind of people. And I like Italian food too, but I
   do like my rice and peas and my cuckoo and so on. (Barbadian
   male teacher, age 43, born in United States)

For immigrants, however, these subtleties of cultural identity are not
called forth by a question about being American. The immigrants are
firmly rooted in their West Indian cultural identity—they perceive
"American" more as a political or citizenship issue. In this political light
the middle-class respondents were more likely to see being American as
something negative. Many of them resented American power and intervention in the Caribbean region. For them becoming American meant
becoming part of a country that had imposed its will on Third World
countries to their detriment:

Because I am from a Third World country, I understand American
interference in all the people's business, I do understand it very well.
They get me so angry because they want to talk about the Third
World as if everything there is not going right because they are not
democracies and this is the ideal democracy. Well it's not. That's not
true. I was in Jamaica for our 1980 elections and I know the American government dipped in it, I know. I'm not going to be on America's side when they are telling me about Noriega down in Panama,
and it's such a great concern of the Americans, you know. Panama

Canal is theirs, but they don't want to give it up . . . I don't think I want to give up my Jamaican citizenship. I don't think I want to give up my loyalty to Jamaica. I've been born a Jamaican, and I'm so grateful to Jamaica for what I am today that I don't really want to disband Jamaica. If I never get to return there, I am still grateful. (Jamaican female teacher, age 41, in United States seven years)

Many of the teachers reported that they were required to apply for citizenship in order to get their licenses. For those who saw becoming American in a negative light, they defined becoming a citizen as a "matter of paperwork," not entailing any sense of loyalty or change in their feelings about where they really belonged:

Even if I have to take an oath and everything else, I would still be West Indian. You know, it would be just for doing it for whatever benefit there is. But then I would still be a Guyanese or a West Indian at heart. And my life and my tradition will remain with me. (Guyanese female teacher, age 33, in United States six years)

Despite the variety of reactions to the label "American," most people recognized that they themselves and their fellow immigrants had changed during their time in America. This process of Americanization was difficult for many people to describe directly because they were also aware that the islands they had come from had changed a great deal. So the benchmark they were measuring themselves against was a moving target as well. People who had traveled back home for visits and who had been in the United States for a long time noticed a great deal of change from economic development in their home countries—both negative and positive changes. The remittances of migrants, the growth of the tourist industry, and direct interventions (in some cases, such as the invasion of Grenada) led to economic developments that people cited as positive. Consumer goods were more available, and immigrants from rural areas reported that their homes had been hooked up to electricity. Televisions and VCRs were much more widely available. Clothing styles changed on the islands, so that there was now little difference between styles there and those in New York.

On the other hand, many immigrants were appalled at how the negative aspects of the United States that they never remembered existing "back home" had suddenly appeared on the islands. Disrespectful children, guns, drugs, and increased racial consciousness and strife were all noted by those making return visits. This was a real disappointment because these immigrants had grown used to seeing such things in New York but remembered their homelands fondly as not containing such horrors.

A visit home would also point up ways in which the islands and the United States are still different and reveal to these immigrants that "they can't go home again." Interestingly, the very people who emphasized that the key feature of West Indian culture they brought with them is the ability and drive to work hard would discover on a visit back home that people do not work hard. The pace of life is so much faster in the United States, and the demands on people so much greater, that when immigrants do return home for a visit they find that they cannot adjust. They see their former countrymen as lazy and with too casual an attitude toward work. Being on "island time" annoys them now that they are used to the fast-paced action of New York City. This woman describes her attitude on her return visit to Trinidad:

> I'm here [in the United States] ten years and when I went back last year for the first time after nine years, I found it was lazy. Why are they lazy? Why are they just sitting all around the place and wouldn't find a job? But that is what I must have been doing when I was there before, you know, because it's so easy, so easy down there and here you have to get up and work and stuff. I would say that [in the United States] you get more independent and more responsible about yourself. (Trinidadian female worker, age 30, in United States ten years)

The view of what happens to West Indians once they come to New York is also double-edged—the freedom many people describe in glowing terms to become more responsible, to be open to new and exciting changes, is for others the freedom to use guns, neglect family responsibilities, become disrespectful, and adopt criminal ways. For many people immigration was a learning experience as they developed new skills and learned to cope with new problems and emergencies without the benefit of extended family members or tried-and-true skills and formulas for dealing with problems:

> I think you gain more experience. Because you have to be, you have to think more constructive than at home. Home, you know, you have people who could brace you. Here you don't know anybody to brace, but Almighty God. So, you have to be more constructive, you are open to more things, you gain more knowledge and everything than back home. So, I think, being over here, I say that you are a step further because you are open—not only to different ways, but people from different countries, you share different views and you gain experience. (Guyanese male worker, age 39, in United States six years)

But these same respondents described the ways in which what one called "the dog-eat-dog" world of New York also undermined the sense of community and care they would have expected from fellow immigrants. Many people also expressed the age-old complaint of the more ethnically identified—some of the immigrants were adopting "American" styles of speech and ways of behavior in order to get ahead, which denied their heritage and somehow left the other immigrants behind. Thus for some becoming American meant adopting a materialist ethic that tended to deny community:

> There are a lot of Jamaicans who come to America and have found a new kind of freedom, and to me they abuse some of the privileges afforded them here. They get very boisterous, loud, carefree kind of attitude, cursing, swearing, doing all kinds of things like drugs. If Jamaicans are like me, I can live with them; if they are not, I don't want to live anywhere close to them. They make too much noise. (Jamaican female teacher, age 37, in United States ten years)

Transnationalism

There is currently a political debate about immigration raging in this country. Some anti-immigration advocates argue that immigrants are not becoming Americans in terms of identity, national loyalty, overall culture, and language. Some conservatives argue that immigrants who cling to racial and ethnic identities foster multiculturalism in the United States and that these competing cultures and loyalties deny the necessity of a core American culture.[30] These writers believe that multiculturalism destroys the political will to become American or "racializes" immigrants once they arrive here. This separate racial, ethnic, or national identity interferes with the ability to become American. Because West Indian immigrants are racially black, the argument about cultural splits takes on added significance for this population.

There is also an academic debate about the nature of incorporation of immigrants into American society.[31] We know that the old models of assimilation, which posit gradual change in immigrants' identities and loyalties from the old country to an American-based ethnicity, have become less and less able to capture the reality of today's immigrants. Some anthropologists and sociologists argue that immigrants today are developing transnational identities—moving back and forth between home and host country with identities that do not evolve from point A to point B, but rather transcend societies and nation-states in a way that changes the individual and both societies, though not in a linear fashion. This new scholarship on transnationalism reflects a postmodern concern with the multiplicity of identities an individual maintains, and the varieties of different experiences "immigration" holds for those of different class, gender, and regional backgrounds. As John Lie describes it, "The idea of diaspora—as an unending sojourn across different lands—better captures the emerging reality of transnational networks and communities than the language of immigration and assimilation."[32] Instead of seeing migration as a move from one culture (the sending country) to another (the host country), involving adaptation and change on the part of the individual, this approach assumes "transnational diasporic cultures."

Immigrants from the Caribbean are central to both of these debates as they are part of a recent migrant stream that is often characterized as circular in nature. There is a great deal of back-and-forth movement between the Caribbean and New York. The ties outlined in the previous chapter between the Caribbean and the United States and the ways in which both societies interpenetrate and change each other also lead to questions about transnational linkages. Are West Indian immigrants undergoing assimilation, similar to earlier waves of European-origin immigrants, or are they developing transnational ties, which keep them much more active in their home-country lives and politics than earlier immigrants ever were?

This chapter has described how the immigrants come to the United States with a portfolio of possible identities—racial identities as black or mixed, national identities as Jamaican or Trinidadian, regional identities as West Indian or Caribbean, along with new possible identities as "immigrant" or "American" or as a "hyphenated American." Their national and regional origins become much more salient and stronger as they come into contact with a wide variety of people from all over the world in the extremely diverse environment of New York City. The cultural, political, and social ties that had given them a regional identity as West Indian or Caribbean even before they immigrated are reinforced in New York where they sense a great deal of commonality with people from other islands, and where they also strongly differentiate themselves from the Spanish-speaking immigrants from other parts of the Caribbean who are very numerous in New York. The immigrants come to think of themselves more and more as West Indians or island people.

All of the immigrants are coming from societies that are pluralist and contain a number of different racial and ethnic groups, so they already have a sense of their subnational identity as blacks. This racial identity is very different from the identity of American blacks because the immigrants are coming from societies in which blacks are the majority and, in most recent historical periods, control the political power. While blackness is stigmatized to some extent in all of the former European colonies, the reality of black political power, numerical dominance, and relative cultural and social freedom contrasts sharply with the American black reality of minority status, political and social domination by a white majority, and relative lack of political power. Thus the very meaning of blackness is somewhat, but not entirely, different for the immigrant pre- and postimmigration. There is a continuity in that the immigrant is used to identifying as black in a pluralist society, and often that identification involves fighting a stigmatized view of being black or resisting discrimination and unfair treatment. But there is strong discontinuity in the experience of going from a black majority to minority society. Blacks are a stigmatized minority in the United States and when others conflate West

Indian identity with that of black Americans, the West Indians find themselves at the bottom of their new society—when many of them, especially the middle class, had much higher expectations.

The immigrants have a great deal of contact with their sending country. The volume of immigration and its concentration within certain neighborhoods of New York City guarantee that the immigrants have a great deal of continuity in the networks they are enmeshed in before and after migration. The technological changes that have occurred in the last 100 years also change the migrant experience. Immigrants can talk on the telephone to relatives and friends back home; they can send and receive letters, cassettes, and faxes with remarkable ease. The closeness of the Caribbean and the ease of air travel mean that there is some back-and-forth movement. Often parents will leave children behind or send them back to the islands for some schooling. For many individuals pinpointing a date of immigration is difficult or impossible because they have visited before moving here, and they make extended visits back home after moving here. There is also a great deal of variation in the experiences people have with regard to the United States, which can be traced in part to their class background or gender characteristics. In general middle-class immigrants have a harder time adjusting to American race relations because they must come to accept that in the United States money does not "whiten" the way it does back home. Women generally find that they have greater freedoms in the United States than they did back home, and they are generally more positive about their new home than the men are.[33]

In those small ways the transnational theorists are correct: a great deal of cultural exchange occurs through the mass media and the back-and-forth movement of people to and from the Caribbean. The multiculturalist ethic in American society at present encourages the maintenance of separate racial and ethnic identities and cultural practices. But I think the notion of a transnational identity or a transnational cultural space is quite exaggerated. Most immigrants come with a dream of going back home, but most also believed that they would stay and make a life for themselves in the United States. While some took part in activities and services offered by ethnic voluntary organizations, the respondents in this study were passive consumers of these services, not actively involved. The immigrants followed political developments back home with a range of interest, from passionate attention to mild passing interest to overall disinterest. However, none of the people interviewed were actively involved in home-country politics. Very few people were active in any specifically West Indian organizations. Cricket teams claimed the allegiance of a few men, and a few people were involved in organizations that created floats for the Labor Day West Indian parade. Aside from church, however, the vast majority of the respondents belonged to no organizations at all.

Yet the contribution of the transnationalist theories is important on a number of other dimensions. Most important, while the old assimilation theories might capture some aspects of the immigrant experience, those theories do not take into account the heterogeneity of the immigration and assimilation experience by class and gender and race. For these immigrants becoming American also entails becoming American black, which they perceive as lower social status than staying a West Indian. This turns the basic assumption of earlier assimilation theories—that American was the higher status identity—on its head.

Often researchers argue that West Indian immigrants are more likely to adopt a transnational identity precisely because if they become American, they are likely to be seen as black Americans; many of the immigrants regard this possibility as downward social mobility, as adopting an identity that can leave them more open to racism and discrimination than if they continued to be seen as foreigners. But maintaining a Caribbean identity to have an "out" to experiencing racism is not the same thing as retaining a transnational identity that changes the assimilation process. Overall the immigrants saw their futures as tied to the United States; they mostly wanted to be seen as Americans and understood America to be a land of freedom and opportunity above all else. Most had not become citizens; the motivation of most of those who did so was to sponsor other family members as immigrants. However, they did not see themselves as loyal to their homelands. Most saw themselves as joining a long line of immigrants coming to this country and hoped that they would enjoy as much success as earlier waves of immigrants. The next chapter will explore how much success these immigrants have achieved in the workplace and whether their desire not to be perceived as black American makes sense given the workplaces they find themselves in.

WEST INDIANS

AT WORK

When Colin Powell was toying with the idea of
running for president in the mid-1990s, media
stories used his West Indian background to
explain his success. In his autobiography Powell himself uses his Jamaican parents' values
and his West Indian roots to explain the development of the good parts of his character.[1] As
the son of Jamaican immigrants, Powell is not alone as a successful West
Indian American. In fact, many black luminaries in United States history
have actually been immigrants or the children of immigrants from the
Caribbean, including Marcus Garvey, James Weldon Johnson, Claude
McKay, Stokely Carmichael, Shirley Chisolm, Malcolm X, Kenneth Clark,
James Farmer, Roy Innis, W. Arthur Lewis, Harry Belafonte, Sidney Poi-
tier, and Godfrey Cambridge.

But there are other black Americans who are also of West Indian origin
whose actions and behavior are rarely tied to their West Indian backgrounds. Louis Farrakhan is also the child of a West Indian immigrant; his
family is from Barbados. Yet the American image of the successful West
Indian is helpful in explaining Colin Powell but not so in explaining
Farrakhan, who is as disliked and rejected by white Americans as Powell
is liked and accepted.

This chapter and the next examine the evidence for and against West
Indian success in American life. The cultural stereotype of West Indian
success overstates many of the differences between West Indians and
African Americans, but there is still evidence of an edge for West Indians
in a few areas. The most striking aspect of West Indian socioeconomic

performance in America is their very high labor force participation rates, especially among unskilled and poorly educated workers.

This chapter briefly reviews the current state of knowledge on how West Indians are doing in the American economy. I then present a case study of exactly the population that is so intriguing in the statistical portrait of West Indians in America—the very low-skilled, yet still employed, workers. Why are low-skilled, poorly educated foreign-born blacks more likely to be employed than comparable black Americans? The interviews with food-service workers and their employers point to three factors—the role of network hiring in providing access to low-skilled jobs in the service economy, the particular characteristics of immigrants that make their assessment of the value of jobs much different than that of natives, and the marked preference white managers have for West Indians over native blacks. This chapter demonstrates how these labor market dynamics lead to the genesis and reinforcement of stereotypes of "successful" West Indians in the minds of whites, native blacks, and even West Indians themselves. The next chapter explores the very special role race plays in both the rather small differential success of West Indians and the quite large differential perception of that success in American society.

HOW ARE WEST INDIANS DOING IN
THE AMERICAN ECONOMY?

The complexity of identity and the difficulty of measuring it exactly among West Indian immigrants, which was described in Chapter 3, has not prevented a great deal of debate about the purported success of black immigrants relative to American blacks. Authors from Ira Reid in the 1930s to Glazer and Moynihan in the 1960s to Thomas Sowell most recently have described the West Indians as more successful than American blacks and have devised a number of theories to explain why.[2] Some of those who tout West Indian success argue that it shows that racism and discrimination are not an explanation for the relative lack of success of African Americans in the United States.[3] Other authors have questioned the "myth" of West Indian success or challenged the theories put forward to explain that success.[4] Lately the debate has become more technical with academics arguing about whether black immigrants in fact do better than African Americans.[5] This is a politically charged debate and the estimates of, and explanations for, West Indian success tend to mirror political differences. Conservative writers such as Thomas Sowell are likely to see big differences and to stress cultural explanations. Liberal writers such as Stephen Steinberg are likely to see little or no differences and to stress structural explanations for the differences they do find.

Perhaps the best known of the analyses of West Indian success is Thomas Sowell's argument that first- and second-generation black immigrants have higher incomes, occupational status, and rates of business ownership than African Americans. He also cites the lower crime rates and birthrates of West Indians. He concludes that this shows that "[c]olor alone, or racism alone, is clearly not a sufficient explanation of income disparities . . . between the black and white populations."[6]

In addition to his claims about first-generation West Indians, Sowell also used 1970 census data on birthplaces of parents to analyze the relative success of second-generation West Indians. He found that second-generation West Indians in New York City who were unlikely to have an accent that would enable a white employer to distinguish them from native blacks "exceeded the socioeconomic status of other West Indians, as well as that of native blacks—and of the United States population as a whole—in family income . . ., education. . ., and proportion in the professions."[7] He concludes that this relative success of West Indians "undermines the explanatory power of current white discrimination as a cause of current black poverty."[8]

Sowell was not the first scholar to note the remarkable achievements of West Indians or to use those achievements to draw controversial conclusions about the experiences of black Americans. The argument that foreign-born blacks are more successful in American life than American-born blacks can be traced back to the work of Ira Reid, a sociologist who conducted a study of foreign-born blacks in the 1930s, published as *The Negro Immigrant: His Background Characteristics and Social Adjustment, 1899–1937*. Reid's work was the source for Glazer and Moynihan's oft-quoted argument that the success of West Indians reflected "the ethos of the West Indians, [which] in contrast to that of the Southern Negro, emphasized saving, hard work, investment, and education."[9] Reid's work has been the only comprehensive study of the black immigrant to date and is a valuable and highly engaging study.[10] But Reid was also faced with the limited data available on West Indians. He based a great deal of his book on entries by West Indians to a Life History Essay prize contest. Contestants entered essays about their experiences as immigrants and described their reactions to specific situations, such as employment and discrimination.[11]

Reid argued that the West Indian immigrants had a high proportion of skilled workers and that professionals made up 4 to 19% of the total number of immigrants arriving during the years he surveyed. Reid estimated "that in New York as high as one-third of the Negro professional population—particularly physicians, dentists, and lawyers—is foreign born."[12] Despite the attention this statistic has garnered, Reid apparently just made up the estimate himself. He offers no statistical foundation for the figure.[13]

More recent academic debates have centered on whether the post-1965 immigrants and their children can also be called a "black success story." Researchers have examined United States census data from 1970, 1980, and 1990 to answer the question, Do black immigrants outperform African Americans? Data from the 1970 census gave a resounding yes as the answer. In a multivariate study that controlled for background characteristics, economist Barry Chiswick concluded that foreign-born blacks who had been in the United States at least ten years had higher annual earnings than native-born blacks.[14] Subsequent analyses of 1980 census data using the same techniques by economist Kristin Butcher and by sociologist Suzanne Model did not find an earnings advantage when foreign-born and native-born blacks with the same background characteristics were compared, but did find an employment and an occupational advantage for the foreign-born.[15]

The debate in the literature has centered on whether West Indians have an earnings advantage over American blacks. Some analyses find a slight advantage; others, using different statistical controls, do not find an earnings advantage. In an analysis of 1990 census data limited to urban blacks, both native- and foreign-born, ages 26 to 64 with positive annual earnings for 1989, sociologist Matthijs Kalmijn finds a distinct advantage in earnings and occupational outcomes for British-origin Caribbeans. He finds that black immigrants and their descendants from English-speaking Caribbean countries are more educated and more likely to be married, have higher prestige occupations, and make higher earnings than native-born African Americans with no Caribbean ancestry.[16]

The literature on the socioeconomic performance of West Indians does agree that they do considerably better than native blacks in labor force participation. Indeed, the propensity to work rather than rely on government handouts that the immigrants are so proud of is borne out in the census data among both the West Indian men and women, but most strikingly among the West Indian women. Foreign-born West Indian women who head households and are thus (if they are legal) eligible for welfare, and foreign-born West Indian men who are disabled, are far more likely to be in the labor force than comparable African-American men and women.[17] Indeed, the high labor force participation of foreign-born black women is remarkable—they are more likely to be in the labor force than any other major demographic group in New York. In 1990 foreign-born West Indian men had labor force participation rates 12.3% higher than native-born African Americans (89.1% vs. 76.8%). Among women the foreign-born exceeded the native-born by 13.8% (83.0% vs. 69.2%).[18] Philip Kasinitz reports that while in 1980 West Indians were less likely to have households headed by single females than was the case for African Americans, even among the more deprived households in this category households headed by West Indian females did better than the poor households headed by native-born females.[19] The West Indians are less likely to be on welfare and more likely to be employed. This high labor force participation rate is all the more remarkable as recent West Indian immigrants were overrepresented in the very lowest education categories.[20]

EXPLANATIONS FOR WEST INDIAN SUCCESS

West Indians may no longer earn more than African Americans when background characteristics are statistically controlled, and there is some question of whether they ever were overrepresented in entrepreneurial activities, despite their reputation as "black Jews." Nevertheless, there are still some ways in which West Indians outperform African Americans.

They are more likely to be employed, less likely to be on public assistance, and more likely to have husband-wife two-earner households. And, while earlier immigrant cohorts have higher educations than later ones, West Indians are recognized as having higher educational aspirations in American society, especially among the second generation.[21] These differences lend some support to Sowell and other earlier writers' arguments about the cultural differences between West Indians and American blacks, for, as Kasinitz points out, "if propensity towards education and two income families are not cultural traits, what are?"[22]

Cultural explanations for a group's outcomes generally imply that the values, beliefs, and behaviors of members of that group explain their success or failures. Cultural explanations imply that members of that group exhibit certain behaviors because of values and ways of dealing with the world that they have learned from previous generations and not because of reactions to the particular situation they find themselves in. Structural explanations point to one's situation within society to account for why certain people succeed or fail. A simplified example is the role of households headed by single females in explaining poverty among African Americans. A cultural explanation, often attributed to the Moynihan report, is that slavery destroyed the African-American family, making it matrifocal. Since African Americans do not value the nuclear family, the reasoning goes, their families break up more often than others. This leads to higher dependence on welfare than in other families.[23]

A structural explanation sees people's behaviors not primarily as reflections of inner values and beliefs but as responses to the environment. Without good jobs to support a family, writers such as William Julius Wilson argue,[24] it makes no sense to marry. Thus households headed by single females form as a response to the economic structure around them, not because of cultural values handed down over generations.

The distinction between culture and structure is of course exaggerated and somewhat arbitrary as cultures respond to structures and vice versa—but the emphasis analysts give to one or the other has strong implications for their analysis and for eventual policy recommendations. If one believes African Americans are disproportionately poor because of their culture, one is not likely to believe that providing jobs is the proper solution to the problem. Instead, strong moral proscriptions against particular behaviors such as childbearing out of wedlock might seem more reasonable.

Authors who stress cultural differences between African Americans and West Indians as explanations for the latter's success point to a difference in the historical conditions of slavery and freedom in the Caribbean and the United States. For instance, Reid argues that the higher ratio of captured Africans to slaves born in captivity in the Caribbean led to a higher degree of resistance and a stronger sense of family among the Caribbean slaves and their descendants: "Coming from the slave clearing house for the United States, the Caribbean Negro has developed into a spirited, aggressive culture-type, whose program and principle of accommodation has been singularly different from that of the American Negro."[25] He also stresses that the absence of a population of poor whites in the islands led to slaves and free blacks being trained in skilled work, whereas in the American South the restrictions on blacks led to less skilled workers among the American slaves and their descendants.[26]

Dennis Forsythe argues that West Indians do so well in the United States because they share the Protestant ethic, which he defines as including "a strong belief in self, discipline, drive and determination." This ethic developed, he states, "because of the West Indians' schooling in the British educational system, their majority status in the Caribbean and the wider 'role frontier' available there."[27] Others argue that majority status provides role models and leads West Indians to grow up believing that "anything is possible" and that their dreams can be fulfilled if only they work and try hard enough.[28]

This theme is very common in autobiographical writings by West Indian immigrants. The Trinidadian political theorist C. L. R. James, who lived for long periods in both London and New York, was asked why he was such a successful person. He responded, "It was because I was from the Caribbean [where] we blacks form a majority. So that our attitude is that things can happen if we will only do it. That's why we are able to go abroad and take part; we have the feeling that we are not defeated in any way."[29]

Of course, cultural explanations for differences in outcomes between groups are hard to pin down. They often rely on impressionistic accounts of how the groups differ, which are enormously influenced by stereotypes that affect how the analyst interprets behavior and beliefs.[30] The debate about West Indian success has often relied on stereotypes about native-born blacks not valuing education, having less ambitions for their children, and being less likely to believe in the American dream. Careful analysis of an exhaustive amount of survey data on this topic by political scientist Jennifer Hochschild has disproved many of these stereotypes about African Americans.[31] Suzanne Model argues that class differences in the Caribbean have created very different cultures within societies, and historical differences across islands have also led to different cultural adaptations. Which of these many Caribbean cultures, she asks, is the culture supposedly carried by all of the immigrants and responsible for all of their successes?[32]

Those who stress structural explanations for West Indian success tend to focus on the selectivity of immigration, the psychological and structural consequences of immigration, and the preference some employers reportedly have for foreign-born over native-born blacks. Immigration is a selective process in a number of ways. Legal restrictions on immigration have selected for literacy in earlier years and, since 1965, for certain occupations, especially nurses (although most immigrants in the post-1965 era come in under family reunification and not occupation categories).[33]

Immigration is also selective in ways that are less easily measured. Even when immigrants and those who stay behind do not differ on measurable characteristics such as education or skill level, one still has to factor in the reality that immigrants are those with the ambition and drive to move to a place where they think opportunities will be better. The personality characteristics this selects for might not be measurable in large data sets, but they could easily lead to aggregate differences across groups.[34]

The psychological and structural consequences of immigration have strong effects on the social organization of immigrant communities in the United States. These structural conditions can have consequences that also explain some of the differences between American blacks and West Indians. Immigrants are more likely than natives to accept low-wage, low-status jobs because the immigrant's sense of self is not as bound up with the job.[35] Immigrants will judge jobs based on comparisons with the opportunities available to them in their own country. In that context, low pay and the conditions in secondary labor market jobs may look good to them. They also do not perceive the same stigma attached to low-status jobs as do natives because, again, their sense of self is tied to the status system in the home country.

Immigrants are also embedded in networks that can provide information and referrals to job opportunities in a way that natives often are not. Since immigration proceeds along chains of networks, most immigrants in an established stream have a chain of contacts that can bring them valuable information and referrals.[36] Both of these factors—the ready-made networks and the absence of an aversion to low-status jobs—could explain the much higher labor force participation rates among unskilled, poorly educated West Indians relative to unskilled, poorly educated native-born blacks.

Finally, discrimination in favor of the foreign-born on the part of white employers can certainly be a factor. Analysts of the situation of West Indians in the United States, starting with Reid, have documented the belief of West Indians that they are treated better by whites when it is known that they are foreign-born.[37] Roy S. Bryce-Laporte writes: "The white landlord, the white shopkeeper, and the white boss will also tell them of their moral superiority over the American black and distinctiveness of their accent, and if British, the grammatical correctness of their English or American—leaving them to believe that they are the recipients of exceptional favors."[38]

During Jim Crow segregation, foreign-born blacks were often seen as exceptions and treated better than native-born blacks.[39] For instance, the Jamaica-born writer Claude McKay was arrested in a sweep of an African-American cafe during World War I to find "draft resisters." He watched in court as the other men who were arrested with him were given jail sentences by the judge. When it was his turn, he explained to the judge that he did not have his draft card with him but that he worked for the railroad. He describes the reaction: "To my surprise as soon as I had finished, the judge asked me if I were born in Jamaica. I said, 'Yes Sir' and he commented 'Nice place. I was there a couple of seasons ago.'" The judge proceeded to reprimand the police officer who had arrested McKay and to dismiss the case. McKay resolved "to cultivate more my native accent."[40] Indeed, many of the people interviewed in this study told similar stories that persuaded them to choose to keep their accents just as McKay did many decades ago.

Yet aside from political pressures to stress one explanation over another, there is no analytical reason that some combination of cultural and structural factors could not play a part in explaining West Indian outcomes. This chapter and the next do just that. I focus on both structural and cultural reasons for West Indian success and for the exaggerated cultural stereotype of that success. The discussion that follows explores the dynamics of employment among low-skilled West Indians in one workplace in Manhattan in order to argue that there are clear structural reasons that explain the legendary capacity for and commitment to work among West Indians—the very attributes that are most often used to argue for a cultural explanation for their successes. The next chapter argues that West Indians have a particular culturally based approach to race relations that also contributes to their success and to the images Americans hold of that success.

American Food Company

Most West Indians in New York City work in the service economy. They are concentrated in the health services, where 22% of New Yorkers from the Caribbean work in hospitals, nursing homes, and home health care,[41] but are represented in a number of other service sectors of the economy. After months of trying to gain access to a hospital to conduct interviews (see the Appendix for a complete discussion), I happened upon American Food as a research site through a personal connection. The mother of one of my former students worked in United States Financial, the corporate headquarters of a famous financial services company in a gleaming downtown skyscraper, and she thought that the cafeteria had the mix of native whites and blacks and West Indians I was looking for. The American Food Company runs the cafeteria, executive dining room, and catering and food-cart service that feeds the 4,000 employees of United States Financial.[42]

In retrospect it is no surprise that I found American Food through a personal connection because it is virtually impossible to just happen upon this workplace. The cafeteria is on the third floor of the United States Financial Building, a new sparkling building that sits next to New York

Harbor. Security is very tight in the building, and employees must present magnetic ID cards just to enter the building. Guests must go to a room to the side of the entrance and give their names and addresses to women sitting at phone banks, who call upstairs to receive permission to issue a day pass, which must be shown to a guard to enter the building and then returned upon leaving the building. This means that, should someone want to come in off the street to apply for a job, it would be impossible. In fact, no one had been hired through a newspaper ad or a direct application without a referral for nine years.

American Food Services is an international food-service company that runs restaurants and cafeterias throughout the country. There are 170 employees in the United States Financial cafeteria. About fifteen managers and office staff manage the operation. We conducted in-depth interviews with sixty-five employees, including nine whites, all of whom were managers (three males and six females); fifteen American blacks, including two supervisors (six males and nine females); and thirty-four West Indian immigrants, including six supervisors and two managers (eleven males and twenty-three females). In addition, we interviewed three Puerto Rican males, two Puerto Rican females, one Peruvian female, and one Bangladeshi male, all of whom were workers.[43] (More details about the sample are provided in the Appendix.) The interviews lasted between one and two hours, and all covered the same core sets of issues—family background, ethnic and racial identity, job history, attitudes and interactions with other ethnic groups, neighborhood characteristics, and political attitudes. In addition, we asked the managers about hiring decisions and their assessments of the strengths and weaknesses of the workforce. The respondents were told that the study was about the impact of immigration from the Caribbean on life in New York City.[44]

While the in-depth interview was my primary way of gathering information, my research assistant and I were present during every workday for about two and a half months, and so we were able to observe the dynamics of the workplace apart from the formal interview situation. When we were not interviewing, we spent time in the main office where employees came in to punch their time clocks, or we sat in a corner of the kitchen area observing the workers, or we sat in the cafeteria and were able to talk informally with employees on their breaks. We were thus able to observe some of the dynamics in the workplace—who took breaks together and how people got along with each other and with their supervisors. In all, we interviewed almost all of the white and American black employees in the establishment and about one-third of the English-speaking Caribbean immigrants. The remaining workers were Haitians, Dominicans, and Puerto Ricans. Haitians were excluded based on language considerations.

Network Hiring

Management was unwilling to give us access to personnel records, but we were able to get a consistent account of how the workplace had changed in the last thirty years. The cafeteria's workforce has been transformed since 1970 from one that employed black American men and women, and older white women who were returning to work after raising families, to a workplace that is now predominantly staffed by foreign-born males and females. The present workers are about 90% foreign-born. The physical plant has also changed. Before the construction of the current modern skyscraper, United States Financial was located in an older New York office building, also in the Wall Street area. The cafeteria and dining room were run by the financial services company in-house. American Food took over the running of the food services for the company in 1981, two years before the move to the current building in 1983. A key difference between the operations in the two buildings is that the older building was more accessible to people coming in off the street and inquiring about jobs. And in fact some of the older employees who have the longest service with the company did get their jobs by "pounding the pavement." In my sample these workers include a white male manager, several American black females, and an immigrant female.

The managers and workers both report that hiring used to be handled through newspaper advertisements and through employment agencies specializing in food-service workers. This changed beginning in the early 1980s. The company has not placed an advertisement in a newspaper in over nine years. Occasionally an agency is used to find a skilled worker—a chef's assistant, for example. However, almost all hiring for the last nine years has been through current employees' social networks. This happens in spite of the fact that there is an official company rule against hiring relatives. The rule is broken all the time because network hiring is easier for the managers. They generally believe that they get a higher quality worker, and they have more control over the workforce because the original worker who recommended the new hire has an interest in that person doing well. One manager describes his point of view on how network hiring is better:

> If a position opens up, and then Ingrid says, my brother needs a job, we won't look at the applications; we tell her to bring her brother. We do it undercover. Because you're really not supposed to have brothers and sisters and husbands and wives in there. But it makes it a little bit more manageable [because] when they do bring somebody in, they tend to be a little bit better workers because of—well somebody like Ingrid [has] been here for ten years. You know? Her brother needs a job. Her brother comes here, he says, "I'm not gonna let my sister look bad. She's been here for ten years and now I'm gonna jerk around and make her look bad? I mean, that's part of her career." (White male manager, age 40)

The remarkable change at American Food in both hiring practices and the demographics of the workforce does not seem to have been a conscious choice by management. Rather, the switch from employing American blacks and a few white women to employing West Indians and other immigrants occurred in the following fashion. Each worker is allowed to recommend someone for a position. If the new person does not work out, then that person cannot recommend any more friends or relatives. If the new person works out well, then not only can the original person recommend another prospect, but the new hire can also. Because of the different value placed on these low-skilled, low-paying jobs by immigrants and by Americans, this rule tends to cut off the networks of the American workers, and yet increases the number of hires from the immigrant networks. Although no statistics were supplied to us, the managers claimed that there was much lower turnover among the immigrants than among American blacks and the white American women. The preponderance of West Indians also does not seem to have been a conscious choice; however, their knowledge of English means that they are preferred for jobs that involve contact with customers. The kitchen jobs are often filled by Hispanics and Thai and Bangladeshi immigrants. In addition, the company has a personnel policy that encourages minority hiring, and the West Indians meet the company's requirements in counting as black employees.

The overall characteristics of the samples interviewed appear in Table 4.1. There are several striking differences among the groups. The black American females were on average the oldest and had been on the job the longest at a mean of 7.1 years. The black American males were more recent hires and were also younger. The foreign-born males and females were also more recent, but both groups had been working there slightly longer than the black American males. Perhaps the most striking differences were in the method of hire of the workers and in the percentage of workers with previous training in food services. Five out of the nine black American females we interviewed got their current job through some formal avenue, whereas all of the black American males and the vast majority of the foreign-born males and females got their jobs through networks. The black American females who got their jobs through formal means either applied at the old premises off the street, answered a newspaper ad, were referred by an agency, or, in the case of two women, were placed in their jobs after completing food-service training programs in an attempt to get off welfare.

There is a strong difference between the black American men and women in how they obtained their jobs. The black American males all got their jobs through recommendations from friends. In two cases the friends who recommended them were foreign-born black males they

Table 4.1 Characteristics of food-service workers in sample interviewed

Birthplace and gender	Number	Average age	Number with training in food services	Number not hired through networks	Average years in U.S.	Average years at job
American black females	9	46	4	5		7.1
American black males	5	31	2	0		4.6
West Indian females	17	36	0	1	12.1	5.7
West Indian males	9	35	1	1	8.8	4.8

Notes: Number does not equal total interviewed because managers were not interviewed about their method of hire, and because some interviews with workers did not include this information. "Number not hired through networks" = number of workers of each ethnic/nativity group who were initially hired through formal means, not through recommendations of friends and relatives.

knew through intermarriage in their families. This gender difference in method of hire also reflects the different periods in which these people were hired. The black American females are survivors from the early days when it was possible to be hired through a formal mechanism; the black American males are more recent hires.

The difference in formal training is also striking. The Americans were more likely to have received training in food services either in school or in previous corporate settings. Since both managers and workers agreed in their interviews with us that no skills were necessary for these jobs, and everything could be taught to workers in a few days' time, it could be that these differences reflect the statistical discrimination that this firm has practiced in hiring. In general, the managers prefer immigrants for reasons that will be elaborated on later. Given this preference, and the fact that many unskilled workers are turned away from these jobs, the American blacks who are hired must impress the person hiring them in some way in the interview. As the managers made clear, all things being equal, they would rather hire an immigrant. The fact that the American blacks who are on the job have had some training may indicate that the training enabled them to get in the door for an interview. This reflects patterns in hiring that have been found in a number of other studies, all of which concluded that formal hiring mechanisms work better for blacks because they provide more objective criteria for employers to make hiring decisions and less opportunity for employers to practice "statistical discrimination" in which they exclude all blacks from consideration because on average they believe blacks will not make good workers.[45]

The microprocesses I have described here freeze out African Americans from entry-level jobs. Roger Waldinger's book *Still the Promised City?* shows on a large scale how network hiring can adversely affect low-skilled African Americans, in effect driving them out of the labor force, while at the same time the labor force absorbs large numbers of poorly educated immigrants. Waldinger shows dynamically how these networks function to change the distribution of groups in jobs. He argues that patterns of network hiring lead to the formation of racial and ethnic niches in employment—the concentration of racial and ethnic groups in industries or sectors of the economy beyond what one would expect, given their proportions in the population. Waldinger traces the patterns of niche formation and succession in New York City over the last fifty years for a number of immigrant groups, including West Indians and African Americans.[46]

Waldinger argues that West Indians have been able to expand their presence in New York's economy in recent decades while African Americans' presence declined because the West Indians were poised to do well in New York's growing postindustrial service economy. In 1940 employed West Indians in New York were concentrated in personal services—notably, domestic services and laundering. African Americans were also highly concentrated in this niche—40% of African Americans worked there. By the 1970s and '80s West Indians established strong concentrations in the expanding health care industry. By 1990 employment in the niches of hospitals, nursing homes, and health services provided employment to 22% of Caribbean New Yorkers.[47] By contrast African Americans were concentrated in public sector employment.[48] This shift into relatively better jobs in public sector employment moved African Americans away from earlier concentrations in personal services. But this shift in opportunities put a bigger premium on education. Most public sector jobs required formal education, which was also rising dramatically among African Americans during this period.

Waldinger concludes that while skilled African Americans are doing well in the niche of public sector employment, with many of them employed in managerial or professional occupations, unskilled African Americans have been locked out of the networks that provide entrée to unskilled entry-level jobs because they no longer control those niches. Those jobs have been taken over by immigrants—both black and other immigrants. Though Waldinger's aggregate statistics show that unskilled, poorly educated West Indians are concentrated in health care and personal services, the contribution of ethnic networks to hiring the food-service workers interviewed in this study is very similar to other niche employment. Networks get immigrants jobs and freeze out African Americans.

Since American Food no longer advertises or uses agencies, it is very clear that networks are the only way a job applicant could even know about the existence of the possibility of jobs and have an opportunity to fill out an application. Nevertheless, as we shall see in the next section, when immigrants and white managers are asked why black Americans do not work in the cafeteria, they argue that they are too lazy to apply and are uninterested in the jobs.

Entry-level jobs at American Food Service pay about $5.25 an hour or $210 a week. This would give someone a gross income of $840 a month for a very strenuous 40-hour week. The yearly income would be $10,080 for a full-time worker. Because the positions are with a major corporation with an internal labor market, include health insurance for full-time employees, and pay slightly better than minimum wage, they are better-than-average entry-level jobs for the unskilled. However, the low pay and general lack of opportunities to advance in salary or job position render them dead-end jobs, resulting in a wage that ensures that employees will be members of the working poor for the rest of their lives. For the vast majority of workers who will not be promoted, the job provides a difficult 40-hour week of hard work, little control over working conditions, and a precarious em-ployment situation dependent on economic conditions. However, there is a steady supply of immigrants who are very eager to land these entry-level jobs, enough so that one 33-year-old white female manager calls the immi-grant network her "upstairs agency": "We have a guy in here who calls us almost every other week—you need anybody, you need anybody? I've got somebody for you, you know. I mean, why go outside? Just go to my agency upstairs and say, got anybody for me this week?"

Skills are generally not a requirement in hiring. Entry-level jobs include dishwashing, serving food on the cafeteria line, fixing drinks, and making sandwiches, as well as general cleanup activities in the kitchen. These jobs can be learned in a matter of minutes or hours. Some slightly more skilled jobs, such as chopping vegetables for salads or cooking soups, can be learned in a day or less. But the managers are explicit that they are looking for certain characteristics in employees, especially reliability, loyalty to the job, and ability to take orders and be "flexible." The managers have enough immigrants who are desperate for a job that they can convey in the initial interview that employees will be asked to work very hard and to be very flexible about doing anything anyone in a higher position in the hierarchy asks them to do. Loyalty to a job that intrinsically should com-mand no loyalty is what the managers are after, and the immigrants fit the bill. These characteristics are important enough that they even outweigh relevant experience.[49]

Those native-born applicants who get a referral to a manager for a screening interview for one of these entry-level jobs are at a distinct disadvantage. Native-born applicants are less likely than immigrants to accept the managers' request for a commitment to an unspecified set of tasks. Rather than seeing the employment as a favor worthy of all one's loyalty to the company and to the manager, the American worker sees the job situation as a contract. For instance, one manager states that in the initial interview with an applicant she asks them, "Are you willing to do anything?" she adds, "If they say yes, I hire them."

Q: Are there people that say no?

A: Yes. I had people come in for a dishwashing job and give me a resume. Does this mean that you wouldn't scrub the floor if I ask you to? And he said, well, if it's not in my job description, no. You know I didn't hire him. (White female manager, age 53)

In fact, this issue of "flexibility" is a source of contention among the workers who are on the job. Many of the Americans related that the immigrants created a situation where everyone was exploited because they were willing to do many different things and did not insist on job descriptions. For instance, one black American worker believed that because the immigrants did not stand up for their rights, all of the workers at American Food were suffering for it, and this allowed management to take liberties with the workers that they should not be allowed to take:

Q: Are there any negative aspects of your job?

A: Well yes. Because I think all of the main focus is on dealing with foreigners. Because, see, they don't know the American system, you know, and they feel they must be cautious because they don't want to do nothing wrong. Basically they don't know their rights, you know? And then, at the job, see, they get the feeling that everybody don't know their rights. So, it causes problems.

Q: What kinds of problems?

A: Well, as far as me, personally, when I punch the clock, I mean, I'm yours, to do. But then, like sometimes, the company's policies are not written; it just seems like they make them up as they go along. You see, and that's what I didn't quite understand, you

know. That's where the conflict always comes in with me. You
see, they [the immigrants] do a lot of things that they don't have
to do, to try to, I guess, appeal to ease their way, you know? Sort
of like, to make less problems for themselves. I guess they would
figure the less problems for them, the better. But then you have
to look at what you consider a problem, you understand? Because, if someone's gonna mistreat you, you know, by taking
away your rights, I mean, that's a problem right there as far as I
am concerned. (Black American male worker, age 28)

In addition to loyalty and flexibility, the managers appreciate that the
low wages paid for the jobs mean one thing to the immigrant worker and
another to the American worker. While these managers and supervisors
do not set the wages for the new hires the way a proprietor of a small shop
would, they seem to benefit from an easier work climate when they deal
with immigrants who do not complain about the low wages and who are
not constantly looking for higher wages:

Americans wouldn't do what immigrants do. They wouldn't do the
work without questions, you know. Immigrants will do anything
because they're here, they have no money, and they're willing to
work for their money. They're willing. Americans, I think, have it
too easy, you know. And I just feel like, you hire an immigrant, right,
you pay him $3 an hour. You hire an American, he won't work for
$3 an hour. He won't. He'll want $7 an hour. That's why a lot of
immigrants get hired, because they'll work cheaper. (White female
manager, age 50)

The immigrants are willing to work for less and to commit themselves
to these entry-level jobs because they use a different metric to measure
them. This Guyanese immigrant describes the sojourner mentality that
allows her to work hard:

That show—*In Living Color*[50]—and it's true, most people that came
from the West Indies they always do more than one job and it's true.
Because you come here with one intention—that you want a better
living and you want to have things that you never had before. So you
don't mind working for it because back home we work real hard. So

when you come up here it's like—the job up here compared to Guyana is like nothing. So you don't mind working hard, you know. To the Americans, it's too much work. And for us it won't be like too much work... You buy yourself things that you never had. You get to do a lot of things. I never had a car in Guyana. Now I have two cars. I never had a lot of things but now I have it. Life is much better. Much easier. (Guyanese female worker, age 29, in United States nine years)

In addition to being willing to work for low pay, the immigrants are not bothered by the low status of these jobs to the degree a person born in this country would be. Because the immigrants exist between two societies—home and the United States—their sense of self is not as tied to the work they do as it would be back home or if they had grown up in the United States.[51] As target earners, the type of work they do does not define their social status in the same way it does for a native. This Guyanese immigrant explains that his dignity is not hurt by doing low-status work here in the way it would be back home in Guyana:

They [Americans] find that it's better to go in line and wait for a welfare check. And you know, that's one of the things that I am totally against. Seeing young body people who could go and do some kind of work, because in America, no job is degrading. No job is degrading . . . In America, when you are a tradesman, you are a big man. More than those who sits in an office. But in my country, everybody wants to have an office job. In America, the main thing is earning, and earning it honestly. (Guyanese male worker, age 39, in United States six years)

While working in a cafeteria all day may not be a great job, many contrast it to cutting cane in the tropical sun or working long hours for much lower wages in an economy where the prices of imported goods have skyrocketed. The immigrants had come to the United States expecting the "streets to be paved with gold":

Back home the impression that I got was when you come to America, so to speak, you coming into a gold spoon. Most people when they go home, they do not tell you the true picture about what is going on over here. So based on what they were telling you, you know, you just tell yourself, well look, from the plane, another couple of days you gonna be in a job. You gonna be working for so much money. I quickly realized that was not so. They never really tell you about the bills and things, you know, that you would have to face. You have to adjust yourself, forget what you was at home, and you actually starting over a new life altogether. But what you have to do is to work to a budget. And you got to know what is your goal. What you want to achieve. And I feel once you know what you want to achieve, and you work hard towards it, you can make it. (Guyanese male worker, age 39, in United States six years)

They found the tales they had heard about wealth and opportunity in the United States to be quite exaggerated. They were very surprised by the poverty and by how hard it was to find and keep a job and a decent place to live. Yet the vast majority of people continued to see the United States as a place of opportunity, mainly because of the educational opportunities they saw for themselves and for their children, and because of the high wages they received for their work relative to what they received back home. All of the immigrants earned more in this country than they did back home and for many the promise of prosperity extended by the United States came true.[52]

This sense that the future would be better and that America was a land of opportunities contrasted with the outlook of the native workers who were doing the same jobs. One American worker saw the job as a "necessary evil" that did not hold much promise for the future:

Q: If you stayed at American Food, do you think you could have a career where you work your way up?

A: I hear people are in there for five to ten years and they doing the same thing. They might make a little bit more money but, I mean, fifteen years and all you get is a plaque, or a dollar bonus, or something like that. That's not money, so I don't think you'll move too far in this American Food so that's why I won't stay long. (Black American male worker, age 33)

Another American worker was well aware of the differences in the ways in which foreigners and Americans assessed the same job. He argues that the immigrants are here on a "work plan," which allows them to accept low wages they should scorn:

Q: So do you think wages would be higher at a place like American Food if there weren't immigrants around to work there?

A: Yes, I think so. I think so. I think the base salary would be. I think the base salary would be considerably higher. And then like the foreigners always say, well you Americans lazy, you Americans this, you Americans that. Due to the fact that we won't work for low wages. In which I feel that is unfair, I mean, we being Americans, I mean, we shouldn't have to work for this less amount of money when we know that we could or should be earning more. And then, see, what the foreigners fail to realize, they come to this country to make a living, too, and then they always talking about going back to their country. So they're mostly here like on a work program. So, I mean, when you come into a country under those circumstances, I guess you would have to take whatever you can get. But, being an American in this country, then, you know, we don't feel that way. (Black American male worker, age 28)

All of the black American workers are aware that the way to be hired at American Food now is to know someone. The low wages and the low status of the job to an American mean that for many it is easy to walk away if some other alternative arises. While the Americans are entitled to recommend friends and families for jobs, most described the ways in which their networks were cut off because the people they recommend do not work out:

They won't let me bring nobody else in because of my brother. Like when I was at the old shop, I got him on, we was working together. That was during the wintertime; during the summer he got in school. He had like a day class. So he had to make a choice between his job and the school. So I told him, go to school, man. So you know, after a while, I couldn't bring nobody in. Because you know, he took school over the job. So I was telling them, he wants to go to school. [They said] "No, you don't bring no responsible people in."

I said, all right. I'm still working, so what am I gonna worry about somebody else for, you know? Let them stand. You know, you can't do that to me 'cause he decided to go to school. (Black American male worker, age 37)

It makes sense to this worker that his brother would choose school over this low-level job, but effectively it cut off his ability to recommend any other friends or family for jobs at American Food. Yet even though the rule covering recommendations for hiring provides a rational explanation for why American Food increasingly hires only immigrants, many of the African-American respondents specifically had heard that there was a systematic bias in favor of the foreign-born in hiring decisions. People reported that they believed whites and West Indians would hire West Indians over American blacks if they had the chance.

Employer Preferences

The American blacks were right. The managers were not at all reticent about describing their preference for immigrants over Americans. White native-born Americans are not employed as workers at all in the site and do not apply for jobs there, so when the managers contrasted Americans and immigrants, they were generally contrasting American blacks with foreign-born blacks and Hispanics. While only one white manager actually described herself and her racial opinions in overtly racist language and attitudes, all of the managers had a clear preference for the immigrant blacks over the natives:

A: If I had one position open and if it was a West Indian versus an American black, I'd go with the West Indian.
Q: And that's because of your experience working with people?
A: Yes. Their reliability, their willingness to do the job or what has to be done.
Q: Are there concrete statistics on this?
A: I don't have them. I just—it's just experience that they have a different drive than American blacks. (White male manager, age 42)

The American blacks did not share the same negative stereotypes as the West Indians and the whites, and they did not use those stereotypes to

explain the dearth of American blacks at American Food. A few argued
that American blacks were often too discouraged to apply for jobs, believing that they would not get them because of their low qualifications or
because of systematic bias against them. One woman who was hired
through formal channels related to her Job Corps training in food service
stated that she did not believe she would be hired when she first applied:
"A lot of American people won't go out there and get these jobs because,
I guess, a lot of them feel like discouraged, you know, like they don't think
they're going to get hired, or—you know—'cause I had cold feet coming
down here myself."

Q: You felt like they weren't going to want to hire you?

A: Yeah. And because, you know, like I knew I didn't have my education—that wasn't together and I just felt like that, you know.
But I knew that I didn't want to be on public assistance so I said,
what the heck, I got nothing to lose, you know. I came down
here. (Black American female worker, age 22)

An older black woman argues that Americans do not apply for jobs at
American Food because they (erroneously in her opinion) expect racial
discrimination to block them from consideration. Americans, she says, are
"so negative about other people. Negative about, oh, I can't get this job
because I'm black. If I was white, or if I was an islander, I'd get that job,
but no, they're not hiring no blacks. They only want Hispanics and
this—that part of them I don't like."

Q: So people would think that? They would think, I won't even apply for a job 'cause I won't get it?

A: Oh, yes. I've seen it happen. You know, where they, oh, no, I
didn't get the job because they don't want me 'cause I wasn't
light enough. (Black American female worker, age 50)

It is clear that the substitution of immigrants for native workers in this
workplace comes about for structural reasons. The company wants flexible workers in a service environment who give loyalty to the company,
accept low pay, and obey higher-ups when they give orders. However,
from the American blacks' perspective these jobs should command no
loyalty. They believe that the pay is very bad, and that workers should not

have to do whatever they are asked to do; they should have a right to a job description. But the immigrants undermine that position. For them, the bargain offered by American Food does not seem on the face of it to be a bad one. It seems to offer a shot at the American dream—if not for them, then for their children. (Perhaps I should say it offers them a chance at the Guyanese dream because it is in reference to home conditions and pay that the job really looks attractive.)

This difference of perception about the relative worth of these jobs and about the treatment workers have a right to expect is very understandable given the different structural situations of the immigrants and the Americans. But the devaluation of these jobs and the desire of the Americans to limit the power of management are not understood by the white managers or the West Indians as a rational response to a lousy job with limited opportunities for mobility. Rather, the whites and the West Indians interpret these reactions as individualistic moral failings of American blacks as workers. The racial stereotypes that float about in our society are easily marshaled to explain what is in fact a more complicated situation. The next section discusses the images each group—whites, West Indians, and Americans—hold of each other, and how those images are generated through day-to-day interactions. The final section focuses on the tensions between African Americans and West Indians that result from this mutual stereotyping.

THE GENESIS OF CULTURAL STEREOTYPES
The Whites' Perceptions

We asked the white managers specifically why there were so few American blacks working in the corporation now, compared with thirty years ago. They claimed that black Americans preferred welfare to applying for entry-level jobs like the ones in the cafeteria, that black Americans lacked a work ethic and the discipline to keep the jobs, and that black Americans wanted more money than these jobs paid. (In economists' terms, black American had a higher reservation wage.) When I asked about white ethnic groups and why they did not come in for these jobs, I got a very different answer. For instance, the supervisor of waiters in the restaurant thought that American blacks do not come in because they are lazy and lack discipline. She thought that Italians do not come in for these jobs because they have other options: "You know, a lot of them go into construction or into their fathers' businesses or they go into Italian restaurants where mostly they deal with Italian customers and Italian bosses."

It was striking that while the managers were aware of how much they relied on network hiring, they still stated that American blacks were lacking in discipline and a work ethic, and that is why they did not work out:

> Very few American blacks have applied for work that I've seen. . . . and the ones we get, they were not successful in retaining their employment. And the conjecture I make in my own mind is, they don't have the self-discipline to hold the job. Have I encountered that among non-American blacks? Yes. But not nearly as significant. (White male manager, age 42)

These whites generally hold a very low opinion of ghetto blacks, distinguishing them from "good blacks"—meaning middle-class or hard-working African Americans. Yet they described most of the blacks they came in contact with at work as ghetto blacks.[53] Many spoke with disdain of women who left their cafeteria jobs because they could live better on welfare. Interestingly, all of them felt this meant that welfare payments were too high and too readily available, not that the cafeteria job should pay enough for a working mother to afford child care. The black American workers who are hard-working, reliable workers, whom these whites see every day, do not disconfirm the stereotypes the managers hold from their everyday lives.[54] Instead, these hard-working blacks are seen as exceptions to the general rule that inner-city blacks are criminal, welfare-dependent, and have too many children.

A key question in the literature on black immigrants is the degree to which whites in the United States are oblivious to ethnic and nativity differences in the black community and see all people with black skin as simply "blacks." While there have been many studies that provide anecdotal evidence from immigrants that they believe whites prefer foreign-born blacks to American blacks in employment situations,[55] there has been only one study that examined this phenomenon in the workplace,[56] and none that have involved talking with whites about what they think.

Among the questions we pursued with these white supervisors and managers were how much they were aware of differences between foreign-born and American-born blacks and how much they were aware of national origin differences among the foreign-born blacks.

All of the whites stated that before working in this worksite they were very unaware of differences between foreign-born and American-born blacks and that they were surprised when they first encountered the differences. The manager of the entire operation told us how he has had to break up fights between West Indians and African Americans and between people from different islands. This surprised him because "I never encountered a situation where blacks would fight among themselves."

The most common way in which the whites learn about the differences between foreign-born and American-born blacks is by talking with their employees about it. For instance, one white male manager described a Jamaican employee whose parents were extremely upset any time she would date anyone who was a black American because they felt all American black males were worthless. He recalled being very surprised by this because to him all blacks were the same. Another manager describes what he has learned from his employees over the years about differences between the two groups:

> I know that the West Indian blacks don't like the American blacks 'cause they get put into the same position as American black people. And they tend more to shy away from doing all of the illegal things because they have such strict rules down in their countries and jails. And they're nothing like here. So they're really paranoid to do something wrong. They seem to be very, very self-conscious of it. No matter what they have to do, if they have to try and work three jobs, they do. They do all kinds of things. They make crafts and try and sell them to each other and whatever. They won't go into drugs or anything like that. Whereas the American black people, right away. I mean, you talk about the ghetto black, you talk about the guy's running around with a gun and drugs. These people don't want to be affiliated with that. But, if you see somebody black, everybody's black, everybody's a junkie, or everybody's got a gun. They really don't like it. They want to be distinguished as Trinidadians, and I

even hear them talk about American black people. They really don't like them. They try to keep their children away from American blacks. I think that the parents know enough to keep them away from American blacks because they see the American black as being a bad person and they don't want their children to fall into this. (White male manager, age 40)

While the whites report that they only recently became aware of differences between foreign-born and American-born blacks, they now describe what they perceive as different values and behaviors between the groups. The whites saw the West Indians as more ambitious, more hard-working, and less troublesome than the African Americans. They also thought the West Indians were less materialistic than the Americans:

I work closely with this one girl who's from Trinidad. And she told me when she first came here to live with her sister and her cousin, she had two children. And she said I'm here four years and we're reached our goals. And what was your goal? For her two children to each have their own bedroom. Now she has a three-bedroom apartment, and she said that's one of the goals she was shooting for. Four years it took her to get there. Now if that was an American, they would say, I reached my goal, I bought a Cadillac. Like, that's what they would say. Or I bought a diamond ring or a watch. This one got her son and daughter each their own bedroom. Now that is a difference. (White female manager, age 53)

The managers use the immigration experience and ethnicity of their employees as explanations for both good and bad behaviors at work. For instance, where American blacks are blamed for their lack of a work ethic and for not showing up for work on Mondays, the immigrants are often granted cultural or ethnic explanations for why they behave in a particular way. One manager explained that when new immigrants were late "on island time" or did not show up for work when it rained, he understood that they just did not understand the "American way of work," and he cut them some slack.

The whites also made analogies to their own immigrant past and ethnicity to explain the experiences of the black ethnics. All of the managers were themselves second- or third-generation descendants of immigrants, and in the interviews they often spontaneously compared the immigrant adjustment experiences of the West Indian workers with their own. The master status of the West Indians in the eyes of these managers for the most part was as "immigrant," and the fact of their black skin was mostly not consequential. Rather, they were appreciated as workers, and they also seemed to be appreciated by these white respondents for their shared experience of the immigration and American assimilation trajectory. The whites genuinely seemed to believe that the West Indian parents were very much like their own white immigrant parents, and that the children of the immigrants would achieve their parents' dream of upward social mobility. The managers generally appreciated the hard work and ambition of the immigrants and for the most part wished them well:

> Like when I grew up, I only knew, from all my relatives, everyone was Polish. You keep your bonds. So, I think in that respect, Caribbeans stay together, as far as the people from Guyana have most of their friends are Guyanese, and you know, Jamaica, it's Jamaicans, and so on and so forth. You have your little backgrounds.[57] (White male manager, age 34)

The idea that their immigrant parents and grandparents sacrificed and achieved mobility is used as the lens through which the white managers understand the experiences of the immigrants. They too are perceived to be sacrificing for the inevitable successes their children will experience. And the immigrants are seen as having to live through a period of discrimination and ethnic exclusiveness:

> I remember, like, seeing movies and listening to my grandfather and all. When he came here, they would call him guinea and this and that. He couldn't get work and all of that stuff. You know? It's the same as that. And now these people are coming—I think that it is just like myself and my son. I didn't let him go amuck. It's the same thing as I think with the Trinidadians. As long as they have their both parents, and their parents are good, I think they'll keep raising them just like that. I think that the Trinidadians—the same thing. They're gonna take care of their children, and they're gonna try to tend to them, keep them away from trouble. (White male manager, age 40)

I was struck by how often the white managers described the experiences of the immigrants as being "just like you and me." Since they did not identify directly with the first generation, they tended to think that it was the children of the immigrants who would turn out just like themselves. Even those managers who expressed very negative opinions about American blacks made many spontaneous comments about similarities between their immigrant ancestors and the current West Indian immigrants. In effect these whites saw themselves in the immigrants, even as they saw the American blacks as "the Other" or as people who shared none of their values and characteristics or those of their families:

Q: So, one of the questions that I have is, what about their children? What will happen with the children of the West Indians?

A: The children, I think, will be fine. Maybe a little spoiled, like, no offense meant, you[58] and I were spoiled, with our parents. But I think they—if they're able to keep them off the drugs and off the streets, they'll do exceptionally well. I think Colin Powell is a great example. He's second generation, and if he should become a candidate for president—I mean, look at all the years that went before. It doesn't say well for . . . people of our country . . . I doubt if I'll ever see one of them [children of the immigrants] in my kitchen because their parents work so bloody hard to make sure they don't have to do that. (White male manager, age 42)

The Immigrants' Perceptions

The immigrants we spoke with are generally well aware of their employers' preference for immigrants as workers, and they are likely to share the whites' perceptions about the superiority of West Indians to black Americans. In fact, the West Indians were much more attuned to minute differences between themselves and black Americans and were apt to chronicle differences between the groups and to point to West Indian superiority in even more arenas than the whites did. Drawing on their experiences in their neighborhoods, their children's schools, on public transportation, in the media, as well as on the job, the West Indians find black Americans lacking in basic values and achievements. They develop very individualistic blaming attitudes toward black Americans' apparent lack of success.

At American Food the line manager in charge of day-to-day functioning of the cafeteria is a Trinidadian woman who has been employed by the
company for seventeen years and worked her way up to this high position.
She shared the same negative perceptions of American blacks as her fellow
white managers—in fact, she was even more forthright in her opinions
that American blacks are terrible workers. She believes that she originally
got her job because she was West Indian and that in general big corpora-
tions like American Food are interested in hiring West Indians. She
thought that American Food is a very difficult company for blacks to
succeed in and that many of the top managers are prejudiced against black
people. However, she has found that the white managers prefer to hire
West Indians and that once people find she is from Trinidad, they are
more likely to appreciate her work. She thinks that on the job her immigrant identity takes precedence over her race:

> A: My ex-boss he was white and he would rather have a staff like
> this with a lot of West Indians because of the problems [he had]
> when he would hire Americans. He would say, "it's a waste." On
> a Monday morning when he looking for his job to be done,
> they're not here. And he always say he liked West Indian people.
> And I think I did benefit from that. I think this is why I'm in this
> position right now through him, you know? And probably be-
> cause I'm black, maybe he wouldn't appreciate me that much. If
> you're working for a place and there's openings for a job, them
> big firms, they like to take West Indians faster than a black Ameri-
> can.
> Q: Why do you think that is?
> A: Because as I was saying, most people know most Americans is
> lazy. Black Americans. (Trinidadian female manager, age 38, in
> United States twenty-two years)

Because of the positive reactions to her national background that she
has received at work and at school from white Americans, she has consciously decided to keep her accent:

> I used to go to beauty school and I can remember going there, it was
> about three years after I came here and I would not open my mouth

to say a thing. Because it was a lot of Americans and I was afraid to speak. And I remember when it was time for graduation, everybody have to get up and introduce their self and stuff like that. And when I started to speak the class went, oh! You know? And the teacher said, you have such a nice accent and you hardly ever speak. And then the kids, they started saying the same thing and after that, you know, be my friend and all this and speak to me. And I was all embarrassed about my accent and here somebody appreciate it and then I decided that I wouldn't try to lose it.

This is a typical experience among the immigrant workers in that they suspect people will be against them because they are foreigners and then they are usually pleasantly surprised when that does not turn out to be the case. But this reaction is usually limited to whites. When it comes to relations with black Americans, the immigrants report a very different reception. This same manager describes her relations and perceptions of black Americans:

A: American people, especially black Americans, they think that West Indian people come here to take their jobs. But the way I feel, this is their place and they have all the opportunities and they supposed to, you know, use it up, but we come from the outside and we see the opportunities and we grab at it and they get upset about us. The average black American will not come here and work for five dollars an hour. They would rather stay home or hang out. But to me, I would take the five dollars and make it do. You know what I mean? And they hate us for that, and that's wrong, I think because we are not here to take anybody's job. Most of the jobs that the West Indian people have here, the Americans wouldn't do it . . . I was talking to one of the employees and she always say, you need to get Americans inside here. But you hire the Americans and they goof off and they like time off too. The Americans work for one month straight, and then after that they start—within a week, they call out sick, late. Most of the employees here is West Indian. [They've been here] fifteen years, sixteen years, seventeen years. The Americans, here, the longest employee I have here must be five years.

Q: Out of a hundred and seventy?

A: About, yeah, about five or seven years. The other ones? About a year, six months, two years.

Q: Do you think they leave because they get better jobs?

A: No. Most of the time they leave, they get fired because they never work. Or they will stay here and never be working, things like that.

Based on all of the other sources of information we have, including interviews with other managers and analysis of the people interviewed, this generalization is highly biased. While there may indeed be higher turnover among the black Americans, the ones who are still on the job have the longest average employment time at American Food. The black American females we interviewed had an average of 7.1 years on the job compared to 5.7 years for the foreign-born females we interviewed. However, these images of black Americans who refuse to work hard persist in the minds of both the immigrants and the white managers.

The other West Indian manager at American Food also argues that American blacks do not last on the job because they do not have the discipline the West Indians have. This manager from Grenada believes that the immigrants are better workers because of fundamental differences between Americans and immigrants:

Q: And what percentage of the people who work for you are immigrants?

A: I would say ninety-five percent.

Q: And why do you think that is? Why is it that immigrants . . .

A: We are very strict. You got to come to work on time. You got to come to work every day. You're supposed to do the work you're supposed to do, when you're asked to do it. I find Caribbean people are more bent to doing this. Most of the black Americans come here and they don't do that. They cannot tolerate discipline. For example, when they don't want to come to work, they don't come to work at all. They come to work late. A lot of excuses for absence. We don't tolerate that. This is the reason why I think we have more Caribbean people here. It's not that more Caribbean people come to interview. It's just that I think more

Caribbean people are able to deal with the discipline. I think that Caribbean people are more—I think they're better. I'm not trying to be biased. But I think they're more ambitious. I think they have a greater sense of purpose. I think that Americans take life very simple. Take life for granted and, I think, they're not ambitious. (Grenadian male manager, age 42, in United States nine years)

These beliefs were not held just by the managers. The immigrant workers themselves were also highly critical of their black American coworkers. The welfare system figured prominently in the explanations the immigrants had about why Americans, compared to the immigrants, seem unwilling to work:

The majority of the black Americans—what I say, is either that they're lazy or they don't like to work. I might be wrong, but by judging from places where you work along with them, if they need something, they work for it. When they get it, that's it. They don't—the majority of them, like, they don't have a plan about what they need with their life. I think this welfare system encourages it. 'Cause in my country, there is no such thing. You gotta work for a living. There is no social security and welfare, nothing like that. (Guyanese male worker, age 39, in United States six years)

Part of the reason the welfare system figures so prominently in the explanations of the workers is that a single mother truly is better off financially on welfare than working at American Food. One foreign-born woman who was working in the cafeteria told me she made $5 an hour, or $200 a week. After carfare and deductions to her paycheck for insurance, she was better off financially on public assistance. When she was on welfare, she was getting $219 every two weeks, along with food stamps and subsidized housing. She chose work over welfare but not for financial reasons—she did so for her own sense of pride.

Several other women described the struggles they were having to stay off welfare, and two described difficulties with the welfare department wanting them to pay some benefits back because once they had started working, they earned too much. Many female workers, both foreign-born and American, discuss these matters at work, and some choose to leave work to go on welfare. This Trinidadian worker sees the choice Americans make to go on welfare as reflecting a lack of values that she has by virtue of being raised as a West Indian:

> That is the lifestyle they adopt. They could always stop and go on welfare. And we have our own lifestyle. And I say, we could do it too because we in this country legally, and we could fall into all these things but it is so much better for you to be responsible and do things on your own than sitting around and waiting for that welfare check to come. Because most of these girls that pass through, they always use that. They say I could stay home, you know, and I could sign up for welfare. You know? And I think it's that that made them that way thinking that they could sit at home and just get that money. You know, instead of coming out and work for it.
>
> Q: Could they make about the same amount of money?
> A: Same thing, yes. Same thing. Same thing . . . When I started working I was making four something. But I just wanted to work. So I say, I don't care how much I make. I'm going to work. And they lazy, and they don't want to go to work. And then they come and say, Oh, I only making four something—I not coming back the next day, you know? (Trinidadian female worker, age 30, in United States ten years)

In a strange twist, the immigrants end up in a position where they describe themselves as teaching and counseling Americans about how to work and how to keep a job. Instead of what one might imagine would be the case with immigrants in a new country seeking advice from the natives about how to get ahead, precisely the opposite happens:

> We had a couple of American girls but they never last because they never used to want to do work. Like, we work. They always want to lay back. So, [we had] one girl that stays, and she follows our lead, because I was her supervisor from start so I just break her in. I say, "You have to learn to work. Get up in the morning and make a living." . . . She would say, "I didn't feel like getting out of my bed

this morning." I said, "But child, you have to be responsible. Get out your bed, this is a job." You know, get out of bed and get yourself here. You know, you really want your job, yes, I really want this job but I be so tired because I went out last night. Well so, go out on weekend. Not during the week. (Trinidadian female worker, age 30, in United States ten years)

The immigrants believe in the American dream of upward social mobility and find themselves in what they perceive to be the very strange position of instructing Americans about how to achieve that dream. This Trinidadian supervisor describes an argument she had with an American worker about the fact that the supervisors are mostly immigrants. Interestingly, in her account both she and the young American worker think there is something unnatural about the immigrants doing better than the Americans. This woman contrasts her individual success with what she perceives as his lack of understanding of what it takes to get ahead:

I said to him, I didn't come here as a supervisor. I came here, and I was poor, I wasn't rich. I started from scratch . . . I was always interested in learning new things and now I'm a supervisor. He said, I don't want to go through all of that to be a supervisor. I think I should be a supervisor. I said, supervise what? How can you supervise if you don't know the job yourself? I said I did every station here. I cooked, I made plates, I made sandwiches, I made soup, I made taco, I made yogurt, I made everything . . . So he was like, yeah, you come here from Trinidad. I said, well you're wrong. Because if I was you, I would be the supervisor because I'm the American, and I wouldn't be the person who was washing the pots. So I said, the immigrant should be the one washing the pots. And you should be the supervisor because you were born here. You let somebody come and take away your stuff from you, so you're wrong. And you have the ambition and the ability, you could get a job doing something else someplace else but you don't want to make the effort. Did you tell anybody you didn't want to wash pots anymore? No, I said . . . You content to wash the pots, so they leave you to let you wash the pots. (Trinidadian female supervisor, age 36, in United States nineteen years)

The immigrants hold on to an image of themselves as disciplined hard workers, and they attribute those characteristics to their strict island upbringing. However, when contrasting West Indians in America with those back home, and in contrasting their own lives back home and in the United States, most people readily describe a more laid-back life in the islands where people do not work very hard. The idea that people back home have it easy or don't work as hard as people in the United States is held at the same time that the immigrants believe it is some sort of inbred trait among West Indians to be superworkers. The immigrants generally do not recognize that it is because they are immigrants that they work in this driven way. After describing West Indians in the United States as extremely hard workers, these respondents go on to explain that they work much harder in the United States than they did back home. In Trinidad, this respondent explains, life was much more easy-going and fun. If it rained, she argued, you did not have to go to work:

> Yes, here it is, "You work!" Down there, you go to work, you miss work and, "Hey you wasn't feeling good yesterday?" and you say, "Nah, I wasn't feeling good," and you stay home. If the rain falls too hard and you feel like staying home, you stay home. But not here. You come out. 'Cause it's—I guess here they make you feel more independent and more responsible than home. You just sit down, you relax and here, they make you feel more responsible. (Trinidadian female worker, age 30, in United States ten years)

So, like the whites who conveniently forget about the hard-working American blacks who *disconfirm* their stereotypes, the West Indians selectively construct and remember cultural traits about themselves that serve to *confirm* their own stereotypes and self-images. Thus West Indian immigrants are able to maintain a view of themselves as hard-working because they are West Indian even as they describe their frustrations with the laziness of West Indians when they return home for a visit.

Black Americans' Perceptions

While the immigrants and the whites believed that there were few blacks at American Food because they did not work hard, most black Americans did not agree with that stereotype, or they turned the discussion around, questioning why the West Indians would work so hard at jobs that offer so little in return. This black American worker agrees with the widespread opinion that the Americans would not work as hard as the West Indians, but he finds it illogical to work this hard for such little reward:

Q: Why do you think that there are so few black Americans working at American Food?

A: 'Cause they don't like to work as hard as the West Indians or people that come from another country . . . There are a lot of West Indians here because they like to bust their butt. You know, they work hard because they need this job. The Americans feel that they don't have to work hard because this is their home, you know, this is where they was raised. A lot of them work too hard. That's sometimes what I see, too hard. You know, 'cause, they like young and they shouldn't be working that hard. That's how I feel. Got a lot of time to go before you gotta go kill yourself like that. (Black American male worker, age 23)

Other workers were very upset by the implication that the West Indians worked harder than African Americans. This worker argues that this perception is mistaken, and it leads to discrimination in hiring:

[The West Indians] have the stereotype that we won't do no work. And they'll come in and do the work for less and work harder. We [Americans] have this attitude that, like, this guy's gonna take my job, my boss is gonna give him the job for less, and in some cases that's true. I've heard a guy I've worked for, he said if it was up to him, he wouldn't hire any Americans, and he'd hire foreigners. This was his words, and he was the boss . . . But I think it is a misperception. (Black American male worker, age 37)

A significant minority of the Americans did not dispute the idea that the West Indians were harder-working and more ambitious. These respondents saw much to admire and emulate in the immigrants:

Q: Do you find that the people from the islands are different than American blacks?

A: How can I say this? I grew up here all my life and I might not think about school and stuff like that that they would think. They come here and they want—they want to get, you know, a position. I mean, you know, so when they go back home it's like, you know, I'm here and I'm working and I'm supervising now and, you know. But most Americans don't really think like that. I mean, not all of them, but some of them they don't really care. But most of [the immigrants] they come here and they feel they want to get something out of it. (Black American female worker, age 22)

The black Americans see the dominance of immigrants not just at the workplace but throughout the New York economy. A few workers made analogies between the dominance of the West Indians in the workplace and the dominance of immigrants among the shopkeepers in their neighborhoods:

My girlfriend would come home and tell me that her friends was talking about this man, this man, either this Korean man or African man who got a newsstand or something. How did he get a newsstand and us black people can't get nothing? You know, she says I hate when they do that because a black person should get as much as anybody else. (Black American male worker, age 22)

In addition to their resentments that the immigrants are surpassing them economically, the Americans hear the immigrants complaining on the job every day about Americans. This black American worker is very much aware of the negative images the island people hold of them:

Q: Have you ever encountered any prejudice or anything like that?
A: Not really, except like the foreign people. They might every now and then they bring up, oh the American people, like we sitting down 'cause we work Saturday and Sunday and we sitting down and they talking about American people don't cook food, you know. All they eat is french fries and hamburgers, you know. And they say, you know, at home, they put on big pots of food and that's the way you supposed to be cooked. And American people they don't know how to keep the house clean and they got rats and roaches, you know, stuff like that. I don't know. I really don't

pay no mind 'cause I guess if I was to get upset, it would make it
seem like what they was saying was true, but you know not all
American people—I mean if you want, if you like french fries
and hamburgers, why not, you know? So what? (Black American
female worker, age 22)

Some of the black Americans dealt with the tensions by distancing themselves and criticizing the immigrants; others, like this woman, dealt with
the tensions by trying to be peacemakers:

Q: Have you noticed any tensions at all between West Indians and
American blacks in New York?

A: Oh yes. Oh my God. Are you kidding? Ah. This is ridiculous. I
mean it's really ridiculous because a lot of it is pure ignorance . . .
They don't like us. And myself included. They think that we're
lazy. We don't try to get out and do things for ourselves. We just
sit back and complain about the white man. What the white did.
Which, a lot of it is true. We lax back, you know, instead of trying to move on, and try to put some of that behind you. But you
try to teach them how some of the black people feel, you know,
and the way they feel. But lots of times when you sit down and
they learn from the history, they can say yeah, I can see why some
of them black Americans are like that, you know . . . I think you
have the confrontation between the black Americans and the
black islanders because the black Americans are not trying to understand the islanders and the islanders are not trying to understand the black Americans. So I listen to them and I try to explain
things to them and they explain things to me . . . You know one
thing about me if they want to say all those things, I don't get uptight about that. I say no, don't feel bad. If that's the way you feel
right now it's all right to say it. You can call me a Yankee, I don't
get offended. Because I know my people have called you people a
lot of things. (Black American female worker, age 50)

But the black Americans' awareness of the stereotypes the immigrants
hold of them makes it very difficult to have normal relations with coworkers on the job. They know the immigrants think they are lazy, and that

they don't like them very much. Even the Americans who said they did not personally have a problem with the "island people" describe a fairly high level of tension on the job. For instance, this woman describes the interactions she has had on the job:

> They can be nasty when they want to be as far as like their attitudes, you know. Some time they just—a lot of times they don't like American people. They say we have a chip on our shoulder about them. It's like they're not too friendly. Like when I first started working here, you know, everybody wanted to know where I was from, you know, they were asking, you know, the first couple of days I was working, where you from, where you from. I said, I'm from here, you know. And then I could see the change like the following day. It's like, you know, I go and I say good-morning and it's like, hm, morning—like if they didn't really want to say it. (Black American female worker, age 22)

A common complaint of the West Indians is that the Americans tell them to go back to their country and do not welcome them to the United States. One of the American workers who acknowledges saying those things to the immigrants explains why he feels that way:

> I hate it when they put this country down. I'll be ready to send them back. You can live, man, but don't put this country down, 'cause it's helping you. It gets me a little upset . . . I tell them, what you doing here then? Yeah, and they always telling me how the sun is shining and all that. Yeah, but they ain't got an economy, man. (Black American male worker, age 37)

Another American worker uses very similar language as he describes his belief that the immigrants try to deceive Americans by putting down the United States while they know that their country is not a good place to live:

> Well, basically, they always saying, well, my country this, and my country that, so I say, well, why didn't you stay in your country? You know what I mean? If obviously, if your country was so that, why you leave the islands to come here? If you feel you want to put down

this one and hype up yours, but you're living here and you left yours, so then I tell them, I don't get that. 'Cause if I felt my country was better than this one, I would not come here. I would not come. (Black American male worker, age 28)

The growth of the Caribbean component of the workforce is also perceived as isolating for the Americans. They describe themselves as a minority on the job:

There's so many—there's so many of them, it's like now I'm the foreigner there, you know, because it's not many Americans up there. I think maybe there's about five or six of us. (Black American female worker, age 22)

While the West Indian accent might be praised by some white Americans for its "British" quality, and it may bring some benefits to the West Indian immigrants, it was brought up often by the black Americans as a source of annoyance and distance between the two groups. Because they feel outnumbered and do not understand the West Indian dialects, the Americans feel paranoid that the immigrants are talking about them. They feel the same way with Haitians and Spanish-speaking immigrants, but it seems to be worse when people are speaking English and one still cannot understand them. To the Americans it seems the immigrants are being more purposeful in excluding them by speaking in their dialect.

This mutual stereotyping and tensions and taunting sometimes make it hard for individuals who are not resentful or angry to interact with people from the other groups. For instance, this black American supervisor describes how he walks on eggshells around the immigrants now:

My neighborhood was mixed—we had a few Jamaican families, one Italian family, a few Chinese. So it was all mixed up. But then I came here, it was kind of different. I didn't understand it then, but before they had that trouble with black Americans—teasing them or whatever about being from somewhere else, so I asked this one girl, like I would say, "Where are you from?" And she got a little nuts, and I never asked that question again. So, the way I know where someone is from now, is if they're saying.

Q: Why would they be upset at you asking where they were from?

A: Like I said, they had a few experiences with other people who
would tease them and say, "You don't have a green card, I'm
gonna call and turn you in." That's a common thing. (Black
American male supervisor, age 39)

These tensions between Americans and West Indians were described to
us by both groups. The primary reason cited for the tensions by the
immigrants is that "black Americans think we are here to take their jobs."
On the job it is very common for the immigrants to be told to "go back
where they come from":

They always cursing the West Indians. I don't think they like West
Indians . . . They feel that we come here to take away what they have,
you know. I mean, they here all the time, you know, and there is so
many things that they could be doing, and we come here and we see
the opportunity and we go for it. So, there is always some American
who would be cursing us, you better go back to where you come
from. (Guyanese female worker, in United States nine years, age 29)

One of the key facts about the immigrants that the Americans stressed
was that the islands they came from were poor and underdeveloped. This
seems to be one of the chief ways in which the Americans counter the
negative impressions the immigrants have of them—by reminding the
immigrants that they are from poor undeveloped countries. It's a way for
the Americans to feel superior on the job to the obviously more successful
immigrants.

The image of the islands as poor is reinforced in conversations with the
immigrants about what life is like in their islands. The Americans realize
that the immigrants are sensitive about the issue, but they stress it out of
annoyance that the immigrants act superior to Americans when in fact
their islands are "inferior":

Yeah, we be saying, "Ain't you glad you here now, even though you
be turning down the place? Ain't you glad you here where you got
nice clothes, shoes, and stuff?" 'Cause, you know, I got this Jamaican
friend. And he told me how Jamaica was, he said before he came
here he never had a pair of shoes. Yeah, they is poor. (Black American male worker, age 37)

The immigrants' nationalistic feelings of pride are often hurt by these insults, and they react sometimes by taunting the Americans with their dominance in the workplace, which they know the Americans are annoyed and embarrassed by:

> The black American that we have working here will always put down immigrants. And he say the thing which is the stereotype saying, "They come here and take our jobs." But as I see it, if he had adapted himself, or adapted different things to get what he wanted, he would have gotten it. Other people say to him, "we are immigrants and we are waiting on tables and working in a kitchen. How does that make you feel as an American doing the same? Don't you feel less of yourself?" (Trinidadian male worker, age 26, in United States four years)

While a few people were sympathetic to the Americans' feelings and could see why they were upset, most thought the situation of West Indian dominance on the job reflected a fundamental difference in attitudes toward work between the two groups. For instance, this worker is somewhat sympathetic to the Americans' resentments, but then when she puts herself in their shoes, she thinks she would have to ask what is wrong with them:

> If I was American I would feel the same way too. You know I don't really blame them for feeling that way. But then I would have to ask myself a couple of questions too. If these people come from wherever they come from and they could do this, I might say, why can't I? You know? . . . The blacks were slaves in the West Indies too and they had to work in the cane fields and whatever, right? I don't know if it's an inferiority complex. I don't know if they [Americans] feel that if they try to make the effort to do something, somebody is gonna slap them down. You know, I mean, what about us, our ancestors were slaves too. What do we do, live on that for the rest of our lives and not try to pull ourselves above that? You know, always walking around like a ripped puppy waiting for somebody to hit you. You don't want to make the time or the effort to try to do something for yourself 'cause he thinks, well if I try, the white man,

he won't give me chance. Try. You know, they can't get you for trying. You have to try . . . I don't know what it is. I really don't understand it to be honest with you. I have lived here almost twenty years and I do not understand why. (Trinidadian female supervisor, age 36, in United States nineteen years)

CONCLUSION

The black immigrants who work at American Food have done very well compared to their black American coworkers. Numerically, they are now the majority on the job. They are told by management that they are valued because they are hard-working in implicit or even explicit contrast to American blacks who do not last long on the job. The American blacks the immigrants encounter on the job tell them to "go back where they came from" and accuse them of coming here to take American jobs. The immigrants also face these hostilities in encounters with black Americans in the streets, on the subways, and in stores. The immigrants definitely perceive this situation as a violation of what should be the natural order of things. The immigrants think that, by right, American blacks should be doing better. The opportunities the immigrants are seizing seem to be inexplicably ignored by the majority of American blacks who are poor.

To explain these behaviors and attitudes, most of the immigrants use their own limited experiences with inner-city black Americans and the ready-made cultural stereotypes that are prevalent in the mass media and that roll off the tongues of the white managers. Thus the immigrants compared their own hard-working, planning, friendly, upward-striving selves with the lazy, welfare-dependent, unfriendly, bitter black Americans. While these beliefs operated at the level of group stereotypes, this did not stop the immigrants from developing interpersonal friendships, romantic relationships, or uneasy alliances with black Americans. The social patterns among the workers, however, were definitely divisive, and very rarely did black Americans and "island people" sit together at lunch break or see each other outside work. The network hiring that creates and recreates the workforce also means that the immigrants often have family and friends at work who look out for each other and with whom to socialize.

Nevertheless, the distancing behavior and negative stereotypes of black Americans do not mean that the West Indians do not perceive racism or racial problems with whites at American Food. To the contrary, the West Indians challenge white privilege on the job and describe many incidents on and off the job of racial bias and prejudice. This is discussed in the next chapter.

ENCOUNTERING

AMERICAN

RACE RELATIONS

5

Comparisons between black Americans and
West Indians often focus on the "culture" of
West Indians as an explanation for their success. Culture here often means a dedication to
hard work and a high value on education, but
there are few ethnic groups in America who
would not claim those particular cultural val-
ues. Can culture really explain any differences in rates of success between
West Indians and African Americans? The previous chapter described
structural reasons for one particular concrete finding about West Indians—their high labor force participation rate. I showed how social networks eased and facilitated their hiring and how their immigrant status
and their different metric for judging a job could contribute to their
longevity in the job. These differences between Americans and West Indians are structural in that they do not imply different values on education
or work but imply instead different social locations for individuals that
lead to different opportunities and actions. The differences described
above were also race-neutral; they were differences one would find between any native-born American and immigrant, regardless of color. Yet
I also showed that these structural differences were often given stereotypical cultural explanations—West Indians value hard work, black Americans prefer to live off welfare.

In this chapter I turn to a specific cultural comparison between West
Indians and African Americans—their interpretations of, and reactions
to, racial discrimination. I argue that the West Indian cultural response to
black-white race relations helps to foster social mobility for many first-
generation immigrants. The cultural reactions to race, discrimination,

and racial hierarchies displayed by the immigrants have two components—the culture associated with being an immigrant and the culture
the immigrants bring with them, the latter the long-term result of living
with the particular racial structures of the Caribbean.

West Indians have a low expectation of sour interpersonal race relations, and this enables them to have better interpersonal interactions with
white Americans than many native African Americans. In addition, their
sense of efficacy, coming from a society with a majority of blacks and with
many blacks in high positions, leads the immigrants to have high ambitions and expectations for their own success. At the same time, they expect
that race will make it harder to rise socioeconomically in the United States
because they know America has racial problems and so they are very
prepared to battle for their rights. This combination of high ambitions,
friendly relations with whites on an interpersonal level, and strong militance in encountering any perceived discrimination leads to some better
outcomes in the labor market for West Indians than for black Americans.
But cultures, as patterned ways of dealing with the environment, change
when the environment changes.[1] The West Indians' notions about race
change over time as their beliefs that race will not hold them back come
up against a reality in which race is still a potent boundary in American
society.

There are three separate components to the West Indians' racial identities and understandings of race—the lack of an oppositional identity, the
expectation of what I call structural racism, and the low expectation of
what I call interpersonal racism. Each of these will be examined in turn.

THE CULTURE ASSOCIATED WITH BEING AN IMMIGRANT

Although blacks were originally brought to the West Indies involuntarily
to work as slaves on sugar plantations, West Indians who emigrate to the
United States do so voluntarily. As voluntary immigrants in the United
States, West Indians display certain psychological and cultural reactions
to American society that are closer to those of other voluntary immigrants
than to African Americans who were absorbed into the United States
involuntarily. Anthropologist John Ogbu makes a distinction between
immigrant "voluntary minorities," who have chosen to move to a society

in order to improve their well-being, and caste-like "involuntary minorities," who were initially brought into the society through slavery, conquest, or colonization. This distinction is very helpful in understanding the reactions to American race relations of West Indian immigrants.[2]

Ogbu argues that the coping responses that different groups develop for dealing with problems of racism and discrimination reflect their histories and social psychologies. Because they use their home country and culture as a frame of reference, voluntary migrants do not react to discrimination and exclusion in the same way as involuntary minorities. In effect they can say to themselves, "Americans might not value my culture but I am from a place where I am valued." Discrimination and prejudice are something they plan to overcome. Immigrants then have a "greater degree of trust for white Americans, for the societal institutions controlled by whites, than do involuntary minorities. Such immigrants acquiesce and rationalize the prejudice and discrimination against them by saying, in effect, that they are strangers in a foreign land [and] have no choice but to tolerate prejudice and discrimination."[3] They develop "immigrant identities" that *differ* from the dominant group's identities but are not necessarily *opposed* to those identities.

Involuntary minorities do not have a homeland with which to compare their current treatment nor to root their identities in. Thus, Ogbu argues, they do not see discrimination against them as a temporary barrier to be overcome. Instead, "[r]ecognizing that they belong to a subordinate, indeed, a disparaged minority, they compare their situation with that of their white American peers. The prejudice against them seems permanent, indeed institutionalized."[4] This understanding of their situation leads the involuntary minorities to conclude that solidarity and challenges to the rules of the dominant society are the only way to improve their situation. Ogbu describes the psychological orientation that develops among involuntary minorities as being "oppositional" in nature.

These "oppositional identities" mean that involuntary minorities come largely to define themselves in their core identities in terms of their opposition to the dominant group. For blacks in America, Ogbu asserts, the very meaning of being black involves *not* being white. A strong value is placed on solidarity and opposition to rules perceived as being against them; when a member of the group is seen as cooperating with the dominant society's institutions, his or her very identity is called into question. In Ogbu's research the young black student who tries to achieve in school is accused of "acting white."[5]

Because involuntary minorities see the rules of the game as stacked against them and permanent, their folk theory of how to make it in society stresses collective effort and group challenges as the ways to overcome barriers set up by whites. Thus individuals who attempt to assimilate and to achieve as individuals often run into strong pressure not to do so: "Crossing cultural boundaries, behaving in a manner regarded as falling under the white American cultural frames of reference, is threatening to their minority identity and security, but also to their solidarity. Individuals seeking to behave like whites are discouraged by peer group pressures and by affective dissonance."[6] Assimilation is thus doubly threatening to the involuntary migrant: they must adopt some cultural practices, such as language and styles of interaction, that are not only different from what they are used to but are perceived as antithetical to their own culture and language. Christopher Jencks notes this difference between European immigrants and African Americans, both of whom faced discrimination but with different psychological consequences:

> For Europeans who came to America because they were dissatisfied with their homeland, assimilation has often been difficult, but it has not for the most part been intrinsically humiliating. European immigrants come with no animus against America and they had reason to believe that if they learned to act like Americans they would be accepted as such . . . In order to become fully assimilated into white America blacks must to some extent identify with people who have humiliated and oppressed them for three hundred years. Under these circumstances "assimilation" is likely to be extraordinarily difficult.[7]

West Indians are a group Ogbu uses to compare with African Americans to show the difference between involuntary and voluntary minorities. West Indians are described as voluntary immigrants who do not experience the same degree of disillusionment and cultural inversion and oppositional identities as African Americans. But West Indians are also the descendants of slaves. Why is it that their initial incorporation into their own societies as involuntary migrants does not create an involuntary minority attitude toward whites when they arrive in the United States?

Part of the answer lies in the differences in racial cultures between the two societies that I will describe below, but the other important variable that explains West Indian racial beliefs and practices is their immigrant status. Judging from the responses of the people we interviewed, the movement to the United States seems to provide the immigrants with a "foreign" status, which makes their reactions to discrimination and prejudice more likely to resemble those of other voluntary immigrants in the United States, than to resemble those of black Americans. (It also leads whites to respond differently to the West Indians than to African Americans as long as the whites see the West Indians' master status as "immigrant" rather than "black." See Chapter 4.) If, as Stephen Cornell and Douglas Hartmann argue, ethnicity can be understood in part as a "narrative" we tell ourselves about our history and our world and our place in that world, the act of immigration tends to erase the slave narrative and replace it with an immigrant narrative.[8] That immigrant narrative includes an optimism about the immigrants' life chances in the United States, even though the immigrants are far from naive about the degree of racial discrimination they expect to encounter. This Trinidadian teacher makes this clear:

> You see I'm not American, and I do not see myself as having been deprived by the whites of America. To the contrary, I came here, I was accepted, I was acknowledged for what I knew, and I am in a position now where I am earning a good salary. I do not view myself in the light of black Americans. (Trinidadian female teacher, age 63, in United States ten years)

Even when they experience prejudice firsthand, West Indians who see themselves as voluntary immigrants have the memory of a homeland to take away the sting:

Q: What were your expectations about whites in the United States?
A: I knew they would think themselves better than me, but I know as a Jamaican I was accustomed to being a person of self-worth so that wouldn't bother me . . . I have experienced prejudice from

whites, but that is how whites are. (Jamaican female teacher, age
37, in United States ten years)

The immigrants we spoke to all had a very rosy picture of race relations at
home, reflecting the "erasure" of the involuntary minority narrative as
well as the stark contrast between the race relations they remember and
the pervasiveness of race and racial conflict they encounter in the United
States. The islands nevertheless have had their share of race problems.
Jamaica has long been a source of black power ideas. Marcus Garvey, a
Jamaican, developed his ideas of black power and pride during his time in
the United States and then brought those ideas back to Jamaica. Barbados
has a long history of brutal relations between its small white population
and its large black population. Trinidad and Guyana are both countries
with sizable East Indian populations. They have both seen bloodshed over
their racial divisions in the last thirty years.

However, one would be hard put to find much description of any of
these ideologies or problems in the descriptions of their home countries
provided by the respondents in this study. For West Indians in New York,
race relations at home are seen through rose-colored glasses.[9] If everything
the respondents said was taken at face value, the Caribbean would seem
the perfect society for peace and harmony between blacks, whites, and
other groups.[10]

Q: Did you expect white people to behave a certain way before you
   came to the United States?
A: Well, to be honest, it's new. In Trinidad—there are white people
   in Trinidad, but the white people in Trinidad is like they all accept you . . . When I was growing up, we didn't have this prejudiced thing. I never knew what prejudice was. So as far as the way
   white people were supposed to react, I didn't know. (Trinidadian
   female supervisor, age 36, in United States nine years)

While the official slogan of the Jamaican government, "out of many,
one," attempts to foster an image of multiracial harmony, Jamaica can
perhaps be described as the West Indian country with the highest amount
of black power ideology and concern with race. This concern with racial
oppression has been fueled by growing poverty and unemployment in the

Kingston slums and by the heavy prevalence of tourism on the island, which brings very rich whites into contact with very poor blacks.[11] But among the Jamaicans we interviewed there was little sense of difficult race relations back home. Even this Jamaican worker, whose only reference point for describing race relations at home are black domestic household workers interacting with white employers, describes the interactions and relations in glowing terms:

> Well, because up here, you know, this racial-racist business different from back home, you know. Different from back home. Back home, mostly blacks always work with whites I say, you know. In the residential area you mostly find the black people, they always work the white. Washes them clothes, clean them house, you know. And they always say the white people handle them so good. People always say that, you know. Yeah, sometime, a lady in my house, she used to work with white lady, and she said the white lady handle her like her own color. Yeah, she told me that. But being up here, everybody is so, you know, different. Like certain streets you can't walk on up here 'cause it's white and, you know, not back home. (Jamaican female worker, age 37, in United States three years)

Given the ways in which class and race intersect and define each other in the Caribbean, it is not surprising that there were some class differences in how respondents recalled race in their home countries. The middle-class teachers gave a more nuanced view of race relations at home. They described race relations in the Caribbean far more positively than race relations in the United States but, to a greater degree than the working-class respondents, described the complexities of the intersection of race and class in their home countries:

Q: What were race relations like in Jamaica?

A: We did not have race, we had class. Yeah, we have class. We have class among black people. The class that we have out there was who was the parents, where do you live? What kind of school did you attend, that kind of thing out there. You could live any four corner of the island if you have the money for a certain area, and even if you're not white, you can live there if you can afford to.

So there was no area that you cannot live. (Jamaican male
teacher, age 41, in United States five years)

Like other voluntary immigrants West Indians are likely to see prejudice
and discrimination as more isolated occurrences, and as temporary barriers to be overcome, rather than as permanent, pervasive symptoms of a
society that has overarching enmity toward them. A West Indian, we were
told repeatedly in the interviews, treats individual whites as individuals
and does not react to whites purely on the basis of skin color. But a West
Indian also does not put up with "racist" nonsense when it does occur:

When I came here, I didn't meet too many of them [whites] in the
beginning. Very few, you know. But I'm a person who takes everybody—how you present yourself to me, that's how I take you. I
don't judge, I don't pre-judge. I don't look at the color and say, oh,
white! Maybe he expects this, maybe he expects that. You know?
Then, when we start to interact, however you interact with me, that's
the way I'm gonna interact with you. So, however you deal with me,
that's how I'm gonna deal with you. I have met some who were very
nice. I have met some who were awful. The awful ones, I deal with
them awful too. And the nice ones, I deal with them nice . . . Just the
way you deal with me, that's how I'll deal with you. Black or white.
(Trinidadian female supervisor, age 36, in United States nineteen
years)

These concerns with "racialism" and with differentiating true racism
from imagined racism reflect a particular experience with race that the
West Indians have carried with them.

THE CULTURE THE IMMIGRANTS BRING WITH THEM

Orlando Patterson has described the difference in how racial relations are
organized in the Caribbean and the United States as a critical difference
between a society in which there is racism (the Caribbean) and a chroni-
cally racist society (the United States). What is this critical difference?
While both societies were founded to a great extent on slavery, the
"American slave society was unique in the complexity and sophistication

of the culture of slavery that it developed and in the extraordinary role slavery and the slave culture played in that development."[12] Contrasting these two types of societies, Patterson argues that in many countries where racism exists, such as England, France, or the Caribbean, "many people there, perhaps the majority, believe in the inherent superiority of whites over nonwhite peoples. Yet they are not racist cultures because this ideology is a minor component in their systems of belief; it serves no indispensable cultural or socioeconomic functions and is not a critical element in the way people define themselves physically and socially. Not so in America."[13] The culture of slavery that existed in the United States from the founding until the civil rights movement, and whose legacy currently persists in the very core of American culture, means that black Americans are "the Other" in the social identities of white Americans. White cultural values fundamentally disvalue African Americans. Racism—the belief in the fundamental inferiority of blacks—is a much larger part of the core American culture in a way it could never be in the Caribbean, where the numbers of white people were never great.

So, Patterson argues that a key difference between the Caribbean and the United States is that the latter is "more terrifying in the all-pervasive presence of the white group and white culture, and the crushing sense of racial isolation and despair" that develops.[14] This is a common theme in the interviews we conducted; the immigrants sense something overwhelming about race in the culture of America, something that they believe has affected African Americans in a very fundamental way:

I'm very disappointed in black Americans because I think they've allowed others to make them feel that they're not important, or it's as if they act the part that has been put on them. They limit themselves because people say that blacks are limited. They limit themselves and they live like that and I don't believe that. (Jamaican female teacher, age 37, in United States ten years)

Ira Reid noted in his 1939 study that the black immigrants he studied all reported that the whites they encountered in the Caribbean did not even come close to matching American whites in their high degree of racial hostility and contempt.[15] That this contempt and hostility take a toll is incontestable; a number of studies document the feelings of rage and sadness African Americans endure every day because of white behaviors and attitudes.[16] Indeed, Cornell West has called the results for the poorest African Americans of living in such a racialized society "black existential angst," which derives from "the lived experience of ontological wounds and emotional scars inflicted by white supremacist beliefs and images permeating U.S. society and culture. These wounds and scars attack black intelligence, black ability, black beauty, and black character daily in subtle and not so subtle ways . . . The accumulated effect of these wounds and scars produces a deep-seated anger, a boiling sense of rage, and a passionate pessimism regarding America's will to justice."[17]

The immigrants describe this difference between the two societies as one where Americans, both white and black, seem obsessed with "racialism." Racialism was the word used to refer to a heightened sensitivity to race, a tendency to regard relations between people in terms of race. The overarching concern with race among Americans was shocking to the immigrants when they first arrived. It was so different from what they were used to back home. Mary, a teacher who emigrated from Jamaica in 1981 at age 29, describes her changing sensitivities on the subject:

> You heard about crime but you didn't hear that you come here and you would be bombarded with this racial thing. And even to this day, sometimes, it's difficult to see things from a race perspective. I still see it as people against people. I find that American blacks, they talk about it, they see it in every incident that happens, it has to be race why this happens . . . You become much more sensitive to it because the television and the radio they pick it up, they say don't you see that, don't you see that. And then you start becoming aware that there is something that's going on, you know. (Jamaican female teacher, age 38, in United States nine years)

Many people we spoke with, both working class and middle class, were especially concerned that their children would develop this attitude of racialism:

Q: Are there any things that you've tried to tell your children as they're growing up about how to be black or how to get along with white people?

A: Well, no, I've never really told them because of black this and
black that. Eventually you will start to become racial. At least I feel
that. You see, I feel that it doesn't matter the color of your skin.
And you know, the minute you will start to look at, oh, he's white,
they're black, and this black isn't gonna do this, you know, eventually it becomes you and humbles your thinking and everything.
You know, like they would say up here is racial. I've never encountered any and I really don't want to. But you know, how I go
about it on a day to day, you meet people, you talk with them.
You know, everybody has different feelings. But you know, for me
to tell them that you're black, you're this, you're that—no, I don't.
(Guyanese female worker, age 38, in United States nine years)

The perception that black Americans are too quick to cry race is intimately tied to the immigrants' long-standing belief that opportunities
exist in the United States and that their own black skin has not, and will
not, prevent them from taking advantage of those opportunities.[18] It is this
belief that racism, while it might exist, can surely be overcome with
determination and hard work that propelled the immigrants to move
from a majority-black society to the United States in the first place. And
there is a strong psychological incentive for the immigrants to believe that
American blacks overestimate the role of race in everyday life and in
limiting opportunity. After all, if you have moved to a society in which
you are now in the minority, and you have done so in order to achieve
success, you do not want to believe that your color will limit that success:

We're not saying that there is not racism, we're not saying that
there's not prejudices. We're not saying that there are not certain
jobs where they put a token black man. We're not saying that. But
you don't have to be negative all the time. I just cannot understand
because I came here, I didn't have a high school diploma from this
country. You understand? But—I mean, I love my job, I'm doing
what I like to do . . . My next step after this will be to have my own
catering business. And that is what I'm working towards now. You
know? So, don't tell me I can't do it. I could do it. [I say to African
Americans] why you can't do it and you're right here? (Trinidadian
female supervisor, age 36, in United States nineteen years)

The idea that while racial prejudice might keep the group down, it will not stop them from succeeding as individuals reflects a long-standing tradition among West Indian immigrants—they fight individually, not collectively, for their rights.[19] Indeed, scholars who studied earlier waves of immigration described how West Indians often stressed their British ties and their foreign status as ways to combat discrimination.[20] In psychological terms West Indians often deal with the stigmatized nature of the black race in American society through a strategy of "exit" rather than "voice." Black Americans generally perceive little possibility for individuals to succeed by "exiting" the category of black people, and thus tend to develop a collective strategy to give "voice" to their lack of equality. West Indians, especially in the first generation and especially when they first arrive, believe that by evoking their foreign status, working hard, avoiding "racialism," and challenging true racism with loud cries of protest when it does occur they can "exit" from the stigmatized black category.[21]

These beliefs that individual effort can overcome racial barriers do not mean that West Indians deny the existence of racism (a charge that African Americans often make and that the immigrants spend time refuting). Rather, the immigrants argue that they are very vigilant in noticing attitudes or behaviors that might keep them from achieving socioeconomic mobility. The immigrants often see racism on the job and in society, and they think that racism should be challenged. In fact, the foreign-born pride themselves in being more likely to stand up to whites when "real" situations occur. Yet their lack of racialism was often pointed to by the immigrants to explain why they got along better with whites than African Americans. This manager believes that whites are more at ease with him because he does not react to them based on their race:

I think—I am a Caribbean American. I see what a person is, right? And if I need something from you, I'm gonna ask for it, regardless of who you are. And like, I'm a person. I mean, color and nationality is secondary and I think that most Caribbean people focus on that point of view. And I think this helps people to get along. You know, if you don't have any preconceived notions. I have no problem with white Americans and I think that from that perspective they treat you differently. In conversations with other black Americans—not all, mind you, some. I seen that some of their basic concepts are so strange, that it keeps them back. You know, their values. (Grenadian male manager, age 42, in United States nine years)

Several respondents consciously tied this difference between West Indians and African Americans to what they perceive as the Americans' preoccupation with the historical experience of slavery. This Jamaican teacher argues that African Americans see slavery in job hierarchies that are merely job hierarchies:

I would think [that West Indians get more opportunities than African Americans in New York] but I don't think it's because of the whites, I think it is because of the blacks. The attitude of the blacks, I see it everyday. And that's—for example, some people will say you are subservient, you are just accepting of everything. It's not a matter of accepting, it's a matter of the work ethic. That a white person is set over you—it's not who is set over you but you came here with a certain work ethic. Somebody is set over you and you do what you are told to do. It's not that you don't have any backbone or that you are subservient or anything, it's just that you are in the workplace and somebody has to be the boss. I think we accept that quicker than American blacks, much more readily than American blacks. American blacks say he's white and he's set over me, that is slavery, and he tells you to do that and it's still the slavery thing continuing. (Jamaican female teacher, age 41, in United States seven years)

Another teacher also pointed out this willingness of West Indians to do jobs that Americans would find degrading because of their ability to separate their sense of self from the job:

To me, Americans still remember and they're really heavy into it, so they don't do certain jobs they wouldn't take either. They don't do it. You know what I'm saying? Most of the maids and stuff you see around here are West Indian people. 'Cause they [black Americans] figure they ain't working in no white person's kitchen. You know 'cause that was a thing of the past. You know they're not thinking

it's money in the pocket. You know they prefer to go on welfare . . .
You know you hardly find any American person who would say
they'd take a maid job or anything like that. They don't want to do
it. You know they feel degraded to be walking out in the park or
wherever and they got two white kids—they babysitting. West Indian person will do it. (Guyanese female teacher, age 33, in United
States eight years)

Thus the cultural beliefs and practices West Indian immigrants bring
to the United States reflect two influences—their status as voluntary immigrants, which leads them to expect hard work and ambition to conquer
discrimination, and their experiences in Caribbean society, which lead
them to expect racial discrimination but to see it as a relatively contained
part of life, not one that suffuses every encounter between black and white.
These expectations are severely challenged by the immigrants' experiences
in American society.

ENCOUNTERING THE REALITY OF AMERICAN RACE RELATIONS

The expectations that the immigrants have about race relations in the
United States do not prepare them well for their experiences here. Most
respondents report surprise at the racial situation they encounter; many
report deep shock. The immigrants come here expecting to encounter
what I call *structural racism*—blocked mobility for blacks in the society
and a hierarchy in which whites have political and economic power. When
they encounter this kind of racism, the immigrants are able to handle
these situations well, mainly by challenging them. For example, they will
apply for jobs and housing they feel they deserve, even if they believe
whites are trying to prevent their mobility.

But almost everyone we spoke to was unprepared for the degree of
interpersonal racism they encountered in the United States—the overarching concern with race in every encounter, the constant role race plays
in everyday life, and the subtle experiences that are tinged with racial
suspicions and overtones. The immigrants' encounters with each of these
forms of American racism will be examined in turn.

Structural Racism

West Indians come to the United States prepared to find racial discrimination. After all, the racial problems of the United States are no secret
throughout the world, and most immigrants are following friends and
relatives who have sent home much information about what life is like in
America after immigration. But when the immigrants imagine the racism
they will encounter here, they base those expectations on the race relations
they have experienced in the Caribbean. Back home whites and light-
skinned blacks were more likely to be in higher socioeconomic positions,
and it was very rare to see a white person at the bottom of the socioeconomic status ladder. Thus while race was not *determinative* of socioeconomic position (many blacks were in a high position), it was *highly
correlated* with it (most high positions were filled with light-skinned blacks
or whites). The immigrants expected blocks to black mobility: while they
could rise to the top, it would be more difficult because whites were in
control and would jealously guard their competitive position.

In descriptions of race relations at home, class distinctions were often
tied to color distinctions; respondents recalled that lighter-skinned people
commanded wealth, power, and top-level jobs:

> Whites were not existing in the community as such. They were
> there. White teachers taught in the schools, but they were volunteers
> from England. You would see American tourists, but what we had
> was sort of a class consciousness in Jamaica which was also corre-
> lated with light skin. Syrians and Chinese and people with light skin
> got the bank jobs, good jobs. (Jamaican male teacher, age 41, in
> United States five years)

But even this story was a dynamic one. Past discrimination in favor of
light-skinned people meant that control of top jobs and power in these
societies was highly correlated with color. However, since independence
in the 1960s and the establishment of the merit-based, yet still hierarchical, school system, many dark-skinned islanders had achieved a great deal
of social mobility.

When they arrived in the United States, both middle-class and working-
class respondents were surprised by the existence of poor whites. Ex-

pecting the United States to be more racist than the Caribbean, they were surprised to find whites in positions where they actually served blacks:

> The class structure really surprised me. Our population is made up of blacks, East Indians who came as indentured laborers, a small percentage of Portuguese, a small percentage of Chinese, very few whites . . . It was the whites who had the key positions. You know, the top positions. And we looked up to them, they were the bosses, they made the decisions. You had to go to them for a job. That was the structure. After independence . . . it started to change and then who did they take? The light-skinned blacks. Those that had the light skin and had the hair and the look . . . So over there, you wouldn't find a white man driving a taxi cab. No way. He wouldn't do anything like that. Not there. Over here, it's common. That's one thing I've been surprised about. Over there, you wouldn't find a white man picking up garbage, being garbage men, no, no no. They had all the important positions, the doctors, the lawyers, the managers. They did not do these menial jobs . . . Here you see white people—they different classes, you have the rich ones and the poor ones, you have the middle-class ones, you have the laborers. You know over there you did not have that. They were only upper class. So that was a surprise. You get in a cab, you expect a white guy to drive you? No. He has a chauffeur. (Guyanese female teacher, age 42, in United States twenty-two years)

Another respondent discusses how she learned once she arrived here that the white tourists she had encountered back home were not worthy of the exalted treatment they had received:

> I can remember when seeing white people there and now I come here, I want to beat up myself because we stop and look at them with so much admiration because they're white. And when I come here I realize that some those that we saw, they just some washed-up white people who just have the fare to come to Jamaica, you know what I mean. They're not elite, you know. They get a fare, a cheap ticket to Jamaica, and they come down there and people run to them like

everybody is so nice to them . . . People would move out of their way to accommodate them because they're white. Nobody thinking of whether they're rich white or poor white. They're white. (Jamaican female teacher, age 37, in United States seven years)

As much as some people were pleasantly surprised to see poor whites and well-off blacks in the United States, their expectations about structural racism here were mostly confirmed. The preponderance of whites in the United States and their positions of power confronted the immigrants daily:

As far as I see, it's a white world. We living in a white world, you know, everything is just white around us. You go to get a job, there's a white man to interview you. You know, it's just that world we're living in. No matter where you go there's a white person. (Guyanese male supervisor, age 33, in United States nine years)

The majority of respondents described their postimmigration years as a process of coming to terms with this reality. The immigrants believe that whites are threatened by blacks who try to advance, and thus they try to keep blacks under them in order to protect their socioeconomic control and relative superior position. This suspicion is often confirmed by their experiences on the job:

Sometimes the white, they feel superior to the Negro regardless of his or her ability. At times you might find a Negro who might be more highly qualified than the white person. And because of the races problem, you find that white person will get the job. It do happen. (Guyanese male worker, age 39, in United States six years)

The expectation of structural racism and the evidence they found for it actually provided a bond for American blacks and West Indians. The theme that whites tried to protect their control of the higher reaches of the socioeconomic structure came through in our interviews with both native-born and immigrant blacks:

I think that white people think that they always have to be the boss over everything. They think that—that was just the way they was brought up, that we aren't better than the whites. We have no blacks teaching in school—like they think that they always have to be the boss of us. That's the bottom line, that they have to be the ruler. They have to be on top. (Black American female worker, age 59)

The middle-class teachers and the food-service workers sounded very similar when they described their perceptions of structural racism in the United States. Even immigrants who were highly critical of African Americans for being too "racial" shared the perceptions of their African-American coworkers that race affected mobility in the workplace. For instance, some immigrants described blocked mobility for black people on the job and the lengths to which whites would go to find a white person for a job when a qualified black was already on-site:

> After I got my master's degree I went to the banks to try to get a job. But you know they would rather choose the young white heir. Even if they have to bring them over from the Midwest, and that's what's happening in New York City. Somebody's grandfather, uncle, or godfather, somewhere they live in Texas and they come right at the mid-management level and they get the jobs. (Guyanese female teacher, age 48, in United States twenty years)

The similarities in both foreign-born and native-born views of racism in the structure of work relations in both the public schools and American Food are striking in comparison with the views of their white coworkers. The whites describe their workplaces as fair and just meritocracies. While the white managers believed charges of racism at American Food were unfounded, there was a widespread belief among the black immigrants and the black Americans that mobility beyond a certain point within the company was blocked for people with black skin, regardless of nativity. And this shared understanding of blocked social mobility due to pure discrimination based on race alone, not culture, provided the opportunity for West Indians and African Americans to go to bat for each other and to see themselves as having common goals and experiences.

At American Food supervisors were especially likely to describe blocked mobility. The comparatively large numbers of black supervisors (all were black) compared to black managers (only three out of twenty were black) testified to the difficulty of moving from the ranks of workers (including supervisors) to management. The supervisors' most common complaint was that while the company often boasted of its internal labor market and worker mobility, the company was likely to "bring someone in from the outside" when there was a management vacancy:

> There's people working here for like excessive amount of years, okay, and they happen to be black. And a white person will come in here and the next thing you know, they're making "X" amount of money more than that person. There's a guy right here right now, he's white, he used to be in purchasing—he used to buy the foodstuffs . . . Now he's been now promoted to manager. He was just with the company for like two years. He's one of the managers. You got people here for like five, seven years. They didn't even ask you if you wanted to apply for it. And this guy have no experience whatsoever, you know, with food, because he just came off the streets, wherever he came from, he happened to know somebody here that hired him downstairs as a purchasing clerk, right? And then he happened to know the executive chef, they were friends, 'cause she's white too, they hang out together. So she just give him a push. Which I think was totally wrong in front of everybody. I was made to understand, this is your boss. Now I can't figure it out. How could he be my boss if he can't even tell me, he can't even explain to me what is a tomato or a cauliflower? There's nothing that he can tell me that I can gain from. (Guyanese male supervisor, age 33, in United States nine years)

Like the immigrants, most American black workers saw systematic racism and discrimination on the job, and they had numerous personal experiences of missed promotions and opportunities owing to their race:

> I had a manager who was prejudiced against me. Harassing me based on my color. I had plenty of chances for a promotion. He denied it. It was left up to him. But he denied it. There was two black ladies working in the office and one Spanish. And there's one more opening. He does not want another black lady in the office. I was due for a vacation, and I said when I come back there will a white woman in that position. Sure enough, when I came back, there was a white woman in the position. (Black American female worker, age 27)

Yet the whites at American Food had very different interpretations. None of them admitted to preferential hiring or promotions for whites over blacks, and some of the whites we spoke to at American Food actually thought that blacks were getting positions at the expense of whites:

> I think there are more opportunities here if you are not white. Because they do push them [blacks] more. I have worked for American Food for ten years, and I think they [blacks], you know, get more today. (White female supervisor, age 50)

Even though all of the whites in the organization held positions as supervisors or managers, whites thought that the company was practicing "reverse discrimination." The whites we interviewed at American Food were all opposed to affirmative action because they believed that it unfairly gave advantages to blacks at the expense of people like themselves:

> When I graduated from college, AT&T had just signed a consent decree with the federal government saying that they would integrate the workplace, and everybody else started. Therefore the white Irish American, say, if I had the ability to work for New York Telephone, chances of me getting a job when I graduated from college in 1971 was slim to none. 'Cause that's when this was signed. (White male manager, age 42)

The white teachers also perceived the hierarchy of the school differently than the African-American and Caribbean teachers. Many of them also thought "the system" was leaning over backwards to accommodate blacks, and none of them thought that special perks or promotions were withheld more often from blacks than from whites.

The achievement ideology of the West Indians prepares them to battle to succeed in the United States. They expect that it will be more difficult for blacks than for whites because they know that whites have more economic and political power than blacks. The immigrants conclude that whites will try to maintain that power and will resist attempts by blacks to enter the higher reaches of society. This is in keeping with the immigrants' understanding and experience of discrimination back home. Their expectations match their experiences, and their interpretations of those experiences match the interpretations of their African-American coworkers and are at odds with the interpretations of their white American coworkers.

While our respondents might have been surprised or disgusted at the extent of structural racism, it fit in with their worldview, and they felt prepared to handle it. Indeed, some people were pleasantly surprised when they learned that whites could sometimes be found in low-level jobs and blacks sometimes in high-level jobs. For some people the degree of structural racism was not even as bad as they had expected. The immigrants were deeply shocked, however, when they encountered the other component of American race relations—interpersonal racism.

Interpersonal Racism

The *interpersonal* racism that the immigrants experience comes in two forms—old-fashioned racism and subtle racism. Old-fashioned racism consists of blatant acts of discrimination and prejudice such as physical attacks or threats, insults on the street, refusals of housing or employment specifically for racial reasons, and hassles or more frightening intimidation by the police. The stories of blatant discrimination told by the immigrants might very well shock Americans who believe that Jim Crow-style racism has been completely eradicated in 1990s America. But the immigrants related episodes of overt racism in housing:

> A: I had applied to get a condo—condominium—and I was told by this lady that they not going to take any niggers in this apartment.
> Q: She said that to your face?
> A: Yes. That turned me off right away. I said, well, I didn't, you know, I'm not going to give up, but still, same time I feel bad to say well O.K., I want to go into a nice decent area and the response that you get is that. (Guyanese female worker, age 29, in United States nine years)

In employment:

> Q: Have you ever been discriminated against for being a black person?
> A: Oh yeah! One time I went to this store, downtown Brooklyn, to get a job and the day before I went into this store and I talked to

one of the girls and she said that they needed girls. So I got up
early in the morning, dressed, had all my stuff ready and I went,
'cause I really wanted the job. And even before the store opened,
I was standing outside and I waited there to meet her. So then
she showed me the boss, it was a white guy. She said that I came
to interview for a job. And he watched me, he watched me really
bad. He just look at me and didn't say good morning or nothing
and he just—so I kinda got scared. I said, but I'm gonna go in
there and get a job. So I went in and I sit down, I talk, and show
him the application and everything. And he said we don't have
any openings. So I said, I was here yesterday and they showed me
that they had a sign up that they wanted help. He said that the
sign came down yesterday evening because we got girls. So I say,
O.K., I'll try somewhere else. But please, keep me in mind. So I
left and I went back about a week after and I went upstairs and
they had two new girls, but they were white girls. My friend told
me, you didn't get your job but he hired two girls after. I said, he
told me he was full. He was filled up. She said, no, those two girls
over there were hired the day after you. So I went back to him because I'm that type of person. I said, why did you tell me that you
didn't want me because you were full and you hired girls the next
day? He said, "Who told you I hired the girls the next day?" I say,
well it don't matter. When I came here you didn't have those
girls. How come you have those two girls? And he was angry, he
was so mad. He wanted me to get out of his store. You know?
And I just look around and I say, I know why you didn't hire me,
but it's not a problem to me, it's a problem to you. And I just
walked off and left him there, you know? Because I felt so stupid
because I've never been treated like that before and I finally was.

Q: Now would that kind of thing happen in Trinidad, do you think?

A: Not really, no. Because I worked in Trinidad and we have white
folks down there. But they don't even look at you no how. You
come for a job and there is an opening, they hire you and you
work. And that's it. And that's why it was so strange to me to see
how it's so—separate whites or separate, I used to be always asking, why? What's the big deal about this? Back home everybody

just live together, do whatever, it never was. You wouldn't even realize you was a black person because you weren't even worrying about it. But when I came here, I said, this is an issue here? Why it's such an issue, you know? This is what I have to deal with if I'm going to live here? You know.

Q: That must have been upsetting.

A: Surely it is, because you not custom of it. I was not accustomed because you never used to look at it. To come here now and separate it—it's so stupid, you know, why you see this person because of the color of their skin, you know. It was kind of upsetting but then when I applied for other jobs, I realized that was the same thing happening over and over. It was—you can stop and see clearer and then say, oh, maybe this is how it is. (Trinidadian female worker, age 30, in United States ten years)

In police beatings of the Rodney King variety:

Q: Have you ever experienced any discrimination since you came here to the United States?

A: Oh yeah, when it was? In October. Yeah, we was going to this party, right? And we was passing down Empire Boulevard coming from Church Avenue—Ocean Avenue there from by Prospect Park, by Burger King here, they had this black guy and his girlfriend in the Burger King driveway and these two cops was beating him. You know? And we was in this cab and this cab driver stopped and we was saying "no, no, no," you know? And they kept on beating him and his girlfriend wasn't saying one thing. And you know, it was sad. It was sad. I mean it was about two or three of them, and then the next cop car came, you know I find they shouldn't have beaten him because he wasn't fighting them or anything. I never know what happened to him after that. But you know, you don't want to get in trouble so you just, just whisper your words. (Trinidadian female worker, age 29, in United States thirteen years)

On public transportation:

I board the subway going to Bay Park, out in Bay Ridge. And I know this is a discrimination area. Because I was told before I went there.

And I went on the train and the train was empty, almost empty seats was there for people to sit. And I went and I sit beside this man. He was a white. And he look at me and he say, what you fucking bitch doing here? You know, like that. I said, excuse me, this is a public place and I didn't come to your house and if you try to mess with me, I think you're messing with the wrong crowd. And he, you know, he look at me like this. So I just get up, I said, I don't want to get in trouble for you. Honestly. I just get up because I would slap his ass out. That for sure, oh yeah. I certainly would. I don't play around. So now I always—when I go on the train, I look where I stand. Now we coming to, where I took the train, this is DeKalb, to Cortlandt, and there is a lot of people coming from that same place which is racism. So when they come up to our area, which is practically black, they don't carry on those things. (Jamaican female worker, age 34, in United States fourteen years)

And in the streets:

Well I was reading, you know, and listening to the news before I came here, and I always know that that was a major problem here in America. Since I'm here, I have encountered a few racial. Because, like it was three years back, it was Christmas Eve night and I was standing downstairs trying to catch a cab and there was this—you know, I was standing there for like thirty-five minutes and each cab that pulls up, you know, would be a white driver, and they would stop and they would slow down, and as soon as they would see me they would just drive off. I was standing there with this bag of gifts. And this white guy came up, he was waiting on a cab too. And he said to me when the cab stopped, he said to me, why don't you go ahead? So I got into the cab and the guy said, no, I'm not taking you. I said, why? I was here before this guy. This guy was nice enough to tell me to go ahead. He drove off. With the bag outside, my feet outside the cab and everything, and I said, boy, this is crazy. And another guy stopped. He did the same thing. He just wanted to pick the white guy up. I said, well, you know, I heard about this, but I never really expected it. (Guyanese male supervisor, age 33, in United States nine years)

These incidents are similar in several ways. Note that each story concludes on a note of surprise that such a thing could happen, and each person relates how he or she was changed by the experience. People who would never look for a "racial" angle now think twice before they accept that a job has been filled or that a cab doesn't stop, or before they venture into a white neighborhood or sit next to a stranger on a subway. There is nothing subtle or open to other explanations about these experiences. They stem from racial prejudice, and the whites who perpetrate these acts are up-front about their disdain for all blacks, including the foreign-born. Any immigrant who had lived in the United States for anything but a short period of time reported having experiences like these. The reactions that appear over and over again in descriptions of these encounters are surprise and shock. Unlike blocked mobility at work, which the immigrants anticipated, these blatant acts of discrimination and raw interpersonal attacks are disturbing because they are so unexpected.

The other type of racism that people experience is the more subtle, modern kind where the perpetrator can deny any racial animosity and claim their behavior is due to other considerations. These subtle experiences often hurt as much or more—the daily hassles, indignities, and "bad vibes" that black people experience constantly in interactions with whites. These include being followed in stores because clerks suspect one might shoplift, whites moving to the other side of the street and clutching their handbags when one passes by, taxis refusing to stop, store clerks who avoid putting money in one's hand because they do not want to touch black skin, or security guards demanding one's identification though they allow coworkers to walk by unchallenged. Subtle racism also includes acts of omission as well as commission—never receiving invitations to coworkers' homes, enjoying friendly treatment from people during telephone exchanges whose attitude turns very cold when they meet one in person, or professors in graduate school acting surprised when one's work is excellent. Both of these types of discrimination and prejudice affect the immigrants profoundly—all the more so because they never expected or imagined how much of it would happen to them personally.

While working-class and middle-class blacks experience both forms of interpersonal racism, the middle class is more likely to experience subtle racism, and the working class is more likely to experience the more direct old-fashioned racism. The working-class immigrants would describe traveling the subways where people would yell at them to stay out of their neighborhoods; the middle-class respondents would speak of trying to get cabs that refused to stop. Both types of incident are due to the race of the victim, yet in the case of the taxicabs, race is not the only possible explanation.

Many of the stories the middle-class immigrants told us about discrimination involved people who refused to believe they could be middle class—for instance, assumptions by sales clerks that they could not afford certain merchandise:

> A: I have had the experience of going to buy something that was,
>   let's say, a high-priced something. You know? And it was like,
>   don't look at this one, because this one is so much and so much.
>   Look at this one, which was less.
> Q: So they tried to steer you to something else?
> A: Cheaper. You know, because you're black. You can't afford this.
>   To me, the implication was, you can't afford it. You're black. You
>   have to look at this. Or I've had instances where I've walked into
>   some place, and somebody is walking up from down behind me.
>   And I have to turn around and tell them, look, I didn't come into
>   here to pick up the store and walk out with it. I really honestly
>   think that they think that we are all a bunch of drug addicts, shift-
>   less, lazy. (Trinidadian female supervisor, age 36, in United States
>   nineteen years)

This female supervisor is experiencing what many middle-class American blacks have experienced—the stereotype that all black Americans are poor. The idea that her class status, which affords her the wherewithal to buy a high-priced computer or car, does not outweigh or modify her race status seems particularly upsetting to her. This vulnerability to interpersonal racism is particularly hard on middle-class immigrants. At home in the Caribbean, money did "whiten" to some degree and acted as a shield against the interpersonal racism that existed there.[22] The teachers felt acutely that they had enjoyed a certain prestige in the community back home, which they did not have here because the same amount of respect was not accorded to teachers and because race was such an overwhelming presence in American life:

> It's different [than the United States] down in Jamaica, but as I told you, in Jamaica it's social class. And there was a way out of it, but it seems in America it does not matter how much money you have or how much education you have, race is still going to be an issue. In Jamaica if you were very black, very dark-skinned, you could always get a good education and gain the respect and adoration of everybody. That was it, nobody would ever again look at you or the color of your skin to ask where you came from, were you a farmer's daughter or anything. No, that would go once you got the education. And the education and social class. But it's not like that here. (Jamaican female teacher, age 41, in United States seven years)

Many teachers were shocked by their experiences in graduate school once they realized that their professors did not expect them to do well academically because they were black. Most had received their undergraduate degrees at the University of the West Indies, where the vast majority of the students were black and the professors did not differentiate among students by race. This teacher describes an incident where she had to question whether race was responsible for the behavior of the professor she encountered:

> The professor was white and the class was mixed, it was like half-black, half-white. And I must have been in the front, I used to participate a lot. I don't know why I took it for granted that he knew my name. The day we were doing the final exam and he was handing out the midterm paper and he handed me my paper. Obviously, he knew me, he just brought it over to me. If he didn't know my name, he should ask me. He brought it and I walked out. When I got to my car, checked the paper out, it was a C. And when I looked at it, it wasn't my name. So when I brought it back, I said to myself, why couldn't he mistake my face for an A? Is it that my face looked like a C? Would he have given a wrong name to someone else? There's not enough to say it's prejudiced, right? These are some of the things because I said, "I'm black, and there's no doubt about that." But

maybe he could have mistaken me for a white A and not given me a C. So I took it back to him and I said, if you didn't know my name, you should have asked me. When I got my paper back, I got an A. (Jamaican female teacher, age 37, in United States seven years)

Experiencing this discrimination begins to change the immigrants' behavior, as this teacher describes:

I had an English class and I had written a paper, and I had done something on children's writing because that's what I like, and the professor read it and he said, was this adapted? I was so upset. I said, well excuse me, this is mine and it's an original. Can you find a duplicate? And he's like "Oh, I didn't mean it that way," but I said that's what you implied. That particular class, I was the only black in it. And I got the impression like you're black and you're not supposed to know how to write, you're not supposed to know how to speak, you know . . . Sometimes you feel as if you are, not a spy, but like you don't belong here. This is our territory, you have no business in this territory. Certain fields, you're black and you count the number in the class with your fingers, and it's why are you here? You are invading. That's the feeling I get sometimes. Because sometimes that can really interfere, you know you're not comfortable, you're not sure you want to answer, you're not sure if you want to say something. (Guyanese female teacher, age 34, in United States nine years)

When immigrants notice discrimination in one area of their lives, they begin to see the subtle racism that exists in other areas:

I have felt it [prejudice]. Like the lecturers at City, they say, "oh, you write so well," or they meet you and they say, "oh you speak so well." Now I don't understand why they should single me out and say I speak so well. It's like it's not normal for that color skin to speak well. And because you have become sensitive to this thing now, you sort of sense it, you know. And at the school where I teach, sometimes you wonder whether it's because you are black that certain things are withheld from you; they [whites] are keeping all the little extra jobs in the school. They know about it, they put up an ad over the time clock, and then you asked if it's been filled or something like that because they had picked out who was to do it already. My district is white and they do discriminate against blacks . . . I often wonder too about some ladies I work with that I often talk to, we are always together. I can get a lift home if I don't have my car, and that sort of thing. And yet they would never like invite you. They're going home for lunch, they're going to have lunch on their back porch and they will not invite you. And you start thinking to yourself, how genuine are these people? What do they think you are going to do if you come to their house? (Jamaican female teacher, age 41, in United States seven years)

In addition to specific incidents, both blatant and subtle, that convince the immigrants to be wary of whites, many respondents reported that they began to pick up "bad vibes" coming from whites—a general attitude of disgust and disdain that is unspoken, yet undeniably about race:

A: White people look at Negroes as though, you know, they don't exist. They think very little of you. It's like you don't have intelligence. And they always try to put you down in that kind of way.

Q: Do you think white people know the difference between Caribbean Negroes and African-American Negroes?

A: No, I think they classify them all as the same. They don't really want to know, you know. (Guyanese male supervisor, age 33, in United States nine years)

The black Americans had the same litany of bad experiences based on race that the middle-class immigrants described, including professors doubting their good performances in university, promotions going to less qualified whites, and treatment akin to a poor or criminal person based on the color of their skin. The teachers saw a great deal of entrenched racism in the schools where they worked; many were concerned that white teachers had low expectations of their black students.

Since a majority of the black American teachers we interviewed were originally from the South, many of them compared race relations in present-day New York with what they remembered from the South. Unlike the immigrants, they did not describe their original home as a place where they experienced no racism—in fact, many told very moving stories about their experiences with Jim Crow racism as young children. Yet several of the teachers from the South suggested that it was easier to be black in the South than in the North because they had attended segregated schools and lived their lives in such a way that they rarely encountered whites. This was not possible in New York, especially as a middle-class person who worked with whites. This nostalgia for the "power" and "freedom" that segregation brought, especially in the schools, has recently been expressed by a number of black writers.[23] The parallels are strong between the immigrants' discussions of the freedoms they felt coming from the majority-black West Indies and the southern blacks' remembrances of their hometowns.

Interpersonal racism begins to undermine the immigrants' belief that they can tell the difference between incidents that are "racial" in nature and those that are not. Over time, the openness and willingness to respond to whites as "individuals" erode. The suspicion that any individual white might treat one badly because of skin color begins to shape every encounter between black and white. Interpersonal racism ultimately undermines the ability of blacks and whites to ever "forget race." The ghosts of past bad encounters influence current encounters. The immigrants learn to expect race to permeate every potential encounter with a white American.

The experiences of Ginny, a 29-year-old Guyanese cafeteria cashier, and Charissa, a 41-year-old Jamaican teacher, illustrate the ways in which interpersonal racism and the expectation of interpersonal racism begin to change the immigrants' overall experience of America and their modes of interacting with whites. Ginny, like most other cafeteria workers, did not have very many areas of her life where she interacted with whites. Aside from work and some fleeting encounters with whites in public arenas such as shops, trains, parks, beaches, and the like, most of her life was spent with other black people. Her friends, her neighbors, and many of her coworkers were either American or Caribbean blacks. Because of the high degree of racial segregation in housing and the ripple effects of that segregation on other institutions such as schools, churches, and parks, there are few areas other than work in which working-class immigrants have sustained contact with whites. Yet Ginny enjoyed very good relations with the whites she encountered on the job. This consisted of the back-

and-forth banter she would have with the white office workers and execu-
tives who came through her line with their lunch every day. Her experiences had generally been quite positive and she had grown to know many
of her regular customers enough to ask about their vacations and their
families, and they would ask in return about her family and her vacations.
Some customers even asked a number of questions about what Guyana
was like and why she had emigrated. Yet Ginny reports that her generally
positive encounters with whites left her unprepared and shocked for the
negative encounter she had recently endured:

> The white people that come to my line, you know, they will greet
> me. They say, hello, morning, good afternoon . . . But one day this
> guy, he came in my line and I was asking him what he have on his
> tray 'cause I couldn't see what he have, and he said, "You can't see
> what I have on my tray? If you don't understand our language, why
> don't you go back to your country and I'm sick and tired of you
> black niggers—all you black people down here—all you niggers
> down here." That's what he said. And I went to get the manager and,
> you know, they told me the next time that he come back they going
> to talk to him. But he came like a lot of times and they never come
> and talk to him. And he was saying it loud and clear, and the other
> whites that was behind him they was surprised to see how this man
> was going on. But—he acts like he has a problem or something, I
> don't know. But it was terrible that he said that, you know. I feel bad
> because when one person mess up with you, well everybody's the
> same thing. (Guyanese female worker, age 29, in United States nine
> years)

Of course, on a cafeteria line all service people will probably experience
rude behavior and lack of respect from customers. But for Ginny and all
of the other workers who witnessed this incident, the use of the term
"nigger" and the racism it laid bare will affect future interpersonal encounters with whites. While most people getting their lunch on this cafeteria line are not likely to ever call anyone a nigger, that one encounter, as
this worker clearly understands, will "color" her expectations and experiences with every white customer who approaches her cash register. Indeed, the story of how black immigrants come to terms with American

racism really is more about how they see *interpersonal* racism rather than *structural* racism. And this involves developing a "sixth sense" that picks up on whites' unspoken disdain, that notices the ways in which whites look at you. The immigrants have to learn for the first time that race in the United States is not just about intergroup conflict over societal rewards, which is what they had expected, but that many whites simply do not see a black person as a human being.

Charissa also had an experience that changed her expectations about race and its effects on her. While Ginny's experience was clear-cut and undeniably about race, Charissa's was more opaque and open to interpretation. But it also changed her expectations about interactions with whites. For most of her interview Charissa was insistent that she did not want to become "racial" in the United States, and she is concerned that her teenage children seem overly focused on racial slights. She feels that black Americans are too consumed by their race:

> I can't help them [African Americans] because they're so wrapped up in racism, and they act it out so often, they interpret it as such so often that sometimes they are not even approachable. If they're going to teach anything and it's not black, black, all black, they are not satisfied, you know. If they're going to teach poetry and it's not all written by blacks—it's strange that they think it should be so. Yes, we did black authors and black writers but certainly we did a lot of British. You know for us that's not new. Sometimes I feel sorry for them, but you find that you just can't change their attitude because they just tell you that you don't understand. You weren't here to feel what we felt. (Jamaican female teacher, age 41, in United States seven years)

Yet she had an experience that made her much more receptive to the advice of her African-American friends. She was attending graduate school to get a master's in education, and she had to take the national teachers test to keep her position in the city schools. The forms for the test included a question on race. The first time she took the test she answered the race question by stating that she was black, and she was certain she had done very well on the test. But when she got the results, she learned that she had failed the test. An African-American friend from one of her graduate classes told her that the test was rigged and that a certain number of blacks who took the test were purposefully failed so whites could pass at a higher number. Charissa was very skeptical about this assertion at first, but the second time she took the test, she left the race question blank and she passed the test. Since that time she has never put her race on any form that asks for it; she believes that many forms require information about race so that blacks can be uncovered and discriminated against.

THE COMFORT FACTOR

In his autobiography Malcolm X wrote about why the white man hated the Negro: "Do you know why the white man really hates you? It's because every time he sees your face, he sees a mirror of his crime—and his guilty conscience can't bear to face it."[24] West Indian blacks provide a black face for whites to look into without seeing the sorry history of American race relations mirrored back. This puts whites at ease, and a cycle of expectations is created. West Indians don't expect strained relations with whites, and whites don't expect strained relations with West Indians. These expectations are often met, and thus race relations at an interpersonal level are smoother for whites and West Indian blacks than they are for whites and American blacks.

I have noted in Chapter 4 that the whites who worked at American Food, most of whom are the descendants of European immigrants, tended to see the immigrants as sharing an "immigrant" identity with them. Yet the basis for the relative warmth all of these whites feel toward West Indians as opposed to African Americans goes beyond their shared immigration histories. Whites sense the lack of opposition in West Indians to their whiteness and report having far friendlier experiences with foreign-born blacks than with American blacks. For instance, this white manager senses exactly the difference that the West Indians describe in how they relate to her as a person who is in authority over them:

> Sometimes I feel that people who come from the islands are more appreciative of their jobs. They consider themselves fortunate. And sometimes I feel that the assistants that come from the South feel that you owe it to them to keep them on when you have some

problems. The island people are a little more open to white people
than the southern blacks who question authority more. And I don't
know how to say it—the West Indians kind of accept the fact that
even though you are white, it is not *because* you are white that you
are dictating to them, but because you are the person in authority.
(White female manager, age 32)

In a widely quoted popular article on relations among American
whites, American blacks, and recent immigrants in *The Atlantic Monthly*,
journalist Jack Miles argues that whites prefer to be with and deal with
immigrants rather than American blacks. Speaking about race relations in
Los Angeles, Miles notes that for Anglos, "Latinos, even when they are
foreign, seem native and safe, while blacks, who are native, seem foreign
and dangerous."[25] Miles describes this as the "comfort factor" and asserts
that whites are more comfortable with black immigrants as well. He notes
that when he was in college, he had a Nigerian roommate whom he felt
immediately comfortable with. The ease of his friendship with his Nigerian roommate showed him how deep an estrangement separated him
from African Americans.[26]

Why did he feel such discomfort with black Americans? He notes that
in the 1960s when he was spending a great deal of time with American
black people, he sensed how they were approaching their relationship with
him: "In the end I felt that even with me they were prepared at every
moment, at every single moment, for the worst, braced as it were, for a
blow. This is what slavery has done to us as a people, and I can scarcely
think of it without tears."[27] The "comfort factor" that whites felt toward
West Indians and their "discomfort" with black Americans came through
clearly in the interviews. A key difference that was cited over and over by
the whites interviewed was the sense of entitlement they detected among
American blacks:

Q: What are the differences [between American blacks and West In-
dians] that you see?
A: From a working standpoint—work ethic? The willingness to
work for a living—among some, as compared to American
blacks. The willingness to be helpful. The chip isn't on the shoulder that you may get from an American black because they're

black, and then a Jamaican person, you can go up to them—I'm
willing to treat them same as me. He's no better than me, I'm no
better than him. And I get that treatment all the time. And I treat
that way.

Q: Where do you think this difference comes from?

A: Uh, their own cultures. I think—this is terrible but I think American blacks sometimes think that they're owed something instead
of working for it. (White male manager, age 42)

The managers' sense that American blacks have a chip on their shoulder is consciously related to the historical experience of black-white racial
conflict in the United States:

This is not the whole group, this is a portion of the group, they
[American blacks] tend to have a chip on their shoulder about the
same thing. Tend to feel that the debt has not been paid by society
and feel that they should get special treatment and take advantage of
the system. Very often I've had people leave here because they can
collect more money on welfare. Stay home and collect welfare. You
know, those kinds of things. (White female manager, age 30)

Whites pointed to a difference between American blacks and foreign-
born blacks in terms of the amount of anger and sense of entitlement they
displayed. For instance, this white teacher was asked to describe what
black Americans are like:

A: I think there's an evolving African-American character as differentiated from a black character. I think that has been around forever. I think that if it's going to be anything, if I could pick a
word, I would say "angry."

Q: Really?

A: Yeah, because I think that there's this sense of "I want what I deserve" happening. (White female teacher, age 26)

In contrast, the immigrants are described by the whites as being willing to
work within the system, as not taking advantage of the system, as not
feeling that they are owed something, and as not being angry and blaming

whites for historical wrongs. So most whites reported that they felt more comfortable with foreign-born blacks than with American-born blacks:

Q: What about West Indians, or people from the islands? What characteristics come to mind when you think of West Indians?

A: Um, from my experience, I think for the most part, they're extremely friendly people. I mean, it just seems like they're friendly. They'll say hello to you, they smile, they wave. (White male manager, age 34)

At the same time, a significant number of the white managers describe the foreign-born as being very outspoken, very aware of race, and very likely to be blunt about what they want. Yet this did not seem to dampen relations between whites and West Indians in the same way that it dampened relations between African Americans and whites:

Q: Do you see ethnic differences between people from the islands and American blacks? Do you notice any distinctions there?

A: American blacks probably feel they, they probably feel that they wish—give more to them. You know what I'm saying? I don't know how to explain it. Whereas island blacks who come over, they're immigrant, they may not have such a good life where they are so they gonna try to strive to better themselves, and I think there's a lot of American blacks out there who feel we owe them. And enough is enough already. You know, this is something that happened to their ancestors, not now. I mean, we've done so much for the black people in America now that it's time that they got off their butts.

Q: Do you think the immigrant blacks will end up doing better economically than the American blacks?

A: Sure. That's because I think they strive for it more. I think they've had, they—I don't think they feel we owe them a living. You know?

Q: But you get that sense from American blacks?

A: I get that sense, oh yeah. Yeah. (White female manager, age 33)

It is not surprising that the immigrants develop the perceptions about white attitudes that I have just described. Race relations have changed enough in American society over the last few decades so that few whites admit to being prejudiced against all blacks and discriminating against them. Yet many of the whites we interviewed for this project were surprisingly open about their negative feelings toward black people.

We spoke to the white coworkers of the immigrants to see how they understood race relations as well as the differences they saw between West Indians and black Americans. Four themes emerged in our discussions with the whites. First, most whites went out of their way to try to convince the interviewers and themselves that they were not racists. Second, the vast majority of the whites felt very uncomfortable with blacks, made negative judgments about black people as a whole, and evaluated their employees and coworkers by the color of their skin all of the time. A smaller minority was blatantly racist and expressed strong resentment about what they perceived as the growing powers of black Americans. Third, most whites did not understand the amount and severity of interpersonal racism blacks endured. Those who did begin to understand those experiences were shocked by it. Finally, given the complexities of American race relations, many whites had a hard time sorting out when race was determining differences they saw between individuals and when race was not a factor.

Most people did not like to think of themselves as prejudiced. Yet a relatively nonthreatening question about good qualities of black Americans was surprisingly difficult for many respondents:

Q: What are the traits of black Americans that you think are the best?
A: Um, this is a real hard question for me. Again, certain blacks, if you—the sense of family is very strong among, you know, certain blacks, but unfortunately, there are just too many black people that don't know who their parents are or there's a lot of, you know, unwed mothers and this and that . . . Oh, God. This is the hardest question you've asked. Can you repeat it one more time? Let me think about this one more time. The characteristics that I . . . (White male manager, age 34)

Others were less embarrassed or reticent about expressing negative impressions in response to a similar question:

I don't have a positive impression of them. I think everybody with a little self-control and a little self-discipline, and I mean a little, can

do a lot better for themselves. And it means, forget the personaliz-
ing. I just mean, come to work every day and stuff like that. (White
male manager, age 42)

Most white respondents were much more able to tap into their negative
impressions of black people, especially "underclass" blacks whom they
were highly critical of. These opinions were not just based on disinterested
observation. There was a direct sense among many of the whites that they
personally were being taken advantage of and threatened by the black
population. One woman's resentment of blacks hinges on her assessment
that they do not work hard (despite the long-term, hard-working employees she manages) and is directly related to her belief that there is much
competition for resources:

Even just observing them and watching them or driving through like,
downtown Jersey City, and you see all these people, I mean, it's a
shame that you have to be terrified going through some sections, you
know? I mean you listen to the news reports, it's always blacks, it's
always blacks, it's always blacks, you know? You want to go out and
like, shake them, wake them up. Hey guys, go get a job. Don't stand on
the street corner drinking a bottle. You know, it's like go out and do
something for yourself, better yourself because the opportunities are
there—but you know what? They find the easy way out. I have somebody working for me who—American black—who got a job here,
and quit four months later because she was collecting more money on
welfare then she was getting here. I think our government has lost
complete control over the welfare system, over social security, and by
the time I'm able to retire, there ain't gonna be anything there for me.
You know, I can't get aid. I'm in the minority now. I can't get school
help. It's not fair, it's not fair. I couldn't get aid in school, I couldn't
get financial aid for school. My father either made too much or I was
white. And that is true today. It's still true today. I don't resent it but I
don't think it's fair either. You know, because we're handing it to
them. We're saying, we're sorry, here you go. You know? Well hey!
What about me over here? You know? How can you not be prejudiced
or bigoted towards American blacks because they don't do anything.
They don't show that they deserve it. I mean if this girl can make more

money on welfare than she can being out there, supporting her-self—when I heard that, when I heard that, and I was like, I was disgusted. I swore to myself, as long as my two legs are able, and as long as my two arms are able, I'm gonna be out there doing a job . . . I see these blacks in Jersey City . . . And the food stamp bothers me. Because I see blacks out there buying food with food stamps eating better than I'm eating. When I was in college, I was twelve dollars a week in college, living on tuna fish and crackers. Yet there were other people out there eating filet mignon. So it just doesn't make sense. I was proud, I said, I'm not gonna go begging or anything. I worked, and that's what got me through. I didn't spend any money through the week. But I don't think it's fair. I don't think it's fair that way. (White female manager, age 33)

Underlying the attitudes these whites profess about black Americans is a sense of personal threat but in even greater measure a belief that black Americans violate the "moral values embodied in the Protestant Ethic."[28] The anecdotes the whites tell of black women quitting the cafeteria while "scheming" to collect welfare reinforce the images they have from the media and their own experiences with urban change that black Americans do not work hard, have too many children, and get government handouts:

Well, I have a million of them [American blacks] in my town where I live. They have taken over the projects downtown where I used to live; now I live uptown. Characteristics? I think they are lazy. I think they are lazy and, now let's say, I don't want to be mean about this but, they just have too many kids. Like, they can't afford to have one or two, and they wind up with twelve. And then that, but if you compare it with a white couple, who will have maybe one, and then you'll turn around and a black couple who, the father usually doesn't even have a job, they have seven, you know? (White female manager, age 53)

While the managers at American Food freely expressed these opinions about blacks to the white interviewer, only one of them really saw herself as prejudiced; when asked about race relations at work, they all thought blacks unfairly saw racism where none exists. One of the chief ways in which the whites reassured themselves and me that there is a race-blind meritocracy at American Food is to point to the black managers and supervisors in the company, all but one of whom are foreign-born.

Ironically, one of the concrete incidents of structural racism at American Food described by many of the black workers was the hiring of a white woman from outside the company to be a supervisor when the black workers thought many of them were qualified for the promotion. The woman who was hired as a supervisor was only 19 years old, although she had worked in food services for a number of years. Perhaps because of her age (she had not yet learned to censor her opinions), this woman was the most blatantly and unabashedly prejudiced of all our respondents:

> I feel that a lot of the stereotypes are true. I mean, they're uneducated, you know, a lot of them are poor. They're rude, they don't know how to carry themselves. Those types of stereotypes . . . They're very showy. Loud. Their music—which I happen to like—some of it is extremely different and aggressive and curses and, you know, fighting. They're very street people, I feel. And I think that some of it's stereotypical, like, you know, but like a lot of the people say they smell, they have, you know, body odor. And I really feel in many ways that it's true. I don't think that because of their hair—I don't think they shower every day. I mean, I don't know it for a fact. And I'm not saying it to be, you know, cruel. But I really, I don't think they shower every day. I don't think they are as hygienic as Amer—like white people. I think that white—not all white people, I think most white people are cleaner, a lot more sanitary and a lot more aware, you know. I enjoy now being more around Italians and white people, and I just feel more comfortable and I don't want to feel tension from other people. I mean, I just—I don't need that in my life. It wouldn't be because, you know, of the color of their skin. It would be because of everything that's involved with the color of their skin.

> Q: Do you think that there are racial tensions now in New York between blacks and whites?

> A: Oh, definitely. Definitely. And I think it's more and more that the blacks are creating it, and I think it's a shame. I think if they would stop blaming us, you know, for everything, then it would

be a little easier . . . And I feel it's a real shame because I love
New York . . . And I hate to feel like I have to leave it because of
that reason. I always feel it will never be all blacks because of, you
know, this right here, this trade center, the financial center. They
couldn't take it over. They couldn't control it. They could be a
part of it, a big part. But I think it's become—whites are becoming—whites are the minority I think now. Factually they are the
minority, which is a shame. (White female supervisor, age 19)

Yet when this supervisor was challenged by the black workers about
receiving her position when black workers with more seniority were
passed over, she was shocked:

We have a monthly shop meeting, and they said this is Suzie, she'll
be running the Super Star Program, so one of the black gentleman
who is a chef in the cafeteria stood up and said, well I feel, why is she
getting hired? How long has she been here? So I thought he was just
asking questions at first. So I said, well, just a month and a half. He
says, well, I forgot exactly the words he used, something like "My
people need jobs" or "I'm here for the minority and why is she
getting the position?" . . . And that really hurt me a lot. I didn't even
want to do my job after that. I felt like, they hate me.

The middle-class white teachers we spoke with also included a few
blatant racists. Most white teachers, however, bent over backwards to
present themselves as accepting of black people, and many felt genuinely
warm toward their black students. Yet quite a few were uncomfortable
with relations with black teachers at their schools and thought that blacks
were too quick to see race as both a source of problems and as a solution
to problems. They resent being told it's a "black thing" when trying to
understand the behavior of their students. While the majority of teachers
believed that having black teachers was important for their black students,
some were concerned that a stress on black role models was being made
at the expense of good education:

We are now going for black role models. Okay? I will never again in
this life do anything because I am the wrong color. We must have
black role models. So we have people who look down on our stu-

dents and then we have people who talk to them in street language, the language right out of the gutter. And they expect to be educated. And then they say this is a black thing. That doesn't work either because children have contempt for them. So we really need better teachers, and we need people who care, who really want to teach children. (White female teacher, age 47)

Given these underlying negative opinions of at least some whites in our society, it is not surprising that immigrant and American blacks experience both interpersonal and structural racism.

CONSEQUENCES FOR THE IMMIGRANTS

There are three main consequences to the West Indians' different expectations and understandings of race relations and the ways in which those expectations and understandings affect their interactions with whites. First, their different understandings of race relations contribute to their tensions with black Americans. Second, their different ways of dealing with race relations lead both to increased chances of social mobility for some and increased chances of bitter disappointment for others. Finally, over time the immigrants become more like African Americans, and their approach to race relations begins to change.

The first consequence—that black Americans and West Indians experience some tensions in how they experience race relations—has been documented in Chapter 3. To summarize, West Indians criticize American blacks for two seemingly contradictory characteristics—racialism and racial docility. The West Indians believe the African Americans are too racial, that is, too likely to cry race in situations where race has nothing to do with what is happening. They also believe that African Americans are sometimes too docile—that they do not stand up for their rights and their dignity because they have allowed the white-majority society to degrade them. For instance, this woman believes that when white managers treat their black employees badly, the black Americans do not handle the situation as well as she would:

[The Americans] being afraid to say certain things. Once you know how to phrase it in the right way, or you don't higher your voice or lower your voice. You could say, listen, Tom, or Bill, you don't have to speak to me like this. Just ask me, could you please move? I'll go. They won't do it. They will just move away instead of correcting your manager and saying, don't speak to me that way, I'm not a dog, I'm not a child. You could speak to me better. That's what I see. And they afraid to say that, like they're afraid of losing their job if they say something. (Trinidadian female supervisor, age 38, in United States twenty-one years)

The black Americans we spoke to thought that the West Indians were naive about race; given enough time in the United States they would come to see that they shared the same interests as black Americans and that their ethnic status was no guarantee against experiencing racism.

Black Americans are more likely to see racism operating in subtle and ambiguous situations than West Indians do. They are more likely to develop a "sixth sense" about whites, to have radar that scans whites for the inappropriate behavior that their past experiences tell them will happen. This is protective when the inappropriate behavior does happen, but at the same time problematic because it makes interpersonal relations with whites strained, and often brings issues of respect into play in hierarchical relations between managers and workers at work and between customers and workers in service encounters.

The second consequence of the West Indians' approaches to race and race relations are the ways in which their racial culture interacts with socioeconomic mobility. Their different approach to race relations can lead to both greater success in the labor market than African Americans enjoy and greater disappointment and rage about blocked social mobility, racism, and prejudice when they do not achieve success.

The whites we interviewed hold deep-seated negative ideas about working-class blacks. They also hold an egalitarian belief system, which makes them eager to find "good blacks" whom they can trust and relate to as "individuals" without the weight of guilt and "chips on shoulders" and past historical wrongs being thrown in their face. To most whites, blacks' skin color acts as a master status that whites believe indicates inferiority. Whites allow for exceptions, usually the black people they meet and get to know—the black "best friends" many whites conveniently have. But these exceptions do not destroy the stereotype of blacks as inferior.[29] After hearing how most of the white respondents speak about blacks when they are not present, most rational people would conclude that blacks would be prudent to be very wary of each white they encounter. The attitudes toward blacks the majority of these whites hold are derogatory; they see blacks as violating the moral code they live by. These whites had a hard time saying anything good about black Americans.

Because immigrants have much less experience with interpersonal racism, they react openly to whites with the idea that whites will respond to their individual personalities and not the color of their skin. In effect, for the immigrants the whites are innocent until proven guilty. Ironically, the immigrants' mistaken assumptions about racism—expecting less of it, and expecting it to be structural and not interpersonal—open up opportunities for the immigrants to do well.

Hierarchical relations on the job are experienced differently by black Americans and black immigrants. Unlike American blacks, the immigrants have more experience in dealing with hierarchy without racial overtones. They are used to taking orders from black supervisors without second-guessing whether those orders are legitimate or rooted in racism and racial hierarchy. So there is not the same sense of suspicion, antagonism, and oppositional identity when they deal with white supervisors on a day-to-day basis. The white supervisors sense this difference and appreciate the absence of racial overtones when they give orders.

These responses to work hierarchies should prove particularly valuable in the service economy. Besides the food-services jobs of the workers in this study, low-level service jobs include office jobs, such as messengers and receptionists, and personal-service jobs, such as home health aides, housekeepers, and nannies. There is a huge potential in all of these jobs for interpersonal conflict between the service worker and the consumer of the service. Work in personal services and nursing homes can involve intimate contact between rich consumers and poor workers. Office work often requires a great deal of deference on the part of the worker. In effect, service work is not only about providing a service but also a particular demeanor on the part of the worker. The best service workers take orders well and are cheerful about it, and not resentful that they have to work for others.

When service workers have oppositional identities where they react to those giving orders with reservations in their mind about whether they are being disrespected because of their minority status, they no longer are cheerful and deferential. Immigrants do not bring the same baggage to a service encounter as any American, white or black, does. Because of their immigrant status, their core identity is not as invested in work relations as that of the native-born. Black immigrants who do not see encounters with supervisors or customers as having racial overtones will no doubt be preferred by supervisors, employers, and customers over black Americans who do. Anyone who has ever been uncomfortable giving orders to a service worker knows that the demeanor of the employee can make a big difference. If the service worker acts resentful of the authority of the supervisor or customer, the encounter is unpleasant. The whites in this study thought that immigrants were more likely as workers to make those encounters more pleasant.

The immigrants are not accustomed to structural barriers and racial ceilings for advancement on the job at the low and mid-levels of hierarchy. When they do encounter incidents of blatant racism on the job or structural incidents such as not being promoted or not getting a raise, they become angry and militant, often raising quite a fuss. The immigrants are also likely to be angrier because injustice when first encountered and not expected is a different thing than long-simmering racial injustice that is always anticipated. The irony we found is that the black immigrants are perceived by the whites to be better workers because they are immigrants. They are perceived to be nicer to be around most of the time because of their separation of work hierarchy from racial hierarchy.

At the same time, the white managers believe that the immigrants are more likely to be outspoken, and some thought that the immigrants are more in tune with differences between blacks and whites:

Q: And you were saying that some groups were demanding?

A: Sure.

Q: Which ones were you thinking about?

A: It's like more of your island people. I mean, they come up with these like superior attitudes, like. You know, who do you think

you're talking to type attitude, you know. They think that because they're here working as a cook or a dishwasher or whatever
they're doing, that they should be paid for it. And every time they
get reviewed, they expect to get a raise and like, wait a minute,
what did you do to earn that raise? It's like we should give it to
you, and I don't like that. I did find that I have a hard time talking to them, to the—'cause most of the people here are like, island people: Trinidad, Jamaica, Panama—you know, they're all
island people. Sometimes you're almost afraid to say something
because you don't know what's gonna set them off.

Q: They get angry?

A: Yeah. They—it's like, angry and belligerent. (White female manager, age 33)

A: It seems that the American blacks are much more prejudiced
than foreigners, yet sometimes I feel that some foreigners do really want to push it.

Q: Push being a foreigner, or push being black?

A: Black, being black. Mostly being black.

Q: But still you kind of feel like, the, the Americans might be a little
bit more prejudiced?

A: I feel they're more—I feel that they—not that they're more prejudiced, I feel they handle it a lot worse. I feel they're a lot more ani-
malistic. Very much so, they're more mean and crude and rude.
You know. They [the immigrants] have a little more class and they
handle it better. I think, you know, they don't yell and scream and
curse. I think they go more—this is just my opinion, but I think
they try to discuss it more . . . The American blacks just want to
blame everything. You know like, I didn't get it because I'm a
black person. They don't take into account that they are uneducated, that they didn't go to school. That, you know, that they
don't carry themselves well. They never seem to take into account.
As compared to where the foreigners, they'll wear suits, and they
dress well, and they try to handle it diplomatically. And I think
they'll get results that way. (White female worker, age 57)

Whites held contradictory opinions of West Indians. They see them as more friendly, more approachable on an individual level, and more cooperative, and, at the same time, more aware of race, more likely to be angry and blunt about workplace race relations, and more demanding and arrogant. This seeming contradiction can be found in a number of studies of West Indians in the United States. They have been described as militant race leaders, with more advanced and confrontational racial ideologies and programs than American blacks. Yet they have also been seen as more conservative, less willing to challenge the rules of the game, and easier to get along with.[30] This mix of confrontation and ambition at a structural level and openness and nonoppositional behaviors at an interpersonal level will have two results at American Food and in general. First, the West Indians will on average go further at American Food, they will become supervisors and managers at higher rates, and they will be better liked at the aggregate level. Second, West Indians will be deeply hurt and disillusioned by racist acts for which they have not developed psychological defense mechanisms such as oppositional identities. By being friendly and open to whites, they open themselves up to bitter disillusionment when the inevitable blatant racist comes along. However, because not everyone is racist, and because there are doors of opportunities open to blacks in American society, at the aggregate level this strategy will lead to success for many West Indians. So this strategy, which opens up each individual to possible hurt, furthers the overall success of the group.

The psychological cost of not being fully prepared for the blocked mobility and especially the strong interpersonal racism that does exist can be high for the West Indian. When West Indians do encounter clear cases of either type of racism, they speak out forcefully about it. Indeed, they have historically had a reputation for militance when it comes to racial issues.[31] Ira Reid noted in 1939 that "the Pullman Company and certain railroads hesitated to employ West Indian Negroes as porters because of their rather vainglorious resentment exhibited when they felt that they had been insulted by passengers."[32]

Because they are more likely to work in integrated job situations, to live in neighborhoods that have some white residents, and to shop outside of their neighborhoods, middle-class blacks are more likely to experience interpersonal racism than are working-class blacks. They are more likely to attempt to get jobs that ordinarily go to whites and to purchase housing in white areas, as well as more likely to ultimately be blocked by racial prejudice as they move toward the glass ceiling. Coming from a country where "money whitens," they are likely to be doubly affronted by interpersonal racism because white people are not responding to the status they feel they have earned and because they had never expected that prejudice could affect them.

Other researchers have noted the particular sensitivity to interpersonal racism that middle-class immigrants exhibit.[33] Reid noted in 1939 that many of the immigrants to New York at that time had chosen to emigrate in order to break the color/class boundaries that would have stopped them back home. He noted that the middle class "express more extreme resentment to any manifestation of discourtesy than the native born Negro is wont to do. Such designations as George or boy are so emphatically resented that some employers refuse to hire West Indian Negroes because they do not make good servants, while many others prefer them because they keep the personal tone at a high level."[34]

Milton Vickerman's study of middle-class and working-class Jamaican immigrant men in New York found some sharp class differences. He found middle-class men were very concerned with race in the United States while working-class men hardly ever complained about the issue.[35] He argues that working-class Jamaican men tend to perceive African-American coworkers as the "enemy" because of the intense competition over jobs. Middle-class Jamaican men see their middle-class African-American coworkers as allies and are likely to see whites on the job as the "enemy." The racial incidents and blocked promotions and raises that the middle-class immigrant men experienced caused them to "become more actively pro-black than they had been in Jamaica and certainly more pro-black than the working class Jamaicans in the study."[36]

The middle-class respondents in this study are more likely than the working-class respondents to experience interpersonal racism but not blocked mobility. Perhaps this is an artifact of the nonrandom sample I ended up with, because one could argue that teachers are less likely to be looking for promotions or social mobility than other middle-class professionals, such as managers or supervisors in large organizations. In fact, the West Indian managers at American Food did report blocked mobility in the form of missed raises and promotions, and that did heighten their consciousness of racial issues. Indeed, the individuals most likely to develop intense racial awareness are those who experience both blocked social mobility and strong interpersonal racism.

But, unlike the middle-class men Vickerman studied, the middle-class immigrants we spoke to, both at American Food and in the high schools, exhibited a great deal of tension and distancing from American blacks. While the middle-class respondents sometimes tempered their descriptions of problems with African Americans by stating that they wished it weren't so, or they thought the two groups *should* come together, their degree of disdain and psychological distance was very strong, as strong in most cases as that of the working-class respondents.

Immigrants who expect structural racism but not interpersonal racism will do very well in American workplaces. With affirmative action and corporate structures the way they are, a black person who aims high, challenges blocked mobility and missed promotions when they occur, and yet manages to maintain very friendly relations with whites and does not make them feel uncomfortable about issues of race can go very far. It is no accident that Colin Powell is the black person who has come closest to being accepted by a cross-section of whites for the highest office in America. His West Indian background gives him this particular set of skills—an ambitious man who aims high, acknowledges the existence of racism and prejudice in American society, and stands willing to challenge it when it affects him, yet a person whom whites of all backgrounds, particularly conservative whites, find "comfortable." Indeed, Powell does not have a "chip on his shoulder" about race.

But what of the West Indian who does not achieve the social mobility of a Colin Powell? What of the person who has middle-class ambitions but does not have the degree of social mobility that cushions the inevitable encounters with old-fashioned and subtle racism? Louis Farrakhan is also a black American of West Indian background, and his fiery militance about racial matters is also reflective of the same mix of racial and socioeconomic expectations. Having grown up in Boston, he reports never having experienced or expected the degree of interpersonal racism he encountered when he traveled to the American South for the first time as a young man. When West Indians experience blocked mobility that cannot be overcome through hard work and ambition and encounter interpersonal racism for which they are not prepared, they can become even more bitter and concerned with race than anyone. Marcus Garvey, Stokely Carmichael, and Louis Farrakhan are black leaders who represent the other side of the West Indian experience in America. At different points in American history each of these leaders advocated a separate sphere for blacks where they could be free of the overwhelming everyday presence of whites and whites' racial beliefs. The black power and black separatism represented by these men emphasize the need for economic power and social mobility, but the psychological appeal of their movements also lies in the idea that blacks should pull back from the possible hurts of interpersonal racism.

The immigrants' experiences with racial incidents undermine and change their initial confidence that they will not become "racial" in the United States. The immigrants describe how the longer they are here, the more they learn to see race operating in interactions where they would not have suspected it when they first arrived. Because of the omnipresence of race in day-to-day interactions and the reality of subtle racial discrimination and prejudice, the immigrants over time become much less confident that they can tell when people are responding to their skin color and not some other characteristic or circumstance. In fact, when long-term immigrants are describing freshly arrived immigrants, they comment on their inability to recognize the racism that is all around them:

> When the Guyanese come, and all the other foreigners first come, they come with the aim of succeeding. If they did not come to succeed, they would not have come. Therefore they do not recognize the subtle signs of racism. They attribute racism to bad manners. (Guyanese female teacher, age 49, in United States nineteen years)

When the immigrants start to see subtle racism, it becomes much harder to maintain their initial militance. Newly arrived immigrants are the most likely to loudly challenge racial injustice and demand proper treatment. Eventually people learn to pick their battles, expending energy and emotions on situations they think they can change or that they know they cannot live with.

Vickerman notes that the Jamaican men he studied "alter their reactions to racism from an active to a passive one—apparently this stems from the stress associated with constant confrontation."[37] Indeed, he found that over time the number of men reporting that they had experienced the same amount of racism as African Americans almost doubled.[38] Tekle Woldemikael also found differences between pioneers, who had come from Haiti to Evanston, Illinois, in the 1940s and 1950s, and those who had arrived more recently in the 1970s. The pioneers reported much more difficulties with American race relations.[39]

The reluctant acceptance that race is affecting the responses of whites to them, in both blatant and subtle ways, serves to undermine the responses of the immigrants to whites. Seeing whites as individuals, not as representatives of their race becomes more difficult. One Jamaican immigrant said that though he had experienced much racism, he still tried to have an open mind:

> You might walk out there, something hit you in the face that this is racial. But if you didn't look for that, you safer to be naive. I don't go out and look for some white person to be mean to me. (Jamaican male teacher, age 37, in United States seven years)

But if enough white people are mean to you, one cannot help but learn to expect it. As Ginny, the cafeteria worker who was called "nigger" by a customer, stated, "when one person mess up with you, well everybody's the same thing." It may be *safer* to be naive, but experience does destroy naivete and, like it or not, the stings of past racial experiences begin to "color" expectations of all personal encounters between black immigrants and white Americans.

So, as the immigrants spend more time in the United States their expectations of interpersonal racism rise, and they report more wariness in their encounters with whites. But no matter how many years they spend here, and however many negative encounters they have with whites, the overall ways in which West Indian blacks and American whites interact generally produce better outcomes for West Indians than black Americans. Whites expect West Indians to be "better blacks"; they find common ground in the West Indians' immigrant experiences. West Indians have an immigrant's faith in the American dream, and their experiences growing up in a black-majority society inoculate them against a bitter attitude that turns off whites in daily interactions (especially in the service industry where many work).[40] At the same time, their strong racial identity and experiences with blocked mobility for dark-skinned people at home inspire the militance and fiery attitudes that lead them to challenge blocked mobility when they encounter it. Many of these characteristics begin to fade over time as the immigrants spend more time in a racist society. Yet most of these characteristics have shaped adults' character and outlook in a way that will not change throughout their lives. But what about the future of this West Indian distinctiveness? Will a particular West Indian identity, encompassing cultural ethnicity, a different way of dealing with racial issues, and a relatively successful socioeconomic pattern persist into the successive generations? It is to this question we turn in the next three chapters.

INTERGENERATIONAL

DYNAMICS

Chapters 2 and 3 argued that the historical
experiences of West Indians and the context of
their reception in the United States created a
particular culture and identity. Because a key
component of that reception is that American
concepts of race and ethnicity serve to classify
the immigrants as blacks, a central task for the
immigrants is to differentiate themselves from black Americans. Chapters
4 and 5 showed how the culture and identities of the immigrants interact
with the structure of the New York economy and American race relations.
I argued that West Indians' identity as immigrants, which includes a
willingness to work at jobs in the service economy, and their cultural
response to black-white race relations allow them to do relatively well in
American society. However, I also argued that the culture that the immigrants bring with them begins to change as they encounter the structure
of American society, particularly the heavy psychological and economic
tolls of American racism. In the next three chapters I turn to the future of
this identity and culture as it interacts with American social structure.
What happens to the children of the immigrants? The experiences of the
second generation that I describe here are best understood after a brief
review of what sociologists know about assimilation among children of
immigrants.

MODELS OF INTERGENERATIONAL CHANGE

Researchers examining the experiences of the post-1965 immigrants and
their children have concluded that the "old line" assimilation model of

cultural and social assimilation moving in lockstep with socioeconomic success is no longer correct. Class mobility for immigrants and their children is no longer associated with increasing Americanization for all groups. Some immigrants and their children become "American" in their identity and cultural behaviors and do not do very well in the labor market, while others who remain very "ethnic" achieve high incomes and educations.[1]

This idea is directly at odds with theories derived from the experiences of European immigrants and their children in the early twentieth century. Those theories predicted that the longer the time spent in the United States and the more their exposure to American culture, the more likely second-generation youth were to adopt an "American identity" and to reduce ties to the immigrant or ethnic identities and culture of their parents. This assimilation was associated with upward socioeconomic mobility in American society. This "straight line" assimilation model assumes that with each succeeding generation the groups become more similar to mainstream Americans and more economically successful.

Perhaps the most complete discussion of the identity and experience of the second generation along these lines is the 1945 study by W. Lloyd Warner and Leo Srole of the ethnic groups of "Yankee City." In the sociological tradition of the Chicago school neighborhood studies, theirs was a six-volume study of the social system of an industrial small city in New England in the early 1930s—Newburyport, Massachusetts—which the authors named "Yankee City." Volume 3 of the study, *The Social System of American Ethnic Groups,* focuses on immigrant adaptation and assimilation, most especially on the transition between the immigrant and subsequent generations.[2]

Warner and Srole describe a generational march of ethnic groups from initial residential and occupational segregation to residential, occupational, and identificational integration and Americanization. The class mobility of the groups from poverty to middle-class status also proceeded in this orderly fashion, which neatly summarizes a straight-line model of assimilation: "Each consecutive ethnic generation pushes progressively farther out of the bottom level and into each of the successive levels above. That the class index of an ethnic group is related to the length of its settlement in the city is a manifestation of the continuous advance achieved in the hierarchy of each new generation."[3] In a chapter on the children of the immigrants in Yankee City, Warner and Srole explore the forces affecting the second generation's relations with their parents' generation and the wider society. They argue that the child's early socialization in the home is oriented to the values and beliefs of the old country through the influence of the parents. But as soon as the child enters into social relations outside the home, the process of assimilation and change to the wider American society begins. The child quickly absorbs values and skills specific for coping in American society and also develops tensions with the parents when the immigrant and the American cultures clash or disagree.

Because the child can absorb change and the new society's values, the child takes the lead for the family in adaptation to the new world. As a result, Warner and Srole argue that the traditional parent-child relationship is turned on its head. Instead of the parent teaching and guiding the child in how to live in society, the child has access to this knowledge in a way that the parent never will. Children internalize the American culture and identity and reject their parents' culture and identity as "foreigners." Warner and Srole believed that these competing allegiances work themselves out in three stages: rebellion and profane behavior, total rejection of the immigrant culture, and final resolution into an ethnic culture that facilitates combining the American and the immigrant social systems. This personality development also facilitates social mobility—for instance, the teenagers they interviewed hated their parents' language so much they would not even answer the relevant questions on the questionnaire. This hatred of their parents' language ensured that they learned English thoroughly and without an accent, thus hastening their assimilation into the same jobs as native Americans.

This model of generational change makes two critical assumptions that may or may not have been true for the white ethnic groups of Yankee City in the 1930s.[4] However, these assumptions are most definitely not true for black immigrants in the 1990s. First, the model assumes that "the American social system" is an undifferentiated whole. It assumes that there is *one* American culture that a child will absorb. That culture is assumed to be the upwardly mobile, self-reliant, and individualistic middle-class culture. Second, this model assumes that the "American" culture and identity are of higher social status than the immigrant culture. This means that it is preferable in the wider society's eyes to be an American than an immigrant. Thus Warner and Srole conclude, "In any judgements of rank, the American social system, being the most vigorous and having also the dominance of host status, is affirmed the higher. Since the child identifies himself with it, his position in the present reciprocal is higher."[5]

In the 1990s black immigrants do not enter a society that assumes an undifferentiated monolithic American culture. Rather, they enter a consciously pluralistic society in which a variety of subcultures and racial and ethnic identities coexist. In fact, if these immigrants assimilate, they assimilate not just as Americans but as black Americans. As we have seen in previous chapters, it is generally believed by the immigrants that it is *higher* social status to be an immigrant black than to be an American black.[6]

Another crucial difference between the experiences of past immigrants and the reception of current immigrants is the economic opportunity structure. The unskilled jobs in manufacturing that gave opportunities for job mobility for the immigrants' children at the turn of the twentieth century have been lost as economic restructuring in the United States has shifted to a service economy.[7] Assumptions in the straight-line model that all immigrants are unskilled and start out at the bottom of the social hierarchy are also not true. Current immigrants are quite varied in the skills they bring with them. Some of them arrive with advanced educational and professional qualifications and take relatively well-paying jobs, which put them ahead of native American blacks (for example, Jamaican nurses). Others are less skilled and face difficulties finding work in the United States.

Aside from these major differences between current Caribbean immigration and past European immigration, one other factor also makes an enormous difference—the fact that West Indians are black immigrants, entering a society where race still determines much of social life. The degree of residential segregation faced by blacks in the United States, whether foreign-born or American-born, has always been, and continues to be, of a much higher order than the segregation faced by foreign-born white immigrants.[8] Even with occupational mobility, blacks are not able to move into higher status neighborhoods in the orderly progression that Warner and Srole describe for European ethnic groups. A further complication for the black second generation is that part of being a black American involves dealing with American racism. As we have seen in Chapter 5, black immigrants and black Americans report a large difference in their perception and expectation of racism in American society. For the second generation, growing up as an American involves developing a knowledge and perception of racism and its effects and subtle nuances. The understanding the second generation develops about American race relations and their role in the racial hierarchy of this country sets them at odds with their parents.

NEW THEORIES OF IMMIGRANT ADAPTATION

New theories that describe the experiences of becoming American for recent immigrants and their children stress the multiple and contradictory paths that can be followed by second-generation children.[9] Some individuals achieve socioeconomic success though retaining strong ethnic attachments and identities, while others assimilate to American subcultures with limited socioeconomic mobility. In a 1992 article entitled "Second Generation Decline," Herbert Gans outlines several scenarios of possible socioeconomic and social integration of the post-1965 second generation. He speculates that the children of the new immigrants could face socioeconomic decline relative to their parents' position because the children of immigrants might refuse to accept the low-level, low-pay jobs of their parents.

The other possibility is that the youngsters who do not "become American" and adopt the negative attitudes toward school, opportunity, hard work, and the "American dream" that their American peers have adopted, but rather stay tied to their parents' ethnic community and values, will end up doing better. Gans thus suggests that straight-line theory could be turned on its head, with "the people who have secured an economically viable ethnic or other niche acculturating less than did the European second and third generations" and those without such a niche "experiencing the poverty and joblessness of second generation decline and becoming American faster than other second generation ethnics."[10]

Using material from a number of different ethnographic case studies, as well as a survey of second-generation schoolchildren in Miami and San

Diego, sociologists Alejandro Portes and Min Zhou make a similar argument. They describe the different outcomes of second-generation youth as "segmented assimilation." They argue that the mode of incorporation of the first generation creates differential opportunities and cultural and social capital in the form of ethnic jobs, networks, and values, which create differential pulls on the allegiances of the second generation. For those immigrant groups who face extreme discrimination in the United States, and who reside in close proximity to American minorities who have also faced a great deal of discrimination, *reactive ethnicity* emerges in the first generation. The second-generation youth whose ties to American minorities are stronger, and whose parental generation lacks the degree of social capital to provide opportunities and protection for the second generation, are likely to develop the "adversarial stance" toward the dominant white society that American minorities such as poor blacks and Hispanics hold. This adversarial stance stresses that discrimination in the United States is very strong and devalues education as a vehicle of advancement.

For those groups who come with strong ethnic networks, access to capital, and fewer ties to minorities in the United States, *linear ethnicity* characterizes the first generation. Linear ethnicity creates social capital—the networks of social ties from church and voluntary organizations that both create links to job opportunities and reinforce parental authority and values vis-à-vis the second generation. Min Zhou points out that parents can have high aspirations for their children but "whether children carry out their parents' wishes can be a matter that extends beyond individual families, since motivation and aspiration do not simply come from their own parents, but from all the families in the community that surrounds young people and from the larger social structure that rewards educational attainment."[11] Groups reflecting linear ethnicity resist acculturation to the United States and ultimately provide better opportunities for the second generation.[12]

A number of ethnographic studies of other recent immigrant groups support the notion of the decoupling of "Americanization" from social mobility. For today's second generation, staying "ethnic" and resisting certain kinds of Americanization may be the key to upward social mobility. For instance, anthropologist Marcelo Suarez-Orozco's study of Central American immigrant schoolchildren found that they maintained a dual frame of reference. They contrasted their experiences in the United States with their experiences at home and developed an immigrant attitude toward school that helped them to do well.[13] Anthropologist Margaret Gibson's study of second-generation Punjabi Sikhs in California developed the concept of "accommodation without assimilation." Whereas young native minority group members saw school achievement as demanding that they give up their specific cultural attributes, the Sikh second generation believed they could acquire the cultural skills and language they needed to succeed in school while retaining their Sikh identities and culture.[14] The Sikh children, like the Central American children that Suarez-Orozco studied, saw success in school not primarily as an avenue for individual mobility or independence but rather as a way to bring honor and success to their families.

In another school-based study of immigrant and second-generation youth, Maria Eugenia Matute-Bianchi compared four different types of children of Mexican descent in a California high school. She found that immigrant children and American-born children who identified as Mexican did better in school than those students who identified as Chicanos or "Cholos," an oppositional identity based on the American race and ethnic classification system.[15]

Anthropologist John Ogbu's theory of oppositional identities, described in Chapter 5, is relevant here. Ogbu argues that involuntary minorities such as blacks and American Indians in the United States respond to the derogatory images held about them by the dominant group and to blocked mobility by cultural inversion—"the tendency for members of one population . . . to regard certain forms of behavior, events, symbols, and meanings as inappropriate, precisely because they are characteristic of members of another population, for example, white Americans."[16] Because these ways of behaving are seen as opposed to the dominant society and not just different from them, involuntary minorities interpret such behaviors as intrinsic to "a sense of collective or social identity, a sense of self worth." For involuntary minorities behaviors such as speaking standard English or conforming to school requirements associated with whites are threatening to group solidarity and to group identity. The important question for the study of second-generation West Indians is whether it is possible for a voluntary immigrant group to evolve into an involuntary minority group. Second-generation West Indians can be seen as possibly developing an immigrant or ethnic identity like their parents or an oppositional identity like their black American peers.

Most research on segmented assimilation stresses differences between groups—for instance, Sikhs do well by remaining Sikh, Haitians do poorly by becoming American blacks. Outcomes, however, vary within groups as well as across groups. Chinese are more likely to develop immigrant ethnicities and less likely to adopt adversarial or oppositional stances than, say, Puerto Ricans. But individual Puerto Ricans achieve socioeconomic and scholastic success, while some Chinese Americans develop an oppositional frame of reference, as the violent youth gang culture of many American Chinatowns clearly attests.

What accounts for variation within groups? Ogbu's caste theory has difficulty in accounting for group variance within oppressed ethnic minorities. Douglas Foley finds a strong class difference among Mexican American youth in southern Texas, with upwardly mobile Mexican American students capable of maintaining some aspects of an oppositional identity, yet succeeding academically and valuing academic success in a way that working-class Mexican American youth values do not allow.[17] Sociologist Robert Smith finds intraethnic variance among second-generation Mexican youth in New York City.[18] He argues that some are developing oppositional frames of reference and are less likely to be successful in the labor market, while others are maintaining ties to their parents' networks, values, and organizations, thereby easing their incorporation into American society. Indeed, some of the literature suggests that the degree to which the second generation maintains transnational economic and political ties to the country of origin may well have a significant influence on its mode of incorporation into the United States.[19]

The following chapters explore the factors affecting West Indian immigrants as they raise their families in the United States. They describe the experiences of these second-generation families and ask which factors sort families into being successful or unsuccessful in their attempts at social mobility. How do families who hold high aspirations for their children translate those aspirations into outcomes? Why do some young people fail in school and in the labor market, despite the hard work, good social values, and desperate hopes of their parents? What are the particular social factors that undermine or strengthen the ties between parents and children in particular families?

This chapter describes the positive and negative factors in American society that affect the chances for success of the immigrants and their children. I explore how the immigration process itself, along with American cultural values about family, individualism, and materialism, affect the Caribbean family. In Chapter 7 I explore the role of racial discrimination and the disinvestment of American society in inner-city neighborhoods and institutions, particularly schools. Chapter 8 looks closely at the relationship between ethnic and racial identity and gender and social class, and shows how becoming American for many second-generation youth is indeed associated with less success in American life.

THE SECOND-GENERATION SAMPLE

To examine these issues I draw on interviews with adolescent and young-adult West Indian Americans as well as interviews with the schoolteachers and the food-service workers who were parents. The second-generation sample included eighty-three adolescents drawn from four sources designed to tap a range of class backgrounds and class trajectories. They include:

1. The public school sample: teenagers attending two public inner-city high schools in Brooklyn, New York, where I did extensive interviewing and participant observation (forty-five interviews).
2. The church and church school-sample: teenagers attending Catholic parochial schools or a Catholic after-school program in the same inner-city neighborhood as the public schools, although most of these students were not themselves Catholic (fourteen interviews).
3. The street-based snowball sample: teenagers living in the same inner-city neighborhood in Brooklyn who could not be reached through a school, either because they had dropped out or because they would not have responded to interviews conducted in a formal setting (fifteen interviews).
4. The middle-class snowball sample: teenagers who had ties to this neighborhood, who either were living there now and attending

magnet schools or colleges outside of the district, or whose families had since moved to other areas of the city or to suburbs (nine interviews).

The two inner-city schools where I and my research assistants interviewed forty-five adolescents were also the locations for most of our teacher interviews. We spent several months in these high schools, which we call Eisenhower and Truman High Schools to protect their real identities. Both of these Brooklyn high schools were troubled places with high drop-out rates, numerous incidents of violence, and crumbling physical plants. In addition to the formal interviews with both teachers and students, we spent enough time, particularly at Eisenhower High School, to do ethnographic observation and to develop relationships with administrators, teachers, and students.

The young people we spoke to included teens who were facing very limited socioeconomic mobility or downward social mobility (respondents we found in the inner-city public schools and the surrounding neighborhood), students who were on an upward social trajectory and had a high chance of going to college (respondents we found in the church groups in the inner city), and teens whose families were doing well and who themselves seemed to have bright futures (respondents we found in suburban, middle-class neighborhoods). Overall, thirteen (16%) of the eighty-three teens were from very poor families on public assistance, forty (48%) were from families with at least one parent working at a low-wage job, and thirty (36%) were from middle-class families with at least one parent in a job requiring a college degree. The ages of respondents ranged from 14 to 27. The average age was 18. The vast majority were ages 16 to 18. We interviewed young people who had spent at least three years in the United States and who had immigrated before age 16. They included thirty-six (43%) who comprise the classic second generation—born in the United States of immigrant parents. Another eleven (13%) immigrated to the United States before age 7. The rest of the sample included thirty-six young people who had immigrated at or after age 7 and had spent at least three years in the United States. The actual age at immigration for these more recent immigrants varied from 7 to 15.[20] My sample probably overestimates the percentage of 1.5-generation West Indians relative to the second generation because I interviewed teenagers and young adults. In the United States as a whole 75% of all children in immigrant families are U.S.-born, 25% fall in the 1.5 generation.[21] Among West Indians ages 1 to 17 in the New York metropolitan area in 1990, 17% were 1.5 generation and 83% were born in the United States. Yet among West Indians ages 18 to 30, 46% were born abroad and immigrated as children or teenagers.[22] In my sample 44% of the teens and young adults immigrated at or after age 7. If I had studied children ages 1 to 17, I would have spoken to far fewer of the 1.5 generation. The respondents' national origins reflect the overall patterns in New York as a whole. The demographic distribution was reported in Table 1.3.

WEST INDIAN FAMILIES

There are some resources available to West Indian families that allow them to protect their children from the worst aspects of American city life. The most important positive factor in the lives of the people I spoke with was the church. Many belonged to an ethnically rooted church, which was comprised of West Indians or often just of people from a particular island. In addition to providing spiritual support, the ethnic churches reinforced parents' ties with other immigrants. These ties between parents are a source of aid and comfort for teenagers. Belonging to a church gives adolescents access to adults other than their parents. Many of the churches also ran peer discussion and recreation groups, which reinforced parental values. A few fundamentalist storefront churches attracted a combination of immigrants and Americans. These churches gave social support to parents and a sense of identity and belonging to the adolescents; many had very active teen and adult programs to ease the transition into life in the United States. Pastors and priests served as sounding boards for parents and teens alike—often cajoling parents into accepting some aspects of the "Americanization" of their teens, while basically upholding the overall values of the parents, which stressed hard work, stability, education, and striving for upward mobility. The key factor appears to be the combination of connecting both parents and teens to social networks that reinforce their values and attitudes as well as the moral and cultural reinforcement that church teachings provide for the messages parents give to their children.

A second positive source of support for parents and children alike were ethnic voluntary organizations.[23] A very small number of people I talked to were active members of ethnic voluntary organizations such as Caribbean clubs. Among middle-class respondents there was some membership in professional or campus-based organizations. For instance, some teachers were members of on-campus Caribbean clubs when they attended Brooklyn College or Queens College. These professional organizations were a source of support for individuals but because they were not multigenerational in their memberships, they did not have the same ability as churches to provide both sounding boards and support for parents as well as networks of like-minded people for teens. While a very small number of the first-generation respondents said they were actively involved in any ethnic organizations, many more, about half, participated in events like dances or sporting events sponsored by these organizations.

The exception to this limited participation was the Labor Day Parade, which was a nearly universal experience.[24] For those people who were involved in designing and building floats or booths, the organization could provide some positive benefits, but all of the respondents in this study were casual consumers of the festivities. They attended the parade and enjoyed the music and food and the expression of ethnic pride, but it did not lead to ongoing involvement in ethnic activities. Some of the boys were on cricket teams, and a number of people reported that they attended the games. These organizations also provided a solid reinforcement of the identities of the second generation as West Indians and also fostered values focused on social mobility. However, unlike the churches, the ethnic organizations did not offer much intergenerational membership and contact. Those who were very active tended to get social support for their participation, but there was no guarantee that the second generation would remain members of the organizations if their parents were also members.

Serial Migration

Americans often imagine the immigration of a family as Mom, Dad, three kids, and some suitcases arriving together on a boat or a plane. This is very rarely true. Many of the families of the second-generation respondents were families headed by single women, reflecting the prevalence of this family form in the Caribbean.[25] Yet even for those Caribbean families we interviewed that were headed by two spouses, in most cases their migration happened sequentially. Of the fifty-three teens interviewed who had not been born in the United States, only three had arrived with both their parents and brothers and sisters as a family unit directly from the islands. One other respondent had arrived together with his parents and brothers and sisters, but from England where they had emigrated and lived first before deciding to come to the United States. Another seven were from households headed by females back in the West Indies. These teens arrived with their mothers and brothers and sisters, and they never lived with their fathers.

The remaining families we have information on (thirty-four families)[26] were split up for some period of time because of the migration process. This process can sometimes take longer than a decade. The children are sometimes left behind with the parent who does not immigrate or more commonly with other relatives, often a grandmother or aunt.

Sometimes the leaving behind of children or the sending of children to stay with a relative or friend instead of the biological parent is intentional and not related to migration dynamics. This is called "child fostering," and it has a long tradition in the Caribbean. In a society where migration has been the norm for over a century, including rural-urban, interisland, and now island to the United States, child fostering has been an accepted way of life. In a study on the prevalence of West Indian child fostering, anthropologist Esther Goody argues that while child fostering is sometimes purposive (for example, in order to send a child to a good school), it is most often a response to some sort of crisis: "the rearing of children by kin in the West Indies tends to be the result of the inability of the parents to provide proper care (whether because they have no joint home or because the mother must work full time)."[27] Under the typical arrangement such children live with their mother's mother or mother's sister. This is not adoption—the biological mother retains the right to reclaim her child. Yet the child who grows up with a grandmother in the role of mother does have a different relationship with his or her mother than one who has been brought up by the biological mother. Goody notes that these children "cannot be depended upon by the mother in her later years in the same way as one she has reared herself."[28]

The immigrants we talked with described both intentional and more crisis-driven child fostering. It is a commonly held belief among the immigrants that the United States is a bad place to raise young children but a place of educational opportunity for older ones, so sometimes children will be left behind on purpose when a parent decides to immigrate. Even if parents want their children with them in New York, the cost and scarcity of good day care often necessitate that children be left behind with a grandmother or aunt. This could be seen as migration-driven child fostering. Intentional child fostering was most commonly for educational purposes. Some of the academically successful immigrant children in the high schools had attended good urban secondary schools in Kingston or Port of Spain because their parents had purposely sent them to live with relatives who resided near the good schools while the parents either lived in rural areas or immigrated to New York. Many of the young adult parents we spoke with had themselves spent part of their childhoods living with their grandparents or aunts while their biological parents were living elsewhere.

Because of its prevalence child fostering is not seen as much of an aberration in the Caribbean. Adults who had been raised primarily by an aunt or a grandmother said that they did not recall feeling "abandoned" by their mothers or stigmatized among their friends. It was a common, and therefore a normal, living situation. Yet the migration experience begins to challenge those norms and creates conditions in which child fostering does have an effect on relations between generations. Serial migration and intentional child fostering both lead to a situation in which the biological parent is not the primary caretaker of the child in early childhood. Most reunions of children and biological parents occur in early adolescence—at junior high school or high school age—often because schooling ends for all but the most gifted students much earlier in the islands than it does in the United States, or because the parents have had time to establish themselves economically before sending for their children.[29] The reunion of young teenagers with parents they barely know can cause some problems between the generations when parents try to establish firm discipline over children they have spent very little time with or often have not seen for over five or six years. One food-service worker, who immigrated at age 16 to live with her mother in New York after growing up with her grandmother in Trinidad, describes the conflicts she had with her mother:

> I lived with my grandmother. It was like, when I was twelve years old my grandmother trust me to go to a party. And when she said be back by ten o'clock, I will come back because I will like to go again, see? But my mother, if I go out, she like she don't trust me. She want to tell me I can't go, if I ask to go somewhere, I can't go. [Because of this] I don't want to stay here no more, I want to go back home. But she says, well this is your home now, you know? So I cried. I cried. I figured if I cried a lot and get sick, she will send me back. So she did send me back—for a year. And then I decided that I wanted to come back up here. (Trinidadian female, age 29, in United States thirteen years)

Yet even though this young woman had such a difficult time living with her mother after their long migration-induced separation, she is currently *intentionally* fostering her young son with her mother in Brooklyn. She lives in East Flatbush and her mother lives in Bedford-Stuyvesant. Her 6-year-old son "does not like living with her," so she sent him to live with her mother one neighborhood away. She thought this was best for him because she had been raised by her grandmother and it seemed a normal, natural thing.

Often these reunions of parents and their children cause problems in the opposite direction than what one might expect. Instead of generational conflict owing to "Americanized" children confronting old-fashioned parents, sometimes the behavior of "Americanized" parents horrifies their newly arrived children. For instance, in one of the schools where I did fieldwork the guidance counselor showed me a letter she received from a tenth-grader who had grown up in the Jamaican countryside with a very strict and religious grandmother. She had recently come to live with her mother, who drank and took drugs and slept around. This young woman was scandalized by her mother's behavior and when she complained to her mother, she was severely beaten. The letter to the guidance counselor described her mother's behavior as "immoral" and asked that she be sent back to her grandmother in Jamaica.

When they are reunited after a long separation, parents and children encounter one another as strangers. Many of the students reported that they learned when they came to the United States that it is not right for a parent to leave a child behind with a grandmother, that it means that the parent does not love the child and that this is "abandonment." Often the parent cannot understand that "American" idea, for the mother herself might have been raised by her grandmother. Social psychologists working with West Indian families blame this separation for many of the strains these families face and tie these strains to teen delinquency in some cases.[30]

Indeed, the teachers in the high schools described the amount of moves and different family situations that teens had to deal with as a major source of tension and stress in the lives of these young people. Often by the time a parent is ready to send for the child left behind in the islands, that parent has found a new partner, and the child not only has to become acquainted or reacquainted with a parent he or she may have never lived with but adjust to a stepparent as well. The living situations get very complicated, including divorces and remarriages. Often the children get caught up in those problems, and their living situations become precarious. Since many of the teachers perceive child fostering and the family separations that result from serial migration as a major cause of intergenerational conflict, they are particularly frustrated when parents threaten their children with being sent back to the islands if they misbehave:

> They have this wonderful banishment, these island people. They bring their children here, and these are a child who is sixteen, seventeen, and you put him in a school that he is not prepared to be in anyway, and he really does not know what to make of it because in the islands you call everyone Miss or Sir and you are polite and so on, and here, teachers yell at the students and students yell back. And they see all these things going on, and within a few months, or a year at most, they have totally changed. Since many of them are not really prepared academically, they begin to follow the lower elements. The kids who cut class, the kids who hang out in the halls. The kids who do possible criminal things and so

on. And when we call their parents into the school, the parents
don't wish to be bothered. Many of them. They will try for a little
bit, but if it doesn't work—they've been here for many years,
they have their own lives, they have their own jobs—they send
the kids back to grandma, or wherever he's come from. And
that's it.

Q: Do the kids want to go back?

A: Oh, most of the time, they do not. That is the ultimate threat.
(White female teacher, age 47)

In a 1967 study of West Indians in Great Britain, psychologists J. P.
Graham and C. E. Meadows found a much higher rate of antisocial behavior among the West Indian boys as opposed to a matched group of white
boys. They attributed this antisocial behavior to the West Indian boys
having all been separated from their parents during the migration process;
most had been left in the islands with their maternal grandmothers.
Graham and Meadows argued that when the children were reunited with
their parents, "they had experienced two separations, one from their
parents and one from their parental substitute. Once reunited with their
parents the children denied recognizing their parents, professed a primary
attachment to the parental substitute, and expressed hostility at being
taken away from their parental substitute."[31]

More in-depth psychological research should be done on this issue to
determine the degree to which separation is the root of any problems
children later develop. Yet it is clear that in the United States at least it is
far less common for children to be fostered away from their mothers, and
the teens in this study learned that very quickly. The reunions of parents
and children that occurred when the children were teenagers often included charges by the teens that their parents had "abandoned" them by
leaving them behind in the islands.

Child Care and Work Hours

While the problems of serial migration and child fostering only affect
immigrant children, the problems of child care and supervision affect all
children of immigrants, regardless of where they were born. The much-
vaunted immigrant ethos of hard work and saving also can cause some

difficult problems that undermine the ability of the children of the immigrants to succeed. Many of the parents of the teens I interviewed worked long hours at low-paying jobs. The mothers were often home health aides or cleaned offices and homes. They worked long shifts, often at night. The fathers were security guards, maintenance men, or cab drivers. It was very common for these parents to work two or more jobs. In fact, many respondents pointed with pride to the TV show *In Living Color,* which had a Jamaican character who was satirically described as having twenty-eight jobs. The immigrants thought the depiction of the hard-working Jamaican was accurate; they missed the satire.

Yet when both parents or a single parent works, there is often no parent at home for the children. Even if a grandmother or other extended family member is present, such relatives often work long hours too. This is very unlike their life in the islands, where most children had an adult looking after them during the day and night. That person might not have been a parent, but most immigrants stressed that at home neighbors, extended family members, and even strangers in their town or neighborhood would take responsibility for watching out for and disciplining children and teens:

> In Guyana we were taught to respect people. Like you live in a neighborhood and people know your parents. If they see you doing something wrong, they will scold you on the street and then they will tell your parents. And your parents would ask you, and if it comes to that you have to get a spanking, you get a spanking. But over here, the American mothers, you can't approach them and tell them, well you know I see Shawn was doing such and such. They'll tell you, "No, not my Shawn." And see that's where the children know that they were doing it, but their parents are there to say no, they weren't doing it, and that's where things get out of hand.
>
> Q: Now do you do that here, look out for other people's children?
> A: Well, to be honest with you, I don't really mix with people here, 'cause I don't have the time. And my kids, when I was living in Flatbush, my mother was living close by and we were a close-knit family. Mostly I would just go visit my mother with the kids.

> They [the children] had their friends and stuff, but like for me to
> have a set of friends to visit, no. (Guyanese female worker, age
> 48, in United States twelve years)

Note that while this woman laments the loss of community responsibility for children that she left behind in Guyana, the circumstances and structure of her life in New York mean that she cannot, or will not, create the web of relationships and friendships she found to be so comforting back home.

Most working parents scraped together money for day care for young children when a relative was unable to care for them. Family or group day care was the normal arrangement. In many families the older children were put in charge of the younger ones as soon as they were able. Teenagers were almost always on their own for some part of the day when both parents worked—often in the case of home health aides, the teenagers would run the house and watch their brothers and sisters when the mother worked as a live-in health aide somewhere else:

> I worry about this coming second generation in this country. I have
> seen kids come in with the strict discipline and then they realize
> what goes on here. And everything about them changes. And it's
> unfortunate but this is what happens. The parents are working and
> they can't supervise them. A woman came in last week and she has
> four children. I think they are eleven, ten, fifteen, and eighteen. And
> because she is undocumented, the only type of employment she was
> able to get was sleep away, where she might be off two days out of
> the week. And there's a lot of responsibility on the part of the
> eighteen-year-old to take care of the other three siblings. And it
> turned out the eighteen-year-old got pregnant. And it's hard, if you
> are working like that. What are you going to do? It's a hard situation.
> (Barbadian male teacher, age 43, born in United States)

For many of the immigrants the adage "it takes a village to raise a child" was literally true back home. This must have been one of the most stark contrasts between island life and life in the United States because it was mentioned repeatedly by the teens we interviewed in response to the question, "What did your parents tell you about what it was like back in the islands?" All of the islands were similarly described by parents to their children as having communal child rearing:

Q: What did your mother tell you about life in Grenada?

A: It's a great place to grow up because you can always run outside and play with your friends. You don't have to worry about gangs and things like that. And if you're in trouble, some adult will stop and help you. If you're doing something wrong, an adult will stop and correct you no matter if they don't know you or anything. They will stop and take the time out. (Grenadian male, age 17, in United States fourteen years)

While the parents, and a few of their children, nostalgically describe a community that helps parents to raise children well, this American-born Trinidadian girl perceives in a negative way the much stricter social control that she would experience were she back in her father's homeland:

I went to Trinidad once, but I would not want to live there. I like New York. New York is better—there it's too hot, and that discipline thing is not gonna work for me.

Q: What is different about the discipline?

A: I mean, talk about torture. I mean, they will beat you for nothing. And wait till you go home. You get it from your neighbor. And the person, he don't even know you. Across the street, all over. My father was explaining to me, you know. One day he made a mistake and he was walking, right? And he didn't say good morning ma'am to this woman. He didn't even know this woman. Do you know that so and so didn't say good morning? Got a beating from his mom, his dad, everybody. The woman did it. They real strict there. (Trinidadian female, age 17, born in United States)

One of the teachers eloquently described how many teens quickly learn that the anonymity and scale of life in New York provide them with a kind of freedom they could not have experienced in the islands:

The kids think that being American means having *freedom*. That is the big thing, freedom. The parents think the kids have way too much freedom. The kids very quickly learn that they want the individualism of America. No one in terms of the community has any control over them. Quickly they say when they first arrive, "You mean no one from my village can tell me what to do?" They come from a place where everyone would know one another, and other people besides the parents could discipline the children. But when they come to the United States, they realize that no one can have authority over them. The kids very quickly adapt to this. They quickly learn that their parents don't have the same authority and social control that they had in the islands. They cannot articulate it the way I would now, but they have moved from a place where there are interlocking institutions, connections so that they are not on their own. They realize that is not true here, and so they are much freer to do what they want. The biggest threat the parents have that we see in the schools is that "we will send them back home." That is what the parents threaten the kids with. For the kids that is the most awful thing because they see being sent back home as being sent to prison. It is a closed society. The kids say, "You mean everyone will know what I do?" (White male teacher, age 45)

Parents who worried about the future outcomes of their children and who saw the difficulties that American children faced blamed those difficulties on the lack of supervision of children, yet they had no answers about how to do it better:

In America, the other problem is, most parents, mother and father, have to work. That leaves the children, most times, to themselves. They have nobody really to sit down to discuss their problems with them, because by the time the parents reach home, they have to do this, do that, it's time for them to go again. You see? That's why in Guyana most women do not work at all, because somebody must be there to have time for the bringing up of the child. So I think that is one of the things which is creating lots of problems with the young children in America today. (Guyanese male worker, age 39, in United States six years)

To me, the problem is that the children are on their own. I taught school back in Trinidad, but when I came home I had to say, where is your homework? Here, I can see the result of the lack of parental guidance. West Indian parents in America now are under the stress of the way of life here. They cannot accommodate that need in their children. They work two, three jobs, yes. Even if they were working one job, sometimes, it's a shift job where they don't see their children. I think also there is a certain, shall we say, loosening of the bonds. For example, children of fifteen being out on the street until ten or eleven o'clock at night. You couldn't see that at home. This is something that also is a cultural shock. (Trinidadian female teacher, age 63, in United States ten years)

Parents who are working all the time, often at two jobs, in order to give their children a better life realize that without adult supervision they are at risk of losing their children to the "street culture" of their neighborhoods. These parents express dismay, anger, and bewilderment that the children do not appreciate or understand their sacrifices when the children don't behave as the parents hope. Yet even though the children often need the social support of the parents in the home far more than they need the material goods the parents are striving for, both the parents and the children are often caught in a relentless race to acquire more material goods.

Materialism

The materialism of American culture poses clear difficulties for these West Indian families, both in terms of the challenges the new-found freedoms to pursue individual gain pose for the adult members of the family, and in terms of the wedge driven between parents and children by the teens' desire for expensive material goods.

Many people commented on the lack of community they felt in the United States. This loss was felt most acutely in terms of the supports that a strong community provides for family values and child care:

The only observation I have to make about family values is that I think a lot of us come here to America and we lose it. The things that used to be important to you as a family, a lot of people come here and it's slipping away. It's not important anymore. And I don't know if it is to get ahead or the money—you have to make the money—why you slack on some of the things that are important. I don't know because we Jamaicans have a really strong family unity where you always in touch with your aunts and uncles. And I don't know of it's the system that doesn't allow you to do it, like if you don't have a phone, you don't hear from me. And children are growing up, nobody is teaching real values anymore. They're not holding on to them. Then again you really can't say Americans are to blame, because some of the things I disagree with here are being done by people who come from West Indies and come here and forget, you know. People who come here and do certain things different from what they're accustomed to—no values, no more morals, and they say, "Oh these Americans do this, let me check it out." They're growing up in other places where they used to have values. (Jamaican female teacher, age 37, in United States seven years)

The stress on individual success and accountability is contrasted with an ethic many immigrants recall from home that stressed family unity and social support:

West Indian family, they stick together. I find that when you come up here and you see the American family, everyone is for themselves. They don't always try to help their sisters or their brothers. It's like everybody try to get where they have to get first before they might help their brothers and sisters. Depends on the family. Depends on the way they were brought up. But the Guyanese you would try to help a brother or sister. You know, because everybody would come and stay in one apartment until they could branch out. But you wouldn't find that most of the time with American families. (Guyanese female worker, age 29, in United States nine years)

This individualism at the expense of family togetherness is experienced in a number of ways; often it is hard for people to articulate how their family life is different, but they are sure it is. One clear difference a number of people commented on is the custom of children moving out of the home at age 18 in the United States, and of parents no longer having responsibility to provide for their young-adult offspring:

Here, here I noticed, your parents more like to get you out on your own fast. Go out there and pay your bills and take your own responsibilities. Hold up your own socks. I done with you. I take care of you for these years and that's it. You know? Because my son gonna be five tomorrow and I be just telling him, I have to take care of you until you is eighteen. I been telling him that already. So, it's kind of funny, you know. Family values I see here are appreciate your family, but when it is time for them to be on they own, they on they own. (Trinidadian female worker, age 30, in United States ten years)

But the culprit many people regard as the most destructive of family values was the desire for money and material gain and the concomitant requirement to spend time away from family at work. This grandmother issued an impassioned plea for immigrants to forget about material gain in order to take care of their children:

When they're here the children are being destroyed because they have to be left unprotected, unsupervised, no time to give them love. Guyana you had what was richer than money. Money, you have today, is gone tomorrow. But you have memories, you have a culture, you have this love, this warmth, that no one can take away from you, and that is what is being destroyed with the new immigrant children right here on this street. When they [the parents] come here, they have no time for the children, they have to continue to work until they die repairing those children . . . Cut your eyes from the American gaiety, look at the children, give them that solid background and love and what you call this confidence, and this reassurance that you are there for them. (Guyanese retired woman, age 72)[32]

All American families are dealing with pressures on their time and finances as two-earner couples become the norm as families strive to maintain a decent standard of living while declining wages make that impossible to do on one salary.[33] But immigrant families face these issues sometimes for the first time because of the nuclearization of the family in the United States. Immigrant families also face some unique pressures stemming from the human dynamics of the often drawn-out immigration process itself.

When the children were back on the islands, one of the ways the parents maintained ties was sending back money and material goods. Indeed, Jamaican social workers coined the term "barrel children" to refer to the children left behind in the islands who receive barrels filled with goods from their parents in America.[34] Long before the children arrive in the United States, they want the fashionable clothes that they have seen people wear in the islands, which have been given to them by relatives in the United States, or that affluent people have bought on the islands:

> The schools don't need to Americanize the kids, because they come with that already. Because they have that copycat idea. Whatever is in America is good for us. They wear big tall boots in Trinidad. Winter boots. You know all year round we have hot weather, but it's the fashion and the style. They see it on the TV and it sells. And when they come up here, they buy the clothes—you know I was surprised to see these sweaters or sweatshirts with the hood that you wear because of the wind and the cold. They would have them in Trinidad. They don't know where to put them on. But they buy them regardless of whether it's suitable or not for their climate. So I don't think it's because they're here. It's because they want to be American. It starts at home, in Trinidad, in the West Indies. (Trinidadian teacher, age 63, in United States ten years)

The media also lead these teens to expect easy access to expensive material goods. One teacher described newly arrived young teens "with *Falcon Crest* and *Dallas* in their heads and they come here and they see the project they will live in and they say, well where is America? Where are the white people?" The parents are proud of the access they now have in the United States to consumer goods that were way beyond their means on the islands. So these hard-working parents have a tendency to want to buy their children material goods:

> Child see a bicycle and they want it, and the parents will put out the effort to give them. What I see back in Jamaica if you want a bicycle, I don't have the money to buy it. It have to just stay, be-

cause you don't have the money to buy it. But here, a child say they want that. The mother always try to give it to them. I don't know why, but they always get it.

Q: Do you think that it's good for the parent to give them the bicycle?

A: Yeah, I feel that. If they want it. 'Cause you see up here, it's easier to buy than back home. (Jamaican female worker, age 37, in United States three years)

On the other hand, the dollar that went so far and the one pair of sneakers that meant so much back home are a drop in the bucket in the United States where small paychecks do not allow the parents to bestow all the material things the kids want, especially fancy clothes for school. One middle-class teen was relatively well-off in Jamaica, but when he came to the United States, he was laughed at by the other kids because he did not have the "right" clothes:

In Jamaica I wasn't that rich. But it's like compared to my other neighbors I might consider myself middle class or whatever. But over here, the hardest thing is going down and see most people just being better off than you. It's going around without having new clothes or not having more money in your pocket or whatever. (Jamaican male, age 16, in United States seven years)

Part of becoming American for these teens is to expect expensive consumer goods, such as fashionable clothes and jewelry, from parents. The parents tend to see these expectations as unreasonable. The teens in turn interpret their parents as refusing to support them in the "American way" that the parents themselves led the children to expect through the economic remittances that preceded their sending for the children. This difference between the expectations of the children and the limited resources available for the hard-working parents leads to an increased susceptibility on the part of the teens to the underground economy. For instance, this teacher describes the pressures hard-working parents face:

A lot of the parents came here and they were working, even doing domestic jobs, to send money home for these children. So they struggling to get a lot of, you know, rich things compared to the other citizens in their country. Once the kids arrived here, they are so accustomed to getting these fancy things that they no longer strive, because it's there. Right? Whereas the parent—a parent told me about a month ago, she said, her child is asking her for a pair of sneakers and it cost a hundred and ten dollars. And she said, you see this pair of shoes I have on? I paid $3.99 for it at Robby's. Now here she's trying her best so she can save the money to buy this for her child. The kids' values change once they're here. They want everything big and fancy. They no longer accept simple things. (Jamaican female teacher, age 36, in United States seven years)

The teachers we spoke with described the intense peer pressures in the high school to dress very fashionably and expensively. For the poor students who just arrive, as one teacher puts it, everyday is Christmas, given the array of material goods that they see available in the United States:

I think it is the availability of so many things, when many things were not available to them before. It's that sudden explosion of Christmas everyday. Christmas everyday, that they are able to buy whatever they want, that they can have so much freedom. These are the great things that this country offers. And unfortunately, materialism is so emphasized that that sometimes is also a downfall. The need to have status items, clothing, automobiles, in particular that they feel that they must have in order to be recognized or to blend in. (White male teacher, age 35)

Indeed, teachers stated that they could tell how long a child has been in the United States by the degrees to which they have adopted expensive American dressing habits.

At the same time that the immigrant parents are scrimping and saving, the easy money of drugs is all around the immigrants in the inner-city neighborhoods they inhabit in Brooklyn. Another incident from my fieldwork makes this clear. One of the math teachers told me he was teaching a remedial class for mostly immigrant teenagers from the Caribbean. He wanted to make a point in math class about interest and decided to try to make it something the students could relate to. He described how he bought his car with a loan, and tried to involve the students in figuring out how to calculate the interest that would be due on his loan. The class's response was laughter—one of their classmates had a much fancier car that had been bought with cash, cash made in the underground drug economy. This teacher told this story to emphasize the degree to which the easy money of drugs undermines the authority of the older generation in the eyes of the younger generation. Parents look like chumps for working so hard at low-paid service sector jobs if their children do not look down on the attractions of the underground economy.

So both the immigrant parental generation and the adolescents associate "becoming American" with access to consumer goods and full participation in a materialist culture. Yet the parents' immigrant metric of what constitutes a good job and a way to gain those material advantages is not shared by their children, many of whom come to expect an easier and simpler way to make it rich in America, such as the underground drug economy that is readily available to them:

> I think that the longer that people are here, the more accustomed they get to the American values. Some of them are positive, naturally. The desire to make money encourages people to become doctors and lawyers and these are very positive. However, the negative things, the pleasure-oriented things that you have in American society, the mass media, the idea of lack of respect for other people, the brashness, the arrogance. This is picked up absolutely. And in addition there's also the drug problem. Larger number of kids who are from West Indian populations are getting involved. And that will just kill a culture. Kids who have never been exposed to this over there become exposed to it over here, and this has a dramatic effect on the parents as well. (White male teacher, age 40)

The question of whether youngsters' ambitions and desires for material goods will be channeled into an academic orientation that will lead them to careers as doctors and lawyers or a present-time orientation that will lead them to short-sighted material gratification and possible involvement in criminal activities will be explored further in Chapter 8. The point to be made here is that for all of the positive things that America's culture of individualism and consumerism brings to these immigrant families, it also brings real challenges to their sense of community, their family values, and relations between the generations. The flashpoint in the West Indian community for disputes between the generations and conflicts between American and West Indian cultural values about family is the disciplining of children.

Discipline

The parents we spoke with believe that physical punishment is the best way to deal with a child who has misbehaved. They are shocked that this is unacceptable in the United States, and consistently told us that it was one of the most disturbing aspects of living in this country. Over and over again, among the middle-class and the working-class immigrants, the issue of corporal punishment and its apparent unacceptability in the United States was described as a very serious problem. That the state can dictate that a parent cannot beat a child is seen by these parents as a real threat to their ability to raise their children correctly. Parental discipline of children was most often mentioned in responses to the very general questions, "How is the United States different from your country?" or "What do you miss the most about your country?" I was very surprised by these answers, as I had expected people to describe the beautiful weather or particular foods or celebrations. Discipline, however, was clearly an issue that was very much on people's minds:

> Q: How was New York different from Guyana?
> A: New York is very different from our country. For instance, the training. Back home, we beat our kids. Over here, you can't beat your kids. It's child abuse. That's the first thing they want to say. Right? You know, well whenever our kids do wrong, something wrong, we beat them. We punish them too. You know and even in the schools, right, our schools, they beat the kids. But over here, the schooling, they don't beat the kids . . . I think it's very bad. I think they should beat the kids. To me, they learn better that way. (Guyanese female worker, age 37, in United States eight years)

> Q: Is there anything you miss about your country?
> A: Well yes, I'm not accustomed to the cold. The other thing is you come up here, it's different in bringing up your kids. Number one, you know, you have no control of them than when you were

back home. This is different when they are here. The people used to say, don't spare the rod and spoil the child. You know, teachers would scold them, and would be able to handle them. But I wouldn't advise anyone to bring their kids up in this town. Always live in the country until they reach an age, then you bring them in; if they choose to work and go to college, then they take it from there. But it's very hard for you to have control of your kids in this city. They adopt the American styles real fast. Back home they were more restricted. And here you find if you try to put pressure on them they become rebellious.

Q: But back there, they wouldn't?

A: No, you know, you would slap them. And you could be more stern with them. Even the teachers and so on at the school, they were able to slap them. They were afraid of that. But here it's different. It's not the American way. Because the first thing, when you beat them, you hear child brutality and things like that. I am kind of afraid of that. (Guyanese female worker, age 38, in United States nine years)

A teacher gave his opinion:

As they say, don't spare the rod and spoil the child. But in this system, if you do that, the child can call the police and you will be in trouble. So that's why some of the parents are finding it hard and the kids know it. They know what they can get away with and they play it into trouble and then what are you gonna do? You're gonna beat them and they'll call the police. 'Cause I, at open school night, I was speaking to parents and he told me one of the kids did call the police. But I guess after talking to the police, the police, I think, give them a warning. Said the next time they would have to press charges. And he's telling me you know because he's from Trinidad and the kid was born there and the kid stays out late, coming in at eleven, twelve in the night. On the telephone all the time and he's talking and not listening. I mean, you could talk, talk, talk so far, and then, when time come to punishment what are you going to do? Can't lock him in the house. You gonna open the door and go out. Now if you lock him out, and if they're under age, the police gonna bring them back. You have to take

them? With my kids I am on them very hard. (Trinidadian male
teacher, age 41, in United States eighteen years)

The issue of corporal punishment came up in two contexts—the issue
of whether parents should be allowed to hit or beat their children, and the
issue of whether teachers and other school personnel should be allowed to
hit children. Both were explosive issues that immigrants experienced as the
most difficult and extreme cultural difference they encountered in moving
to the United States. In fact, I believe that the issue of corporal punishment
in the home and the schools and the wider philosophical differences about
child rearing that this issue touches on represent the key behavioral and
cultural change that assimilation to America calls for among West Indian
people. It is a widely discussed, contentious issue in the public schools and
in the West Indian community. It brings many West Indian immigrants
into direct conflict with the American state, in the form of the Department
of Social Services. And, like the contentious issues of Muslim girls wearing
scarves in French schools or male African immigrants who have more than
one wife, the issue of corporal punishment brings up very hard questions
for multiculturalists. West Indians see corporal punishment as an integral
part of their culture and as the best way to raise their children. How then
do we reconcile respect for that culture with the duty of the American state
to protect the welfare of children?

While the immigrants and their children believe that it is illegal in New
York for parents to hit their children at all, the law does not outlaw
spanking. It does prohibit excessive force, and teachers are required to
report parents if they leave any mark or welt on their children.

Strictness in dealings between parents and children does seem to be a
key component of West Indian culture. It has been commented on by a
number of scholars who have studied West Indians both at home and in
the United States.[35] In fact, the former Prime Minister of Jamaica, Edward
Seaga, in his earlier life as an anthropologist wrote an article on the use of
corporal punishment in the schools of a rural Jamaican village.[36] David
Lowenthal noted that corporal punishment was an accepted, even taken-
for-granted, aspect of West Indian child rearing:

Upbringing is felt to require physical chastisement; parents regularly
resort to the rod. Outsiders may interpret frequent beatings as

symptoms of parental insecurity, but West Indians consider them normal and appropriate. Flogging is considered essential not only for effective punishment but for education; teachers vie with parents as disciplinarians. Beatings are no evidence of cruelty, opines a local authority; people of nearly all classes in Jamaica who are very violent with children at any other given moment are often at other times very loving and warmhearted.[37]

West Indians are not the first or the only immigrant group to experience these challenges to their methods of child rearing. Historian Selma Berrol describes the same friction between parents and children and the same concerns of social service agencies about Italian and other southern and central European families in the beginning of the twentieth century:[38]

When a son criticized the decor at home for being too Italian, his father beat him. This was also the fate of a daughter in another family who came home later than the hour her father had specified. One young girl attempted to wear lipstick at age 13, which brought about a harsh scrubbing from her mother. Resentment at such treatment sometimes escalated into crisis; even if their youth and poverty forced them to stay at home, immigrant children left their parents in terms of culture, behavior, and affection.[39]

The West Indians' perception that Americans don't hit their children is actually mistaken, yet it does pick up on recent changes in norms about corporal punishment in the United States. According to sociologists Murray Straus and Denise Donnelly,[40] the laws in all fifty states give parents the right to hit a child with an object provided no serious injury results. Figures on the prevalence of corporal punishment[41] show that 90% of toddlers had experienced some form of corporal punishment, and 52% of the adult population of the United States recalled having experienced corporal punishment as a teenager.[42] Yet Murray Straus and Anita Mathur show that norms about corporal punishment have been changing rapidly for some segments of the American population in the last few decades. They note that while no state outlaws corporal punishment by parents completely, in the way the country of Sweden now does, the laws in the United States have been changing:

> Other categories for adults with responsibility for children (such as foster parents and craftsmen supervising apprentices) previously also had the right to use corporal punishment. Today essentially the only type of person besides a parent who can legally hit children is a teacher or other school official. Moreover, despite opposition from most teachers' organizations, this is changing rapidly, and by 1990 27 states had banned the use of corporal punishment in schools.[43]

This change has been uneven across U.S. regions, racial groups, and social classes. In 1968 "there was almost complete consensus concerning the cultural norm which permitted and expected parents to use corporal punishment. At that time 94% of the U.S. adult population approved of spanking a child."[44] By 1994 the percentage of Americans who approved of spanking had decreased to 68%. But the decline in approval of corporal punishment was greater among whites, among the highly educated, and among people who did not live in the South. Thus in 1994 there was much less normative consensus on the issue.[45]

Indeed, African Americans have a much higher approval of corporal punishment than whites. (African Americans had an 84% approval versus European Americans who had a 66% approval.) Some recent research about this issue shows some southern black Americans experiencing some of the same frustrations as the West Indians in this study because of the disparity between their method of discipline for their children and that of more mainstream parents. Lynne Vernon-Feagans studied low-income African-American children in rural North Carolina and compared them to a group of middle-class families in the same area. She noted that "physical punishment was the norm and other relatives and respected adults were obliged to physically punish children for transgressions, even if they were not their own children." While the middle-class whites lectured or talked to their children, the low-income African Americans used physical punishment.[46]

Parents in rural North Carolina had the same fear as the New York West Indians that the government could interfere with their chosen method of child raising:

One mother told us that after she had recently spanked her 5-year-old daughter for disobedience, the child threatened to tell the social worker she was being abused. The mother was somewhat surprised that such a young child could already play one adult's value against another's for her own benefit. The mother told us that this conflict between her strong-held views about the value of physical punishment and the more mainstream view had caused many of her friends and family difficulty with the social service system and the schools.[47]

Since the law does allow parents to hit their children, the real dispute between immigrant parents and the state departments of child protection is about the line between allowable physical punishment and discipline and actual child abuse. Some scholars argue that any amount of corporal punishment by parents can have serious negative consequences for children. Murray Straus, the foremost sociological expert on family violence in the United States, believes this to be the case. He and coauthor Denise Donnelly conclude: "Corporal punishment of adolescents is particularly likely to be harmful because as existing evidence shows, it is associated with an increased probability of violence and other crime, depression, and alienation and lowered achievement. Although not tested in this article, we suspect that corporal punishment is also likely to interfere with the development of independence and to humiliate, antagonize and infantilize adolescents."[48] Yet other scholars argue that to deny ethnic minority parents their preferences in something as private as how to raise one's children is wrong. George Hong and Lawrence Hong conclude that adequate definitions of child abuse and neglect should include ethnic minority perspectives and that "[o]ne has to find a balance between honoring society's obligation to protect children and providing safeguards for minority groups from unwarranted interference in their preferences and practices."[49]

Vernon-Feagans concludes that it is a myth that all physical punishment is the same as child abuse and that the research literature has a strong middle-class bias:

> Much has been written in the middle-class research literature about the "evils" of physical punishment of children and the myth has been created that physical punishment borders on child abuse. No

doubt there are families in which physical punishment can lead to abuse, and coupled with poverty and the stress of family life, this form of punishment may indeed be dysfunctional, but the judicious use of physical punishment should not be dismissed as merely a "bad" parenting practice without understanding its roots and its effect on the children.[50]

The overwhelming majority of people we interviewed believed that there was a moral obligation of parents to discipline their children, and if the parents did not beat them, children would turn out badly. In fact, the absence of physical punishment was often cited as the cause of the problems of juvenile delinquency that people saw among Americans:

> Q: Have there been any times you feel you have benefited from being a person from the Caribbean?
>
> A: Yes. And this is more personal than anything else. I was explaining to this guy the other day, to me being from the Caribbean, you have a little bit more sense of respect. And that, you know, you are brought up learning to respect, to obey. You know over here they won't scold the kid with a lash or anything because the cops are going to be on you. Back in the Caribbean we had the wild cane. This is like a very slim thing. When you misbehave that cane is on you. Over here you can't do that. Over here they can't discipline children and that is why I think they have a lot of problems, a lot of delinquents. It stems from the home. (Trinidadian male teacher, age 41, in United States fourteen years)

Because the immigrants believe that it is the good parents who physically punish their children and the bad ones who do not, the parents were very forthright about "beating" their children:

> Because home, a twelve-year-old at home and a twelve-year-old here is two different things. A twelve-year-old at home is a twelve-year-old child. A twelve-year-old child here is a twelve-year-old man. You know—he out on the street by himself because if he was twelve home and six o'clock come and it getting a little dark and he not home, prepare yourself you are gonna get licks when you cross that door because why you let outside getting dark and

you not . . . But here you just see twelve-year-olds on the train by themselves and going places by themselves and if the parents scold them, that is child abuse. I didn't know about child abuse until I come here.

Q: And how will you raise your son?

A: Well, my son is raised as a West Indian child because he is only five. But if he do something that he not supposed to do, I give it to him good. And I tell him, you never do that again and he would say, yes mommy . . . But he is strange, because sometimes my mother be so strict with him and if he want to say something, he will say it anyway. I say, boy, you have this American thing in you that I'm gonna beat, you know? (Trinidadian female worker, age 30, in United States ten years)

One of the first things children learn when they arrive is that parental beatings are considered child abuse in the United States, and they can report their parents to child welfare:

If my mother hit me, all I gotta do is go to the child welfare agency and say, look at what my mother did to me, and they come and they arrest her. My mother says you can't even touch a kid nowadays without getting into trouble for it. (Jamaican male, age 18, in United States fifteen years)

Many teens do report their parents. Two of the teachers and three of the food-service workers we talked with had encounters with the police over beating their children. The parents are outraged that the state can come between a parent and a child. Indeed, many parents spoke defiantly of how they would beat their children regardless of the consequences:

When I came here my father was telling me, oh you cannot hit a child as long as it's here. 'Cause they will call the cops on you. But I'll be telling my father, there's no way I'm gonna bring a child in this world, and if I want to hit him, and he's done something wrong, and they decide to call the cops, then he gone have to live with the cops, not with me anymore. 'Cause when I was coming up, my mother would hit me, with a belt. She did this thing called a tambering rod. She picks it off a tree like a branch, she splice it together, and she would beat us with that. And that's to discipline us. So when I bring a child into this world, I prefer to discipline my child, and then let him call the police, 'cause the cops going to take him or her if they call them. (Barbadian female, age 19, in United States four years)

One teacher told us the following story about a father who defied anyone preventing him from disciplining his children the way that he wanted to:

Haitian kid decided to get one of the new kinds of haircuts—one of those flattops. And he got home and his father beat him. Matter of fact, when he came to school he pulled up his shirt, and I saw the fist mark right there. And we called Social Services and they sent a representative to the house. And the father was about, maybe six foot ten, ten zillion pounds. And he let the worker know that yes, I did it. He cuts his hair like that again, I'll do it again. The father said, he comes in here looking like these Yankee kids. And if he comes in here doing it again, he would do it again. At that point the worker left and that was it. End of story. (Barbadian male teacher, age 43, born in United States)

We heard of one case where a teenager was misbehaving very badly. The parents tried to discipline him and threatened him with a beating, but in turn he threatened to call Social Services to report his parents. The parents bought the child a one-way ticket back to Jamaica and forced the teenager to go home. When he got off the airplane, many members of his extended family met him in the airport and beat him very badly right then and there.

Some parents, however, are trying to learn new ways to discipline their children. Some of them learn new techniques from their children, who explain how their American or Americanized friends are disciplined. Some parents are forced to consider change because of encounters with the Social Services Department or because of referrals to family therapists because of a child's problems in school. But it is difficult to change behavior that the parents think is the right thing to do and that is such a private and ingrained part of their own upbringing. The African-American guidance counselor at Eisenhower High School describes how he tries to convince the parents to use other techniques to deal with their children:

We have to deal with a child coming into school and he has a bruise or you can see he has been verbally abused. You have to report that. In this society here, we don't allow that. That is the law. I try to talk to the parent about how we try to talk to the child as opposed to beating the child. And that stuff they learned from their parents, to their parents, on down the generations. That is part of their culture now. However, in parent training programs when they come to talk to me, I try to make it another way to deal with, a way to talk with a child. But a lot of that will probably continue, and it means that when we report it to the system of child abuse, the social worker might go to the house and investigate. And I have to call the parent after that and let them know, this is what you have to do in America. And I will let them know that when you move from Haiti, or wherever, any part of the West Indies, that's something you have to be faced with here. And personally, I understand what they are saying. They say, "It's the only way I can keep my daughter in line." I say, "But in America you don't do it. And you have to see your daughter get out of line." I don't know what's worse really. (Black American guidance counselor, age 50)

Parents who have sought help from community mental health centers for dealing with their troubled teenagers are referred to group sessions for West Indian parents to discuss their difficulties and to share coping mechanisms. One worker's 16-year-old daughter had run away and was now living in a group home run by Child Protective Services; the parent told me with true astonishment that she had learned in the group sessions that she should give her teenage daughter "privacy." She said the word with the utmost disdain—as if people who would recommend privacy for a 16-year-old were completely out of their mind. She planned to continue searching her daughter's possessions for anything illicit.

But the main thing parents are introduced to in these sessions is the idea that they should talk to their children, that they should share emotions and feelings with their children and be open to the children's emotions and feelings, and that instead of physical punishment they should use techniques like denying them privileges. It is difficult for these parents to change. One teacher who was told never to hit a child when she was angry exclaimed, "But when you are calm, who wants to hit?" It still seemed to her that physical punishment was the only way to control an unruly child. A few parents did say they were trying the new technique of talking, not hitting:

> Where I'm from you don't talk to parents that way, you don't say what's on your mind. You don't get a chance to express yourself. And here, it's more free speech. I'm even practicing. Although I couldn't tell my parents anything, I try to open up to my children so that they can talk to me about anything. (Jamaican female teacher, age 37, in United States seven years)

This second-generation teacher described the frustrations he feels about raising his children so differently than the way he was raised:

> Q: What is the best way to raise kids, the American way or the West Indian way?
> A: I try to talk to mine, which is frustrating, you know. So, you know, I have teenage daughters and I have the two little ones, the two foster ones, sometimes it's difficult 'cause I like talking, 'cause I like to hear what the kids have to say. But I have created lazy children. You know, I want your chores on Saturday, well, you know, there's not going to be any real punitive kind of, we're not gonna do them. And that's a frustration. You know, my day, we had an old belt. Well, actually, she used to give it to me with the cuckoo stick. That's the stick that is used to turn the cornmeal. And you have to take it. You'd go sulk and you would learn. But because you try to do things in this modern way, I don't know if it works. I don't have bad kids, but they're lazy as hell. And, you know, that's the bottom line. So I tend to think the old-fashioned way is better, but you just can't do it here. (Barbadian male teacher, age 43, born in United States)

Not one of the teenagers we spoke with was completely opposed to the use of physical punishment. Many defended their parents' practices and argued forcefully that they would raise their children the same way:[51]

Q: Do you think Haitian parents have a different way of raising their children than Americans?

A: Yeah, yeah. West Indians are fucking strict. Strict, strict, strict. It's like now Americans, white and black, they are scared to punish their kids because their kids could dial a phone and call the police. Play that shit with a Haitian parent or a Jamaican parent, you all get beat. You'll get yourself chained up to the radiator, like that girl on the blocks. Try to do that stupid shit.

Q: If you were to have kids, how would you raise them?

A: Yo' the same way my parents raised me. Believe me, believe me, when I have my kids yo' if he did something stupid, he gonna get hit, he gonna get hit. Word. Cause I seen how yo' that shit helped me a little bit, you know? Now I see what's up. (Haitian male, age 19, born in United States)

Q: Do you think Jamaicans have a different way of raising their children than Americans do?

A: I think a Jamaican parent is more stern with their kid than an American parent. Then again, in Jamaica a parent could like spank her kid, give her kid a good spanking and so he will listen. But in America, if you do that, this system is against it. They say, well you know, you can't beat up your kid or you'll go to jail.

Q: Which way do you think is best?

A: Well, a beating is good. A good beating is good sometime, you know. I don't think you should murder the kid, you know. Just, if he deserves a good beating, give it to him. In the right places. You know, on his butt, on his foot. But I think the Jamaican is good because there's a lot of kids turn out to be good kids when they finally grow.

Q: If you had kids, which way would you raise them?

A: Oh, the Jamaican way, definitely. Actually I don't really like the American way of raising kids 'cause as you can see, I mean most of the violence and crime that's going on right now it's done by the young kids, youth, all ranging from age fourteen to twenty-one. (Jamaican male, age 22, in United States six years)

The teens we spoke with did not think that Social Services was protecting them or looking out for them. Rather, they echoed the parents' concerns that Social Services came between parents and children and was responsible for high rates of delinquency among youngsters in the United States:

> In Jamaica the families try hard to raise their kids properly, you know. When you do something wrong, they beat you or something. But up here, do something wrong and they beat you, some neighbor going to call Social Service that you're beating your kids and you're doing all this and so you have more guidelines to follow. But in Jamaica, you raise your kids better 'cause there's no Social Service come knocking on your door saying why you doing this to your kid, you know . . . [With Jamaican parents] if you don't follow guidelines then you're in trouble, a lot of trouble, you know. (Jamaican male, age 18, in United States eight years)

But the majority of the students we spoke with said when they grew up and had children, they would try to combine West Indian strictness with American freedoms and openness. The students identified "talking" and "withdrawing privileges" as American ways of punishment, and even if their parents were not using these methods, the teens anticipated using them with their own children:

> Over there, if a child misbehaves, they give them a spanking or a whipping. Over here, they talk to them and they punish them.
>
> Q: Which way do you think is best?
> A: I believe a little bit of both because a child need discipline, but they also need space. You know, a little bit of both.
> Q: If you had kids, which way would you raise them?
> A: A little bit of both. I would be strict up to a certain point, but I'll be flexible. They could talk to me, you know, I would say OK, but I'm not gonna be like, oh well, this is what I think, and what I think is gonna go. You know, I am going to be flexible. (Jamaican female, age 17, in United States three years)

Clearly, the second generation is caught in the middle on this issue—while few completely condemn the way their parents are raising them, very few completely endorse it. Most try to find a middle ground, arguing that they will take the best of both worlds—some discipline from their parents' methods and some leniency from the American methods. It remains to be seen how the next generation of West Indian Americans will raise their own children, but it is likely that discipline is a cultural practice that will be very modified in the next generation.

The Dilemma of Teachers

This clash between American and West Indian methods of child rearing and discipline manifests itself in the schools in two ways. First, teachers deal with adolescents who are being beaten at home and are often required by law to report the parents of their students to Social Services. They are often caught in the middle—representing laws, procedures, and customs they don't entirely agree with, but that they have to explain and endorse to their students and their parents. Second, teachers must deal with a situation where they are prohibited from using corporal punishment on their students, but both parents and newly arrived students expect it.

Some teachers agree that parents should beat children, either because that is how they deal with their own children or because they empathize with parents who have a long tradition of handling their children this way. Not surprisingly, West Indian teachers are most likely to be sympathetic to the West Indian parents:

> In my day there was corporal punishment.
> Q: And do you think that's a good thing?
> A: Yes. 'Cause I know from myself and a lot of people it did more good than bad. And I mean, at any age group, no matter what you do, there will always be kids who are definitely bad or rotten as you might want to say it. No matter what you do you won't be able to reach them. But then I think with the discipline, some who might tend to go to the other side, it helped bring them back. (Trinidadian male teacher, age 41, in United States eighteen years)

Another teacher agreed:

> I think a parent can get out of control using a cane. I still think that a little whipping now and again helps to keep a child on track. That doesn't necessarily mean that you are going to abuse a child. You can do it with caution. But I am sure there must be some control to say,

hey this is the limit. I think that's one of the reasons why children here generally have gotten so out of hand because they know that if the parents do anything, they can call up. A lot of parents feel, you know, what can I do? A lot of them are at that point of "What can I do?" . . . I usually suggest, do you have an uncle or is there a brother who, you think, will be able to have a firmer grip, who could counsel the child? So I usually recommend having another person, usually male, and if that fails, I usually say, just try to get some professional help. (Jamaican female teacher, age 36, in United States seven years)

Even American teachers who might not use such discipline methods themselves can readily see the predicament the immigrant parents find themselves in when they can no longer use the methods they would normally resort to:

When you are having trouble with a child who is running in the halls, not going to class, beating up other kids, acting as a spy for a gang, you know, lookout type thing. And you know that the child is into actual criminal activity, what do you do when you ring up the father and the father is under court order as an abusive parent? Who do you speak to? What do you tell him? You can't imagine how difficult it is. (White female teacher, age 47)

This teacher is sympathetic to the island parents and does not think they are abusing their children, yet her duty to report them is an issue in her relationships with her students:

I tell the students that they have to understand, there's certain things that I can keep secret. If they tell me about a pregnancy or something like that and they don't want me to call the parent, I will honor that. I tell them they should tell their parents, etcetera, etcetera. But with child abuse, I know it's not my decision whether I should call. I have to. I discuss it with the guidance counselor and I tell the student I have to do it. For instance, I know I have a girl right now who is having tremendous problems with her father. She will not tell me what is going on until I cannot call or I cannot do anything about her, until she is over eighteen. But when someone under eighteen tells me, I think that although they don't want it [the call to Social Services], there's also a wish for it because they are having such a difficult time. But they really would like something done. And usually it's a matter of these parents not knowing that they cannot hit the way they did in the islands, and once they understand that we don't sanction that, then it resolves. So it's really just a matter of getting accustomed to our culture. You know I don't think it's particularly child abuse. And I do understand what the parent is saying and I do understand the parents' frustration. (White female teacher, age 46)

The image of African-American teenagers in the neighborhood who are behaving in criminal or violent ways is not far from the surface in all of these discussions of parental discipline. The immigrants are very afraid that their children will become the "out of control" children they see around them in their neighborhoods. Among the food-service workers, parents talked about "losing" their children to the streets. Teachers also worried about whether they could keep their children from becoming involved with the wrong crowd of peers. Then when the parents use a method of discipline that they know from their own growing-up experiences works, they are told they will get in trouble with American authorities. Nevertheless, the teachers, who very much appreciate the parents' fears, also sometimes see those methods of discipline causing emotional damage to their students:

If you have Caribbean parents, they are going to discipline you differently. All this talking whatever, forget about it. And they believe strongly in it and I don't blame them in many respects. But you can't brutalize a child physically. At the same time if you want to give a smack here and there, I don't mind. But there's so much you can do, and there are sometimes parents who go crazy because they've been really working themselves up, genuinely trying to make a better future. There is one boy now who is so afraid of his father. And the father wants those boys not to get caught up in what's happening to the African-American black males and he's trying to keep them straight, and both kids are so fearful of him right now. Maybe it's the right thing to do right now, but at the same time, the child is suffering emotionally . . . [She tells the story of another young teen who was beaten up by her mother.] The kid kind of learned to cope. Submerge everything. 'Cause what would you do? Would you pull a child out of a home like that? The child is being fed as far as the father is concerned. She has a place to sleep. What more can you ask? Emotional well-being is not one of the issues for the island people. (Guyanese female teacher, age 43, in United States twenty years)

But even teachers who disagree with using corporal punishment with adolescents are in a difficult position on this issue. One white American teacher told us that she had a student who was doing poorly in her class, and she knew she should call his parents to discuss it, but she did not. She was afraid that if she indicated any problem with the way the child was performing, the parents would beat the child. Another teacher told how she had called a parent because a young man in her class was acting very badly. The next thing she knew the parent and the young student were in the principal's office, and the mother was yelling at her son to get on his knees before the teacher to beg her forgiveness. The teacher perceived this as the student being humiliated by the parent, and thought that it just made matters worse when the student returned to her class the next day and was even more of a behavioral problem. She concluded that the West Indian methods of discipline

> don't really work. There has to be a better way of handling your kids because I have seen that demeaning just doesn't work. I think the brand of discipline that they use is just inappropriate. Especially in our culture where we are told to talk things out. But when you say, "OK Johnny sit down," and he'll look at you like you are nuts. Because they are used to having people hitting them. And responding to them in this way, they'll look at you as being a real weakness. (White female teacher, age 43)

Corporal Punishment in the Schools

Immigrant parents, children, and teachers have experienced schools back in the islands where corporal punishment is an integral part of school life and discipline. It comes as quite a shock to all three groups when they learn that all forms of corporal punishment are forbidden and illegal in New York City schools. Many parents do not know what the schools are like and do not know that the strict discipline they experienced in schools on the islands is not what happens in New York City public schools. Many are very upset by this, and some ask the teachers to please beat their children if they misbehave. As we have seen, this makes some teachers who do not believe in corporal punishment very uneasy. For those West Indian teachers who do believe in corporal punishment, this parental permission to beat their children is very welcome. One assistant principal told us that he had discovered that one of his West Indian teachers was routinely beating a student in front of the entire class because this teacher had the permission of that one student's parent to do so. The teacher thought the public beating helped him maintain control over the rest of the class because of the power of the example. The principal had to suspend the teacher because his behavior was against school rules and the law.

One West Indian teacher spoke about such parental permission and believed that it helped her maintain control in the classroom:

> Some of them will come and tell you that if their child misbehaves, I give you permission to hit him. I'll give you permission to do it. Of course, you are not supposed to. But I mean they are giving you a certain amount of leeway. The other thing they say is he has to listen to you. I am telling you and if, you know, he doesn't, complain to me and I will take care of him at home. So if a child knows this, there is more control. All I have to say to that child is I will be making a call to your parents. You know then he gets his act together. (Guyanese female teacher, age 48)

This is an enormous policy problem in the schools. Principals have to warn their teachers not to send negative notes home because often the students will come back to school black and blue. Parents come to school and want to know why the children are not beaten in school by the teachers, an accepted and respected part of Caribbean school discipline. This same teacher describes her frustrations with not being able to use a system that she thinks works well back home and that she sees very negative consequences from not using here in the United States:

> Back there corporal punishment is allowed, and the child knows if he misbehaves he will be getting a spanking from the teacher. And if he's real bad he'll be referred to the headmaster. They have some strong person do the paddling. Then because the community is so

closely knit, the teachers know the parents, the parents know the teachers so the child knows his mother will be seeing the teacher any time and if the teacher makes a comment to the mother, he knows he gets punishment at home also. So it's reinforced because you all work together for the good of the child. Over here, they do not believe in corporal punishment, it's against the law, because it's all considered abuse—child abuse. Now back home children know they will be punished. They will feel it. Some kids are tough and they know they'll be getting a beating, but they know they'll take a beating. But that's a very small number who would have that type of attitude. Most kids will conform. You could call it forced discipline, but it works. The teachers are respected. Some kids who are born over there, used to that discipline when they come here and it's more or less lax—if they don't do their homework, the teacher just says, Why didn't you do your homework? It doesn't bother them much. You know they don't feel any punishment. They allow themselves to change. They follow what the others are doing and they get wild. When they come here and they notice, Oh, I could get out of my seat and I could scream out and nothing happen to me. And they take full advantage of those things. And then they really don't get that good of education. They lose out on a lot of things.

Even teachers who don't approve of corporal punishment note that it is difficult to deal with students who have been brought up in that system and then enter the New York system. When students have been accustomed to corporal punishment for minor infractions in island schools, the methods of discipline in New York schools sometimes do not work with them. Imagine the surprise of youngsters who move from the islands to New York during their school years. They are used to a school system where teachers expect complete respect, where corporal punishment with canes is regularly administered, and where close ties between parents and teachers mean that they have no ability to act out in school without their parents hearing about it. This young man who immigrated at age 9 as a fourth-grader describes his shock:

School was very strict in Jamaica. You miss your homework one day and they beat you with a cane in front of your whole class. So it was a little bit of pressure to do well down there. The big thing between the schools down there and here were, the first day I went to school, the kids were cursing at the teacher and they were throwing things all over the place. It was just out of control and I couldn't understand what the heck was going on. I thought I was on another planet or something because I couldn't understand. They wore whatever they wore. In Jamaica we had to wear uniforms. Every day. And you had to wear a tie, a vest, and a jacket. And the teachers were very strict. Very, very strict. It's not like here at all where the kids are basically out of control. I think that I myself might have done better in school in Jamaica than I did here because it was entirely too much freedom, I thought. (Jamaican male, age 22, in United States thirteen years)

The methods used to discipline teens in the New York schools seem very ineffective to some of these youngsters. Compared to being beaten, punishments such as being yelled at, suspended, or even transferred to another school seem almost laughable:

In Jamaica they discipline you if you get out of hand. Up here, it's like, you do it, don't do it again. You do it again, they suspend you. You come back, you do it again, nothing they can do about it. They transfer you to another school. You do the same thing. You get away with it. So you know the rules kind of stink. (Jamaican male, age 19, in United States six years)

The folk theory among most students was that West Indian students were better behaved than Americans because they grew up in stricter households and had more discipline instilled in them at home. One exception to this general characterization was that many people, both students and teachers, believed that some West Indians became particularly uncontrollable when they came to the United States and realized they were not subject to the social control they had experienced back home:

West Indian kids get more in trouble than Americans because when they come up here, right?, they see the other teachers can't hit them so they think they could do anything they want. Now they free. (Grenadian male, age 14, in United States four years)

The West Indian teachers lamented over and over again the lack of respect they felt in the United States compared to the high degree of respect teachers were accorded back in the islands. The immigrant students we spoke with noted this as one of the starkest differences between schools in the islands and here. Teachers in New York did not receive respect from their students; in fact, they were cursed, insulted, and threatened:

> The system in Grenada is better. Because back in Grenada you look at the teachers as another parent to you. But up here, you could mistreat them, curse them, anything you want. But in Grenada, if you say any foul language, you get detention, or if they don't want to give detention, they beat you in front of the class. (Grenadian male, age 18, in United States nine years)

> Here you can just say anything to your teachers. We can't do that in Jamaica.
> Q: What would happen if you did that in Jamaica?
> A: Get a whipping. A beating that you will never forget. And you can't go home and tell your parents because you'll get another one from them. (Jamaican female, age 18, in United States seven years)

In the vast majority of cases it should be recognized that this is not an issue about child abuse per se but about culture clash. West Indian social workers and parents argue that they can tell the difference between parents who are in control of themselves and yet beat their children, adolescents included, with an object like a strap or a stick, and parents who are actually physically harming and abusing their children. Yet the laws in New York make some of the practices parents genuinely believe in—like beating a child to the point where welts appear—illegal.

The methods a person uses to raise and discipline children are clearly a cultural behavior—and they are a behavior that people hold close. If child protection measures call for a change in those cultural behaviors, as the laws currently do, then there should be some public recognition that this is clearly an assimilation issue. The United States is imposing cultural values about how to raise children on immigrants whose practices and beliefs are very different. Some churches and other programs have recognized this and are actively trying to change behaviors through education and social support.

But in general this issue has not received the public airing and debate that it should. Currently, the United States requires parents to make an enormous leap of faith in changing their discipline practices. The state asks them to abandon the methods they grew up with and argues that it is better for their children. Yet these parents see American children as un-ruly, undisciplined, and often frightening examples of what happens when kids get too much freedom. Especially in inner-city neighborhoods, the immigrants see American children who are not beaten by their parents, but who are dropping out of high school, getting pregnant, or getting involved in crime and drugs. In short, these parents believe that the government tries to deprive them of their chosen technique for disciplin-ing their children, while offering no other alternative of how to teach respect and good behavior to teenagers.

If the United States is going to impose its laws on the immigrant parents, as it has the right to do, then it should be a clear political decision that child protection trumps multiculturalism. And far more attention should be paid to the fact that what the Department of Social Services and the teachers, churches, and other social service professionals are doing in New York is a type of forced assimilation.

Race and Discrimination

Another factor that clearly causes problems between the generations is the interpretation of race and discrimination in the lives of these families. As we have seen in Chapter 5, the parents grew up in a situation where blacks were the majority. They do not want to be "racial" in the United States—meaning that they do not want race to play a big part in their lives. Yet their teenaged children experience racism and discrimination con-stantly and develop perceptions of the overwhelming influence of race on their lives and life chances that differ from their parents' views. These teens experience being hassled by police and storeowners, being turned down for jobs they apply for, and being attacked on the streets if they venture into white neighborhoods. This makes them angry and resentful about the whole issue. The media also project images that tell these students that blacks are disvalued by American society. Parents urge their children to strive for upward mobility and to work harder in the face of discrimination, but the kids think their chances of attaining success by doing so are very slim.

These different interpretations of the role race will play in one's life also create a gulf between parents and children. Parents will tell their children to strive for upward mobility and have high aspirations, but often the peer group and the children's own day-to-day experiences tell them the color of their skin might make it difficult or impossible to meet those aspirations. The differing responses of immigrant and second-generation teens to the role of race will be examined in more detail in Chapter 8.

Researchers such as Ruben Rumbaut[52] and Carola and Marcelo Suarez-Orozsco[53] find that immigrants and their children sometimes do worse the longer the time spent in the United States. In addition, Rumbaut finds that even when one controls for a host of individual characteristics, such as socioeconomic status and language ability, there are still strong national origin differences in how well immigrant children do. Although downward assimilation is not true for all immigrant families, and human, political, and social capital can provide for much happier outcomes, there is some evidence that the United States can actually erode some of the strengths immigrants bring with them. The ethnographic material I have sketched here shows some social factors that put strains on immigrant families and may contribute to the declines in aspirations, academic achievement, and hard work among immigrant children that surveys such as Rumbaut's uncover. In the next chapter we turn our attention to the institutional and physical locations in which immigrant and second-generation children come of age—the schools and neighborhoods where these West Indian children study and play. In both neighborhood and school settings race plays a very important role in shaping the experiences and life chances of the second generation.

SEGREGATED
NEIGHBORHOODS
AND SCHOOLS

Because West Indians are black immigrants, the vast majority settle in neighborhoods that are predominantly black. This has profound implications for their lives. Racial segregation for blacks is unlike segregation for any other ethnic or immigrant group. It is far more extensive in scope, and it is not mitigated by class—segregation is just as severe for middle-class as for poor blacks. In their book *American Apartheid,* Douglas Massey and Nancy Denton describe the segregation indices for black Americans in many U.S. cities, including New York City, as constituting hypersegregation—indeed, an American form of the racial separation of apartheid.[1] This chapter explores the impact of such segregation on second-generation youth as they experience it in their neighborhoods and their schools.

A voluminous literature has developed on the effects of residential segregation, concentrated poverty, and inner-city life on individual outcomes of American minority group members.[2] Massey and Denton show that active discrimination and institutional racism lead to declining city services and declining private investment in residentially segregated neighborhoods.[3] This is reflected in the experiences of the respondents in this study. Levels of street violence, the overall ineffectiveness of the schools, and the cultural consequences of living in neighborhoods with concentrated poverty all coincide to lead to negative effects of segregated inner-city residence for West Indian immigrants and their children.

Massey and Denton conclude that "quantitative research shows that growing up in a ghetto neighborhood increases the likelihood of dropping out of high school, reduces the probability of attending college, lowers the

likelihood of employment, reduces income earned as an adult and increases the risk of teenage childbearing and unwed pregnancy."[4] This is
partly because racial segregation of the type experienced by black Americans concentrates poverty and its effects, and subjects all ghetto residents
to the cultural and structural effects of such poverty.

The vast majority of the people we interviewed lived in the predominantly black Brooklyn neighborhoods of Brownsville, Bedford-Stuyvesant, East New York, Flatbush, and East Flatbush. These neighborhoods
all exhibited many of the most common problems of segregated neighborhoods. Some of the West Indian teachers interviewed lived in the middle-
class West Indian neighborhoods of Cambria Heights in Queens or
suburban towns such as Hempstead on Long Island or Mount Vernon in
Westchester. While these suburban areas were safer and had better housing, they were also predominantly black. When white ethnic group members achieved middle-class status, they were able to move out of ethnically
segregated neighborhoods. In effect, their socioeconomic mobility allowed them to purchase residential mobility. Blacks in the United States
have not been able to convert their socioeconomic mobility into residential mobility. American blacks are "equally highly segregated at all levels
of income."[5] In New York, for instance, in 1980 "black families earning
under $2500 per year experienced an average segregation index of 86,
those earning more than $50,000 experienced an index of 79."[6] Even when
they move to the suburbs, middle-class black immigrants are still highly
segregated, much more so than other immigrant groups.[7]

Because of the concentration of poverty in black residential areas, this
segregation of the middle class also means that middle-class blacks have
more reason to worry about the influences of their neighborhoods on
their children than do comparable middle-class members of other groups:
"Compared with children of middle class whites, children of middle class
blacks are much more likely to be exposed to poverty, drugs, teenage
pregnancy, family disruption, and violence in the neighborhoods where
they live."[8]

Some of our respondents did live in mixed-race neighborhoods, such
as Crown Heights, Canarsie, and Midwood. Crown Heights is an area that
has a middle-class and working-class black population and a long-standing West Indian immigrant population, as well as a strong Hasidic Jewish

population. It was the scene of racially charged riots in the summer of 1991, the summer before I interviewed people there. Canarsie and Midwood are predominantly white neighborhoods that are currently receiving an influx of middle-class black residents, the vast majority of whom are West Indian.

Most people do not choose to live in an all-black neighborhood because they want to avoid whites. The typical experience for immigrants is that they arrive in the United States and choose to live near friends and family who came before them—and are currently living in West Indian or black American neighborhoods. A few people recognized that white neighborhoods were better in a number of ways, but the racial composition of the neighborhood is a factor in their decisionmaking. While they desired the amenities they saw in some white neighborhoods, they wanted to make sure they would be "comfortable":

> I am hoping to get out of this neighborhood. I think for you to have a true feeling of what United States is, you can't live around so many blacks. I find that in the white neighborhoods and the white schools, their children are exposed to more difficult things, more opportunities are there, exposures are there, whatever. So if you want your child to get a balanced view of what he is going to face out there, I think he shouldn't be subjected just to blacks and Jamaicans. So I am just shopping white areas. There is some things they advertise on tv, you can't find it in a black supermarket. So I would prefer to live where there are opportunities. Not that I am going to go somewhere where just whites live and my child's going to be uncomfortable, but I am going to find some place where there is a more balanced population. (Jamaican female teacher, age 37, in United States seven years)

And this concern is well-founded. It is not easy to be the first black person to move into a white neighborhood. One woman whose experience is described in Chapter 5 was told by a landlord that she did not rent to "niggers" when the woman tried to get an apartment in an all-white neighborhood. Many middle-class West Indians have played the role of pioneers in many white neighborhoods, buying houses in previously all-white neighborhoods, such as East Flatbush in the '70s, Canarsie in the

'80s, and Midwood in the '90s, in order to have access to safer streets, better schools, and higher quality housing. Yet these pioneers pay a price. In the period of my fieldwork there had been several firebombings of black-owned houses and real estate offices that had helped blacks buy houses in the neighborhood of Canarsie.[9] The firebombed homeowners were all West Indian immigrants. Middle-class immigrants who have the financial ability to live in the suburbs or the better neighborhoods of the city often choose not to because of the experiences of these pioneers:

> I would love to live in the suburbs. But I would not live there, not now. Because too many things are happening. I would not want to go live in a white neighborhood. Not because I think anything derogatory or negative about them. But because of what is happening. You don't know who is who. I feel more comfortable in a mixed neighborhood. If there are blacks over here, and blacks over there, and a white here, and a white there, I would be more comfortable. I feel safer because I know I am moving in here, but these blacks, when they moved in with these whites before, and they are still living here, I feel safe coming here now. I am not going to be a pioneer. I don't want to be the first one to move in the block. No. I'll rather be safe. Things are happening out there. (Guyanese female teacher, age 48, in United States twenty years)

While many of the adults blamed young people for the problems in the neighborhoods—noting that kids were out of control, involved in drugs and crime, and preyed on the community—most of the young people we spoke with wanted to live in good neighborhoods, free from violence and fear. One young man admitted to carrying weapons, being a gang member, and participating in a number of illegal activities. He came from a two-parent middle-class family, who had purchased a house in the relatively better East Flatbush neighborhood. He told us that he and his friends respected that his parents lived in a good neighborhood, so they took their illegal activities someplace else:

> Mostly me and my friends are here. We just sit on the steps. That's our place right there. You don't do stuff around here. If you want to

do something, we go to Flatbush. We go there [when we are going]
to rob a store. (Jamaican male, age 17, in United States ten years)

Most people were very dissatisfied with their neighborhoods, most
particularly with the level of crime and fear they lived with. The reasoning
that the teens give for why their neighborhood is good or bad tells a lot
about the kinds of conditions people get used to living with. For instance,
this Bajan respondent describes her current neighborhood of Flatbush as
very good because she has not yet witnessed open shooting on the streets:

Flatbush is better than Bed-Stuy. To me, there are more West Indians living here than Americans. When I was living in Bed-Stuy it was
so bad. I mean I can just look down on my window and people
downstairs, they'll be shooting all over the place. I was looking
through my window one day and I look across the street and there's
this guy—this man walked up to this other guy and shoot him, just
like that. (Barbadian female, age 19, in United States four years)

Indeed, respondents describe their neighborhoods as fair or good despite
conditions that most Americans would find absolutely intolerable:

Q: And how would you rate Crown Heights as a place to live?
A: I wouldn't call it terrible, but it's somewhere close to that because
on my specific block, it's not bad. They do have drug dealers at
both corners. But that tends to keep the neighborhood peaceful
from anybody starting trouble or anything. But it's not like it's a
safe neighborhood. There are shootouts and a guy got shot like
right in front of our door downstairs. A stray bullet came
through our window, and my mother got mugged a few blocks
away. (Jamaican male, age 16, in United States seven years)

These neighborhoods are neither a source of support nor a community
of like-minded people, as our nostalgic and often inaccurate images of an
"ethnic" neighborhood might have us imagine. Instead, these neighborhoods are viewed by many of their inhabitants as "toxic." Many people who
lived in the worst areas made it a point not to interact with their neighbors—they went to work and came home, making an effort not to see or
talk to their neighbors. Their churches were ethnically and not neighbor-

hood-based. They tried to keep their children from the dangers of the surrounding area. Many students said they spent little time in their neighborhoods or with other people—they concentrated on their families and their
school friends and tried to minimize the influence of the neighborhood:

> I don't really talk to anybody from my neighborhood. I don't hang
> out. I just go home. And I stay in my house or I go to work or I go
> the store, but I don't talk to anybody. (Guyanese female, age 18,
> born in United States)

Those respondents who lived in housing projects were very worried not
only about crime and violence, which everyone agreed was worse in the
projects than in private housing, but also about the stigma attached to
their children for living in housing projects:

> I worry about my kids. I ended up in the projects. And I realize it's
> the wrong choice. My kids are not into the drugs. But they hang out.
> And the cops just see a lot of black kids and they just approach them.
> You know there are things that I can't deal with. I have been through
> that with my youngest son. Because of living in the projects you
> eventually start getting treated as, you know, a bad element. You try
> to pull your children in one direction, but you feel for their safety.
> (Guyanese female worker, age 38, in United States nine years)

For those in the worst neighborhoods it is difficult to overestimate the
effect that the problems of the neighborhood have on their day-to-day life:

> I live in the Brownsville area. My neighborhood. It's very scary.
> Q: Why is it scary?
> A: It is, because you are coming home at night and you can just hear
> pow, pow, pow. You are coming down the street and there's no-
> body you are seeing and then you just see people appear from no-
> where. Like in alleys, yards, schoolyards. Mugging, robbing you. I
> have been robbed twice since I have been living here. They take
> everything I had. I had my green card, my social security, my
> money for rent, everything . . . I would give anything to be in a
> good neighborhood. The building that I live in, it's so much.
> They have people that don't live there and they come in there
> and they smoke crack. OK, my boss tell me take a cab home. The

cab drop me off in front of my building. I come up. Turn the key, when I go in, the elevator's stuck. I keep pressing and pressing and pressing. After like a half an hour it come down, there's two crackheads in there smoking. It's so bad. (Guyanese female worker, age 26, in United States ten years)

SEEKING A BETTER NEIGHBORHOOD

The experience of many families is that they seek out integrated neighborhoods or all-white neighborhoods that they see as desirable places to live, but then as soon as they move in, the neighborhood starts to go downhill. The whites move out, more blacks move in. The classic tale related by the working-class parents and the urban high school students was that they lived in core neighborhoods of Brooklyn—Crown Heights, Flatbush, Bedford-Stuyvesant—when they first arrived. Then after a number of years the family could afford to buy a house or pay higher rent, and so they moved to the East Flatbush, Canarsie, and Midwood sections of Brooklyn, areas with more single-family and two-family houses, backyards, and lawns. But the peace and security the families were seeking were elusive; redlining and white flight meant that the quiet, integrated neighborhoods the families were seeking were not stable. And the blacks who moved in were not like their own families—they were the "wrong" kind of people:

Q: And how is your neighborhood as a place to live?
A: East Flatbush is a good place.
Q: And in the future is it going to get better or worse?
A: I don't really see it getting better. It's going to get worse. 'Cause you got like the wrong kind of people moving in to the area. And when they come, they bring like trouble, violence and stuff. 'Cause they come with their guns and they just hang out on the corner. And it's a nice area, you know. A lot of nice houses and everything. It's mostly white, but you have a lot of blacks living there now. (Guyanese female, age 18, born in United States)

A teenager from Tobago felt the same way:

I moved here from Tobago when I was in the sixth grade. We lived in Flatbush and boy, over there it was very bad. Neighbors would

play blasted music and they didn't have no consideration for anybody else and people were driving crazy and a whole bunch of things
were happening. So we moved over here. We live in East Flatbush.
When we first moved there, it was very quiet and peaceful but things
are starting to act up, you know? Accidents are happening and late
at night you will hear gunshots. It seems as far away as you move
from it, you always—bad things always come and catch up. So right
now it is bound to get worse. (Trinidadian female, age 17, in United
States seven years)

The experience my respondents report with racial change and its socioeconomic and social consequences is not just a result of bad luck or bad
people. Middle-class immigrants seeking better schools, services, and
housing stock and less crime spend their hard-earned money purchasing
housing in predominantly white neighborhoods. At first they are successful—the neighborhood is much better than the ones they left behind. But
individual white prejudices about living near blacks as well as institutional
discrimination in the form of bank redlining and discrimination in credit
lead to white flight, declining property values, and decreasing investment
in the neighborhood. While many people—white or black—caught up in
the experience are likely to see this process as an inexplicable "inevitable"
decline due to the behaviors of black people, Massey and Denton describe
the structural forces and decisions that underlie this decay:

> To the extent that property owners perceive a decline as possible or
> likely, they have little incentive to invest in upkeep and improve-
> ment on their own buildings, because money put into neighbor-
> hoods that are declining is unlikely to be recouped in the form of
> higher rents or greater home equity. As a result of the initial disin-
> vestment by a few owners, therefore, others are led to cut back on
> the money they invest. With every additional property owner who
> decides not to invest, it becomes increasingly likely that others will
> reach similar decisions, even if they are otherwise disposed to main-
> tain their buildings. At some point a threshold is crossed, beyond
> which the pattern becomes self-reinforcing and irreversible. Racial
> segregation makes neighborhoods where blacks live particularly vul-
> nerable to this sort of disinvestment and decay. Poor blacks are

more likely than the poor of any other group to be trapped in neighborhoods caught in the grip of such downward spirals, because segregation acts to concentrate poverty and all things associated with it.[10]

As the cost of owning or renting a house in the neighborhood drops and whites are no longer interested in moving into the neighborhood, poorer blacks are now able to afford living there. The middle-class black "pioneers" in the neighborhood watch helplessly as the "undesirable poor" former neighbors they had moved away from follow them into the new neighborhood:

> There were very few blacks in the neighborhood and now some started moving in. It's my own Jamaican people, and they are making the neighborhood worse. As soon as blacks move in, the neighborhood it goes down. The late nights and they have boys coming in and you can tell it's drugs. And they don't have on any shirts. It's hard for me to say. You know what I mean? I don't want to downgrade my people, but they bring with them this thing. (Guyanese female, age 49, in United States twenty-nine years)

As the tax base declines, the crime rates increase, the housing stock deteriorates, and the neighborhood "spirals downward"; the middle-class and working-class black residents once again suffer the consequences of concentrated poverty and re-segregation.

The experience of moving into good neighborhoods only to watch them decline over time leads to a real sense of pessimism about the future. The American dream of home ownership for these immigrants can become a nightmare as they always seem to be just one or two steps ahead of the "bad element" who poison their living conditions:

> I think the area is going to get worse. Because when I first moved there, it was very quiet and it's like it was a predominantly white neighborhood when we moved there and then they started moving out and, you know, we have a lot of violence now. This area is becoming very bad. 'Cause I used to live in Crown Heights. We got used to the guns and the drugs and the buildings. We got used to that, it was a part of your daily life. When we lived in Crown

Heights, the whole first floor was a drug house, and cops coming every day, checking. And we all knew what was there, we always kept our mouths shut, 'cause we didn't want nothing to happen to us. Then when you move into a house, that's the reason my mother bought it, 'cause she said, she didn't want to worry about that. You have to be safe, you can run outside. Now you gotta wonder, what are you really safe about? (Haitian female, age 18, born in United States)

The changes that happen in the neighborhoods make these teenagers sound like old-timers as they reminisce about "the way things used to be back in the good old days" when they first moved into the neighborhoods they now live in:

Over the years the neighborhood has gotten worse. Like when I was smaller, you know, we could go outside anytime, you know, without anything happening. We couldn't hear gun shots. Now like, when I am getting old, it's like people shooting, you know? (Guyanese male, age 16, born in United States)

Ironically, the only neighborhood that was described by a few respondents as getting better, rather than getting worse, was Crown Heights. The Crown Heights riots had happened the summer before our interviewing. Because of the riots a number of new programs had been started in the neighborhood for youths—including basketball leagues and the Crown Heights youth initiative—which included after school-activities for black youths and discussion groups for black and Jewish children. For some these activities were working, but for others there was still a considerable gulf between the black and Jewish populations:

After all these things about the Jews and the Americans and the West Indians, I still see everybody, you know, participating in things with each other and different groups. I see Jewish people coming in the park and playing basketball. And it's real fun to see them playing ball with us, and they always get picked out to play with us. We have basketball, we have the Police Athletic League, we have a Youth Service League. We have a lot of things that people could share in. The summer is coming up and we are gonna be joining basketball

and baseball teams. So I think it is a real good place to live. (Barbadian male, age 18, born in United States)

Yet another teen we spoke with has a very different take on what is
happening in the same neighborhood:

> I have lived in Crown Heights fifteen years and it is a terrible
> place to live. Because the Jews don't like the blacks and the blacks
> don't like the Jews. So we always fighting.
> Q: Why don't the blacks like the Jews?
> A: The way they act, like on the street, you know, if you were walk-
> ing, they will take up the whole street. If you say excuse me, they
> make a smart remark like, walk in the streets, or something like
> that. So we don't get along with each other. But it's a safe place.
> (Trinidadian female, age 14, born in United States)

While many respondents were angry as they described better treatment
by the city of Hasidic Jews than blacks, the residents of Crown Heights did
benefit from increased police presence, as compared to other neighborhoods our respondents lived in. The decision of the Hasidic Jews to
collectively stay or move into Crown Heights despite the black population
that lived there creates an anomaly in the world of American apartheid—an integrated neighborhood.[11]

THE IMPORTANCE OF SCHOOLING

Living in an all-black neighborhood can increase the pressures on West
Indian families—exposing them to crime, declining private investment,
and a declining tax base for city services. Yet perhaps the most important
consequence of living in these neighborhoods for West Indian families is
the exposure it brings to the neighborhood schools. The hopes of these
immigrant parents for a better future for their children hinge on the
children doing well in school. Schooling has always been seen as the path
to upward mobility for the children of immigrants, but one can argue that
the stakes are even higher now because of changes in the economy.

The children and grandchildren of the European immigrants who arrived in the peak years of immigration at the turn of the twentieth century

benefited from the spectacular expansion of the U.S. economy between 1940 and 1970. Barry Bluestone describes the conditions that shaped the success of the European second and third generation: "In the U.S., real average weekly earnings [grew] by 60 percent between 1947 and 1973. Median family income literally doubled . . . And over the same period personal wages and family incomes became tangibly more equal . . . Along with growth and greater equality, poverty declined across the nation."[12] The existence of secure, well-paid manufacturing jobs meant that blue-collar workers with a high school degree or less could attain a stable and secure middle-class lifestyle during this period. They managed to do this even though many southern and eastern European immigrants and their children did not acquire much formal education. Selma Berrol notes that first- and second-generation Poles usually did not go beyond the sixth grade. It was not until the 1950s that Poles and Italians began to accept the idea that their children's lives should be improved through formal schooling.[13] In the early twentieth century historian John Bodnar found that "while 60 percent of native born white children began high school, less than a third of the German and less than a quarter of the Italians did so." Bodnar also found "that by 1910, less than 10 percent of the Italian, Polish, and Slovak children stayed beyond the sixth grade in Buffalo, Chicago, and Cleveland."[14] The postwar economic growth created a great many well-paying blue-collar jobs that paid a family wage to workers who may not have had a formal education. Thus a middle-class lifestyle was available to the children of European immigrants during the twentieth century. This economic growth also helped to close some of the wide gap between blacks and whites from the end of the Depression through the early 1970s.[15]

This level of economic growth and widening opportunities was not sustained after the early 1970s. Over the past two decades, the U.S. economy has been "restructured" by a shift from manufacturing to services and rising inequality between rich and poor, especially in the nation's urban centers.[16] Some have described the result as an hourglass economy, with many jobs for highly skilled workers in professional services and information processing and many unskilled low-level jobs. This is especially true if the structure of men's occupations is examined.[17] The unionized blue-collar manufacturing jobs that supported middle-class lifestyles have become scarce. One result has been to increase the value of formal education in the labor market: "In 1963, the mean annual earnings of those with four years of college or more stood at just over twice (2.11 times) the mean annual earnings of those who had not completed high school . . . By 1987, the education to earnings ratio had skyrocketed to nearly three to one (2.91)."[18]

These disparities intensified in the 1980s. During this decade the average real wage of male high school dropouts fell by 18 percent, while male high school graduates suffered nearly a 13 percent real earnings loss. Only men with a master's degree or more registered an increase in inflation-adjusted earnings, while college graduates stayed about the same.[19] This happened partly because all the employment growth in the economy during the 1980s came in the services sector, where wages polarized between high school dropouts and college graduates four times faster than in goods-producing industries.[20]

These changes in the economy mean that the economic ladder that allowed earlier immigrants to climb slowly from poverty to a middle-class lifestyle has been changed. In effect, the ladder is missing the middle rungs.[21] Low-skilled immigrant parents can barely get by on the wages they earn from low-level service jobs. High-paying service jobs are available for workers with college and graduate degrees and specialized training. But middle-level factory and other blue-collar jobs are scarce. As a result the second generation of today's immigrants must achieve a great deal of educational success relative to their parents' backgrounds. The children of West Indian food-service workers and nurse's aides must either finish college and get well-paying jobs in the high end of the economy, or they face the same job prospects as their parents without sharing the characteristics of immigrant status that make those jobs attractive. The guidance counselor at the high school where I did my most intensive fieldwork, Eisenhower High School, describes the situation well:

The parents feel like there's a job out there [for their kids]. Because you can always go and do someone's housework, or you can be a nurse's aide, or you can help out. But these are youngsters now coming up and they don't want a job like that. And they don't have the skills for other things, so they may have a child themselves. They may get pregnant, have a child, and then they go through the welfare syndrome. Teenage pregnancy, food stamps, that has been happening to quite a few of them. (Guyanese female teacher and guidance counselor, age 42, in United States twenty-two years)

Unlike the Poles and Italians who could drop out of high school and still achieve socioeconomic mobility, the West Indians have to reach the top half of the hourglass economy through formal education. Yet getting the education they need is even more difficult, given the neighborhoods the immigrant families find themselves in.

Neighborhood Schools

New York City's school system is mammoth in size. There is a total of 1 million students, 260,000 of them high school students. There are 66,000 teachers, and a yearly budget of $6.65 billion. The high school system in New York is built around neighborhoods. Students are supposed to attend their neighborhood high school, unless they apply to and are accepted by any of the special magnet high schools. These magnet high schools include some of the best high schools in the country, Stuyvesant High School, the High School of the Performing Arts, and the Bronx High School of Science, as well as lesser known but still specialized high schools, such as Brooklyn Technical High School and the Edward R. Murrow High School.

The academic standings of the neighborhood high schools, not surprisingly, generally follow the socioeconomic status of the surrounding community. The two high schools where I interviewed students (here called Truman and Eisenhower) served the Crown Heights, Flatbush, and East Flatbush neighborhoods of Brooklyn. This area contained about 25% of all of the second-generation and a slightly higher percentage of the 1.5-generation West Indian youth in New York City. (Yet about half of all 1.5- and second-generation West Indians in the entire New York area live in Brooklyn and are zoned for either the two schools I describe here or the three neighboring public high schools.) The high schools neighboring the two I studied are actually slightly worse both in terms of educational outcomes and violent incidents, and I was denied entrance to them. Thus while the two high schools described here are close to the bottom of the high schools in New York City and thus

overstate the problems facing all West Indian children, they pretty accurately reflect the neighborhood schools available to at least half the
West Indian youth in urban and suburban New York. The other half
of West Indian youth do not face schools in as dire a condition. Table
7.1 gives the distribution of West Indian children and teenagers by
neighborhood. These schools had changed a great deal in the last few
decades, as had the neighborhoods surrounding them. Eisenhower had
been a top-ranked neighborhood high school with a very good reputation up until the 1960s. In past decades Truman had an average reputation and less academic distinction than Eisenhower, but had a number
of illustrious graduates who had gone on to fame and fortune.

Both of these high schools were now ranked very low both in terms of
academic achievement and the amount of violence present in the school.
They had official drop-out rates of 19% and 11%, but the actual graduation rates were much lower, less than 50%, as all of the high schools in
the city play statistical games to reduce their official reported drop-out
rates.[22] In other words, Eisenhower, a four-year school with 2,600 enrolled
students, graduates 175 seniors each year.

These schools were places of great heroism among teachers and student
success despite the odds, as well as places of despair, fear, and resignation
to extremely low standards. The neighborhood problems of poverty, drug
use, and violence did not stop at the school doors; in fact, these problems
were generally more visible at the schools than in the immediately sur-

Table 7.1   Residence of West Indian youth by age and generation

Location	Age 1–17			Age 18–30		
	2nd generation	1.5 generation	All	2nd generation	1.5 generation	All
Crown Heights/ Flatbush	25.3%	26.2%	25.5%	22.2%	31.3%	27.1%
Brooklyn	39.1%	40.5%	39.3%	38.0%	44.4%	41.4%
New York City	72.8%	78.8%	73.9%	75.5%	81.2%	78.6%
Total N.Y. metro region	109,634	23,027	132,661	21,151	24,549	45,700

Source: 1990 Public Use Microdata Sample, 152 PUMA areas in tristate metropolitan New York City.
Note: Table does not include second-generation individuals residing outside parents' household.

rounding neighborhoods because both schools drew some of their students from even worse neighborhoods that were close by.

Savvy parents, many of them middle class, who lived in these neighborhoods did their best to keep their children out of these schools. This meant sending them to private or parochial schools or to the citywide magnet schools. Several students from these mostly West Indian neighborhoods attend Harvard University each year. But none of these students have attended the local neighborhood schools; they come from private schools or from the premier city academic schools like Stuyvesant. The teachers at Eisenhower and Truman blamed specialized high schools for some of the problems at the neighborhood high schools:

> Syphoning off by the specialized schools kills every other academic school. I think that if we had the hundred kids that are zoned to come here but go to those other schools, they would be the movers and the shakers of the school. They would do the plays and the things that would get the other kids involved. If we had those really dedicated, high-level kids, we would have more things to offer all the kids. They would kind of like drive the system to offer them various activities. That's the dream. The reality is that we don't have that certain segment of kids who choose to go to the specialized high schools. (White male teacher, age 45)

Some teens end up attending Truman or Eisenhower not out of choice but because their parents cannot afford Catholic or private school, and the students failed to win admission to the competitive high schools. However, many of the students attend the local schools because the parents do not understand the system and fail to understand the problems their children face in the local schools. Many immigrant parents are under the mistaken impression that their children are much safer attending local schools because they will not have to travel on the subways or into neighborhoods the parents do not know at all.

Violence in the Schools

Violence and the fear of violence dominated school life for the teachers and the students at Eisenhower and Truman High Schools. In this they were not alone. In the school year of the fieldwork, 1990–91, guards detected and confiscated 1,779 weapons in the city schools. In that year there were 3,843 serious incidents reported by the Board of Education. Serious incidents include assaults, robberies, sex offenses, and drug and weapon possessions. There were fifty-six reported incidents involving guns, including shootings of sixteen students, five teachers, two parents, and one police officer on school grounds. Six students and one teacher were killed in school-related incidents. These statistics should nonetheless be interpreted warily. Some principals over-report incidents to get better security. Others under-report so they do not get a bad reputation. Yet Eisenhower and Truman were at the extreme end. In the ten years preceding the study both schools had seen students killed on school grounds. Both schools had experienced mass disturbances with students rampaging through the building and police being brought in for crowd control. In addition, many incidents that happened just off the school grounds also contributed to the fear in the schools. Classmates of students in both schools had recently died off-campus in shooting and stabbing incidents. Drug dealers were present near school grounds every day so that students who walked to school had no choice but to walk past them. Both schools were among five schools designated that year by the New York City Board of Education as the most violent in the entire school system.

Even though I had read a great deal about the problems in inner-city schools and I thought I understood how many serious issues there were to deal with in urban high schools, I was still deeply shocked by my experiences in these two schools, most especially Eisenhower High School, which was in worse shape than Truman. Despite the efforts of a number of excellent teachers and guidance counselors, the general situation in Eisenhower was quite troubling: the number of weapons entering the school was enough to color all interactions between teachers and students, the academic standards of the vast majority of classes were not sufficient to prepare a student for a competitive college, the problems of teen pregnancy and drug and alcohol use were widespread, and the odds of a freshman graduating four years later were appallingly low.

My first day at Eisenhower set the tone for the fear and uncertainty I felt during my time there. After all my struggles to get access to the high schools (see the Appendix), I was very happy to be there. I arrived on time for my appointment with the principal and saw that there was a long line of students at the front door of the school. It turned out that this was one of the "surprise" days where metal detectors were brought to the school. The designation of the school as one of the most violent schools in the city system had occurred earlier that year, and the mayor had pledged metal detectors to try to keep out weapons. But since the city did not have enough metal detectors, teams were sent to the five worst schools on different days to set up the detectors. The random nature of when the detectors would show up at the school was supposed to be a deterrent to bringing in weapons.

On the day that the weapons detectors were there, a large security van was parked in front of the school. They might as well have put up a big sign saying, "Use another entrance if you have weapons." Because that is precisely what the students did. The students were all supposed to enter the one main door, and all of the side doors to the school were locked from the outside. Because of fire regulations, however, the side doors could not be locked from the inside. So some students would get in by going through the metal detectors, then create a commotion that would attract the already overwhelmed security guards to one part of the building, while another group of students would go to a side door and let in their friends, none of whom went through a metal detector. I saw this happen on every occasion that the metal detectors came to the school. The teachers and administrators knew about it. As a result no one believed the school was weapon-free even on the days that the metal detectors were there. (Of course, there also was nothing preventing the students from bringing in a weapon and hiding it somewhere in the school.)

On my first day at the school I made it by the metal detectors (they were handheld detectors, much like the ones used when people set off the walk-through detectors at airports). Since I was a guest in the school, I had to stop at the security desk to sign in, a routine I would go through every day of my time at the school. The security guard took my name and asked if it was my first day in the school, and I said yes. She looked at me gravely and said, "Be very, very, careful." Other security guards warned me about staircases not to use because of the kids hanging out on them. I later learned that assaults on teachers and students had often occurred in the less-traveled stairways.

My most frightening experience happened one morning at 11 A.M. when a drunk or drugged-out student went crazy in the area where I was doing interviews. The area was filled with small tables and chairs, which at that time were occupied by a number of students who were talking and horsing around. This young man suddenly started yelling about nothing in particular and threw the movable chairs at the walls. Everyone else began to scream and run away. The teachers responded by retreating to a safe area away from the student, getting as many other students in the safe area with them, locking the doors, and calling for security. I later learned that teachers need to react this way because their own personal safety is in question if they try to intervene with a violent student because they do not know whether the student has a weapon. The security guards came quickly and subdued the student and took him away to the assistant principal's office.[23]

As my interviews with both students and teachers at Eisenhower progressed, I became more concerned about safety in the schools. Everyone told me about the number of weapons being carried by the students. A series of fires were set in the school during the time I was interviewing. I was told that they were not being reported at first to the police because the school was trying to preserve its reputation. Ultimately, however, several serious fires brought the police and fire departments to the school. The students I interviewed told me stories of other students who had been wounded or killed near the school:

Q: Do kids bring weapons into this school?
A: Just last week on Thursday there was a whole bunch of crowding on the second floor. There was a fight here and a fight there, people were pushing each other, running to see the fights. And then you would break up one, the next one would start. So I don't know. One guy pulled out a gun. And start pointing it on the second floor, right? Then another guy pulled out another gun, and started pointing it. So everybody was running down the hallways, back and forth and back and forth. And eventually they didn't catch the guy. They took everybody outside. Everybody came outside and there was still fights going on outside. People fighting, beating up. They were jumping kids. And the police are standing

right there, looking, and they didn't do anything. One Haitian
boy, by himself, got jumped by a whole bunch of kids. Got
slashed. Got his face scarred up from the pavement . . . And so
then everybody just left and went home. I don't know, everybody
wants to leave this school. Nobody wants to stay here anymore.
On Friday half the kids weren't in school 'cause they were scared.
(Trinidadian female, age 17, in United States seven years)

The fear was ever-present for these kids and definitely affected their ability
to learn:

It's like every day you come in here, you are wondering, oh, are
you gonna make it through another day of school or something.

Q: Really?

A: Because you have kids who get stabbed. Then a lot of things.
Fights break out over nonsense. You know, "Oh she looked at me
funny," or you know, "Oh, he stole my girl." Some real nonsense.
It's like it makes no sense. It's just not necessary . . . People have
knives and stuff like that. Guns. But nobody get shot in here, but
we have people who have been stabbed. They set a girl's hair on
fire. Craziness in this school. (Guyanese female, age 18, born in
United States)

The presence of weapons was very obvious to these teens. When I asked if
there was anything they would want to change about their schools, the
most common reply was that they wanted the unruly kids controlled, and
they wanted the weapons out of the school:

Truman is a scary school. When I first started, I hear from a lot of
kids that Truman is a bad school and all of that. I was scared myself,
you know? A lot of things happening. Every second there's a fight,
you know, in the halls . . . This guy who was playing volleyball once,
he was playing and a gun fell out of his pocket. (Jamaican female,
age 19, in United States three years)

Because of this fear of guns and knives most students we talked to wanted
the metal detectors to be installed permanently—not only one or two days
a week. This was said with some sadness as more than a few students noted

that the presence of the detectors made them feel like they were in jail. As one student put it, "white kids don't have to go through metal detectors to go to school."

In this atmosphere of fear most teens did not blame other students for carrying weapons. In fact, it was often the nice kids who felt the need for a weapon because they had been hassled so much and feared so much for their own safety. The atmosphere was like the Wild West—everyone thought everyone else was carrying guns and that they should carry guns for their own safety:

> I know some people who still get guns in the school, my friends, some guys I know.
> Q: Why do they bring guns to school?
> A: Because they feel, it's just that they feel once they have a gun they protected. Nothing can happen to them, you know? But a gun is gonna hurt somebody. 'Cause if you and somebody arguing, and you don't have a gun, you're not gonna argue 'cause you know you don't have a gun. But if you have a gun, you know, you're gonna end up arguing and stuff 'cause you can shoot them or whatever. (Jamaican female, age 16, born in United States)

There are no statistics on how many students actually carry weapons, but in an inner-city school it is very common. In a nationwide survey conducted by the *New York Times,* 31% of white teenagers and 70% of black teenagers reported knowing someone who had been shot in the last five years. Among black teenagers, 54% reported that they worried about being a victim of a crime, and the crime they most worried about is being shot.[24]

One young man we spoke with who admitted to carrying a gun had already been shot, not in school but on the streets. He dropped out of school eventually, but he was one of the students who was often in fights and who intimidated other students. But he too described being scared most of the time, especially when he was younger:

> It's just that too much big people, there's big guys there. Big, big guys. I mean guys that would rob you after school for tokens. They do. They rob you after school for tokens. They walk in a bunch and

they rob you after school for tokens. I used to always have to cut school just to leave early so they wouldn't rob me or something 'cause I wasn't having it. And one day this guy just pulled out a knife on me and said, yo, I want your tokens. And I was like, you better get out of my face, 'cause if you don't have the knife we could do this, you know? (Jamaican male, age 17, in United States ten years)

The unpredictability of the violence comes through in many of the students' accounts. Walking through the hallways is dangerous because of the risk that one might inadvertently bother someone with a weapon. As a result, as noted earlier, it is often the small kids, the kids who are not in gangs and get good grades in school, who end up carrying weapons for protection:

I touch this guy by accident. It was like right there in the hall [he points to the hall outside of the room we are interviewing in]. All the kids are right there. And I touched him, I brushed against him. He said, why you hit me? I said, I ain't hit you. I just kept on walking. And he came behind me and then I stopped. I got to the classroom upstairs and I stopped in front of the door and he grabbed me. And I said I didn't hit you and I tried to walk away and he hit me in the face. It was a black American guy. And the Jamaicans, my friends, they see this happen and they stopped the guy . . . But because of what happened, I had to come home that same day early. I missed like two classes because my face was all red and everything. My nose was bleeding. (Jamaican male, age 18, in United States three years)

This young man was both very short and doing well in school. He was thus a prime target for kids who wanted to harass him, and after we turned off the tape recorder for the formal part of the interview he admitted that he carried a gun for protection. He said that while most kids carried knives, it was still possible to come up against someone with a gun:

You brush up against the wrong guy and you can just feel that lump. You're like, oh God, I hit the wrong guy and you turn back quick. Most of the guys carry knives. You probably see seventy-five percent of the guys carry at least a blade or a knife or something.

The teachers are also very frightened by the weapons that are in the school and the degree of violence and disruption, issues that came up frequently in the interviews:

> For the first time in eleven years I felt myself making decisions. Should I walk up the stairs and walk to the cafeteria—which was the safest of the two? And I feel, well, the cafeteria, because you know if you get food thrown at you, well it washes off, it's done, right? . . . I know we had a lot of fires, and I doubt there was ever any report to the Board of Ed because there was never any fire personnel here. The last two fires have been reported because there have been fire personnel here. (White female teacher, age 58)

The situation is very frustrating for the teachers because there seem to be no easy solutions. Weapon detectors were desired by most teachers but it was clear these devices would not eliminate the problem of violence and weapons:

> Violence is a very serious problem. They have no problem settling anything with violence. The most trivial thing, and that goes for girls and boys. Many of them fight for status. It makes them "bad," people look up to them. But all of them will fight at the drop of a hat . . . We had two murders here before we had metal detectors. Ten years ago I stood on the sidewalks outside of Eisenhower and identified a dead student for the police. The next year there was another dead student. If you live with violence and accept it as a way of life, you will find a way to commit it. Yes, you can stop them from bringing in their guns and you can find the knives, but we play musical chairs with these children anyway. You have a knife at Eisenhower, you get sent to Truman, you have a knife at Truman, we send you to Lee, you have a knife at Lee, we send you back to Eisenhower. These kids just go round and round. You don't do anything to attack conflict resolution. (White female teacher, age 47)

The New York City school system guarantees an education to every child, and a school is unable to really expel a student under the age of 16. When a student does something violent or has severe behavioral problems, the last resort for the high school is just to transfer him or her to another neighborhood high school. And in return the school must then take a "bad kid" from another high school. Even teachers who don't want the old system to return do not know what to suggest for a new system; however, they know the current system is not working:

> We cannot discipline if each child has a constitutional right to attend a public school, and that if the bad child in this school just gets sent to another school, but in return we have to get the bad child from that other school. We have to take the really dangerous child that might be carrying a gun or might be violent. That might hurt you. I do think we have to examine that issue. Without discriminating against anybody and without making anybody feel like a leper. Because we don't function well. But I don't know how we're gonna get across that. I don't know. (White female teacher, age 40)

In addition to the constant fear of weapons, teachers described their fears of being assaulted, pushed down stairs, and having things thrown at them:

> Q: Is violence a serious problem here?
> A: Yes, very serious. For example today, on this very day, there are weapons checks going on that you see on the side of the school. This side of the school has police trucks and vans, and students are constantly being scanned for weapons. I think the biggest problem has been the number of incidents we have had this year, just simply involving throwing things at teachers, pushing teachers down flights of stairs. I myself almost had an eardrum blown out when an M-80 exploded several inches from my ear at my old school. (White male teacher, age 40)

Some teachers deal with this danger by trying to avoid dangerous situations. Teachers walked each other to their cars after school and tried to avoid situations where they thought they were most at risk:

> I would rather not walk out of the school during lunch periods when some of the riffraff is sitting around on the stairs, steps . . . I know just by going to the dean and knowing what goes on here, there are weapons that are confiscated from the kids. Weapons, I mean,

there's one thing having a knife fight, there's another thing having a gun in the building . . . One of the things I have learned over twenty years is that one way of not dealing with things is by not getting out in the halls and confronting kids. And that's one of the reasons I like my job [doing scheduling]. I can escape the chaos and sit in front of the screen. (White male teacher, age 45)

RACE AND THE SPIRAL DOWNWARD

How did the schools descend to this level of violence, chaos, and deteriorating academic performance? Race certainly plays a major role. Both Truman and Eisenhower High Schools are among the seven high schools in the city that the Board of Education calls "racially isolated"; in other words, they are segregated schools that are all-black. In a 1990 column in the *New York Times*, journalist Sam Roberts commented that there had been a public outcry in South Africa when statistics were released showing that only 42% of black high school students there were passing their competency exams. Roberts pointed out that among the seven "racially isolated" high schools in New York, the failure rate for basic competency exams was worse. In the high schools where I did fieldwork less than 2% of the students who were afforded a diploma received a New York State Regents Diploma, the diploma that signifies a strong academic program of college preparation courses. Citywide, 23% of graduating public school students received a Regents Diploma.[25]

The guidance counselor at Eisenhower estimated that among those who actually receive a diploma, about 70% go to college and 10% go into the military. Of those who do go to college, 40% go to a two-year college, and 60% go to a four-year college. She had no statistics at all on how many drop out of college and how many finish. Anecdotally, she knew that a number of students never even finish their first semester of college.

Parents who drop their children off at the school door every morning and pick them up at the end of the day often have no clue about what is going on in the school. In a small Caribbean school it would be impossible for a teen to arrive at school and spend the day there but never attend class, yet that is precisely what some of the troubled students at Eisenhower did. They spent day after day hanging out in the hallways or right outside the school. Their parents thought they were getting an education but they were just marking time and disrupting the school atmosphere for the other students and teachers. This math teacher describes the frustrations of a parent in this situation:

> By the time they reach sixth grade the basic skills have to be there and they are not. A parent comes up here to me and says, "Why is my child not in sequential math?" I tell him the child can't cope with it because he doesn't have the skills built up from before. The parent says, "Why did my child not get the skills built up from before? I have been sending my child to school every day. I have not heard about any problems, he always got good grades in math. So how come you tell me he can't do the math?" (Guyanese female teacher and guidance counselor, age 42, in United States twenty-two years)

Sociologists of education have stressed that one of the reasons middle-class children do well academically is that parents have the "cultural capital" to reinforce what is learned in school, as well as the resources and know-how to closely monitor a school's performance. Some West Indian parents, including the teachers we interviewed who had children in the system, did know how to monitor their children's performance. A number of teachers told us about intervening with a school guidance counselor or teacher who was not encouraging their own children to do well, or who had assigned their children to a lower academic track, or who had let students choose too few rigorous college prep courses. But many of the West Indian parents do not know enough to be equally involved in their children's education. Working-class parents often don't know the differences in the kinds of academic courses their children are taking. Middle-class parents often erroneously believe that their children's schools are like the schools they attended back in the islands:

> In Jamaica the parents, they don't really participate because they trust the teacher to do this type of job. And here when they come they have the same impression that OK well, I am sending my child to school and I know the teachers going to do the best. And it's not like that. A lot of teachers they are like, "Oh really, these West Indian parents, they don't really care about their kids because I don't see

them involved." But they don't understand these parents, they say, "Well you know this is the teacher's job and I trust that the teacher knows how to do the job well." So they put all their trust into the teacher. (Guyanese female teacher, age 48, in United States twenty years)

Another teacher echoes this sentiment by comparing West Indian parents with African-American parents:

Many of the West Indian parents believe that the teacher is right always. So if you find that you are in trouble with a teacher, and although you might be right, you have a difficult time explaining that to an old-fashioned West Indian parent. I find that many of the black American parents, many of them, children of the sixties and the seventies, they tend to be a little harder on the teacher, a little more suspect. But the old-fashioned West Indian parent is difficult to get them to believe, well, possibly the teacher might be wrong. (Barbadian male teacher, age 43, born in United States)

The trust that the parents have that the schools are looking out for their children is often misplaced. So even though, as one student put it, the reputation of Eisenhower is that "only stupid and bad kids come here," many of the students said that their parents insisted that they attend the local school because they did not want them traveling on buses and subways:

I want to transfer from here [Truman]. I want to go to John Dewey High School or Graphic Arts. Dewey has a whole class for drama. My grandmother said I should work with what Truman has. I shouldn't try to go to a school that has the things I want. I should stick with a school that has the things I don't want. She was trying to scare me. She was like, "Oh, if you go to school by Coney Island or Manhattan, you know they have guns there." Always trying to scare me. And Truman's not even that good. They have guns here. (Trinidadian female, age 15, born in United States)

The guidance counselor at Eisenhower complained that this approach to keeping kids placed locally extended to college choices for the best students, who were accepted at a number of colleges. Many parents insisted that their children turn down scholarships to competitive schools because they wanted them to live at home and attend Brooklyn College or Hunter College. They were fearful of what would happen to their children, especially their girls, if they were allowed to go away to school.

The white managers in charge of hiring at American Food whom I described in Chapter 4 had definite ideas about West Indian workers being better than African-American workers. This was reflected in their hiring practices. There is also an image in the popular culture of West Indians as the "model minority." Thomas Sowell, for instance, argues that second-generation West Indians do better in educational achievement than African Americans.[26] We asked the white and black American and West Indian schoolteachers we spoke with about differences between West Indian students and African-American students. While the teachers noted differences in discipline and behavior and in attitudes toward race,[27] they did not generally conclude that West Indians were better than their African-American peers in terms of school work at the present time. Instead, the teachers described a range of abilities among the immigrant and native-born students. The distribution of the immigrant students in terms of achievement was bipolar—the newly arrived students were by far both the best and the worst students in the school.

A number of older teachers conceded that the stereotype of the West Indian as the better scholar fit their experience in the late 1960s and early 1970s. However, beginning in the mid-1980s until the time of my field-work in the early 1990s, the distribution of West Indian students shifted. This reflects changes in the migration stream to the United States. The earlier immigrants of the late '60s and '70s were often arriving under occupational visas—a great many of them were recruited nurses. The stable, mostly white, middle-class neighborhood surrounding Truman High School did not have many black families. The few Caribbean black families who bought houses in the area at that time were well-educated middle-class families. They had students who excelled in school.

As the immigration stream diversified over time, the class distribution of the immigrants changed, and a number of poor and working-class immigrants entered the United States. In central Brooklyn the 1970s saw a great deal of white flight, and the area around Eisenhower changed to an all-black neighborhood, with a still sizable middle-class population of

West Indian immigrants, along with poor people who came in after real estate prices fell and after a number of apartment buildings fell into disrepair and rents were lowered.[28] The class mix of the students at Eisenhower and at nearby Truman changed downwards, and the diversity in the class origins of the West Indian immigrants increased.

Indeed, the longtime teachers at Eisenhower all described the past few decades as a "downward spiral" in terms of the academic quality of the students, the discipline in the school, the overall distribution of the teachers who choose to work there, and the academic standards in the classes they teach. These teachers most definitely tie this downward spiral to the changing racial composition of the school—not to the influx of immigrants per se. Black and white teachers alike believe that the Board of Education had a conscious policy in the 1970s and 1980s of preserving some white and integrated schools in Brooklyn by opening a new high school in an all-white neighborhood and by changing the neighborhoods from which high schools in black areas drew their students. These teachers state that the changing demographics of the immediate Eisenhower neighborhood would not have resulted in an all-black school if the Board of Ed had not decided to "save" other schools in white neighborhoods by changing the feeding patterns of all of the high schools. As a result of these changes Eisenhower abruptly lost middle- and working-class white students, who were rezoned into high schools in all-white areas, and began to be assigned poor black American students from the neighborhoods of East New York and Brownsville as well as from the changing (in terms of class distribution) population of black immigrant students from Flatbush, East Flatbush, and Crown Heights.

As one teacher described the changes in the late 1970s and early 1980s, "In the beginning the American black kids were tougher. The West Indians were very, very refined ... We had a lot of tough American black kids that wouldn't think twice of throwing the teacher out the window." The middle-class West Indian students began to transfer from the school when the discipline problems became acute after the inclusion of poor American students from rough neighborhoods:

In the middle 1970s they opened [another high school in a white neighborhood], and many of the white students just bolted from the school. Bolted. And as a result the school was left with middle-class black students, you know, who were doing quite nicely. However, there began inclusion into the school of students from East New York and other neighborhoods, poverty-stricken, and these students were performing rather poorly on basic competency tests. This encouraged other middle-class black students to opt for other schools—these students traveled many, many hours to go to other schools. And this, therefore, continued the basic decline. (White male teacher, age 40)

In addition, the West Indian students themselves also became more diverse as poor and working-class West Indians began to migrate into the area:

In 1979 a lot of the students we got were students who had been to school in the West Indies and who came from very stable homes, and they were well prepared to do academic work. But there was a change on the part of faculty and there was a change on the part of the students because every year the quality of the students became poorer and poorer. And we were beginning to get, not students who came from the cities and who came from private schools, we began to get students who came from the back woods, who barely spoke English, who spoke what they called "English Creole," who could not read and write at the same level. Students, some of whom had only third-grade educations and had not been in school in years. At the same time the staff had to change what we taught. We had a new chairman who felt that those children could not cope in terms of reading level or experience with what we taught before—we used to teach the classics, Dickens, Shakespeare, Thomas Hardy. We taught Sinclair Lewis. When I came back [from maternity leave in 1979] we taught Paul Zindel, which is about a fifth-grade reading level. It was very different. (White female teacher, age 47)

In math the same changes occurred; a school that used to offer all kinds of advanced math classes found its remedial math classes overflowing and struggled to keep a calculus class for the handful of students who were able to take it. This caused some of the best teachers to want to leave the school for a school with better students:

> Most teachers who come here really want to teach math. If they wanted to teach remedial math, they would have become elementary school teachers. You know, they want to teach trigonometry and they want to teach all this stuff. And you give them a program and they have three or four classes of remedial math, they get bored. They look to get out. The trade-off is if you get the people who don't really want to teach math, but are in teaching 'cause they need the job and the money, they like teaching the remedial math, because they can handle the math. They're perfectly happy. (White male teacher, age 45)

The downward spiral feeds on itself because as Eisenhower develops a reputation among teachers as a dangerous and unsatisfying place to teach, it becomes a very unpopular choice for any individual teacher. Since the schools award teaching choices based on seniority and on which teachers are in demand by principals, good teachers who have some experience will get the opportunity to leave and teach at a better school. Thus schools like Eisenhower and Truman, which have students who need the best teachers available, have staffs that are comprised of three groups. There are young inexperienced first-time teachers who get assigned to Eisenhower because they have the least seniority and it is no one else's first choice. Some of them may end up being good teachers and thriving in the challenging environment of the high school, but the majority will give up teaching within a few short years. In any case, their inexperience is no match for conditions that would try the abilities and patience of even the most accomplished and dedicated teachers. The second group is comprised of older, burned-out teachers who are marking time until retirement. These teachers are either not motivated enough to seek another job in the system or not good enough to be offered one. They go through the motions of teaching but no longer have much energy or spirit for their students. They are often referred to as the "deadwood" of the system:

> There are teachers in the school who I know from the inside don't do anything. I can walk up and down the halls and

see them doing nothing. As much as my students say, hey, give us a free period, I hate babysitting, but they are getting free periods in other classes during the day.

Q: You mean teachers sit there and don't teach?

A: Yeah, they teach for maybe ten minutes, and then they stop. There are card games going on in the back of the classroom. Not by subs, this is the regular teachers I am talking about. When I see some of the dreadful teachers they are giving some of these poor kids, I said if I were one of these kids, I wouldn't go to class either, you know. I think that we've got some real deadwood. (White male teacher, age 45)

Students speak in disdain of teachers who are afraid of students and stoop to academic dishonesty:

I don't think that it is right for teachers to help kids out on tests. I think he was scared of the kids. 'Cause they would curse him out. In order for them not to—he was scared so that he would give them the answers to the test so they would go home and study, and during the test the next day, he would leave the classroom and then the kids would cheat—well nobody was in the classroom to stop them, so they would cheat and stuff. And when report cards came, he would ask them what grade do they think they deserve on their report card? (Trinidadian female, age 17, in United States seven years)

There are many reasons why teachers would get to the point where they do not care about teaching and about their students—hard and dangerous working conditions, school and district politics, relatively low pay and prestige, difficult students, and the like. Often, however, the interpretation some students have of why these teachers do not care about them is that the teachers are white and the students are black. Because these schools are completely segregated with an all-black student body, and because the rest of these students' lives are also likely to be highly segregated, white teachers are often the only "representatives of their race" these kids know in person. The students had been told by a number of teachers that they did not care about the students because the teachers would still get paid whether the students learned or not:

From what I am hearing I hear from other students that the teachers just don't care. All in all they just, you know, because it is a black school. That is what the kids say. (Trinidadian female, age 18, in United States four years)

The black teachers in Eisenhower they care a lot because you know they are saying, well, we know what you are going through and everything. We want you to get ahead. But there's a lot of teachers in here they are like, yeah, we care and everything. But behind your back, oh, those black kids, they don't know anything . . . White teachers are like, they come and they tell you, I don't have to teach you. I get paid anyway. They'll sit there and let you do anything. They say, bang your heads on the wall, kill yourselves, I don't care. It's like if they have a few students who have a discipline problem they say they're acting up, they can't control the class, so they finished our class. See, that's how you are. I ain't gonna bother to teach. For a whole week I went to class without a teacher. There was no teacher. And they getting paid? But no black teacher would do that. It was like, you and you, to the dean's office. The rest of the class, those that want to learn, stay. Those who don't they can leave. And the white teachers, most of them in this school, they don't care. As long as they get their paycheck. (Haitian female, age 18, born in United States)

Two of the West Indian teachers also told us that it was clear to them that many white teachers did not have the same standards for black kids that they did for whites:

Just about twenty-five to thirty percent of the teachers are minority. In an all-minority school, okay? And the kids and them know it. They say, oh the teachers, as soon as school is over they jump in their cars and they drive out to Long Island and they don't care about us. (Trinidadian male teacher, age 41, in United States eighteen years)

Many of my colleagues and myself share the opinion that the public school system is not doing as much as they could for these kids. Their perception is that these are minority kids and therefore their expectations are lower . . . The parents like me, who look out for their children, cannot get walked over. I'm talking about a parent who is a nurse's aide, and trusts the schools totally to handle the welfare of the child. And the child gets channeled into various programs and classes. And they say it's not as true anymore but I think it is true to a certain extent. (Guyanese female teacher and guidance counselor, age 42, in United States twenty-two years)

The final group of teachers—the dedicated, experienced master teachers—are the real heroes of this story. They truly believe in what they are doing with their students. They know how to teach students of all ranges and abilities. They go beyond the call of duty—devoting extra hours helping students and spending their own money to help students who need carfare or to buy lunch. They talk to parents, they help students with personal problems, they respect their students as people. The racial and ethnic backgrounds of the teachers made little difference in those the students identified as the really good teachers. They are white, black, and West Indian. The teachers who really made a difference in their students' lives combined a respect and true affection for their students with a very firm sense of standards, goals, and discipline. Some of the hardest teachers in the school were also some of the most respected and loved—as long as the rules and discipline that they enforced were matched by a true respect and understanding for their students. This music teacher was one of the very best teachers in the school:

It's not just—in my case, teaching them music. That's the last order of business. You have many more concerns that have to be addressed. They have problems at home. They have economic problems, they have parental problems, they have educational problems, and I try to help them go to class and do well in class. And they come to me when they have had an argument with a parent, or they don't have money to get on a bus, you know, or they don't have money to have lunch. And it's a multifaceted job today. It's not just teaching a subject matter, that's far from it. And that starts to wear you down. My own family is concerned about me because they see me spending more time here than I do with my own family. And I say, well I know but I feel that there's a need for it. And they say, it's a lousy job but somebody's got to do it. But I don't look at it as a lousy job. I just feel that someone has to do it. And there are many teachers that also have that same feeling. And the students feel it. The students know it and they feel it and they gravitate. (White male teacher, age 45)

DIFFERENCES IN SCHOOL SYSTEMS

The fact that West Indian students were both the very best and the very worst students in the high schools reflects the difference in the educational systems of the West Indies and the United States. The West Indian educational system is modeled on the British system. It is a pyramid in structure and while all students get a primary education, only a select group of students can proceed to high school and beyond.[29] There are also vast differences in quality among the primary schools, with urban schools generally offering better educations than rural schools. The islands also differ. Barbados has a very good reputation for its school systems. Guyana may have had a good school system for some of its students in the past, but the economic decline of the last decade has led to severe problems in its school system. Jamaican and Trinidadian students from urban areas generally have good preparation, while those from rural areas are much less well prepared:

> Immigrant students that we have are students who did not have a sound educational standard, because they were the ones who would not have entered high school. Here in this country they're forced to go to high school. So we have a pattern of them who are not of the caliber for high school, and they are here and they're struggling. And sometimes it probably gives a bad impression that, hey, they're from the islands, their standards are low. They're not just low, it's just that these are not students who originally would go to high schools. So we have a lot of them here, we have to water down courses just to meet their needs because they can hardly read or write. You know they were going to go to vocational schools. So I think there's going to be a need for us to have some sort of vocational system here for these students. (Jamaican female teacher, age 36, in United States seven years)

Thus students arriving from the West Indies after having gone to school for some number of years have very different educational profiles depending on where they attended school. Those who were in the strong educational track in the selective primary and secondary schools in the islands with good educational systems have an extremely strong educational background. Those who were attending primary school in a decimated school system such as Guyana or in a rural area of Trinidad where compulsory education laws were laxly enforced could arrive at the doorstep of the American high school at age 17 or 18 unable to read or write. Thus, as noted above, the best and the worst students in these New York high schools were West Indians.

The influx of these unprepared students also contributed to the downward spiral of the high school because they lowered the standardized test scores that savvy middle-class parents use to assess the schools they consider sending their children to:

> A kid comes in; because the kid is fifteen, sixteen years old, we put them in the tenth grade, which is one of the grades they use to rate the school. Comes June, the kid takes the Regents Competency and fails. Kid was in my school for six, seven months. OK, I have to make up for all that. The kid fails. Now they have a statistic which shows that so many percent of the kids have failed. So now they take all the kids in the school and they put out a list showing that only thirty-seven percent of the tenth grade is gonna achieve competency in math. And the chancellor wants seventy percent to achieve competency. And you get a principal who comes in or an administrator who comes in who doesn't have the slightest concept of the difficulties we're facing with these kids, what's coming in. And they don't want to hear from me. All they know is that their boss is looking for that percentage to go up . . . The clamor for statistics means that they don't really have a concept of the difficulties that the kids and the teachers face. And they want an easy way to rate schools and departments, and it doesn't exist. Especially with the problem we're discussing, with the immigrant mixtures. (White male teacher, age 45)

The West Indian students encountered the best and the worst aspects of the American school system, with both happy and tragic outcomes. Instead of the restricted and structurally elitist British system they left behind, the immigrant students encountered the free-flowing, unrestricted, democratic, yet also deeply flawed American system. The newly arrived students from the best schools in the Caribbean were able to take the honors courses still offered at the high school. Teachers who are starved for responsive and bright students lavish attention and hopes on these students, and every year Eisenhower graduates approximately ten students who get scholarships to private schools like Syracuse and New York University or who get into branches of the State University of New York like Stony Brook or Albany. Once every year or two there is a memorable student who qualifies for a highly competitive college—in the last ten years Eisenhower has sent a student to MIT, to the University of Pennsylvania, and to Columbia. Almost every teacher I interviewed told me about these students by name, with the pride that every teacher everywhere takes in a student who excels. Most of these very successful students have not spent their entire schooling in the New York school system. They are recent immigrants, who had at least their primary schooling back in the islands. Occasionally, an American-born student of West Indian origin will also be in this group. Usually these students are from middle-class families who provide a strong support to the efforts of the schools.

But the average and below-average students from both the islands and the United States can just as often be victims as beneficiaries of the New York school system. The strengths of the system—the opportunities it offers to all students regardless of ability, the democratic nature of the schools, the wide variety of subjects and activities in the schools, and the special programs offered for students of low abilities and bad academic preparation—are balanced by the weaknesses of the system—the lack of control and discipline in the schools, the presence of weapons and the resulting fear, the racial segregation and prejudice, the large size and the resulting bureaucracy, and the spillover into school of the social problems affecting the kids.

The strengths and weaknesses of the school system are intimately and hopelessly intertwined; the reason there are opportunities and hope for all students is because no one is turned away. This is also the rationale that teachers have for struggling with students with severe problems who disrupt their classmates and for teaching to a lower level of comprehension. The democratic nature of the schools and the free interaction between teachers and students and among students lead to more creativity, spontaneity, and even fun in learning for many students. Yet it also contributes to the discipline problems and the perceived lack of respect of students for teachers and of students for each other that plague the schools.

The students and teachers agreed that the best part of the New York school system was its openness, the almost unlimited opportunities it extended to students regardless of their previous academic records or abilities. For many of the teachers who came here as adults to further their own educations—getting a bachelor's or master's degree in teaching at the City University of New York—the availability of college for anyone who manages to graduate from high school is one of the best things about America. This Grenadian teacher describes what he loves about the American system:

> In the British system there are not enough slots at the high school level, and then to go on to college. Their contention is that high school and beyond is only for certain people. And so if you haven't studied from day one and put in your hours of homework and what have you in study, then by the time you take the exam you won't be ready . . . Whereas here in America you can basically slide through almost twelve years and then get into a college, do fantastically well, and then transfer to another college. And for those twelve years when they look at the record, they really don't care because that first year of college you have done phenomenally. So now they say you've matured, you've woken up, the whole thing. You can't do that in the British system.
>
> Q: So which system would you prefer for your own children?
> A: American. Given the freedom and the opportunity everybody has—at least initially the same opportunity to be and do what they want. (Grenadian male teacher, age 46, in United States twenty-six years)

The sentiments of this teacher that the chance for higher education was much greater in the United States and that this was a very good thing were shared by a number of other teachers. Yet this teacher was the only one to say unequivocally that he preferred the American system for his own children. The other teachers we spoke with could describe the good aspects of the American system, but most of them thought that their own children would do better in the West Indian system. This teacher is typical:

> In Jamaica, I think there is some type of discrimination because if you did not pass certain exams, you wouldn't get into high school, whereas here you know everyone gets the opportunity to go to high school and college. I think that's the one good thing about American education where I don't think we have it that much in the West Indies.
>
> Q: Which system would you prefer for your own child?
> A: Jamaica. As a matter of fact, my son just went to Jamaica, he is going to be going to school there for one year. Because I think you know these public schools are failing the children. They need to make some changes. I mean they are not fitting the needs of the children. I mean these children are going wild all over the place and they are not learning a thing. No respect. Nothing.
> (Guyanese female teacher, age 48, in United States twenty years)

Many teachers (and some students) recommended having children attend primary schools in the islands, where they receive a very solid and strong education, and then bringing them to the United States when they are high school or college age in order to take advantage of the opportunities here. This is in fact the strategy of many families who believe, based on all of the factors discussed in this chapter and in Chapter 6, that the United States is not a good place for young children. Many families send for their children or only begin the migration process after their children have exhausted the educational possibilities available in the islands.

Because they were trained in the West Indian system, some of the West Indian teachers can be the least forgiving of the downsides of the American system. The New York school system has employed a large number of West Indian teachers, and many people we spoke with gave us some good reasons why West Indian students benefit from having West Indian teachers. Aside from the obvious benefits of their acting as role models for immigrant students, West Indian teachers are also often cultural translators in the schools, explaining particular behaviors of the immigrant students to the American teachers. For instance, in the islands students are expected, as a sign of respect, not to make eye contact with people in authority. But American teachers are annoyed when students refuse to look at them and take it as a sign of disrespect. West Indian teachers can explain these and other behaviors to their colleagues.

But sometimes West Indian teachers do not share the same philosophy of education that the school system espouses. Teachers trained in an elitist educational system are occasionally very disrespectful of students of low ability or preparation who would never have been present in a class of an equivalent level back in the islands. Surprisingly, West Indian teachers were often criticized by some of the best teachers in the schools for their disrespect toward their students. One principal explained to me that some of the West Indian teachers in the school, especially in science and math, were actually graduates of the University of the West Indies, who did not want to be teachers but who realized they could make far more money as a teacher in New York than as a businessperson or government bureaucrat in the islands. Some of these individuals did not believe that their students, regardless of whether they were West Indian or American, should be in school:

> I never expected that I would see illiterate students in a classroom in a high school because back home you have to take an exam to get in. So if you cannot read or write, you just don't get into high school. So I'm still not a hundred percent sure that it's really to our advantage to have everyone in high school. (Jamaican female teacher, age 36, in United States seven years)

We asked the students who had been in both the West Indian and New York school systems about the strengths and weaknesses of the different types of schools they had attended and about which system they preferred. Not surprisingly, the students who are themselves doing very well in American high schools and who attended very good schools in the West Indies for earlier grades, are generally very positive about the West Indian system. These students either were totally disdainful of the American system and supportive of the West Indian system, or wanted to combine the best aspects of each system. Many students said they did very well when they first arrived in New York because school was so much easier here:

> I think the education back in Barbados is better than here 'cause when I come over here, there was stuff they were giving me here that

I already learned in Barbados, like math and English. The only thing
I had to get used to was American history. (Barbadian female, age
17, in United States three years)

But for students who are coming from Guyana or from schools in Jamaica
and the other islands that are not on the academic fast-track, the U.S.
schools seem superior in most ways. The differences in perception of
school life in the United States are like night and day. Whereas the academically successful students think school in New York is laughably easy,
the average and below-average students are more challenged by their
course work in New York:

> When I was in Jamaica, education really wasn't the thing down
> there. It's like you got enough to survive. And up here now, they
> push education. You know they want you to be somebody. (Jamai-
> can female, age 18, in United States seven years)

> In Guyana I had it easy. But they had it so easy like, that you don't
> learn much. If it's easy you don't pay attention. Up here you have to
> pay attention to get by . . . It seems like the teachers care more here
> than in Guyana. (Guyanese male, age 19, in United States six years)

Other students described how they were expected to drop out of school at
age 16 or 17 in the islands, and they appreciated that they were afforded
the opportunity to keep going to school in the United States. Many of the
immigrant students also commented favorably on the teaching styles in
the United States, as opposed to those on the islands:

> I get better grades here because I think the teaching is more geared
> to me. Back there it's a formal setting. This works better for me,
> maybe because I am older now and I want to get out of high
> school now. This system works better for me. But for other people
> it might not be the best, 'cause they like, get relaxed, and then
> they don't do the work. (Jamaican female, age 18, in United States
> three years)

> Q: What is better in the system here than in Jamaica?
> A: The way the teachers teach. They teach, you know, they show you
>   that you must have patience. They have patience with you. They

keep, you know, asking if I have questions, repeating it. If there is anything you don't know you could just understand. You could fail a class there, you could move on. But here, you know, you have to stay until you really know the stuff. (Jamaican female, age 19, in United States three years)

CONCLUSION

In Chapter 6 I described the difficulties and the strengths of immigrant families. Even families with the best intentions and the greatest ambitions for their children face difficult structural forces that affect their children's chances for success. In this chapter I have examined the effect of neighborhoods and neighborhood schools on the experiences of the second generation. West Indian immigrants and their children are funneled into inner-city neighborhoods where families are exposed to declining city services, crime and violence, and deteriorating housing stock. Racial segregation means that working-class West Indian immigrants are likely to find themselves either in, or in close proximity to, neighborhoods of concentrated poverty. Middle-class immigrants are also likely to end up in neighborhoods that are predominantly black. Even people who try to move to better neighborhoods seem to be followed inexorably by a cycle of neighborhood resegregation and economic decline.

And just at the point in history when formal education is most crucial to future economic and occupational success, these immigrants also are funneled into foundering inner-city schools. The New York school system struggles valiantly to provide the American dream of equal opportunity of education for all youth, even the academically unprepared. Yet the particular problems of academically unprepared immigrant youth and of an increasingly armed and violent society that does not stop at the schoolhouse doors conspire together to make it very difficult for these immigrant children to achieve that dream.

In the next chapter we turn our attention to the future trajectories and identities of the children of the immigrants. Will the 1.5- and second-generation West Indians do as well or better than their parents, or will they experience the downward social mobility that their parents dread and that neighborhood schools make more likely?

IDENTITIES OF THE
SECOND GENERATION

Chapter 3 described how first-generation immigrants from the West Indies identify themselves according to their national origins, going to great lengths to differentiate themselves from black Americans. These immigrants have a particular culture that reflects their status as immigrants. This culture is an aid to their assimilation process and to their relative success in the economy. The last two chapters have shown some of the difficulties first-generation West Indian parents face in trying to raise a family in New York. The materialist U.S. culture, an oppressive racial environment, and segregated city schools and neighborhoods pose serious obstacles to the children of West Indian immigrants. This chapter focuses on the identities and beliefs of adolescent West Indian Americans, both second-generation youth (those who were born in the United States of West Indian immigrant parents) and the 1.5 generation (those born in the West Indies but who immigrated to the United States as children).

The dilemma facing the children of the immigrants is that they grow up exposed both to the negative opinions voiced by their parents about American blacks and to the apparently more favorable responses of whites to foreign-born blacks. However, they also realize that because they lack their parents' accent and other identifying characteristics, other people, including their peers, are likely to identify them as American blacks. How does the second generation handle this dilemma? Do they follow their parents' lead and identify with their ethnic identities as Jamaican or Haitian or West Indian? Or do they try to become "American" and reject their parents' ethnic immigrant identities?

Specialists on West Indians in the United States have speculated about the identity choices the second generation will make. Some researchers suggest that the second generation will hold onto their ethnicity and emphasize their distinction from American blacks, so as to remove themselves from the negative stereotypes of blacks in the United States, and, perhaps, to maintain some sense of superiority over American blacks.[1]

Other researchers argue that the second generation will shift toward developing a strong racial identity, reject their parents' ethnicity, and primarily identify themselves as black Americans. For instance, Susan Buchanan Stafford predicted that the children of the Haitian immigrants she studied would be brought closer to black Americans out of a common racial identity. She believed that they would primarily identify themselves as blacks and consider their ethnic identity as Haitians less important. Whether their ethnic identity played an important role in the second-generation's identity would depend on how strongly their parents stressed their Haitian heritage.[2]

Empirical research on the identities of the second generation is sparse. In a study of Haitian Americans in Evanston, Illinois, in the 1970s Tekle Woldemikael found that the second generation mostly identified as black Americans. He found that the first generation stressed their differences from American blacks but the second generation faced pressure to become "not so much American, but Afro-American"; "Afro-American students pressured the Haitian students to adopt their dialect, speech and dress styles and ways of behavior."[3] In an in-depth study of the experience of several West Indian children in New York City schools, Suzanne Michael also stresses the influence on these children of the Afro-American children in school and on the streets.[4]

I found some clear divisions in the ways in which the second generation balanced their race and ethnic identity. This variation in racial and ethnic identity was related to attitudes toward school and work and to the socioeconomic backgrounds and trajectories of these youngsters. Some of the adolescents I and my assistants interviewed agree with their parents that the United States holds many opportunities for them. Others disagree with their parents because they believe that racial discrimination and hostility from whites will limit their chances of meeting their goals. By contrasting the ideas these youngsters have about their own identities and the role of race in American society, I find a great deal of variation within the West Indian group. Some Jamaican Americans, for example, are experiencing downward social mobility while others are maintaining strong ethnic ties and achieving socioeconomic success.

The key factors for these youths are race, class, and gender. The daily discrimination that the youngsters experience, the type of racial socialization they receive in the home, and the understandings of race they develop in their peer groups and at school affect strongly how they react to American society. The ways in which these youngsters experience and react to racial discrimination influence the type of racial and ethnic identity they develop. The most important influences on how these young people experience race are the class background of their parents, the type of neighborhood they grow up in, the schools they attend, and their gender. Youths who grow up in poor households in inner-city neighborhoods are most likely to adopt an "oppositional identity." Middle-class teens from integrated neighborhoods and schools are more likely to adopt an "ethnic identity." Girls and boys differ in the meanings they attach to these identities and the extent to which they see these identities as mutually exclusive.

THREE PATHS OF IDENTITY DEVELOPMENT

The interviews with the teenagers suggest that while the individuals in this study vary a great deal in their identities, perceptions, and opinions, they can be sorted into three general types: those identifying as Americans, those identifying as ethnic Americans with some distancing from black Americans, and those identifying as an immigrant in a way that does not reckon with American racial and ethnic categories.

A black American identity characterized the responses of approximately thirty-five (42%) of the eighty-three second-generation respondents we interviewed. These youngsters identified with other black Americans. They did not see their "ethnic" identities as important to their self-image. When their parents or friends criticized American blacks or described what they perceived as fundamental differences between people of Caribbean origin and American blacks, these youngsters disagreed. They tended to downplay an identity as Jamaican or Trinidadian and described themselves as American.

There were definite elements of an "oppositional identity" among the American-identified teens. They were more likely than the ethnic and the immigrant teens to describe racial prejudice as pervasive and more limiting of their own individual chances in life. They talked of the school as representing white culture and white requirements much more often than the other teens. They also were more likely to report that they would describe someone as not "acting black" or as "acting white." The ethnic and immigrant teens were aware of these terms but were much more likely to see them as problematic and less likely to use the terms to describe other people.

Another twenty-six (31%) of the respondents adopted a very strong ethnic identity, which involved a considerable amount of distancing from American blacks. It was important for these respondents to stress their ethnic identities and for other people to recognize that they were not American blacks. These respondents tended to agree with parental judgments that there were strong differences between Americans and West Indians. This often involved a stance that West Indians were superior to American blacks in their behaviors and attitudes.

A final twenty-two (27%) of the respondents had more of an immigrant attitude toward their identities than either the American-identified youth or the ethnic-identified youth. Most, but not all, of these respondents were more recent immigrants themselves. A crucial factor for these youngsters was that their accents and styles of clothing and behavior clearly signaled to others that they were foreign-born. In a sense their identity as an immigrant precluded having to make a "choice" about what kind of American they were. These respondents had a strong identity as Jamaican or Trinidadian but did not evidence much distancing from American blacks. Rather, their identities were strongly linked to their experiences on the islands, and they did not worry much about how they were seen by other Americans, white or black.

While the identity choices made by the young people did not differ by gender, there tended to be a strong relationship between the type of identity and outlook on American race and ethnic relations that the youngsters developed and their social class background and/or their social class trajectory. The ethnically identified youngsters were most likely to come from a middle-class background. Of the total of eighty-three second-generation teens and young adults interviewed, 57% of the middle-class[5] respondents identified ethnically, whereas only 17% of the working-class and poor respondents identified ethnically. The poorest students were most likely to be immigrant- or American-identified. Only one out of the thirteen respondents whose parents were on public assistance identified ethnically. The American-identified, perhaps not surprisingly, were also more likely to be born in the United States. Of the American-identified 66% were born in United States, as opposed to only 14% of the immigrant-identified or 38% of the ethnically identified. The patterns of identity choice by social class are presented in Table 8.1.

Parents with greater education and income were more able to provide better schools for their offspring. Some of the middle-class families had moved from the inner-city neighborhoods they had originally settled in to middle-class neighborhoods in the borough of Queens or to suburban areas where the schools were of higher quality academically and more likely to be racially integrated. Other middle-class parents sent their children to Catholic parochial schools or to citywide magnet schools like Brooklyn Tech or Stuyvesant. These youngsters were thus far more likely to attend schools with other immigrant children and with other middle-class whites and blacks, although some of the Catholic high schools the students attended were also all-black in enrollment.

The children of middle-class parents who did attend the local high schools were likely to be recent immigrants who had an immigrant identity. Because of their superior education in the West Indies these students were the best in the local high schools, attended honor classes, and were

Table 8.1 Parental socioeconomic status by adolescent identity

Identity	Parental SES		
	Poor	Working class	Middle class
Ethnic	8%	20%	57%
Immigrant	46%	35%	7%
American	46%	45%	36%
Total	100%	100%	100%
	N = 13	N = 40	N = 30

Note: "N" indicates in each column the number of respondents on which percentages are based.

bound for college. The children of middle-class parents who were American-identified, pessimistic about their own future opportunities, and adopted antischool ideologies were likely to have arrived early in their lives and to have attended New York City public schools in inner-city areas from an early age.

The social networks of parents also influenced the type of identity the children developed. Regardless of social class, parents who were involved in ethnic voluntary organizations or heavily involved in their church seemed to instill a strong sense of ethnic identity in their children. Parents whose social networks transcended neighborhood boundaries seemed to have more ability to provide guidance and social contacts for their children.

The Ethnic Response

All of the second-generation respondents reported comments by their parents about American blacks that were very similar to those recorded in our interviews with the first generation. The differences were in how they interpreted what their parents were thinking. In general, the ethnic-identified respondents agree with their parents and report seeing a strong difference between themselves and black Americans, stressing that being black is not synonymous with being black American. They accept their parents' and the wider society's negative portrayals of poor blacks and want to avoid any chance that they will be identified with them. They describe the culture and values of lower-class black Americans as including a lack of discipline, lack of a work ethic, laziness, bad child-rearing practices, and lack of respect for education. They contrast these with their parents' values, which include education, strict discipline for children, a strong work ethic, and social mobility. They try to impress others that they are Jamaican or Haitian and most definitely *not* black American. This allows them less dissonance with their parents' negative views of American blacks. They do not reject their parents' culture and identities but rather reject the American social system that would identify them as black American and strongly reject the African-American peer group culture to which they would be assigned by whites and others if they did not consciously transmit their ethnic identities:

I see my ethnicity and my race as one and the same. Ethnically I am West Indian, more so than just black. A West Indian black has a lot more things going on with it than just good old black. I think West Indian gives more—a stronger identity than to say just black. (Saint Thomas female, age 20, in United States fourteen years)

Although society may define the second generation on the basis of skin color, the second-generation ethnic respondents believe that being black American involves more than merely having black skin. As a result their self-identification is almost always at odds with the identifications others make of them in impersonal encounters in American society, and they must consciously try to accentuate their ethnic identity:

Q: What do other people think you are?
A: I am quite sure they think I am a black American.
Q: Do you ever tell them that you are from a West Indian country?
A: Oh yes, I make it very clear. Sure. It's important. Because of the way I think in general. It's a difference in the way I act, in the way I carry myself. In my priorities and everything I do. I don't think like the average black man, I would say. (Saint Thomas male, age 27, born in United States)

Forms and surveys constantly request that these second-generation respondents declare their race. Rarely if ever do the forms allow for a West Indian identity. For some of those with strong ethnic identities, this was not a problem, but a sizable number of respondents told us that they try to check "other" on these forms:

Q: When a form or survey asks for your race, what do you put down?
A: Oh boy, that is a tough one. It's funny because you know when we fill applications I never know what to check off, you know. I'm serious. 'Cause they have Afro-American, but they never have like Caribbean. They do have white, Chinese. To tell the truth I would like to be called Caribbean, West Indian. Black West Indian. (Jamaican male, age 25, in United States twelve years)

When they have black listed, I put other, Jamaican. When they say black, they mean black American. So I don't list that because I am not black American. (Jamaican female, age 20, in United States twelve years)

In addition to perceiving themselves as "better" than black Americans, these young people also differentiate themselves from black Americans in terms of their sensitivity to racism, real or imagined. Some of the ethnic-identified second generation echo the feelings we heard from the first generation that American blacks are too quick to use race as an explanation or excuse for not doing well:

Black Americans, they think that every little thing a white person does to a black person is discriminating. But an island person has a different view . . . We really don't see any discrimination. (Guyanese female, age 17, in United States eight years)

The second-generation respondents who are doing well try to understand how it is that they are so successful when black Americans are not, and often they chalk it up to family values. They say that their immigrant families have close-knit family values that stress education:

I think one of the things that I can say about coming from a West Indian home is that, unlike people in America, West Indians do not see themselves as any different than anyone else. So that they don't have the baggage that black Americans have about being inferior to white people, about having been slaves, and that sort of thing. So that when I know that when my mother came here, she didn't assume any particular role. She took advantages of opportunities that were available to her based on her socialization and her education. She was not at all inhibited by the fact that she was black. That did not mean anything to her at all. (Nevis female, age 22, born in United States)

Aware of, and sometimes sharing, the negative images of black Americans that the whites they encounter believe, the second generation also perceives that whites treat them better when they realize they are not "just" black Americans. When asked if they ever benefited from their ethnicity, they responded "yes":

Many people look at me and they say your eyes, your complexion, is a little different than the average person, why is this? Well, I'm from the

Caribbean, I'm part Indian and also French. Automatically their interest is peaked. It seems as though a lot of barriers are dropped, and they want to know so much about where I'm from and, you know, there's this—oh this wonderful person, you're so different than the rest. (Saint Thomas female, age 20, in United States fourteen years)

The dilemma for the second generation is that while they have a strong sense of their own identity as one very different from black Americans, their West Indian identity often is not clear to other people. Both whites and blacks usually identify them as just black Americans and do not notice that they are ethnically different. This dual identity also exposes the second generation to a great deal of racism. When whites learn that they are second-generation immigrants, the whites are likely to let them know that they think of them as exceptions to the rule—the rule being that most blacks are not good people. However, these young people also know that unless they tell others of their ethnicity, most whites have no idea they are not black American. One young woman spoke of her conflicted feelings of recognizing these distinctions:

At my workplace I was hired because I was Jamaican. They fired all the black Americans, and the lady, I asked her how come she hired me, and she said, well, because you are different, you are Jamaican . . . I am the only black person who works there, and one time we went out [after work] and this girl [I work with] was having a fight with her boyfriend, and she said to come here, and he said, "What do you think I am, a nigger?" And one of the other girls turned around to me and said, "Oh, don't get offended, you are not black anyway." I was so upset. I was upset because I was like, I'll just be caught in between. I was like, what am I? Purple, green, yellow? Even though I don't like to be labeled just being black, I am black. I don't know. (Jamaican female, age 20, in United States twelve years)

There is a great deal of relief in realizing that whites will treat one better, but also anger and ambivalence because one also understands that people can't always tell that you are not black American. Many of these young people coped with this dilemma by devising ways to telegraph their identities as second-generation West Indians. Although some felt that the way they talked or the way they walked clued others into their West Indian identities, many adopted very conscious strategies of identity presentations. One girl carried a Guyanese map as part of her key chain so that when people looked at her keys, they would ask her about it and she could tell them that her parents were from Guyana. Another young woman described having her mother teach her an accent so that she could use it when she applied for a job or a place to live because she and her mother firmly believed that West Indians were far more likely to be chosen than black Americans. Others just try to somehow work their background into the conversation when they meet someone. Maintaining a specifically West Indian identity means that these young people are very conscious of their presentation of self, and this is true when interacting with both white and black Americans.

In the public high schools where there was a large West Indian population, the ethnically identified teens described tensions over cultural differences such as language that caused the West Indians and the African Americans to keep their distance from one another. Some of the ethnically identified youth who lived in inner-city Brooklyn thought that they were safer around other West Indians and reported being afraid of crime at the hands of black Americans:

> If you see a gang of West Indians on the street, maybe one of them might harass somebody but, when you see American black people, you see a lot of them—they'll push people around, they beat people up . . . If I ride on the bus and I see American kids in the back of the bus, I won't go to the back of the bus. If I go on the bus and I see Jamaican kids at the back of the bus, I'll think twice, but I won't definitely not do it. My experience is the Jamaican won't mess with you. They seem to be calmer in their ways. I mean, they want their nice clothes and nice car, just like the Americans. But American black—they'll go out and steal it. While the Jamaicans, some of them might steal, but most of them want to work for their stuff. They want to be proud of their stuff. (Jamaican male, age 18, in United States fifteen years)

For those who came earlier or to parts of the country where there were few West Indians, the tensions with black Americans were strong and often pushed the West Indian kids toward whites rather than toward blacks:

I was eight years old when I first came here and I did everything to try to break my accent and to be American because I was afraid because they always made fun of me. But then the more I became American, I didn't like it because I was losing my thoughts. And the kids would just make fun of me and say go back to Jamaica, go back to Africa. They would call me all those names. I hated it. It continued until junior high school and then I didn't hang out with black Americans anymore because I don't like the way they make fun of me. But the white Americans they accepted me for how I was. They didn't make fun of me or anything. (Jamaican female, age 20, in United States twelve years)

Some who did want to identify with, and be included among, black Americans reported that black Americans called them an oreo or accused them of "acting white." The teens who associated with many black Americans felt pressure from their peers to be part of the group and to identify as black American. These teens would consciously talk about passing for American at some points and passing for Haitian or Jamaican at others by changing the way they talked or acted:

When I'm at school and I sit with my black friends and sometimes I'm ashamed to say this, but my accent changes. I learn all the words. I switch. Well, when I'm with my friends, my black friends, I say I'm black, black American. When I'm with my Haitian-American friends, I say I'm Haitian. Well, my being black, I guess that puts me when I'm with black Americans, it makes people think that I'm lower class. . . . Then if I'm talking like this [regular voice] with my friends at school, they call me white. (Haitian female, age 17, born in United States)

The ethnic-identified young people were more likely than the American-identified to attend West Indian cultural events, specifically West Indian churches, or to belong to sports teams that were made up of all West Indians. The annual West Indian Labor Day Parade in Brooklyn was often cited as something that gave them pride in their identities:

Labor Day is very important to me. I mean all the West Indians come out, the parade, the music, and the food, and you are just sharing with everybody. It's very nice. All Americans, black Americans, white Americans. (Jamaican male, age 25, in United States twelve years)

The American Response

The American-identified second-generation respondents differed in how little they stressed their immigrant or ethnic identities to the interviewers. They follow a path that is more similar to the model posed in the straight-line theory. They stress that they are American because they were born here and are disdainful of their parents' lack of understanding of the American social system. Instead of rejecting black American culture, they embrace many aspects of it. This brings them in conflict with their parents' generation, and most especially with their parents' understandings of American blacks. The assimilation to America that they undergo is most definitely to black America: they speak black English with their peers, they listen to rap music, and they accept the peer culture of their black American friends.

The American-identified young people do not seem to be aware of the scholarly literature, backed up by the perceptions described by the ethnic and immigrant respondents, that the foreign-born have higher social status than the American-born. Not one of the American-identified respondents voiced the opinion of the overwhelming majority of the ethnic respondents that whites are more apt to like the foreign-born. In part this reflected the differences in the groups' contacts with whites. Most of the American-identified teenagers in the inner city had almost no contact with whites, except for teachers. The larger number of middle-class teens who were ethnically identified were more likely to have white classmates in citywide magnet high schools, in parochial schools, or in suburban schools or workplaces. In the peer culture of the neighborhood and the school, the American-identified teenagers describe a situation in which being American has higher social status than being ethnic.

The peer pressure to be American led some kids to consciously try to "pass" as American and deny their West Indian background:

When I first came here, I wanted no part of being Jamaican. 'Cause when I first came here, they made fun of you. It wasn't a good thing

to be Jamaican. I didn't want to deal with that. Where you from? I'm
from here. I'm from here. I tried my best not to, you know, use the
Jamaican slangs. I tried to be as Americanized as I possibly could.
(Jamaican male, age 27, in United States nineteen years)

Most of the American-identified youth included their ethnic identities as
background, but none of them adopted the stance that they were not in a
major sense black American. When asked about her ethnic background,
one respondent replied:

A: I put down American because I was born up here. I feel that is
   what I should put down . . .
Q: What do other people think you are?
A: Black American because if I don't say . . . Like if they hear my parents talk or something, they always think they are from Trinidad .
   . . But they just think I am black American because I was born up
   here. (Trinidadian female, age 17, born in United States)

While the ethnic respondents had strategies to correct others who thought
of them as black Americans, the American-identified respondents thought
that was a natural assumption, which they let stand:

Q: So when forms or surveys ask about your ethnic group or ancestry, what do you put?
A: If they have black, I put down black. If they have Afro-American,
   I would put that down because it's a wider term into who I am.
Q: So what do other people think you are? Do they think you are
   black American or Bajan?
A: Those who live in my neighborhood know of my mother and so
   they will call me Bajan. But those who, like I just meet, or even
   those in the neighborhood don't really consider me Bajan, because like I don't have an accent. I don't really seem like I am
   from the West Indies. You know to me and to them, I, like, blend
   in, so they would consider me, you know, a black American . . .
   My mother tell me that I am Bajan, but I can't really say that I
   am because if you ask me so much about being a Bajan, I
   couldn't tell you because I haven't experienced it. I know about
   being a black American because I lived here in America most of

my life and I experienced those types of things . . . You know just because your parents is [from the West Indies], it's not just on your parents, it is who you are yourself. And if you are going to tell a person you are West Indian, or you are from the West Indies, and you haven't really experienced nothing of there, and not really from there, and know nothing about it, then how can you be from the West Indies? (Bajan male, age 17, born in United States)

In fact, these teenagers contrast being a black American as being more stylish and with it than being from the islands. When asked about the images others held of people from the islands, most of the teens described neutral attributes, such as styles of dress. However, many of the kids who identified as Americans also described negative associations with the immigrants' identities. The Jamaicans said most people thought of drug dealers when they thought about Jamaicans. A few of the teens also intimated that the people from the islands were backwards in not knowing how to live in a big city, both in terms of appreciating the wonders of the city and in terms of being street-smart in avoiding crime and hassles with other people. As for the former attribute, the teens described people from the islands who were not accustomed to shopping in big malls or having access to the wide variety of consumer goods that they did in New York:

Q: What comes to mind when you think about Jamaican people?
A: Jamaicans have like a country-style attitude. Like a prehistoric type. I don't know—old. Like they are not used to the technology, the new stuff. Most of the things they would do would probably be called like old-fashioned or something. (Jamaican male, age 17, born in United States)

Some of the young people told us that they saw little if any differences between the ethnic blacks and the American blacks. Many stressed the Caribbeanization of black New York and described how all the Americans were interested in being Caribbean now:

It used to be Jamaicans and American blacks did not get along because everyone was afraid of Jamaicans. But now I guess we are closer now. You tell an American that you are Jamaican and it is no big deal. Americans are acting more like Jamaicans. Jamaicans are acting like Americans.

Q: What do you mean by acting like each other?

A: Sure there are a lot of Americans out there speaking Patois. And then all the Jamaicans are coming over here and they are like "Yo, what's up" and they are like that. Pretty soon you can't really tell who is Jamaican and who is American. (Jamaican male, age 17, born in United States)

In some of the schools and neighborhoods of New York, West Indians are the majority or a sizable minority of the black population. So, while fewer new immigrants report the kind of peer pressure to "become" completely American that people experienced even ten years ago, the Caribbeanization of black New Yorkers also means becoming black American is less of a leap for these youngsters. While a few ethnic-identified young people saw this cultural blending, it was mentioned much more often by the American-identified:

Nowadays more people are getting into reggae and stuff and finding about the music and the cultures. What I really like is when you stand at a street corner sometimes, and people start in playing calypso and stuff and all sorts of people come around and dance and have fun with each other. I love that. That's one thing I like about my culture, the music just brings people together. That's one thing I like. (Jamaican female, age 16, in United States ten years)

But the parents of the American-identified teens have expressed to their children the same negative impressions of American blacks that the ethnically identified young people reported. These teenagers report many negative appraisals of American blacks by their parents:

My parents they say that the kids over here are too wild and the boys over here, most of them are in jail. Stuff like that.

Q: Do you agree with them?

A: No, not really. They always look at the bad things. They never look at the good things, the positive things. All the black people that's in college. The black kids that are in college, that are trying to finish high school. But they only look at the black kids that are in jail and that are dropping out. That's all they want to believe. They want to believe that Guyana is the best place to raise a child. (Guyanese female, age 17, in United States eleven years)

Often the teens indicated how much they disagreed with their parents' negative opinions:

Sometime I get upset at my mother 'cause she use the term nigger, and I don't like that . . . She has these feelings against black Americans because of how they treat her when she first came here . . . But since I lived here, I know that it's not all of them that's that way. There's a few. But I know some Bajans, even my cousins, when I hang out with them, it's not so rosy, how my mother would say either. There's some Bajans that act as wild as black Americans. (Bajan male, age 17, born in United States)

In marked contrast to the ethnically identified respondents, however, the American-identified teens either disagreed with their parents' statements about American blacks, reluctantly agreed with some of it but provided qualifications, or perhaps, most disturbingly, accepted the appraisals as true of American blacks in general and *themselves as American blacks*. This young Trinidadian American swallows her parents' stereotypes and directly applies them to herself:

Q: How close do you feel in your ideas about things to West Indians?
A: Not very close. My feelings are more like blacks than theirs. I am lazy. I am really lazy and my parents are always making comments and things about how I am lazy. They are always like in Trinidad you could not be this lazy. In Trinidad you would have to keep on working. (Trinidadian female, age 16, born in United States)

This Haitian-American teen tries to disagree with her mother and to temper her mother's interpretations of American blacks:

Q: Are there any characteristics or traits that come to mind about Haitian Americans?
A: Not really. I don't really—'cause most people are Haitian American if they are born here . . . Like me, I don't know if I act like a

Haitian or do I have Haitian characteristics, but I'm mostly—like everything I do or like is American . . . My parents they do not like American blacks but they feel that they are lazy. They don't want to work and stuff like that from what they see. And I feel that, um, I feel that way too but sometimes it won't be that person's fault, so I try to stick up for them. And my mother is like yeah, you're just too American. (Haitian female, age 17, born in United States)

This young Guyanese-American woman's use of the pronouns *they* and *we* shows that she includes herself in the stigmatized American black group as she describes how she does not agree with her parents:

Q: Do you think Guyanese have a stereotype of American blacks?

A: They think *we* are not civil. People don't know how to control themselves. And *they* are too loud. Their parents don't know what they are doing.

Q: Do your parents believe these stereotypes?

A: Yes, some.

Q: Which ones?

A: The ones that American blacks are out of control. And like my father does not trust black Americans as much as other people.

Q: Do you have the same ideas?

A: No, not really. I don't. Well, sometimes they [American blacks] can't be civil. But like as a teenager I can understand. My parents are adults; they can't understand. Sometimes they [American blacks] are not civil. But they feel like they should be themselves because they have been put down too long. I think that is the only part of the stereotype that is true. Other than that I think they are just a good race. (Guyanese female, age 17, in United States eleven years)

While the American-identified young people come to terms with their parents' images of American blacks, they do not do so in a vacuum. It is not just their parents who criticize black Americans. These youngsters are very aware of the generalized negative view of blacks in the wider culture. Interestingly, while the ethnic young people had many stories of whites preferring West Indians to American blacks, the American teens thought whites could not tell the difference or, in a few cases, thought whites preferred African Americans to West Indians. In answer to the question "Do whites have an image of blacks?" all of them responded that whites had a negative view of blacks, which saw them as criminal, lazy, violent, and uncaring about family. Many of the teenagers prefaced their remarks by saying that they did not know any whites but that they knew this is what whites thought because of what they had seen in the mass media and through their own encounters with whites in buses, trains, and stores. These encounters mostly involved incidents such as whites protecting their handbags when the teenagers arrived or store clerks following them and expecting them to shoplift. This knowledge that the society in which they live disvalues them because of their skin color and their identity affected these teens deeply and shaped the content of the American black identity they adopted.

The Immigrant Response

The more recently arrived young people who are still immigrant-identified differed from both the ethnic- and the American-identified youth. They did not feel as much pressure to "choose" between identifying with or distancing from black Americans as did either the American or the ethnic respondents. Strong in their self-identifications with their or their parents' national origins, they were neutral toward American distinctions between ethnics and black Americans. They tended to stress their nationality or their birthplace as defining their identity. They also pointed to their experiences growing up and attending school in a different country. This young man has dreadlocks and a strong Jamaican accent. He stresses his African roots and lets his Jamaican origin speak for itself:

Q: What is your ethnicity? For example, when forms or surveys ask what your ethnic group or ancestry is, what do you put?

A: African.

Q: Do you ever put Jamaican or anything?

A: No, not really. Only where Jamaican comes up is if someone asks where you're from. I'll say I am from Jamaica.

Q: What do people usually think you are?

A: They say I am Jamaican.

Q: They know that immediately?

A: Yeah.

Q: How do they know?

A: I change my voice. I don't have to tell them. I think it's also because of my locks sometimes and the way I carry myself, the way I dress. (Jamaican male, age 22, in United States six years)

While ethnically identified Jamaican Americans are aware that they might be seen by others as American and thus actively choose to present themselves as Jamaican, immigrant-identified Jamaicans could not conceive of themselves as having a choice nor could they conceive of being perceived by others as American:

Q: Do you think of yourself as an American sometimes and as a Jamaican sometimes?

A: No, fully, one hundred percent Jamaican. I think no time as American, always Jamaican. I have no time to be American.

Q: But sometimes when I mentioned American blacks, you sometimes included yourself in that category?

A: Well, I mean, we are all black, yeah, you know, but I am a black West Indian. People think I am West Indian, a black West Indian. The way I dress. You know, there is a certain West Indian way to dress. The way we walk. I have dreads. You know, a lot of things you associate with Jamaica. (Jamaican male, age 23, in United States twelve years)

This certainty among the immigrant-identified respondents about where they belong is different from both the ethnic-identified and the American-identified young people. While the ethnic and the American teens have more or less chosen a way of identifying, a large number of both groups describe "passing" back and forth between identities. For instance, this American-identified young man describes having "two personalities":

I think of myself as West Indian sometimes and American sometimes. Like if you hang out with your friends, some are West Indian and some are American. You hanging out with your American friends and they ask you what you are, you might say that you are

American just to be in with them. And then when you are with your
West Indian friends, you might say you're West Indian to be with
them. (Trinidadian male, age 15, born in United States)

None of the youth we classified as immigrant-identified described this
type of code switching. Indeed, when the immigrant teens talked about
their racial identities, it was in a West Indian, not an American, context.
So the immigrant-identified kids were more likely to describe themselves
as "colored" or to describe racial disharmony at home rather than the
idealized view of racial harmony in the islands that the ethnic-identified
second-generation youth inherit from their parents.

Indeed, if there is any evidence in this study of a transnational identity,
it is among this group. When it comes to the meanings attached to racial
and ethnic categories, the immigrant-identified respondents tend to resist
American ways of thinking. A crucial factor that allows these young people
to maintain this identity is that their accents and styles of clothing and
behavior clearly signaled to others that they were foreign-born. The immigrant-identified were so sure about their identities being known to
others that they did not mention consciously trying to "manage" their
identity and telegraph that identity to others:

Q: How important is it to you that your friends think of you in
terms of your ethnicity?

A: Oh, very important. You know I try hard not to lose my roots,
you know, when I come to the United States. A lot of people who
come here try to lose their accent, you know. Even in the workplace, you know, because they fear what other people might think
of them. Even in the workplace. Me, I never try to change, you
know, the way I am. I always try to, you know, stay with them,
the way of my culture.

Q: So it's something you want people to recognize?

A: Yeah, definitely. Definitely. Absolutely.

Q: Why?

A: Why? I'm proud of who I am, you know. I'm proud of where I'm
from and I'm not going to change because somebody might not
like the way I walk, talk, or dress, you know. (Jamaican male, age
23, in United States twelve years)

The importance of birthplace was stressed repeatedly by the immigrant-identified as they stressed their difference from American-born co-ethnics:

Q: What would you put on a form or survey that asked about your ethnicity?

A: I'll say I'm Jamaican. You gotta say where you come from.

Q: And do you think of yourself more as a Jamaican or more as an American?

A: I think of more of a Jamaican 'cause it's, I wasn't born here. I was born in Jamaica and was there for fourteen years.

Q: And what about kids who are born in America, but their parents were born in Jamaica?

A: Well, you see, that is the problem. You see, kids whose parents are Jamaican, they think that, well, they are Jamaican. They need to recheck that they're Americans 'cause they was born in the country and they wasn't born outside the country. So I think they should, you know, know more about American than Jamaican. (Jamaican male, age 19, in United States six years)

Most teens in this category were recent immigrants themselves. Some who adopt this strong identity with the immigrant country were born in the United States, but the combination of strong family roots on the island, frequent visits, and plans to return to live there when they are older allows them to think of themselves as not really American at all. This is especially easy to do in the public high schools where there are large numbers of freshly arrived youngsters from the islands:

Q: What do you think your race is?

A: Well, I'm black. I consider myself black. I don't consider myself black American, Afro-American, and stuff like that because it's hard to determine, you know, for a person as an individual to determine himself to be Afro-American . . . I'll be more a Guyanese person because certain things and traditions that I am accustomed to back home, it's still within the roots of me. And those things have not changed for a long period of time. Even though you have to adapt to the system over here in order to get ahead

and cope with what is going on around you. (Guyanese male, age
19, in United States three years)

While the ethnics tended to describe people treating them better when
they learned their ethnic origins, and the Americans tended to stress the
antiblack experiences they have had and the lack of difference between the
foreign-born and the American, the immigrant teens spoke about seeing
much anti-immigrant feelings and discrimination and responded with
pride in their national origins.

The immigrant-identified teens are different from either of the other
two groups, in part because of how they think about who they are not as
well as how they think about who they are. These teens have a strong
identity as Jamaican or Trinidadian, but this identity is related more to
their interactions with other Jamaicans or Trinidadians rather than their
interactions with black or white Americans. These youngsters identify
with their homelands or their parents' homelands but not in opposition
to black Americans or to white Americans. They are likely to be immersed
in the immigrant community, to have friends who are all the same ethnicity or from other islands. They tend to be more recent arrivals. Unlike the
ethnic-identified, however, they do not distance themselves from American blacks, and they have neutral or positive attitudes and relations with
them.

These identities are fluid and change over time and in different social
contexts. There are cases we found of people who describe being very black
American-identified when they were younger who became more immigrant-identified when they began high school and found a large immigrant
community. Most new arrivals to the United States start out as immigrant-
identified and the longer they are in the United States the more they begin
to think of themselves in terms of American categories. The kind of social
milieu, especially the school environment, the child faces has a strong
influence on the outcome. A school with many black Americans leads to
pressure to identify racially; likewise a neighborhood or school with many
immigrants makes it possible to avoid thinking much about American
categories. In the face of much pressure in the neighborhood school environment to not follow the rules and to not succeed academically, youngsters who are doing well in school and value education increasingly come

to stress their ethnic backgrounds as an explanation for their ambition and success.

CONTRASTING IDENTITIES

In some sense each of these identities can be seen both as an embrace of a particular identity as well as an opposition to another identity. The American-identified youth are in fact assimilating to the American black subculture in the neighborhood. The sheer numbers of the immigrants and the second generation also indicate that the American black culture is absorbing Caribbean influences as well. When these youth adopt American black cultural forms, they do so in distinction to their parents' ethnic identities and the wider mainstream white identities. These students adopt some of the "oppositional" pose that American black teenagers have been observed to show toward academic achievement, the idea of America, the idea of opportunity, and the wider society.[6] They are also opposed to their parents' ideas, stressing that what worked as an outlook, a life strategy, and a child-raising technique in the islands does not work in the United States.

These teens tend to adopt a peer culture of racial solidarity and opposition to school authorities. Because every young person is aware of the negative images held by whites and the wider society of black Americans, the acceptance of an American black identity also means the acceptance of the oppositional character of that identity. Oppositional identities, John Ogbu clearly argues, are self- and group-affirming identities for stigmatized groups—defining as good and worthy those traits and characteristics that are the opposite of those valued by the majority group. What is clear from the interviews is that this stance of opposition is in part a socialized response to a peer culture; however, for the most part, it comes about as a reaction to the teens' life experiences, most specifically, their experience of racial discrimination. The lives of these youngsters basically lead them to reject the immigrant dream of their parents of individual social mobility and to accept their peers' analysis of the United States as a place with blocked social mobility where they will not be able to move very far. This has the effect of leveling the aspirations of the teens downward.

The American racial classification system, which pushes toward an either/or designation of people as black or white, makes the immigrant option harder to hold onto. When others constantly identify an individual as a black, and refuse to make distinctions based on black ethnicity, there is pressure on the individual to adapt his or her identity to that outside identification—either to say, yes, I am black, and to accept categorization with black Americans, or to resent the characterization and strongly make an ethnic identification as, say, Trinidadian American. The American myopia about ethnic differences within the black community makes the middle-ground immigrant identity unstable.

The American-identified teens also voiced more positive appraisals of black Americans than did the ethnically or the immigrant-identified teens. Their descriptions also reflect the reality of living in neighborhoods where there is a great deal of crime and violence. A majority of the American-identified teens said that a good trait of black Americans is that they work hard and they struggle. These are the very same children whose parents describe black Americans primarily as lazy and unwilling to take advantage of the opportunities available to them. The children seem to be perceiving a reality that the parents can or will not.

Many of these teens live in neighborhoods and attend schools that are all-black. So, aside from teachers, these young people have almost no contact with white Americans. This does not stop them from absorbing whites' negative stereotypes of blacks. But unlike the middle-class blacks who come in contact with whites who tell them that they are "good blacks," these youth live in urban areas that are associated with crime, they dress like typical black urban youth, and they talk with Brooklyn accents and black American slang. When they do encounter whites in public places, the whites do not ask about their parents' backgrounds:

Q: Have you ever experienced any discrimination or hostility in New York?

A: From being Trinidadian, no. But because of being black, you know everybody stereotypes. And they say, "blacks they tend to steal," and stuff like that. So like if I am walking down the street and a white lady go by and they smile and I smile, they put their bag on the other side. (Trinidadian female, age 16, in United States three years, immigrant-identified)

The parents of these teens grew up in a situation where blacks were the majority. The parents do not want their children to be "racial" in the United States. They define "being racial" as being overly concerned with race and using race as an excuse or explanation for lack of success at school or on the job. The first generation is likely to believe that while racism exists in the United States, it can be overcome or circumvented through hard work, perseverance, and the right values and attitudes. The second generation experiences racism and discrimination constantly and develops perceptions of the overwhelming influence of race on their lives and life chances that differ from their parents' views. These teens experience hassles by police and store owners, job refusals, and even attacks if they venture into white neighborhoods. The boys adopt black American culture in their schools and wear flattops, baggy pants, and certain types of jewelry. All of this contributes to their "cool pose" image, which in turn causes whites to be afraid of them. This makes them angry and resentful. The media also tell these youngsters that blacks are disvalued by American society. While parents encourage their children to strive for upward mobility and to work harder in the face of discrimination, the American-identified teens think their chances of success by doing that are very slim.

This creates a very wide gulf between the parents and their children. These parents are absolutely terrified of their children becoming Americans. For the children to be American is to have freedom from the strict parental controls of the immigrant parents. This is an old story in the immigrant saga that one can see in novels and movies about conflicts between Jewish and Italian immigrants and their children. But the added dimension in this situation is that these parents are very afraid of the downward social mobility that becoming an American black represents to them. And these parents have that idea reinforced constantly in the comments made to them by whites that they are better than American blacks.

One question I asked about how things had changed since the civil rights movement shows the different perceptions of the teens about race in U.S. society. The ethnically identified give answers I suspect most white Americans would give. They said that things are much better for blacks now. They state that they now can ride at the front of the bus and that they can go to school with whites:

> Things are much better now. 'Cause I mean during the sixties, you couldn't get into white high schools. And you couldn't drink from the same water fountain as whites, you had to go to the back of the bus. Now it's a lot of things have changed. (Guyanese female, age 18, born in the United States, ethnic-identified)

The irony, of course, is that we were sitting in an all-black school during the conversation where these accomplishments were touted. The vast majority of the American-identified teens told us that things are not better since the civil rights movement. They think that the change is that the discrimination now is "on the down low," covered up, more crafty:

> It's the same discrimination, but they are more careful of the way they let it out. It's always there. You have to be very keen on how to pick it up. But its always there. But it's just on a lower level now. (Grenadian male, age 17, in United States three years, American-identified)

Some of the American-identified teens pointed out that we were in an all-black school, and they concluded that the fight against segregation had been lost. The result of these different worldviews is that the parents' view of an opportunity structure that is open to hard work is systematically undermined by their children's peer culture but more important, by the actual experiences of these young people:

> It's worse now because back then at least you know who didn't like you and who like you. But now you don't know who's after you. I mean, we don't have anyone to blame for anything. I mean, we know what we feeling. We know when we got there to get a job, we can't get a job. We know it is our color . . . If you know who your enemy is, you can fight him. But if you don't know who your enemy is, you can't fight him. And they're tearing you down more and more and you don't know what is going on. And there's a lot of undercover racist people out there, institutions and firms and corporations, that's directly keeping people out. (Jamaican male, age 22, in United States six years, immigrant-identified)

This American-born Trinidadian girl points to the difference between de facto and de jure rights for blacks. She is taught in school about the accomplishments of the civil rights movement, and her mother tells her all the time not to be "racial," yet her peer group and her own "mental map" of her surroundings give her a very different picture:

Q: Do you think things are better for black people now than they were before the civil rights movement?

A: In some ways I would say yes and in some ways no. Because, it's like they don't say that you can't go in this neighborhood anymore. But you know you really can't, because there will be trouble if you do. I mean you could go there, but you know you will get those looks and stares and everything like that.

Q: What neighborhoods can't you go to?

A: My friends say Sheepshead Bay is bad. They say Coney Island too, but I have to deal with that. They say by South Shore, around there. And near Kings Plaza. They say over there. And by Canarsie. They say that's really bad. (Trinidadian female, age 15, born in United States, American-identified)

On the other hand, the ethnically identified teen, whose parents are more likely to be middle class and doing well, or who attend parochial or magnet schools and not the substandard neighborhood high schools, see clearer opportunities and rewards ahead, despite the existence of racism and discrimination. Their parents' message that hard work and perseverance can circumvent racial barriers does not fall on unreceptive ears. The ethnically identified youngsters embrace an ethnic identity in direct line from their parents' immigrant identity. Such an identity is partly in opposition to their peers' identities and partly in solidarity with their parents' identities. These youngsters stress that they are Jamaican Americans, and that while they may be proud of their racial identity as black, they see strong differences between themselves and black Americans. They specifically see their ethnic identities as keys to upward social mobility, stressing, for instance, that their parents' immigrant values of hard work and strictness will give them the opportunity to succeed in the United States, whereas black Americans without those values will fail. This ethnic identity is very much an American-based identity—it is in the context of American social life that these youngsters base their assumptions of what it means to be Jamaican or Trinidadian. In fact, often the pan-ethnic identity as Caribbean or West Indian is the most salient label for these youngsters as they see little differences among the groups, and the most important thing for them is differentiating themselves from black Americans.

Middle-class teens discussed feeling sometimes lost because their parents had not taught them how to be black in American society and perhaps had not equipped them to deal with American racism. Yet the inner-city teens had no such complaints. Once again the difference is in the social milieus of the two groups, as one young Haitian inner-city girl responded:

Q: Is there anything your parents didn't tell you about how to get along as a black person in America that you think you would have wanted them to?

A: Whatever they didn't tell me, I learned in school. So, I don't really have a problem in dealing with other people or black Americans. (Haitian female, age 18, born in United States, American-identified)

Some middle-class teens reported that they wished their parents had given them specific advice about how to live as a black person in the United States because when they do encounter racism, they are unprepared for it. The American-born teens were dismissive of the advice about race they did receive because they disagreed with their parents' lack of racialism:

My mother thinks that anything the white have they earned. She doesn't feel that white people are racist. Like whenever we say something like say we will be at school and one of us thinks that a white kid in one of our classes got off more than he should have, she'll say that's not true, that they worked for what they got and they earned it, probably more than we did. (Trinidadian male, age 15, born in United States, American-identified)

The two groups also differed in their plans for racial socialization of their own children. The ethnic respondents wanted to pass their ethnic identities along to their children:

Q: If you were to have children, are there any things you would tell them about their heritage?

A: I would tell them about being West Indian and where my family comes from and I would also explain to them the American history of slavery. I think that's very important. Because when living in America, when people see you, they don't see you as being a West Indian or see you as being any different. They see you as being a black American who comes from slavery or from poverty until you get to explain who you are to them. (Bajan male, age 25, in United States twenty-three years, ethnic-identified)

The American-identified respondents were more likely to think that their children would just naturally absorb what they needed to know:

Q: How do you think your children will identify?

A: Black American. 'Cause they're gonna be raised in a black American society and most people will ask them where they're from, they're gonna have to say America 'cause that is where they were really brought up. (Trinidadian female, age 17, in United States five years, American-identified)

One heartbreaking response we received from a Guyanese boy who was American-identified showed how the American kids felt that their parents really did not know how to prepare them for life in New York City. He had recently received a new bike from his parents and when he took it out for a ride, some American kids stopped him and demanded the bike. When he refused to part with it, they stabbed him and ran away with it. We asked if he thought his children's life would be better or worse than his own:

Better. Because I am from up here, and I will know more things than them. And you could say I would be wiser than them. I could tell them things like . . . Like you see how I got stabbed? I could tell them, you know, don't get the bike, you know. I would get them a cheap bike, so that this type of thing would not happen to them. Things like that. (Guyanese male, age 15, born in United States, American-identified)

The ethnic and racial identifications of these teens were also correlated with what they thought of being American. While both groups contained individuals who spoke in somewhat patriotic terms of the privileges of being American, there was a difference in the overall interpretation of American identity described by the teenagers. Ironically, the American-identified teens had more negative things to say about being American in the abstract:

Q: What does it mean to you to be an American?

A: To be an American? The question's kinda hard for me 'cause I don't believe in the American dream. My parents believe in it because that's what they came here for. But I don't know, for me, the American dream. I would have to see equality among everybody. You know there's a lot of corruption and prejudice in this country and racism. People always brush it under the rug. But I'm very, you know, vivid about that. So, I'm like, the American dream, does it exist? Or is it a myth or something? I think it's something they portray to attract people to come here and to work for what they call the American dream is. And they actually getting a bum rap. The American dream does not exist, unless you have money. (Haitian female, age 18, born in United States, American-identified)

Q: What does it mean to you to be an American?

A: American? Well, I live in America, so I call myself American. But America is just like—we were brought here to do work for Americans. So like, we work for Americans really. (Jamaican male, age 17, born in United States, American-identified)

The ethnic-identified respondents, who were also more likely to be middle class, often gave more positive appraisals:

Q: What does it mean to you to be an American?

A: To be an American, is to, one, be free. I think that's the main thing we have in our Constitution and the Declaration of Independence. Free to vote. Free to express our ideas. Free to go out and do what we want to do. That may be to go out and start our own business. I think that being an American gives the individual the opportunity to make the choice to succeed, to be better . . . I felt like an American when I went overseas to Europe and talking to people there. I probably have never felt prouder to be an American. I think most of the time I feel proud to be an American when I am away though. Or when America as a whole has done something great. Most of the time though I think of myself as a West Indian. (Montserrat male, age 22, born in United States, ethnic-identified)

GENDER AND IDENTITY

The meaning of "being American" also varied by gender. Although there was no overall difference in the numbers of boys and girls in the choice of identity adopted, there were significant differences in the meanings attached to being American. The two main differences were that girls were under greater restrictions and control from parents than boys, and racism appeared to have a different impact on boys than on girls. Boys discussed being black American in terms of racial solidarity in the face of societal exclusion and disapproval. Girls also faced exclusion based on race, but they discussed being American in terms of the freedom they desired from strict parental control, which was a much more salient issue in their own lives.

Strictness of Parents

All respondents thought that West Indian parents were much stricter than American parents and that the former were even more strict with girls than with boys. The girls also reported far more restrictions placed on their activities and movements by their immigrant parents than did the boys. This reflects differences in gender roles and parental expectations about gender between the United States and the Caribbean. The girls see how things change for their mothers and fathers in the United States and perceive different expectations of behavior by their parents for boys and girls. Among the first-generation immigrants we spoke to, the women were more satisfied than the men with the changes that had occurred in their lives following immigration. The women reported having more personal independence in the United States and more secure employment outside the home.

While the ethnic-identified adolescent girls were likely to point to their parents' strictness as a very positive factor in their lives and stated that they would bring up their children the same way, the American-identified girls responded to this differential treatment by criticizing their parents for being too strict and for not understanding American culture. One girl said:

> My mother's strict, she don't give me that much privileges, and at some time I said to them, you know, I wish I had an American parent because, you know, they would be—I'm not saying they would let me on the loose but I would have some kind of freedom. That's not a word that should be in our vocabulary, you know, because I am not allowed to go to parties. (Haitian female, age 16, born in United States, American-identified)

This young Jamaican woman compares her relative lack of freedom to the freedom she believes American teens enjoy:

> A: The black kids I know, compared to the Jamaicans I know, there are certain things you can't do. The black Americans where I live, they can hang out on the street certain hours and things like that. The Jamaican families they don't permit that. You aren't allowed to do, especially with my father, the girl would do certain things, the guy can do certain things.
>
> Q: Like what kind of things?
>
> A: Well, according to my dad we are not allowed to get phone calls from guys. He was more strict with us. My brother, he was free to do anything. (Jamaican female, age 20, in United States twelve years, ethnic-identified)

Many of the American-identified girls pointed to the freedom their brothers had to stay out late, date, talk on the phone, work at part-time jobs, and so forth, and were upset that they did not have the same privileges. They saw their American classmates having much more freedom and definitely believed the restrictions on them grew out of their parents' island background. For instance, this Guyanese girl points to rigid parental role expectations that she does not agree with:

> I have a friend and her brother gets to—she's a year older than

her brother. They're a year apart. She has to stay upstairs, wash the dishes, clean her room. But he gets to go out, come back in, two, three o'clock in the morning.

Q: Do you think that's good?

A: No, you should treat them equally. (Guyanese female, age 17, in United States eleven years, American-identified)

My mother, when she hear about boys, she just get crazy. All she think about is that you're gonna get pregnant and drop outta school and stuff. She don't think about—the only reason why I didn't get pregnant is because I respect myself. You know. And I wanted to finish school and stuff, and not because she real strict. She think 'cause she being strict, that's why I am doing well . . . Some of my friends that got pregnant they come back to school after they had their kids and stuff. The strictness of the mother doesn't make a difference. 'Cause the mother ain't gonna be with them all the time. They could cut school and go see a boy and stuff. They think it's working but it's not. (Jamaican female, age 16, born in United States, American-identified)

Frequently, these negative perceptions about the strictness of West Indian parents reinforced an American identity in the teenagers.

Reactions to Racism

Ironically, although parents monitor girls' activities more than they do boys' activities, the boys face a more violent environment than do the girls because of the differential effects of American racism. The boys reported far more racial harassment from whites and from the police than did the girls, and they felt less at ease when they left their all-black neighborhoods than did the girls. The types of incidents reported by the boys included instances of gangs of whites threatening them or starting fights with them when they ventured into white neighborhoods. Common situations faced by both girls and boys were being followed in stores because they were suspected of shoplifting or people recoiling in fear in public places, such as the street, subway, parks, and anywhere the youngsters encountered whites. A girl from Guyana describes this situation:

When you're on the trains, and like white people start holding their

> pocketbooks because they think you're going to rob them, or walking down the street, they'll cross the street and stuff like that. (Guyanese female, age 17, in United States eleven years, American-identified)

She goes on to say that this type of thing, although it happens to girls, is much more likely to happen to her male friends. This was a common perception, and the boys described being hurt and very angry by white people's reactions to them:

> The white ladies on the street, they see us coming and they stop and the women start looking in the window. And like quick, look in the window until you pass by and then they start walking again. Like one time I was going to summer school. And this old lady was at the bus stop and she turned around, and I was walking, and she started walking. And I walk pretty fast, and I was walking behind her. And I caught up to her and she stopped at the bus stop. And I was going there too, and so I stopped to see if the bus was coming. And the first thing I see the lady do, she was walking so fast. The first thing she took her bag off, and she put her arm through it, and she had it on like this [across shoulder]. (Jamaican male, age 18, in United States fifteen years, ethnic-identified)

Some of the ethnic-identified youth, like this one, blame their treatment on whites who confuse them with black Americans. This young man told the interviewer that if this woman had known he was Jamaican, and not black American, she would not have been afraid of him. The ethnic-identified respondents assume that whites have valid reasons to be afraid of a black American on the street but not of Caribbean Americans:

> Especially with the black Americans, you know? They [whites] see hip-hop music or just with a certain wear, you know, with their pants baggy and you know? And they don't really see us as someone productive. That's how they stereotype us. Black people as thieves. As thieves. Yeah, you know, when we walk on the road because we dress a certain way, they feel intimidated by us and all, they would hold their handbags and things like that. That has happened to me a lot of times, you know. (Jamaican male, age 21, in United States ten years, ethnic-identified)

The American-identified teens did not describe these behaviors as understandable; rather, they saw racial prejudice by whites as the cause, and racial solidarity among blacks was important to them in the face of such pressures. Rather than looking to the police as a source of safety from attacks by whites in local neighborhoods, the males had many stories of being singled out by police in a threatening way for things they did not do. This Grenadian boy was stopped at a train station and pushed against the wall by a police officer who yelled racial slurs at him and his friends when they were on their way to their summer jobs. He said his friends and he had concluded:

> Because what happen really with the cops nowadays, don't care what
> they do. They just want to manhandle you anyhow because the law
> is in their hands. They think they could do any and anything what
> they want to do to you. (Grenadian male, age 18, in United States
> nine years, American-identified)

In the two high schools where we interviewed, it was far more likely for girls to graduate than for boys. The girls also perceived having more job opportunities than did the boys. The message that boys derive from the behavior of whites, the police, and these educational outcomes is that they are unwelcome in mainstream society. This appears to create a rigidity in their attitudes toward racial solidarity that is not present so much among the girls. Two pieces of evidence in our data that suggest that boys pay acute attention to racial boundaries are that boys are more likely to suffer social stigma if they speak standard English among their friends and that they were more likely than the girls to report that they accuse others of "acting white."

In effect, girls experience less overt hostility and exclusion by mainstream society, and boys experience a greater number of attacks on their rights to be full-fledged members of society. In terms of identity I think this creates more of a direct choice for the boys. The African-American identity many of them adopt has an adversarial or oppositional character to it, inverting many of the values of mainstream society and prizing racial solidarity very highly. The girls also experience exclusion and denigration by the wider society, but in not as virulent, direct, and all-encompassing a manner; as a result the black identity adopted by the girls is not as sharply differentiated from the mainstream as that of the boys.

All of the youngsters interviewed described behaviors that were considered to be "acting white." These included speaking standard English, having white friends, listening to "white people's music," walking a particular way, and refusing to adopt particularly "black" ways of doing things. While the girls could describe these differences and point to other girls who "acted white," the boys had more polarized opinions about it. For American-identified boys the phenomenon of "acting white" or speaking standard English was a very important way of describing others and determining with whom they could be friends. "Acting white" for the boys was also often associated with challenging masculinity. According to a few respondents, both boys and girls, a girl could use standard English and not be ostracized by her peer group for doing so, but a boy who used standard English could have his masculinity questioned. This teen describes someone who acts white as "like a faggot":

Q: Do you know anyone who acts white?
A: Yeah.
Q: What did they do to make you think they are acting white?
A: Well it was a combination of acting white and being a faggot. It was a combination. He used to, like there are certain things he would do. He would be around us and we'd be talking in a certain tone of voice and he would just sound different. He wouldn't sound like us. And then, yeah another thing, he never had a girl. He never had no girl. And we were like, damn dude, what's wrong? (Jamaican male, age 17, born in United States, American-identified)

Ethnic-identified boys usually denied that "acting white" was a real phenomenon. They were proud of their ability to code-switch in speech, although many of them said some of their classmates would accuse them of "acting white" for behaving that way:

Q: Do you know of any black people who act white?
A: I wouldn't say they act white. I would just say that they speak

properly and use the correct English as opposed to broken English when that's how they act black.

Q: Has anyone ever said that about you?

A: A few times.

Q: How did that make you feel?

A: Well, I didn't notice it really. Because I know what I am doing as opposed to—if they know what they're saying. [They are saying] you are different. 'Cause that's how I like to be. I don't like to be a follower. I always like to be a leader. (Guyanese male, age 18, in United States four years, ethnic-identified)

Acting white and speaking standard English were not the same for the girls, and they were far less likely to say that they would describe others as acting white or that they would choose their friends on that basis. They had more leeway in choosing to code-switch and to speak standard English when the situation called for it:

Q: Do you speak black English as well as the way the teachers speak?

A: I think I speak both. Like if I'm in school I speak, you know, white American proper English, everything. But if I'm with my friends and, you know, we joke around, and I speak black American.

Q: Do you think most kids can switch back and forth?

A: I think it's easier for girls.

Q: Why?

A: I think guys, they want to put up a front or something to say that like if they with their friends they won't talk like right English or correct English, they'll talk the way their friends do even if their friends are not there. They want, I don't know. They'll talk the street language, just to say that "I'm a guy and I am not this," and I think for them if you speak correct English it is like a putdown, I think. So they won't speak it. They think, "If you're talking correct English, you're smart and you shouldn't be smart" . . . It's among the guys. A girl would not say anything like that to a guy. But a boy would say, "Oh why you talkin' like that for, what's wrong with you?" (Haitian female, age 17, born in United States, American-identified)

So while an equal number of boys and girls chose to be ethnic or American or immigrant in their social identities, this choice appears to be harsher and more all-encompassing for the boys than for the girls. Girls appear to have more leeway. They are able to claim a racial identity, maintain a stance of racial solidarity, and also to be more bicultural. Anthropologist Signithia Fordham also found a gender difference in her study of black Americans in a Washington, D.C., elementary school.[7] Although those students did not have an alternative ethnic identity to choose when accused of "acting white," some developed a "raceless" identity in order to conform to mainstream educational requirements. She says this appears to be much easier for the girls than the boys and that the girls also appear to be "much less victimized [than the boys] by the fact that they are required to live in two worlds concurrently."[8]

Similarly, for the boys we studied, choosing not to conform to specific ideas of black racial identity appears to also challenge their gender identity. Girls, who are less violently stigmatized in the wider society for their race, seem to have more latitude for adopting a bicultural identity. However, stricter control of girls and the pressures toward less equality for girls in Caribbean households will push these girls toward desiring an American lifestyle, which includes more freedom to date, less discipline, and greater equality of sex roles.

An ironic element of our findings is that although the parents typically appeared to believe that teenage girls were more in need of their protection, the boys see fewer opportunities in their future, are under more peer pressure not to do well in school, and experience more overt racial hostility and violence than do the girls. Because many black girls perceive less racial exclusion from mainstream society, they may feel less desire to develop oppositional or adversarial components of racial identities than do boys. Girls may be more flexible and fluid in their racial and ethnic identities and adopt an oppositional racial identity that does not completely forestall another type of identity. Concretely, this may mean that the boundaries between an ethnic-identified and an American-identified adolescent described here might be sharper for males than for females and more consistently maintained by males than by females. Males who identify with the mainstream or with their parents in opposition to their peer group may be less able to move in and out of an American black identity than are girls, for whom the oppositional component of an American identity may not be as important.

CONCLUSION

Some of the distancing shown by the ethnically identified teens in the sample vis-à-vis underclass black identity and behaviors can also be found in middle-class black Americans. Sociologist Elijah Anderson has noted that middle-class blacks in a gentrifying neighborhood in Philadelphia use various verbal and nonverbal strategies to convey to others that they are not from the ghetto and that they disapprove of the ghetto-specific behaviors of the blacks who live there.[9] Being an ethnic black in interactions with whites seems to be a shorthand way of conveying distance from the ghetto blacks. Thus the second-generation black immigrants reserve their ethnic status for use as an identity device to stress their distance from poor blacks and to stress their cultural values, which are consistent with American middle-class values. This same use of an ethnic identity is present among first-generation immigrants of all social classes, even those in racially segregated poor neighborhoods in New York.

The second-generation teens in the segregated neighborhoods with little chance for social mobility seem to be unaware that status as a black ethnic conveys higher social status among whites, in part because as of yet they don't have all that much contact with whites. The mass media convey to them the negative image of American blacks held by whites but does not convey to them the image among intellectuals, middle-class whites, and conservative scholars such as Thomas Sowell that they have cultural capital by virtue of their immigrant status. They do get the message that blacks are stereotyped by whites in negative ways, the all-black neighborhoods they live in are violent and dangerous, and the neighborhoods of whites are relatively safe. They also encounter a peer culture that values black American cultural forms. The much-vaunted immigrant culture of struggle, hard work, and educational success that their parents try to enforce is experienced in a negative way by these youngsters. They see their parents denying them privileges that their American peers enjoy, and unlike the middle-class youth, they do not automatically associate hard work, lack of dating and partying, and stress on scholastic achievement with social mobility. In the peer culture of the school, ethnically and immigrant-identified teens are apt to be the best students in the class. In the neighborhood inner-city schools newly arrived immigrants who have attended better schools in the islands tend to outperform the students who have spent their lives in the substandard New York City public schools. This reinforces the association between ethnicity and school success—and the more American-identified adopt more of an adversarial stance toward school.

In their study of Yankee City in the 1930s W. Lloyd Warner and Leo Srole reported that it is the socially mobile white ethnics whose ties to the ethnic group and the ethnic identity decline. It is the individuals who are stuck in the lower classes who turn to their ethnic identities and groups as a sort of consolation prize:

> Our class system functions for a large proportion of ethnics to destroy the ethnic subsystems and to increase assimilation. The mobile ethnic is much more likely to be assimilated than the non-mobile one. The latter retains many of the social characteristics of his homeland . . . Some of the unsuccessfully mobile turn hostile to the host culture, develop increasing feelings of loyalty to their ethnic traditions, become active in maintaining their ethnic subsystems, and prevent others from becoming assimilated. But, generally speaking, our class order disunites ethnic groups and accelerates their assimilation.[10]

The process appears to be exactly the opposite for black immigrants and black ethnics. The more socially mobile the individual, the more he or she clings to ethnic identity as a hedge against racial identity. Less mobile second-generation West Indians see little advantage to stressing an ethnic identity in the social worlds they travel in, which are mostly shared with black Americans. Stressing an ethnic identity in that context risks being described as "acting white," as rejecting one's race and accepting the white stereotypes that they know through their everyday lives are not true.

The changes in race relations in the United States since the 1960s are very complicated and most surely involve a mixing-up of class and race. Some white Americans are striving to identify the difference between ghetto inner-city blacks, whom they fear and do not like, and middle-class blacks, whom they do not fear and would like to have contact with, if only to prove to themselves that they are not racist or in a more formal sense to meet their affirmative action goals.

Middle-class blacks realize this and try to convey their class status to others in subtle and not so subtle ways.[11] The immigrants also exploit New Yorkers' tendency to use foreign-born status as a proxy for the class information they are seeking. The white New Yorkers we interviewed do notice differences among blacks, and they use ethnic difference as a clue for the class difference they are seeking information about. If the association found here between social class and ethnic identity is widespread, this perception could become a self-fulfilling prophesy. It could be that the children of poor parents will not keep an ethnic identity, and the children whose parents achieve social mobility will keep the ethnic identity. This will reinforce the image in the minds of whites of the "island people" as the "good blacks," thus giving the edge in employment decisions and the like to the ethnic black over the American black.

On the other hand, it remains to be seen how long the ethnically identified second-generation teens will continue to identify with their ethnic backgrounds. This is also related to whites' racial judgments about identity when it comes to blacks. The second generation does not have an accent or other clues that immediately telegraph their ethnic status to others. They are aware that unless they are active in conveying their identities, they are seen as black Americans, and that often in encounters with whites the "master status" of their black race is all that matters. It could be that by the time they have their own children, they will have decided that the quest to not be seen as a black American is a futile one.

IMMIGRANTS
AND AMERICAN
RACE RELATIONS

9

This book has addressed three questions. Who are the West Indian immigrants coming to American society and in what ways are they becoming Americans? In what ways are West Indians doing better than American blacks and what explains their success and their image as a model minority? And, finally, how are the children of the immigrants doing, and how are their identities and understandings of American society and race relations similar or different from those of their parents? After briefly reviewing my answers to these three questions, I turn here to one final question. What does this study of West Indians tell us broadly about our own society and specifically about the present and future of American race relations?

IMMIGRATION, ASSIMILATION, AND IDENTITY (BECOMING AMERICAN)

The debate over immigration we are witnessing today focuses on two outcomes among the immigrants—political loyalty and economic success. Will the new immigrants become patriotic and loyal citizens of America? Will they love their new country the way past immigrants are described as doing? These concerns focus on issues of identity and belonging. They reflect a fear on the part of some Americans that transnational ties and multiculturalism will prevent or delay the "Americanization" of new immigrants. If new immigrants keep a strong tie to their homelands or become hyphenated Americans, will this affect our civic culture? Are we creating such a heterogeneous population, with so few directives to abandon previous loyalties and identities, that we will have so little in common that the very idea of America will not survive?

The second locus of concern is economic. Will new immigrants succeed in the economy or will they or their children become a welfare burden or members of the criminal underground? Critics of current levels of immigration argue that even though the United States was able to absorb very poor and unskilled immigrants in the past, the emphasis in today's economy on skills and education and the hourglass shape to today's economy indicate that new immigrants might not ever achieve the same degree of socioeconomic mobility as earlier waves of immigrants.[1]

The nonwhite complexions of the vast majority of today's immigrants exacerbates these worries over immigration. Those who worry about political incorporation are concerned that nonwhite immigrants will not follow an ethnic immigrant model of assimilation and participation in the nation's political life but rather will follow a minority racial model of exclusion and bitter disappointment.[2] Economic incorporation is also seen to be more problematic for nonwhite immigrants. Continuing racial discrimination means that new immigrants of color will have a harder time being hired and a harder time translating their education into occupational success and higher earnings. Some nonwhite immigrant groups will also face a more difficult time in translating their economic success into residential mobility and social integration at the highest levels of American society.

Earlier, simpler models of the relationship between immigration, identity, and assimilation tied together identity, political loyalty, and economic integration. Becoming American meant learning the language, voting, adopting the culture, and achieving economic security for oneself and social mobility for one's children. A number of studies of the European immigrants and their children who arrived in the nineteenth and early twentieth centuries were conducted based on these theoretical expectations. The simple answer from these studies was that by the second generation most people had become hyphenated Americans. By the third generation the descendants of the original immigrants were very thoroughly American, with a continuing emotional and cultural, yet very rarely behavioral, tie to their ethnic ancestries. In these "straight-line assimilation studies" successful incorporation into society was taken to be more or less automatically associated with loss of ethnic, social, and cultural attachments.

Recent decades have produced many critiques of this model of identity and assimilation. Ethnic and racial identities and American identity have been shown to be very complex, even in the case of European immigrants. A large number of European immigrants went home, and many went back and forth, establishing transnational ties. The unproblematic idea that people with identity A (say, Italian) transformed themselves into identity B (say, American) was too uncomplicated. As Nathan Glazer and Daniel Patrick Moynihan noted long ago, many "Italian" immigrants did not come to think of themselves as Italians until they arrived in this country.[3] The identity many immigrants had based on their national origin was often not coterminous with their ethnic origin. Jews immigrated from Germany or Poland or Russia; though some Jews thought of themselves as Germans at one point in time, most would not have defined themselves as Poles or Russians (although that is exactly what the census asks them to do; a person cannot tell the census that he or she is Jewish since that is a religion and the government does not collect data on religions). Postmodern critiques of the concept of identities stress the ways in which class and gender differences both in the sending countries and in America mean that while people may nominally have the same identity, that identity can be very different for the rich and the poor or for men and women.

Empirical research on later-generation whites concluded that very few people ever became unhyphenated Americans. The end point to assimilation is still very fuzzy. While the descendants of Italian immigrants may intermarry and exhibit few cultural Italian traits, this does not mean that they no longer identify as Italian.[4] Finally, models of European immigration, settlement, and ethnic change have been criticized for being too individualistic. People migrate in social networks of relatives, friends, and neighbors. These networks provide a social environment at the micro level of both the sending and receiving societies that have enormous influences on the meanings attached to identities and the types of identities adopted by people.[5]

However, one facet of these earlier models of identity and assimilation has always been central—that it was higher social status to become American.[6] Becoming American was coupled with economic success. Yet the experiences of post-1965 immigrants and their children challenge this central assumption. In fact, especially for nonwhites, remaining immigrant- or ethnic-identified can lead to greater success in the labor market and beyond. The theory of segmented assimilation and the idea of second-generation decline reviewed in Chapter 6 both suggest that there are major benefits to being firmly ensconced in an ethnic or immigrant community—access to social networks with ties to jobs, social networks, and institutions that support parental authority over children, and protection from the stigmatized identity and discrimination directed toward native racial minorities.[7]

As I have shown in Chapters 2 and 3, West Indians are perhaps the quintessential postmodern peoples. The influence of the capitalist system, the interpenetration of cultures in the created societies of the Caribbean, and the long-standing role of migration in the everyday lives and life cycles of the people there all point to the kinds of situational, multilayered, and socially constructed identities that are said to characterize the modern world. And, as I have shown in Chapters 3 and 8, the identities of these immigrants and their children must be understood in context. The identity chosen by any one individual is always chosen in relation to others and can change in different situations. Yet current power relations in the United States are such that West Indians face a very particular situation shaping their identity choices. Assimilation implies becoming black Americans, who have traditionally been the most stigmatized and abused people in American history (along with American Indians). If anyone has an incentive to either maintain loyalty to another country or to maintain a transnational identity, these West Indians do.

The story of how the West Indians become Americans, which I have described here, reflects many of the complications and changes that demand a more complex model of what it means to become American. I have paid particular attention to the ways in which class, gender, and generation have shaped the individual identities adopted by Caribbean immigrants, the ways in which race and ethnicity interact and intersect for these immigrants, and the ways in which these characteristics shape how white Americans categorize and react to the immigrants.

My argument in this book is that middle-class families and the institutions and environments in which they live provide more support for the maintenance of a distinct West Indian identity and for sharper "cultural" boundaries around the group. Working-class and poor families live in neighborhoods and work in institutions in which their children come to see little difference between themselves and African Americans. In part this is also because the concentration of West Indian immigrants in New York and their large presence in the city have "Caribbeanized" native black New Yorkers. Class shapes how race and culture are used in the development of identity. Middle-class second-generation West Indians use their cultural identities to claim an American identity as a member of a "model minority." While not denying their racial identity as black, these youths distance themselves from the underclass image of American blacks. Working-class second-generation youths become African Americans.

The findings I have reported here may surprise many readers, as they go against popularly held conceptions of immigrants and how they are becoming Americans. For instance, the people most likely to resist Americanization were the middle-class teachers, not the working-class foodservice workers. Recall Warner and Srole's 1945 study of European immigrants where they suggest ethnicity is a sort of "consolation prize" for people who do not achieve social mobility.

Yet even among the teachers we interviewed, it was a minority who showed active resistance to becoming American. Most people very much wanted to be American, even though they thought that America was in many ways still a "white world." Among the second generation about a third of the sample was classified as immigrant in their identities. The few teens who were born in the United States and yet maintained an immigrant identity were the closest I found to any evidence for a sustained transnational identity. Indeed, they were very likely to have traveled back to see their relatives in the islands or were even sent back there for schooling, child care, or summer vacations. Yet most of the people with an immigrant identity were more recent immigrants. It also seemed the most difficult identity to maintain, with constant pressure to come to terms with how others were identifying you—as black American.

But teens who did travel back and forth between New York and the islands were the exception. Most immigrants could not afford to send their children back to the islands nor to travel there much themselves.

Among the food-service workers, only six out of thirty-four immigrants had ever been back to visit their homeland. Most of these working-class people could not afford visits or even frequent phone calls back home. They were struggling to get by in America and as much as they liked to entertain thoughts of retiring back home to the islands, most people were very firmly planted in the United States. Even among the more economically secure teachers, travel back to the islands was still seen as a big expense. Only nine of the twenty-five teachers we interviewed had traveled home within the last ten years.

Most of the immigrants we spoke to, like earlier waves of immigrants, came to the United States for very selfish and individual reasons. They wanted to make a better life for themselves, and they realized they could make more money in the United States than they could back home. There was a greater possibility they would be employed here than back home, and for a significant proportion of people, there were more educational opportunities available in the United States.

Yet the debate over immigration has misplaced its emphasis in asking whether these new immigrants *want* to be American. It is not political or ideological considerations or a policy of multiculturalism that will keep them from assimilating. Choosing to become American for these immigrants is an economic decision. They come here to have a better standard of living for themselves and their children, and they are becoming American as the way to do it.

Yet the economic payoff seems to go to those who are the least Americanized among the post-1965 immigrants. Why? For one thing, American culture seems to have a bad effect on the children of immigrants. The less Americanized they are, the better they do in school, the more time they spend on homework, the less materialist they are, and the less they challenge their parents' and teachers' discipline and authority.[8] Discrimination is the other key to this puzzle. The more immigrant or ethnic the immigrants are, the more likely they are to have access to jobs and information from social networks, and the more likely employers are to prefer to hire them than native minorities.

If there is a problem then in the Americanization of the immigrants coming into our society, it lies not with the immigrant but with American society. And most especially with the problems of the urban areas many poor immigrants find themselves in. Those public policy analysts who are concerned about whether current immigrants are showing loyalty to America should be less concerned with abstract questions of civic incorporation and continuing transnational ties, and more concerned with the paradox of current American society. The best Americanization program for earlier waves of immigrants to the United States was not civics lessons in public high school but rather the enormous economic payoff to immigration that the descendants of European immigrants enjoyed. Today's working-class immigrants, who come for many of the same reasons as earlier immigrants and who also seek the same economic payoff, are rewarded for maintaining strong ethnic ties and punished for assimilating into American minority communities. A clear concrete example of this dynamic process from this research is the belief on the part of some second-generation youth that it is best to cultivate a West Indian accent because it opens doors to housing and employment. Those same doors are shut to American blacks from those same neighborhoods. This study suggests that the kinds of discrimination members of America's native minority groups encounter is an important part of the process of assimilation that should be central to the immigration debate. In other words, we should not just be asking as a society, "How can we structure our immigration policy and our institutions to facilitate immigrants adopting our civic culture and becoming American?" We should also be asking, "What can we do about the pervasive inequalities in American life that often mean that becoming black American or Mexican American leads to a less bright future than remaining an immigrant?"

WEST INDIANS AS A MODEL MINORITY

For decades liberals and conservatives have squared off over the question of whether structure or culture is responsible for the problems of black Americans. Conservatives are likely to blame the culture of black Americans for their failures, arguing that black Americans have a "victim mentality" that keeps them from taking advantage of the real opportunities that do exist in American society. Thomas Sowell, for instance, points to the success of West Indians in American society to show that racial discrimination cannot triumph over the "correct" cultural values. Liberals, on the other hand, point to the immense structural problem of poverty and racial discrimination as an explanation for why black Americans are not doing well in American society. They have usually argued that any attention to the culture of black Americans is "blaming the victim" and takes away from the real task of blaming the structure of society for the problems of black Americans.

In Chapters 4 and 5 I explored the differences between West Indians and African Americans in two areas—low-skilled labor force participation and attitudes and experiences with race relations. The story conservatives tell is that West Indians are a "model minority"—a group that, despite black skin and sometimes humble beginnings, triumphs over adversity and exhibits a strong work ethic and a strong commitment to education. This image of a model minority is the image of themselves that the immigrants prefer, and it is this image they use in differentiating themselves from black Americans. The actual empirical evidence lends some small support to this stereotype—West Indians do have very high labor force participation rates. Yet many careful analysts have concluded that other claims of West Indian success have been overstated. By 1990 they did not earn any more than comparable African Americans, and their education advantage had narrowed because of rising African-American education levels and declining levels of education among more recent immigrants.

I have argued that white preferences for hiring West Indians, a different metric for judging the worthiness of jobs, and dense social networks that connect individuals to jobs explain much of the differences between natives and West Indians in labor force participation. I have also argued that, given these structural reasons for West Indian success, any group that found itself in the same position would behave in the same ways.

I do give more credence to cultural explanations for West Indians' attitudes and behaviors around race relations. And I argue that the particular West Indian approach to black-white race relations can lead to acceptance and socioeconomic mobility in the service economy.

The immigrants' preparation for and militance about structural racism, together with their lack of anticipation of interpersonal racism, lead to more comfortable relations with whites on the job, as well as ambitious and vigilant monitoring of progress in job hierarchies. In an age of affirmative action West Indians have the potential for success; they push for promotions and perks, yet they have easygoing relations with whites. According to one teacher, her principal, under pressure to hire more blacks, actually asked "where could he find some Jamaican teachers like [her] to fill his quota?" The food-service company we studied had an extensive internal labor market, and aside from one black American supervisor, all of the promotions of blacks from within went to West Indians. The food-service managers, as their comments demonstrated, were not at all reticent in expressing their strong preferences for foreign-born over American-born blacks.

In arguing that there are cultural expectations about race that explain some of the dynamics of West Indian success in the service economy, I am not in agreement with the classic "cultural" explanations for West Indian success put forth by other analysts. The beliefs and practices I am describing do not stem from historical differences generations ago but rather from recent experiences in the Caribbean as well as from the immigration process itself. Indeed, the structural realities of American race relations quickly begin to change the beliefs and behaviors of the immigrants and most especially of their children.

All too often "cultural" explanations of West Indian success appeal to whites because of their wish to believe that it is something in African Americans' own behavior and beliefs that is responsible for their low status in American society. This is a preferable explanation for whites who do not believe that there is continuing prejudice and discrimination in American society. Whites who want blacks to "forget about race and past injustice" profess that, if they do and shed their "victim mentality," blacks will then do well. The experiences of the immigrants I describe here show a very small kernel of truth in that argument. A lack of expectation of interpersonal racism does make whites feel "comfortable" and does provide a small advantage in the workplace. But the weight of the evidence in this study leads to a very different overall conclusion. It is the continuing discrimination and prejudice of whites and ongoing structural and interpersonal racism that create an inability among American, and ultimately West Indian, blacks to ever "forget about race." Whites' behavior and beliefs about race and their culture of racist behaviors create the very expectations of discomfort that whites complain about in their dealings with their black neighbors, coworkers, and friends. That expectation is not some inexplicable holdover from the long-ago days of slavery but rather a constantly recreated expectation of trouble, nourished by every taxi that does not stop and every casual or calculated white use of the word "nigger." If the West Indian experience teaches us anything about American race relations, it should refocus our attention on the destructive and everyday prejudice and discrimination whites are still responsible for.

THE FUTURE OF THE SECOND GENERATION

Analysis of the experience of West Indians in the United States shows how quickly structure does affect culture. Within one generation, structural racism—the institutional racism of substandard schools, racially segregated and disinvested neighborhoods, and the discrimination of employers who fear urban black men in their workplaces—combined with interpersonal racism—the racial killings by modern lynch mobs, finding oneself followed in stores, stopped by police, and called nigger on the street, and being "looked at as if we have germs on our skin"—have worked their effects on people. Rightful anger, correct diagnoses of blocked mobility, and prudent protection of one's inner core from these assaults give rise to cultural and psychological responses that are best described as "disinvestment" and oppositional identities. To protect oneself from these indignities, some blacks in the United States detach themselves, especially from education, redefine social norms, and see behaviors such as doing well in school, speaking standard English, and so on as oppositional to their very core identity.

The story I have told here is on balance a sad one. Declining city services, a materialist U.S. culture, failing inner-city schools, an economy that offers little hope to the least educated, and a society where black skin still closes doors and awakens hatred can destroy the chances of people who have sacrificed a great deal for a better life. Many West Indian immigrants face the real prospect of stagnating standards of living or intergenerational downward mobility. While a significant minority of immigrants and their children will be rewarded for immigrating with significant social mobility, many others, indeed a majority, could face bitter disappointments. This study, because of the limitations of the nonrandom and relatively small sample, cannot ascertain what percentage of second-generation West Indian Americans will do better or worse than their parents. Because the census does not ask a birthplace-of-parents question, it will be very difficult for any studies to address the question of how well second-generation West Indians are doing in the economy. An important finding here should inform future studies that use the subjective ancestry question on the census to identify West Indian Americans. If less successful children of West Indians identify as African Americans and the more successful identify as West Indian as I described in Chapter 8, and if we continue to gather data in a subjective fashion on West Indians and their descendants, the image of West Indians as a model minority will continue to garner statistical support. But such support will be reflecting the situational identities of these second-generation youth and not some statistical reality.

The key factor brought to fresh light by the West Indian immigrants' experiences is the role of continuing racial inequality—the institutional failures in our inner cities to provide jobs, education, and public safety—in sustaining a cultural response of disinvestment in the face of discrimination rather than increased striving. A lifetime of interpersonal attacks based on race can lead to bitterness and anger on the part of an individual. A community of people coping with economic marginality and a lack of any avenues of institutional support for individual mobility leads to a culture of opposition. That culture might serve individuals well for those times when it protects them from the sting of racism and discrimination, but ultimately as a long-term political response to discrimination and exclusion it serves to prevent people from taking advantage of the new opportunities that do arise. Those opportunities are reserved by whites in power for immigrants who make them feel less uncomfortable about relations between the races and especially about taking orders from white supervisors or customers.

One of the African-American teachers eloquently describes how even one act of cruelty or disdain by a white person can have long-standing effects on a young black person and on the whole cycle of black-white race relations:

> I have had this happen to me so let me relate this incident. I have been going or coming from a building and held the door for some old white person and had them walk right past me, as if I am supposed to hold the door for them. Not one word, a thank-you, or an acknow-

ledgment of your presence was made. A seventeen-year-old, when he has something like that happen to him, the next time he is going to slam that door in the old lady's face, because I had that tendency myself. I had the hostility build up in me. The next time it happens I won't do that because I am older, but when I was seventeen it might not have made any difference to me that this was a different old lady. I would have flashed back to that previous incident and said I am not holding that door for you. Now that old lady who may have been a perfectly fine individual, who got this door slammed in her face by this young black person, her attitude is "boy, all those people are really vicious people." Her not understanding how it all came to pass. That on a large scale is what is happening in our country today. That's why our young people are very aggressive and very, very hostile when they are put in a situation of black-white confrontation. They say to themselves, "I am not going to let you treat me the way you treated my grandparents, or the way I have read or seen in books or movies that they were treated." I would rather for you to hate me than to disrespect me, is the attitude I think is coming out from our black youth today. (Black American male teacher, age 41)

The policy implications of this study lie in the ways in which the economic and cultural disinvestment in American cities erodes the social capital of immigrant families. The families need recognition of their inherent strengths and the supports necessary to maintain their ambitions. The erosion of the optimism and ambition of the first generation that I saw in their children could be stopped if job opportunities were more plentiful, inner-city schools were nurturing and safe environments that provided good educations, and neighborhoods were safer. Decent jobs, effective schools, and safe streets are not immigrant- or race-based policies. They are universal policies that would benefit all urban residents. Indeed, the strengths these immigrant families have may be in part due to their immigrant status, but the problems they face are much more likely to be due to their class status and their urban residence. Policies that benefit immigrants would equally benefit Americans.

But, in addition, the experience of these immigrants tells us that we must recognize the continuing significance of interpersonal racism in creating psychological tensions and cultural adaptations in the black community. The cycle of attack and disrespect from whites, anger and withdrawal from blacks, and disengagement and blaming behaviors by whites must be broken by changing whites' behaviors. This involves policies that specifically address racial discrimination. The immigrants' tales of blatant housing and job discrimination directly point to needed vigilance in protecting all blacks in the United States from unequal treatment in the private sector. The more difficult problem is dealing with the everyday subtle forms of prejudice and discrimination that also plague foreign-born and American-born blacks. We cannot pass laws forbidding white women from clutching their handbags when black teenagers walk past them. We cannot require old white women to thank young black men who show them courteous behavior. Those kinds of behaviors can only change when whites no longer automatically fear blacks and when whites begin to perceive the humanity and diversity of the black people they encounter.

The real correlations that exist among race, poverty, and criminality can explain some of the fears of whites that make them behave badly.[9] Policies that improve the situations of blacks in the overall class structure of society could remove whatever true correlation there is between poverty, race, and criminal behavior. But what is really needed in the final analysis is for whites to no longer see blacks as the "other" but rather as the "self." Why was it so much easier for the white managers we interviewed to describe the immigrants as "like you and me" and the American blacks they worked with as "those people"? If whites saw the basic humanity and individuality of the black people they encountered, they might perhaps think of how they themselves might feel if strangers on the street assumed they were criminals and clutched their handbags or quickened their pace. Sadly, the color line and the ingrained stereotypes and segregation we have constructed in American society since slavery all too often prevent and undermine human connections between whites and blacks in American society.

THE FUTURE OF THE COLOR LINE IN AMERICAN SOCIETY

The West Indian immigrants who are the subject of this book are part of the large wave of immigrants who have arrived in the United States since the change in the immigration laws in 1965. This wave of immigrants is predominantly nonwhite and mostly from the Caribbean, Latin America, and Asia. The influx of these immigrants has forever changed the demography of the United States. Before 1965, race relations in the United States were largely a dichotomy between blacks and whites, apart from a small nonblack, nonwhite population of Asians, American Indians, and Hispanics. Joe Perlmann notes that in 1970 blacks were 66% of all nonwhites in the United States.[10] They became 48% of all nonwhites by 1990, and the Census Bureau forecasts that they will drop to 30% by 2050.[11] In 1960 when the Census Bureau did not include Hispanics in the nonwhite category, nine-tenths of those classified as nonwhite were black.

How will this wave of immigration affect American race relations? Where will the color line be drawn in the twenty-first century? Do these demographic changes mean that color and race will take on new meanings in American society? Aside from the often-asked question of whether immigrants take jobs from black Americans, how does the existence of nonwhite immigrants affect the relations between blacks and whites?

A simple model of the impact of immigration on American race relations rests on the assumption that the major division in American society will continue to be between people we historically have thought of as white and those who are nonwhite. This model is often the one envisioned in discussions of population projections of racial and ethnic groups into the future. In 1990 *Time* ran a cover story, which asked, "What Will America Be Like When Whites Are No Longer the Majority?"[12] The "rainbow coalition" that Jesse Jackson tried to enlist in his 1984 presidential campaign speaks to this idea that nonwhite groups in the United States have common cause in challenging the white-majority privilege and that these nonwhite groups could come together politically. The popular term "people of color" also implies such a model. If these assumptions were true, immigration and the increasing diversity of American society would empower black Americans as the new immigrants would become allies to black Americans in challenging white hegemony.

Recent scholarship on the historical absorption of immigrants in the nineteenth and early twentieth centuries provides some reason to be skeptical of such a simple model. Groups such as the Irish and southern and central Europeans were originally seen as fundamentally "racially" different from established white Americans. In the nineteenth century Irish immigrants were referred to as "niggers turned inside out," and Negroes were referred to as "smoked Irish."[13] Yet over time the category "white" absorbed these European groups by identifying them as "not black." By consciously and assiduously distancing themselves from black Americans, these groups became white. In fact, historian Noel Ignatiev entitled his book on this subject, *How the Irish Became White*.

Even groups we still think of as racially distinct from whites have used some of the same tactics. Sociologist James Loewen argued that Chinese immigrants and their descendants in the Mississippi delta in the period from 1870 to 1960 succeeded in changing their racial position. Loewen found that the Chinese, who were considered nonwhite legally and socially in the mid-nineteenth century, slowly changed their status so that by the 1960s they were accepted as equivalent to whites in that area. The price they paid for such social movement was the ostracism of Chinese who had married blacks and continued social distance between blacks and Chinese on every level. Loewen's book opens with the following quote from a white Baptist minister in the delta: "You're either a white man or a nigger here. Now, that's the whole story. When I first came to the Delta, the Chinese were classed as nigras. [And now they are called whites?] That's right." In effect, the Chinese accepted the color line in Mississippi as a price for stepping over it.[14]

Speculating about the identities of the post-1965 non-European immigrants, historian Gary Gerstle proposes that they could also put themselves on the white side of the color line: "Whiteness is a cultural category, not a biological one; its boundaries were stretched once before to admit immigrants from southern and eastern Europe and they can be stretched again to accommodate a wide range of people who today are considered non white. It may be too that Hispanics and Asians will want to pursue whiteness much as the Irish, Italians and Poles did before them, as a way of securing their place in American society."[15] One can see evidence of this occurring now, especially among Hispanics and Asians. Many Asian groups such as Koreans, Chinese, and Japanese have achieved far more economic success and structural assimilation with whites than have black Americans. Koreans have taken over many of the middleman minority positions in the nation's black ghettos that once were filled by Jewish

Americans. There is some evidence that whites are much more accepting of Asians and Hispanics than they are of blacks. Intermarriage rates between whites and Asians are quite high. Among native-born Asians, ages 25 to 34, over 50% have out-married.[16] Residential segregation is also very low for Asians, even for first-generation Asians. The tensions between blacks and Koreans in the L.A. riots, as well as documented tensions between Hispanics and blacks in many neighborhoods, point to a lack of solidarity based on nonwhite status alone.

West Indians, however, are a very extreme test case for this argument regarding social construction of race. It is relatively easy to imagine Chinese or Koreans being socially defined as nonblack or even white, but is this a possibility for people who come from societies where they have long identified racially as black? Despite their black skin, can West Indians distance themselves from black Americans and become nonblack?

The historians who stress that race is a cultural, not a biological, category would lead one to believe this is possible. Indeed, some scholars such as Paul Gilroy and Anthony Appiah argue that racism now is rooted in cultural definitions and explanations, not biological ones. Arguing that since World War II there has been a decline in outright racist thinking, especially in racial essentialism based in biology, Gilroy notes that racism now "frequently operates without any overt reference to either race itself or the biological notions of difference that still give the term its common sense meaning. Before the rise of modern scientific racism in the nineteenth century the term race did duty for the term culture. No surprise then that in its postwar retreat from racism the term has once again acquired an explicitly cultural rather than biological inflection."[17] Gilroy defines this as a shift from vulgar to cultural racism. Reuel Rogers notes that American cultural pluralism allows this cultural racism to flourish.[18] According to this line of thinking, in the 1990s American blacks are not doing badly in the economy or overrepresented in the prison system because of biological inferiority (as old-time vulgar racists would argue) but because their "culture" is lacking.[19]

Indeed, one can see this cultural distancing among the immigrants we spoke with. They argued that they and other West Indians like them merited inclusion in American society because of their strong work ethic, value on education, and lack of pathological behaviors. By asserting a cultural identity as an immigrant and as a member of a model minority, West Indians make a case for cultural inclusion in American society. By asserting an immigrant or an ethnic identity, West Indians can make a case that they are culturally different from black Americans. This is a strategy that many new immigrants can adopt. But when Koreans "become American" by distancing themselves from the underclass black image in American society, the status of the group itself improves. This is the process that seems to have worked for the Irish, the Poles, and even the Mississippi Chinese. But when West Indians and middle-class black Americans do it, there is a boomerang effect. It may help individual black Americans and West Indians, but it leaves intact and reinforces stereotypes of blacks as inferior.

Middle-class black Americans face this problem of self-definition quite often. Because of the ingrained images of African Americans as unworthy and as failures, middle-class blacks have not been able to develop a "symbolic ethnicity" that goes along with their socioeconomic status. As I have argued elsewhere, middle-class white ethnics have been able to selectively identify with their ethnic origins, picking and choosing which aspects of their backgrounds they will continue to practice and identify with.[20] As they achieve in society, the images of their groups change. Jews are no longer seen as particularly talented athletically, Irish are no longer seen as stupid. Over time two things happen with European groups: middle-class individuals can pick and choose whether to identify ethnically at all; if they do identify, they do so with a group that maintains its positive characteristics and loses its negative ones as the group itself increasingly comes to be known by its middle-class successful members and not by its poor immigrant members. Most Irish Americans no longer even recognize the term "paddy wagon" as an ethnic slur against their supposed proclivity for criminal behavior. Instead, politicians of every ethnic background flock to Saint Patrick's Day celebrations to become "Irish for a day."

For middle-class blacks both aspects of a symbolic ethnicity are missing. Because being black is a racial identity, people with certain somatic features—dark skin, kinky hair—are defined as blacks by other people regardless of their own decision about how they wish to identify. Racial identification does not allow for "passing" except for a very few light-skinned people. And the group itself is not seen as changing. For most nonblack Americans the image of blacks as poor, unworthy, and dangerous is still potent, despite the very real success of many black Americans and the growth of a sizable black middle class. The existence of an urban underclass of poor blacks who exhibit "ghetto-specific behaviors," no matter how small a proportion of black people in America they actually are, reinforces and shores up cultural stereotypes American whites developed long ago to justify and shore up slavery itself.

Middle-class black Americans often face whites who are so convinced that all American blacks are poor, criminal, hostile, or nasty that they will not even admit a nice successful person could be black. This black American teacher describes this reaction:

> I had a white person I work with say, "that Mary, she is not white, she is not black." Or people say I'm better or I'm different. To me that's ignorance. They probably feel that I would feel better if they said that. When you don't know, you say a lot of stupid things. (Black American female teacher, age 34)

The white coworker who wanted to say that Mary was not like her image of a black person had to say that she was raceless—neither white phenotypically nor black culturally and behaviorally. For many whites who have an image of West Indians as a model minority, identifying a person as a West Indian provides a useful label. A West Indian is a successful black—a person who may have black skin but who is not "the other" nor part of the group that is defined as "not like us." This white teacher describes the positive image many white Americans have of West Indians:

> Q: What is your impression of West Indians?
> A: They are educated. They have high values for education. A lot of times their accent is more British than American. It's sort of somehow people with a British accent, you always think that they are really intelligent no matter what they say. (White female teacher, age 32)

In reviewing the responses of the whites we interviewed, it is clear that the images of race and ethnicity that "fit" with the immigrants are more acceptable to the whites than the images they hold of African Americans. West Indians are seen often, although not all the time, as immigrants. And whites see themselves as the descendants of immigrants. This allows a shared history and, in some ways, a shared future that whites have trouble visualizing with black Americans.

Yet for blacks and whites to move beyond the color line, and to prevent new Americans of many different origins from accepting that color line in order to be on its advantageous side, we must move beyond both cultural and vulgar racism. By taking seriously the experiences of West Indian immigrants and their children, I hope I have shown how much race still shapes everyday life for those defined racially as black in our society. If the color line is redrawn to make a sharp distinction between those identified socially as black and those who are not, this could be disastrous for black Americans. Four hundred years after coming to this country and 100 years after the end of slavery, another generation of black Americans would see new immigrants from around the globe leapfrog over them to greater inclusion and success in American life. The result of such a scenario would be bifurcated outcomes for new immigrants, with those who are socially defined as white or nonblack doing well and those defined as black doing poorly.

W. E. B. Du Bois wrote in 1903 that the problem of the twentieth century is the problem of the color line, and that a veil separates black from white in America.[21] As we enter the twenty-first century, the tragedy is that America has sold West Indians a bill of goods—a universal ideology of inclusion that in reality is based on defining blacks as "the other," the people who can never really be Americans. The story of West Indian immigrants is the dance they, black Americans, and white Americans do around this central contradiction—their status as immigrants lets the newcomers see, dream, and even visit behind the veil, but their children's and grandchildren's status as Americans may close it once again.

APPENDIX

NOTES

INDEX

APPENDIX:

NOTES ON METHODOLOGY

When I set out to do this study of West Indian immigrants and their children and their black and white American coworkers, I did not think that I would run into very many methodological problems. I had already written a book about ethnic identity using the in-depth interviewing technique.[1] I had learned a great deal doing that book about the logistics of interviews, and I had even done some limited participant observation. This project, however, turned out to be much more complicated and to involve many more ethical dilemmas and methodological problems than I had ever envisioned.

I ended up fashioning solutions on my own or with the help of friends and other ethnographers. I found little written advice in the literature about how to cope with a large number of important field questions: How do you preserve your own and your interviewers' personal safety when doing research in crime-ridden inner-city neighborhoods? How do you do research within workplaces without letting managers and supervisors dictate the conditions of the interviewing? Can a white woman study issues of racial identity and race relations with a black population? How do you deal with the myriad ethical issues that evolve in the course of the fieldwork? For instance, how do you decide how much to pay respondents, and then how do you manage the payments? To what degree should you adhere to what you told your grant proposal funders, and to what degree should you do what you think is the right thing in the field? How much do you get involved in the lives of the people you study?

Of course, other researchers deal with these issues all the time, but I have found that frank discussions of the reality of the research experience are much rarer than sanitized discussions of "research methods" or vague advice about how to construct an interview schedule in the abstract.[2] In this appendix I discuss in some detail the many issues that arose in my research and how I handled them, with the hope that such a discussion will provide some practical tips, advice, and reassurance to other researchers who encounter similar problems and barriers as well as insight for the general reader into the research that produced the book.

Because I was interested in the social process of identity development among the immigrants and their children, I decided to interview people in context—I did not design the study to be a study of individuals alone, but individuals within a context in which they interacted with other people. So I wanted to interview the immigrants and their black and white American coworkers because I was interested not only in how the immigrants identified and saw themselves but how they perceived how others saw them. I also wanted to interview those "others" to see whether the immigrants were accurately understanding how others saw them and to understand the dynamic process of identity construction. Because of the strong patterns of residential segregation, and of segregation in other aspects of people's lives, I believed that the workplace was the only site where such interaction among so many different groups of people would take place. I also was interested in how social class might affect these patterns, so I designed the study so that it would take place among working-class and middle-class immigrants. This meant that I needed a middle-class worksite with sufficient numbers of Caribbean immigrants, black Americans, and white Americans. I also needed a workplace with the same mix of unskilled working-class people. Because I also wanted to study the second generation, I first came up with the idea that I would contact the children of the immigrants that I interviewed in the workplace. Because this design included so many different class, ethnic, and age groups, it also meant that I would be doing a large number of interviews—150 was the total in my original grant proposal. This immediately led to questions of site selection to find the sample and to logistical questions of how to manage doing such a large interview study.

SITE SELECTION

I began the process of site selection in June 1991 by examining data on employment patterns of West Indians in New York, and I decided that a hospital (or hospitals) would be the perfect worksite. Black immigrants were concentrated in hospital employment, and hospitals had both middle-class nurses and doctors and white-collar workers and technicians, along with working-class maintenance and cleaning personnel, food-service workers, and other laborers. I decided this would be the perfect mix of both ethnic and racial groups and social classes. I also thought the hospitals would be a good place to conduct interviews since they have so much public space such as cafeterias, lobbies, and the like.

GAINING ACCESS TO RESPONDENTS

While this reasoning was sound, and it was this design that the funders approved, it proved impossible to actually accomplish. I tried many avenues to try to gain access to a hospital, but I was never successful. I began by choosing hospitals that were in the neighborhoods that West Indians concentrated in. I called and wrote to the public relations offices of several hospitals. Hospitals were not set up to approve studies that involved their employees, and they certainly were not set up to approve studies that involved so many different levels of their employees. The large city hospitals were also in the middle of a crisis. Several major investigations were underway about mismanagement that had led to deaths or improper patient care. It became clear as I hit brick wall after brick wall that people suspected me of claiming to study the racial identities of employees while actually planning to study the ways in which the hospitals were not functioning properly. I tried using some personal contacts at different hospitals; they got me at least partly in the door, but in the end the legal departments of two different hospitals where I got furthest in the door denied my requests for access.

As I sought help from a variety of New Yorkers with my problem of locating a workplace with West Indians, I became aware of a central distinction between academic work and journalism. Most people offering me advice about how to find "Caribbean people" to interview were thinking of me as a journalist. Journalists find key informants who tell them a story about something. So, for instance, a journalist who wishes to understand the experience of West Indian immigrants would talk to the director of a neighborhood agency who deals with such immigrants, or the priest in an immigrant parish, or an academic who studies immigrants. Then the journalist has a story of upward mobility, extreme social problems, interesting rituals—whatever narrative makes sense to the journalist after the key informant interviews. The journalist next looks for sample "real people" to describe the experiences the journalist knows to be true of the group. So if the story the journalist gets from the key informants is that this particular immigrant group is succeeding because of self-employment, he or she will ask around until a self-employed person is found who will tell that story.

Most people I sought advice from were trying to find people for me to interview along those lines. So I told them I was interested in identity, and they should simply refer me to people who were self-identified as West Indian. Most of my network contacts were disturbed that I had not spoken to leaders of the immigrant community who would tell me about the problems the people faced before I went out and spoke with "the people." But the nature of my research project was such that I did not want to find what the self-described leaders of the community would tell me to find. This is enormously important in research on identity because leaders have a very pronounced interest in claiming strong identities among those people with the "potential" to have that identity.[3] It may be that what I found ultimately rings true with community leaders (and that has been my experience when I have talked about my work). But it was important to me that I not choose interviewing sites based on a preconceived notion of what I would find, or that I not begin with a convenience or expert sample.

I considered other industries and worksites. Almost everyone to whom I explained my problem had recently had a taxi ride with a Caribbean immigrant and suggested taxi drivers as a sample population. But how much interaction do taxi drivers have with each other?[4] And in the end this suggestion did not work because there are very few white or black Americans who drive taxis in New York. Almost all the drivers are immigrants.[5] I tried nursing homes as well. While they did not pose as big a problem as hospitals for access, and while there was some variation in the employment and class level of the workers, I could not get access to one that was big enough to have the requisite numbers of workers of different racial and ethnic backgrounds as well as different social classes.

By October 1991 I was beginning to despair that I would ever have a study. I had already decided that gaining access to the children of immigrants from the sample would not work as a way to study the identities of second-generation adolescents. The number of immigrants who would have to be contacted at work to yield a big enough sample of the second generation would be extremely large because not all immigrants would have children in the high school and young-adult age group, and not all would be willing to have their children interviewed. There was also the problem of where these interviews would take place if the children were contacted via their parents. The worksites would bring people in from all over the city, and then I would have to track down the children and interview them in their homes. I decided that a more efficient route would be to interview adolescents through the public schools. They would not be the children of the adults I had interviewed, but they would be facing many of the same types of family issues, and I would be able to observe the adolescents in a context where I saw them interact with others.

Gaining access to the public schools was a nightmare. I began by deciding which high schools were in the neighborhoods where the West Indian students were located. I wrote to the principals of these high schools. I also tried to call the Board of Education to find out how to go through its review process. It was extremely difficult to get anyone to answer the phone or return a phone call. It took me several weeks of phone calls to the wrong places before I received a written set of guidelines from the Board of Ed about doing research in the schools. Several layers of permission from different parts of the bureaucracy were needed. Principals of the schools needed to approve the project, as did the superintendent of the districts the schools were in, as did the main Board of Ed office. It was very unclear to me which layer of bureaucracy needed to be approached first—some teachers and administrators told me to contact the principals first; others told me to go through the central administration.

The rejection from the hospitals was relatively clear-cut—there seemed to be a chain of command, and if I were persistent in calling I could finally reach a person who seemed to have the authority to turn me down. Dealing with the Board of Education was, on the other hand, a truly Kafkaesque experience. Messages seemed to go into a black hole. Secretaries would scream at me that the person I asked for would not be in for days or weeks. Receptionists were angry with me for calling back persistently when my calls were not returned. In fact, the secretaries in the school offices truly succeeded in intimidating me. I shudder to think about the effect they have on a relatively uneducated immigrant, new to the country, who is trying to find information or even to protest or change some treatment of a child.

I decided I needed help. My mother had been teaching teachers at Brooklyn College for thirty years. I began to use her contacts and knowledge of the system. For example, I am a professor at Harvard University and have a Ph.D. I tended not to use the titles of Professor or Doctor when I introduced myself on the phone to people because, frankly, it seems obnoxious and pretentious to me. So when I left messages, I would say, "This is Mary Waters calling. I am a sociologist from Harvard University." I thought that if I sounded on the phone like a nice person who was not being pretentious, then the secretaries would like me and give my messages to whoever could approve my project. My mother told me not to do that. I needed to say I was Dr. Mary Waters, a PROFESSOR from HARVARD UNIVERSITY doing a very important study. This new strategy got me a little bit less yelling from the secretaries. But not a lot of action.

Meanwhile, I did fill out the forms and prepare the application to the central office of the Board of Education. When I went to hand it in, the secretaries said I needed a letter from my professor approving my project. Obviously the office is accustomed to handling many graduate students who are doing projects in the schools for their dissertation. I *was* the professor, I told them, getting more pretentious and obnoxious as time went on. They had me sign the form where it said that the professor should sign. I waited for board approval while I still tried to track down the supervisors and the principals of the schools I wanted to work in.

In the meantime through sheer luck I found a workplace to do interviews. A former student of mine who was living with his parents in New York called me, and we got together for lunch. I told him my problem. (By this point I had become very boring and was telling everyone my problems.) He said his mother worked in a major corporation downtown; when he ate lunch with her there, he had noticed that exactly the mix of people I wanted to study worked in the cafeteria. All the supervisors seemed to be white, and the workers included many West Indian people and several black American people. I asked him to check with his mother whether his perceptions seemed correct. She said they did and gave me the name of the manager of the cafeteria. I called the manager and explained who I was and that I wanted to interview his employees about their experiences with immigration in New York. This manager, a white male, said indeed he had a ton of immigrants working for him. He asked me to send him a letter describing what I wanted. I did, and two days later he gave me approval as long as I did not interview the employees on work time and as long as I did not conduct interview on the grounds of United States Financial[6]—the company where the cafeteria was located. I could do so anywhere in the skyscraper complex that was not within the floors of United States Financial. After five months of writing letters, making phone calls, going to meetings, filling out requests to human subjects committees, all with no avail, I was suddenly "in" after two phone calls and one letter. And I was really "in." Although I had to be vouched for everyday to get through security in the lobby in order to go to the cafeteria, once I was admitted I was free to hang out in the cafeteria as much as I wished to observe the workers, as long as I did my interviews in another place.

This worksite was not perfect, but it met many of my requirements. It had a mix of unskilled, generally uneducated West Indian immigrants and black Americans. The whites were all in supervisory positions, but this allowed me to ask a great deal about hiring practices, which I knew was a sore point in relations between West Indians and black Americans. In late November 1991 I was able to begin interviewing. The timing was an added bonus because the money I was offering for the respondents ($25) was especially attractive for people who were about to do Christmas shopping.

But I still needed people for the middle-class sample, and it was clear I could not find enough middle-class people at the cafeteria worksite. It then occurred to me that schoolteachers would fit the bill. There were sufficient numbers of West Indian teachers in the public school system, along with sufficient numbers of black Americans and white Americans. And school teachers definitely had a college education and qualified as middle class. I decided to try this strategy. Gaining official access to interview teachers would involve another whole round of permissions through the Board of Education, as well as through the local district, which was currently in the midst of severe disarray owing to charges of financial mismanagement. I was weary from my earlier attempts to get into the high schools, and I did not feel that I had the time to jump through the necessary hoops. I decided instead to interview teachers using a snowball sampling strategy in elementary and high schools with a number of West Indian students, concentrating on teachers in the two high schools where I had sought permission to interview students.

Meanwhile, my proposal to interview the children was snaking its way through the layers of bureaucracy. The Human Subjects Committee at the New York Board of Education came back with a provisional approval. I had submitted my interview schedule along with a standard proposal, but the committee had problems with some of the questions. One objection was to a question I proposed about language: "Do you sometimes speak proper English and sometimes speak slang with your friends?" The committee felt that designating black English as slang could be damaging to the self-image of the youngsters, and I was asked to change "slang" to "black English." I had come up with "slang" in pretesting because that was the term the youngsters themselves used, but I did not want to argue with the committee and jeopardize my proposal. Of course, this entire process was to prove extremely ironic when contrasting this micromanaging of my proposal with the complete chaos that prevailed in the schools I studied, and the complete freedom I had in the schools once I was in the door. While I obeyed the bureaucrats and asked the teens about speaking black English, I often had to clarify myself in the face of their blank stares by saying, "You know, slang, broken English."

Six months after I began trying, the central office of the Board of Education and the Superintendant of Brooklyn High Schools approved my project. However, though I had requested four schools, I was denied access to two of them. I was told my choices did not have the West Indian concentrations I needed. I later learned that a more likely explanation was that these schools were even more dangerous and chaotic than the two I was allowed into. One of the schools I was not allowed to study, Thomas Jefferson High School, was the scene of a number of murders of students in previous months. I promised to protect the anonymity of the two schools that I did study, and so I call them by the pseudonyms Eisenhower and Truman throughout. After gaining permission from the principals of the two high schools, I entered the schools in January 1992.

CHOOSING THE SAMPLE

The reviewers for both the Board of Education and the Russell Sage Foundation (my funding source for the study) had asked that I choose the students for the interviews randomly. The Board of Ed reviewers were particularly concerned because I was going to pay the respondents $10 for participating. In the end, however, I found that if I randomly chose all my respondents in the schools, I would have a very unrepresentative sample. I was required by the Human Subjects Committees of both Harvard and the New York Board of Ed to get parental permission in writing before I could interview a student younger than 18. In a large public school like Eisenhower or Truman this selected for students who attended homeroom where the slips were distributed, who filled out a preliminary screening questionnaire I distributed to all students, who could remember to bring the permission form home and back to school, who had contact in the evenings with a parent or guardian, and who wanted to participate in something officially occurring in school. An enormous number of students did not meet all these criteria, and it systematically selected for the most responsible, mature, and interested students.

At Eisenhower High School this was partly remedied because a guidance counselor took me under her wing. She looked at the list of second-generation students I had selected for interviewing and told me which ones she would send for first. Over time she added names to the list with advice like "I really want you to talk to Keisha; she is having a very hard time with her parents and her friends." Or "you should talk to Ricky; he is at risk of dropping out." She reminded students to return their forms and ran interference for me with homeroom teachers who did not follow up on missing students or parental permissions. At Truman High School I had no such help, and I was more at the mercy of my inadequate list of second-generation students. Often I would request up to twenty names before I would get one student who had a signed permission form and who showed up at the appointed time.

The guidance counselor at Eisenhower, whom I call by the pseudonym Mrs. Montgomery, also informed me that I should not exclude Haitian students. In my original grant proposal to Russell Sage I had included Haitians as one of the groups I would study. The anonymous reviewers of that grant proposal had all said they did not agree with that decision. Because Haitians were refugees, did not speak English, and did not share many elements of West Indian culture, they were very different from the other groups I was to study, so I had agreed to exclude them. When the questionnaires came back from the students, I eliminated all the Haitians.

But Mrs. Montgomery told me in no uncertain terms that it would be impolitic not to include Haitians. As I learned more about the atmosphere in the school, I agreed with her. The Haitians had very low status in the student hierarchy; they endured a great deal of teasing, exclusion, and ridicule. The other students would claim that the Haitians were practicing voodoo on them or that they had AIDS. As soon as I started interviewing, and it became known that I was offering $10 and the chance to get out of class to be interviewed for an hour or more, all of the students in the school wanted to be interviewed. If I had said I was willing to talk to all children of immigrants except those from Haiti, I would have reinforced vicious stereotypes that hurt the feelings of the Haitians, and I would have lent official sanction to the informal shunning and exclusion of all things Haitian that occurred among the students. This decision to include the Haitians posed another dilemma for me later when I had eight excellent interviews of Haitians, and I had to decide whether to analyze them together with the other West Indian adolescents. In the end I did include them in the analysis, and their words appear in the book. I was sensitive to any issues, such as language, that might differentiate the Haitians from the other teens.

ENLARGING THE SAMPLE

I became more concerned about the lack of representativeness of my sample. As I spent more time at Eisenhower, I recognized the degree of chaos and the large numbers of students who never make it to senior year and certainly would not respond to the college counselor. I worried that we were missing the core of students who hung out in the hallways, the ones who carried weapons and intimidated the students who were doing well in school. I knew I needed to interview a few of these students in order to have a sense of the range of experiences among the second generation. (I never thought I would be able to get a random sample that would allow me to statistically generalize to the entire second-generation population, but I wanted to be able to describe the range of experiences of the second generation as an exploratory qualitative study.) To solve this dilemma I knew I could not go through the schools. I also knew I would have to conduct interviews with these minors without parental permission. This is how I came to have a street sample.

I got the name of a young man who had done some interviewing for another New York ethnography on drug dealers. He was a graduate of Truman High School who was now attending college and was himself a second-generation West Indian. I called him and told him I wanted some interviews done with kids who had dropped out of school. He said he could find them through his own neighborhood connections and those of his younger brothers. He eventually did fifteen interviews with kids whom he found through the neighborhood. Although this was just about the most "unscientific" sampling one could imagine, I believe that it provides a better overall picture of the range of experiences of the second generation than one could have with a school-based random sample. In fact, given my experiences, I believe it would be impossible to get an accurate perception of the subjective experiences of second-generation youngsters in different life experiences through a simple random sample administered through the schools. This arrangement did pose another ethical dilemma, however, because I authorized interviews of minors without parental consent, something I had promised the institutional review boards I would not do.

There were two more types of youths I knew I was missing. Not every local student attended these neighborhood schools. The teachers I was interviewing indicated that many of the best students attended citywide magnet schools or private schools. In addition, the neighborhoods themselves, while containing some middle-class families, were bound to be different than suburban middle-class neighborhoods. Because my goal in the study was to tap the range of possible experiences among the second generation, I decided to try to find two types of second-generation youth—those whose families were well-off financially (the upper middle-class sample) and those who were from a more modest middle-class background but seemed to be on an upward trajectory, having enrolled in college or with a bright chance for going to college. Both of these groups were found through snowball samples.

The middle-class sample included young people whose families had moved from Brooklyn to suburban Long Island, New Jersey, or Connecticut, as well as one youth whose family lived in Brooklyn but who attended a citywide magnet school. I found these youths through contacts in the neighborhood and in Eisenhower and Truman High Schools.

The church-school sample was composed of youth who currently attended or had recently graduated from Catholic parochial schools in Brooklyn. I found these youths through an after-school program at a nearby parish and through Catholic high schools; however, only half of these students were actually Catholic. (The Catholic schools had minimal bureaucracies. An alum of one nearby Catholic school, I explained my project to the school principal who still remembered me; she gave me instant approval, connected me with other principals who approved my visits to their schools, and connected me with a local parish organization. The entire process of gaining access took a few days.) The occupations of the parents of the church-based sample were very similar to the occupations of the public school parents. Yet these parents were paying tuition for their children to attend much more rigorous and college-focused high schools. There were nine interviews from the middle-class sample and fourteen from the church-based sample.

THE ATMOSPHERE AT THE PUBLIC HIGH SCHOOLS

Space was at a premium at both of these old overcrowded high schools. Although I requested private space to do the interviews, neither school could give me exactly what I needed. There were absolutely no empty classrooms or offices during the day at either school. At Truman I was directed to the school library. Students who had a free period would be in the library sitting at desks, talking and carrying on. The very unpleasant librarian was not happy to have me interviewing students there and did nothing to help me stake out a private corner. I became more emboldened over time and took over a corner of the library and did not let others come and sit there. Still the curious would come and sit near me during interviews and taunt and tease both me and the students I was interviewing. On one occasion a boy flashed a knife in my direction when I told him to stop threatening the student I was interviewing. I did not say anything to the school authorities because I did not want to get a reputation with the students as a snitch, and by this time I knew a large proportion of the students in the school were carrying weapons of some sort.

At Eisenhower I was set up in the basement in the college advising section. There was an office for Mrs. Montgomery to do her advising, and whenever she was at a meeting or teaching a class she let me interview students in that private space. When she was in her office, I moved outside to the general reading area where there were a number of tables and chairs. Students spent free periods congregating in this area because there was no place else to spend the free periods, and because it was safer there than in the cafeteria. Often the students who were hanging out there made so much noise and disturbance that it was very difficult to conduct an interview. I also had to constantly watch out to make sure that students were not overhearing the sometimes very personal information my respondents were reporting.

The large numbers of students who were hanging out in this interview area proved to be a great boon to my research, however. The question of trust and access was a very serious one in this research. Would young black students answer honestly my probing questions about their family life, their racial identity, their behaviors, and their beliefs about touchy issues like race relations and weapons in school? I had hired an African-American student from Harvard to do interviews for me because I was worried that my race, gender, and age would make it difficult for students to trust me. Because of the method of approach to the students that developed, I also felt that I was too identified with officials of the school, and that students would be afraid I was collecting information in an official capacity.

ESTABLISHING RAPPORT WITH THE RESPONDENTS

Before I began this project I had thought that I could establish rapport with the students by telling them that I had grown up nearby and knew all about the neighborhoods of Brooklyn. In my fantasy of how this would work, I would explain that I grew up in the area, that my parents lived locally, and that, even though I taught at Harvard, I still had "Brooklyn roots." I could not have been more wrong! My background did seem to allow some degree of rapport when I shared it with the teachers, but when I told the students I was from Brooklyn I was met with blank stares and occasional hostility. It did little to impress these students because they had lived their lives in Brooklyn and did not know people from other parts of the United States. They did not know the level of ignorance outsiders have of Brooklyn, and so my so-called "special knowledge" of neighborhoods and street names and high schools was actually "common knowledge" in their view. Most unexpected to me of course, but very understandable once I became aware of it, my white skin became more of a marker to these kids when it was associated with the white neighborhood my parents continued to live in. Instead of the type of bonding I thought would take place "We are all from Brooklyn"—my invocation of where I grew up evoked such responses as "That's where the white people live" or "My brother got beaten up when he went to that part of town." When I told one of the students that if I had gone to public high school instead of Catholic high school, I would have attended Midwood, she explained how the students at Midwood refused to have an exchange program with Eisenhower because they were too scared to come to an all-black school. Being an outsider who was visiting from Massachusetts rendered me more interesting and less threatening to the students.

I also had thought that my affiliation as a professor at Harvard might have proved intimidating to the unskilled workers and to the students. Some of the unskilled workers had heard of Harvard, but none seemed intimidated by it.

Though a few of the teachers seemed uneasy about my affiliation with Harvard, they also seemed most reassured when I told them I had grown up in Brooklyn and was a "local girl made good." The security guards at Eisenhower usually heard "Howard" when I said "Harvard." Since they seemed to like Howard better than Harvard, I let that slide. The academically oriented students asked me about getting into and applying to Harvard. I encouraged them to apply, even though I knew that the valedictorian and smartest student in the school had combined SAT scores of 900, which did not bode well for anyone's acceptance at a very competitive college.

Because the process of choosing students for the study and having them return a parental permission slip took a long time, I had my research assistant, Ritchie, with me with nothing to do. Ritchie was a Harvard senior, taking a semester off to be with his family after his father died. He is a very good-looking and charming young man, who had grown up in Brooklyn in a working-class household. He was also a star football player at Harvard. I chose him to do the interviews because of his good rapport with people and also because he is a black American. The football playing proved the icing on the cake. I paid Ritchie to just hang out in the area at Eisenhower where the students hung out. The girls immediately wanted to talk and flirt with him. The academically inclined boys wanted to talk about college and how Ritchie had gotten in and how he had found it to be. Many of the nonacademically inclined kids also wanted to talk to him about football and also just about life. He was very popular.

Ritchie spent a few weeks getting to know the kids and occasionally doing an interview or two. After a week or so the students began to ask him about me. Was I really a professor? What was I doing this study for? Was I OK? Ritchie vouched for me. He told them about the study, that I was writing a book, and that I was a good person. I immediately noticed a change. During the time I spent hanging out between interviews, students began to ask me if they could get interviewed. A few students asked me to bring in the books I had written. Students began to ask my opinion about things. Some would say hi to me in the hallways or on the street outside. Over the five months we were there Ritchie and I conducted many formal interviews, but we also learned a great deal about the students through informal interactions. Although we conducted eighteen formal interviews at Truman over a three-week period, and many of those interviews were very similar to the Eisenhower interviews, I shifted my attention to Eisenhower, and I gathered more information and more material from there, conducting twenty-seven formal interviews with students. I also conducted teacher interviews at Eisenhower, but not at Truman because of the access problems I was having at Truman.

USING INTERVIEWERS

In the end the project included 202 formal interviews, 140 of which I did myself. The rest were done by a crew of research assistants. In my previous project I had done all of the interviews myself. There are a variety of opinions about this subject. Some methodological purists argue that when the researcher does not do the interviews herself, she loses the closeness of the ethnographic interview, and the work is less good. Others argue that a white woman cannot interview black men and women about race, and that a woman cannot get the same level of cooperation from men that she can get from women. At first I was convinced by the race-of-interviewer argument that only blacks could interview blacks, and only whites could interview whites. I was further worried that, given the tensions and distance between West Indians and African Americans, I needed to match on immigration status as well.

I had hired research assistants who were ready to start in the summer of 1991. But I did not get into a site to do research until November 1991, and I did not complete the interviewing until June 1992. I lost the original group of handpicked research assistants, who were black immigrants, second-generation black immigrants, and African Americans, because of the timing problems and because they had to go back to school. I was able to hire an African-American male student—Ritchie, described above—to help me with interviews in November. But once the interviews started to be lined up, we needed to be ready to go. So out of necessity, rather than let the opportunity to interview slide, I began to interview the blacks as well as the whites. My student also did a number of the interviews with black Americans and immigrants. We compared notes on the interviews, and I immediately had the interviews transcribed so that I could try to compare the interviews for any signs that my race was biasing results. Life history interviews are each very different from one another, and this makes them difficult to compare. I especially concentrated on the questions about race relations and discrimination. We found that the interviews with African Americans conducted by Ritchie elicited more antiwhite sentiments and incidents of discrimination than the interviews I did with African Americans. The differences seemed pronounced for the African Americans. The immigrants seemed to report the same degree of antiwhite sentiments and experiences with discrimination to Ritchie as they did to me. The one interview that Ritchie conducted with a white manager was the only interview with a white out of the total of twenty-five conducted that did not include antiblack sentiments. I concluded that it was important to match on race of interviewer for white and black Americans, but it was less important to match for the immigrants. Ritchie and I also both felt that while he did not have much problem interviewing women, he did a better job with the young men than I did. Later in the spring I hired two West Indian graduate students to help with interviews of the school teachers and the food-service workers, and I tried to match as much as I could on race and immigration status in later interviews.

There are a number of reasons why a white American would be more comfortable with foreign-born blacks than American blacks. I discovered that I was much more at ease with the immigrants than with the African Americans. For a while I rationalized that it was because it was easier to explain what the project was about to immigrants, and that it was easier to interview the immigrants because they wanted the story of their immigration to be told. I think there is something to that. But I also am embarrassed to say that I found it easier to interview foreign-born than American blacks because I too am at greater ease with the foreign-born for many of the same reasons my white respondents reported in this study. The foreign-born blacks did not evoke the same feelings of guilt in me about race relations that black Americans did, and I did not sense as much personal anger and distancing from me with the immigrants as I did with the African Americans. It is indeed a sad finding that race relations make Americans more uncomfortable with each other than with outsiders; it is a personally sad and sobering realization that I found it true for myself as well.

THE LINE BETWEEN INTERVIEWING AND PARTICIPANT OBSERVATION

I would not describe this research project as being just an interview study. Because the interviews, which are the meat of the project and the source of most of my material, were based within institutions where people interacted over a long period of time and where I had access to people at times other than the interviews, the study has elements of an ethnography. Certainly my experience in Eisenhower High School involved a great deal of participant observation. I overheard and saw a great deal of interactions among students other than those I interviewed. I attended some classes, I roamed the halls, I went to the cafeteria. I went to the home of one of the teachers. I gave some teachers rides home. I grew attached to a few of the students I interviewed. On the other hand, I did not get as involved in the life of the Truman school or in the other public schools where I interviewed a few teachers, and I don't know how the study would have turned out if Truman school had been my only entrée.

At American Food I also got to know people in the office over time, and I hung out in the cafeteria and observed people together on breaks. My research assistant and I were invited to the company Christmas party. I was out of town at the time, but he attended and gave me a detailed description of what happened there. He also had a very good time.

The involvement I did have at American Food and Eisenhower High allowed me to make some observations about the relation between what people did and what people said. For instance, some people at American Food who described many differences between American blacks and West Indians were observed taking breaks with individuals of different backgrounds or sitting together with these coworkers when they ate their lunches in the cafeteria. At the high school I was able to observe the ways in which some white teachers talked disparagingly of their black students with each other, and I also witnessed the extra hours of dedication that other white and black teachers put in to help their students.

Sometimes the ethnographic experiences served as reminders of the real limits of the interview approach. Toward the end of my fieldwork at Eisenhower, I arrived at school early one morning to find Mrs. Montgomery, my model of sanity in a field of chaos and despair, in tears. One of the seniors had been arrested the day before. She was charged with throwing away a baby she had given birth to alone on her mother's living-room rug. The baby was found in a garbage can outside the apartment building where this high school student lived. Apparently the 18-year-old had been too frightened to tell anyone about her pregnancy. She had recently won a scholarship to a state university for the following year and was set to graduate in a few weeks. She kept the pregnancy a secret from all of the students at school as well as from the teachers and her family. She wore baggy clothes and had skipped gym the last few months. She was a child of a Caribbean immigrant from Jamaica.

I had interviewed her! A few weeks before she gave birth alone in desperation and threw her baby away, I had spent an hour or more with her discussing her family and her relations with her parents, and asking questions about how old she wanted to be when she had children and how old she wanted to be when she got married. She was not a good interviewee. Even though she was outgoing when I met her hanging out in the school, she answered most of my interview questions with one-word answers. I immediately listened to the interview when I heard news of her arrest. There was no sign at all of what she was going through. I would not expect her to have blurted out her secret to an interviewer when she had kept it to herself for so long, but it made me wonder about how many other secrets, relevant or irrelevant for the research, people were keeping from me.

This tragedy provided another rich research opportunity. Students were very upset by the news, and a number of girls gathered in Mrs. Montgomery's office to discuss how they felt. By this time I was an accepted part of the scene in that office, and I sat by as the students discussed their feelings about teen pregnancy, parental pressures to succeed, and how much future opportunity they had. I learned some valuable things that day but only due to an opportunity that arose because of a tragedy.

SAFETY ISSUES

A number of issues that came up over the course of the research related to concerns about my own personal safety and that of my research assistants. The first issue came up in the design of the study. I had decided to apply for money to pay respondents. Partly I did this because it seemed to be the thing to do. I had heard about other researchers who were paying respondents; moreover, according to the ethnographers I consulted, payment was the best way to ensure cooperation among the widest range of respondents, not just the people who were eager to talk because of their own agendas. It also seemed to me an ethical thing to do because I was taking the time of these respondents and also drawing out their words and feelings in order to produce a book.

I decided to pay adults $25 and adolescents $10 for taking part in the interviews. I do not know how I came up with these figures; I think I made them up based on what would make me agree to be interviewed.[7] But the problem immediately arose about how to pay the people. My grant money flowed through Harvard University. The university could cut a check for each individual I interviewed but only after receiving a social security number and permanent address. The check would then reach the person several weeks after the interview. That would not work.

Perhaps I could have written a personal check to the teachers, but that would have included my home address and phone, which I did not feel comfortable giving out to people I did not know well. And the food-service workers could not be paid by check. Most poor people do not have checking accounts; to cash a check they usually have to patronize a check-cashing store where they are charged exorbitant fees for the privilege of getting their money. I had to give the money to the people in cash or money orders. Money orders also provided problems for the people who wanted to cash them as well as problems for me in obtaining them.

So, despite my fears, I decided to use cash, and I tried to take whatever precautions I could about handling the money. I prepared for each interview by putting the cash in a sealed white envelope, and I asked each person whom I interviewed not to open the envelope until he or she went home. I also tried to balance my desire for a private spot for the interview with my desire to be in a public space in case someone found out I was holding envelopes with cash in them and decided to rob me. I rationalized that since I rarely did more than two interviews a day at American Food, or three a day at the high schools, that I was not carrying any more cash than most people carry in their wallets. Yet I was still very uneasy.

WHITE STUDYING BLACK

Aside from the more specific question of the race of an interviewer and its effect on responses, a far more general question exists about whether a white researcher can or should study black people in the United States. The question contains a number of assumptions and subquestions. Can whites really understand race relations and the lives of blacks when they not only do not experience the same things, but when white researchers are implicated in the whole process by virtue of their skin color? Will black people be honest with white researchers about their experiences? Will they refrain from criticizing other blacks because of the tendency not to want to air dirty laundry in front of others? Will they not be honest about their negative feelings toward whites because they don't want to hurt the feelings of a white researcher? Will researchers misunderstand what they find because of their limited knowledge of black culture? And in the most extreme cultural relativist point of view, is it possible ever for outsiders to understand and not distort the experiences and beliefs of a group of which they will never be a part?

There is a long history of scholarship on race in this country that fuels this debate. Some of the most moving and sympathetic accounts of black life have been written by white researchers, for example, *Tally's Corner* and *All My Kin*.[8] Yet black people in America were too long kept from telling their own stories and have suffered from having their experiences misinterpreted by white outsiders.

On the other hand, the proposition that only blacks should study blacks is very problematic. Does that mean that only insiders should study insiders? Does that mean that black scientists should only study black topics? Does that mean that a black sociologist interested in sociology of religion should only study black churches, or one interested in ethnicity should only study black people? I believe that one's personal characteristics cannot help but influence the work that one does. I know I include gender in studies of immigration and ethnicity more than some of my male colleagues do, not necessarily because they have a bias against women but because they do not think about it. But I also do not believe that because I am a woman I should only study women, and that I have nothing to contribute to a study of immigrants, for instance, that includes men. I do not think that black sociologists should only study blacks. I also think that outsiders as well as insiders can study any phenomenon. The perspective in the resulting work will bear the imprint of the person doing the research. An insider and an outsider will not see exactly the same things or interpret things exactly the same, but that does not make one perspective automatically invalid.[9]

Race is enormously important in our society, but it does not define the entire human being. One of the most important aspects of a work like this is that it should make clear that whites, blacks, and black immigrants are alike in many ways as people. They share the same hopes and values and some of the same experiences. I know this experience has changed some of my perceptions and challenged some of my preconceptions about race and about how I personally use race to judge people. Because I teach race and ethnic relations and I think about American race relations, I have had many discussions with friends, colleagues, and students about the experiences of black people in white America. I knew about middle-class experiences with discrimination, so I was not very surprised when the interviews yielded a great deal of information about the vast amount of interpersonal racism the black immigrants and their children faced and about how much it hurt them. This research experience, however, was the first time I have spoken at any length with young poor black males.

I learned a lot through those interpersonal encounters, and I hope these lessons have come through clearly enough in the book for the reader to have learned the same things. One is that I was shocked at the degree of physical violence these youths had experienced at the hands of whites. I too had internalized the idea that these youths were so tough and violent that they were never afraid of whites. I thought naively that if the students at the school learned that I had grown up nearby, it would be a source of bonding; this reflects my lack of knowledge about the degree to which white ethnics use threats and acts of physical violence to keep blacks out of their neighborhoods.

I also learned about my own tendency to stereotype and about the effects those stereotypes had on young black males. One experience I had while interviewing the food-service workers makes this clear. I had been searching for a quiet place to conduct interviews at United States Financial. It was the week before Christmas and the shops in the lobby of the skyscraper complex were becoming more crowded, which meant that the benches in the lobby area were also becoming crowded and louder. I began looking for quieter places. Part of the logistics of the interview process involved asking the women in the office to send people down after their shift to the lobby bench where I had set up shop that day. So, for instance, I would say send the 3 P.M. person down to the bench outside Crabtree & Evelyn. And at 3 P.M. I would just wait there and one of the food-service workers would show up. (This spared me having to go through security between every interview to get upstairs to the cafeteria to meet each interviewee. The security guards grew tired of calling upstairs for me four or five times a day. They would not make an exception for me and issue some sort of ID card because I was not an employee.) One particular afternoon in the week before Christmas I had found a particularly deserted part of the lobby that was in a section where no stores had yet opened. One walked down a busy corridor and then turned left and there were some benches, but it was not a corridor that led to anywhere else except to empty storefronts. So I set up shop there, very pleased that I had finally found a place without blaring Christmas music, which had been making it very hard for my transcriber to make out the words of the respondents.

I was sitting there alone when I saw a young black male come to the end of the corridor. He saw me and then abruptly turned and started looking in a store window, around the corner from me. Then he eased out into the corridor, looking behind him back down the corridor where there were some people. He was looking at me and then looking away in what I immediately perceived to be a guilty or sinister way. He was dressed in baggy pants that were hanging down low on his body. He had high-top sneakers and wore a sweatshirt with the hood pulled up over his head, covering half of his face. His hands were buried inside the sweatshirt.

I was sure he was there to mug me. My heart started racing. I looked around. I was trapped. I had my silly white envelopes filled with $25 in cash next to me, and my expensive tape recorder and microphone were set out on the bench. I was all alone, and there was no one else in this corridor to nowhere. The young man was coming toward me now, looking at the same time in every direction. I thought he was checking whether he might be noticed by anyone else who could later report on the robbery that was about to happen. I started to gather up my things with the thought that I could make a run for it to the open stores. He walked up to me and said, in what I perceived to be a very menacing voice, "Is this the place to get interviewed?" I said yes; he told me he was from the food services and wanted to be interviewed. He sat down, I paid him his $25, and we began a very long and heartfelt interview.

My hands were shaking as I put the microphone on him. I was busy thinking that my close call with a violent encounter had just been averted. He was not very talkative at first, but then he started talking about his grandmother who had raised him and he opened up quite a bit. He talked about how active he was in his church. He was working full-time in the food services but he hoped to go to school to become a pilot someday. In short, he was a very good person. He loved his grandmother and did all kinds of things to take care of her, he was deeply religious and very active in his church, and he had the hopes and dreams of any 19-year-old and was working very hard to see if his could come true. Then I asked about discrimination. He told me how he did not have much contact with whites but that he knew he scared them. He told me how hurt and angry he felt when people crossed to the other side of the street when he walked by. He told how it almost made him want to hurt white people because they seemed to expect it from him. I was the sympathetic interviewer, but I was feeling a great deal of guilt. I too had typecast and stereotyped him. I had reacted like all those people whom he met on the streets, except I got to hear directly how it made an innocent person feel to be perceived as a mugger. I came to understand how angry and hurt it made him and how utterly unfair it seemed to him.

But I did not want to accept unqualified blame—he did look scary to me. So I strayed from my interview schedule and asked some other questions. I said I had always wondered why some guys wore their sweatshirt hoods like that, even indoors when they were not cold. He said he did it for privacy. He liked the feeling that he was able to walk about, and people were not able to see what he thought or felt. I was not completely satisfied with that answer. I wanted him to see that he looked scary to me, so I asked him if he ever saw people on the street who were scary to him. I guess at the time I thought he might reply, "Yeah, people like me." Instead he told me about being chased by a gang of whites when he had been coming home from a football game and found himself in a white neighborhood. He was chased for a long time and escaped by jumping onto an outdoor subway track and running along it, hoping a train would not come before he could lose the white guys and be able to climb out of the tracks. He said that when he saw people like those guys he was very afraid.

I had been trying to get this young man to see that the "cool pose" he adopted was intimidating to whites and caused people to be afraid of him. I was partly trying to do this because it was clear that he was upset that whites were afraid of him. But I also wanted to absolve myself of some guilt for having those same fears of him a few minutes earlier. What I learned was that the people who looked like my own brothers, the whites who dressed in T-shirts and blue jeans with belts, seemed dangerous to him. I vowed after that interview that I would no longer stereotype young black males, and that I would see them as individual people.

A few days later I was going for a walk in Central Park with a friend of mine who was visiting from out of town. We were walking along a busy path and up ahead could see a group of four young black males. They looked like the young man I had interviewed. We were coming to a fork in the pathway, and my friend said, "This path does not seem safe; let's walk on the road where there are a lot of bicyclists." The young men were on a path that snaked into the woods. I began to lecture my friend on how bad it would make those boys feel to see us run away from them by walking on the road. They were probably not bad kids, and we were stereotyping them by being afraid to walk past them. We had slowed down to have this discussion, and I was about to insist that we take the more deserted path when we heard sirens. The young men pulled out a very large butcher knife and tossed it in the bushes and began to run. We found out that they had just robbed a passerby at knifepoint. My friend immediately pointed out to me that they could have been on that secluded path because they were ready to mug someone else.

I tell both of these stories because I think it is clear that there is no easy answer to the question of stereotypes and urban fear and crime. Black men are unfairly stereotyped as violent; on the other hand, urban crime is a reality, and there are certain class and race cues that people use to decide whether they are in danger. Neither is clear-cut.

Another aspect of race relations that has affected this project lies in the presentation of the findings. Some of the opinions about American blacks that the immigrants hold are highly negative. I was very worried about describing these negative images of American black people in talks I would give around the country on my research. I was repeating some of the most negative stereotypes about blacks it is possible to have in our country. The first time I gave the talk to an audience that included black people I was very worried. Would they think I believed these stereotypes because I was repeating them? Would they think I had fabricated these respondents? Was the very act of a white woman saying negative things about blacks, even though I was quoting from black respondents, offensive? I looked out at the audience, and the black people were nodding in appreciation of what I was saying. The comments afterwards were always that I was telling it like it is—that their grandmother thought that, or that they knew West Indians thought that, or that they as West Indian immigrants thought that. The only challenge about doing this work was posed by white graduate students who did not think that whites should study blacks.[10]

ETHICS

A number of ethical issues arose during the research, some of which I still do not have answers for. One of the ethical issues was whether I should be paying the respondents. The argument for paying people is that I am taking their time so they should be compensated in some way for it. On the other hand, is the payment a form of coercion for poor people and adolescents? The teenage students needed their parents' permission to participate. One day a parent called to complain bitterly about the fact that I had offered his son $10 to take part in the study. My field notes recall the conversation:

> He said that he was very upset that the kid was offered $10. He wanted to know why. I told him that it was an incentive for the kids to participate, and that it was to compensate them for their time. He said that it was unfair to offer $10 to the kids, that all his son wanted was the $10. He said that his son was too young to understand the dangers of being interviewed. "What if his son grew up to be a politician? His words that he gave to me could be used against him." I tried to tell him that I guarantee anonymity, and I could not "go back to my files" as he said I would. He said that there was no way that it could be controlled. How could his son know what would be used in the book? Suppose his son said something that was highly unusual and it stood out in the book? Ten dollars was nothing to sell all that information that you could not get back.
>
> I told him that I understood his concerns and that was why it was completely voluntary, and if he did not want his son to take part he could say no. He said that was why the $10 upset him so much because his son could not understand why his father was saying no. He said that it caused conflict in the family because all his son could understand is that his father was denying him the chance to get $10. He asked why all of a sudden was there money to take part in a survey? They didn't pay him money to open his books, and that was what was important and his son never opened his books.
>
> He said that maybe I had already figured out that he was from the Caribbean, and being from a small island he understood that things can come back to haunt you. He moved here and he went into a store and he saw a postcard that was taken of his friends, and the picture was taken without their knowledge and the postcard was now being sold and it was something out of their control. He said tourists come down there and they want to take pictures or they want to take a part of the country, and they think because they have money they can do this. What kind of a message

did it give this kid to offer him money to take part in the survey? All the kid knows is that there are people at school whom he thinks are smarter than his father who tell him to take part, and then the father looks stupid and he denies his son money.

Then I tried to explain to him what the book and the study was about. I said that Chinese and Japanese and Irish and Italian were recognized as having their own cultures in the United States but that black immigrants have not been, and that I wanted to understand how much of the background was passed along from generation to generation. He said that it was all who had money. The reason the Caribbean did not pass along the background and preserve it was because they did not have money. Then he said that his son was born here in Brooklyn and that he did not know anything about back there; he had not been to visit. He said what did kids that young know? They did not know anything. They would just have to come home and ask their parents, and half their parents would lie anyway. I said that I had been interviewing the kids and that they did have things to say. He did not have an answer for that.

I told him he had made some important points and that I would think about what he said. I said that it was a difficult decision to try to decide to give the kids $10, but that it was a decision that was supported by the Board of Ed. I told him that he also had valid concerns about the study, but that I had gotten approval at the Board of Ed, the Superintendent of Schools, and the principal. I also said I completely respected his decision not to take part, and that was why I had included the phone number so that if someone had any questions they could talk to me about it. I also said I was sorry if I had caused him any problems or conflicts in his family. He was calmer then and thanked me for calling him back and said each person has the right to their own ways of doing things. I ended the conversation by telling him that his son was fortunate to have such a concerned and active father. He thanked me for that, and we parted on good terms.

I think this father raised some very valid questions. People do not know what future problems they are letting themselves in for when they take part in a study like this. They do not have a good reason to trust a stranger to guarantee them anonymity. And, perhaps most important, it is the person with the power and the money who gets to tell the story of the other people, whether it is by stealing their images for a postcard or using their life histories to write a book on immigrant identity. While I do not deny that there is an element of coercion in the offering of the money for the interview, I believe the amount of money was not great enough that people would do it against their will. I also think that all of the people who take part in the interviews ultimately enjoy them a great deal, and there is not much risk that their lives will be compromised by taking part in the study.

Paying the respondents brought up another ethical issue, however. In order to be reimbursed by the grant through Harvard I needed to submit forms with the names, addresses, and social security numbers of the people I interviewed. Because some of the people I interviewed could be undocumented immigrants and others were definitely involved in criminal behaviors such as carrying concealed weapons and dealing drugs, I had designed the study to be anonymous rather than confidential. A study that promises confidentiality is one where the researcher retains the name and address of a respondent but will not divulge that information to anyone. The researcher promises to keep the name a secret by changing identities and the like. This is a tenuous promise because, unlike a lawyer who is protected by attorney-client privilege from having to divulge a client's guilt to a court, a social scientist can be required to turn over records. A few social scientists have gone to jail rather than submit the names of or evidence prejudicial to their respondents. Because I was collecting data that was potentially harmful to my respondents, I promised that I would keep the records in such a manner that I could not identify them. This meant that I would not keep any identifying material on the respondents. I did not mention their names on the tapes, and I can honestly say that for most of the respondents I cannot reconstruct who they were.

The requirement to collect names, addresses, and social security numbers for reimbursement purposes made this more difficult. I had to immediately keep those pieces of paper containing this information apart from the tapes and transcripts. I also had to decide what to do about people who were undocumented immigrants. Though most had social security numbers, a few told me they did not. I told them to make one up, or in a few cases I left it blank.

The question of how to explain the project to potential interviewees also posed an ethical dilemma. It was not much of a problem to decide what to say to the immigrants themselves. I could tell them I was studying the experience of West Indian immigrants in the United States. The same was true for the children of immigrants. For the white and black American coworkers, however, the reasons I wanted to speak to them were not as clear. I told them I was studying the experience of New Yorkers with immigration both in the past and currently. I found that by asking the blacks and whites about their own family histories, they were more at ease and less likely to worry that I was trying to find out if they were racist. Of course, to some extent I was trying to find out if they were racist, and I was specifically trying to understand how they reacted to West Indian immigrants. This was a shading of the truth that I felt was necessary to gain cooperation of the nonimmigrants and that I felt was not harmful to them. It remains to be seen whether they might find fault with what I told them I was doing, and what I ultimately did with their words.

Many of the questions I faced came out of the dilemma most ethnographers have to come to terms with: How much involvement should there be with the subjects of the research? I do not know the correct answer to this question, but I think it is one of the thorniest we face as researchers. Many day-to-day questions arose that I had to make a snap decision on with little guidance from the professional social science community about what the correct answer might be. In the inner-city schools it became clear to me that the type of relationship I was establishing with the students was unusual for them. The students were used to one-way communication from whites toward them in their neighborhoods, with little give and take. White teachers and administrators were authority figures who told them what to do. Mainstream television and other media told them what white life was like. But very few whites listened to them and answered their questions. So the students I interviewed had a great deal of curiosity about what my life was like. I felt that it was important to answer those questions and share some of my opinions and feelings with the students; at the same time I often found myself in over my head. Troubled teenagers who were not happy with their home situations asked my advice. I did not know what to say. A few of the students I spoke with seemed very troubled; one talked of suicide during the interview. After the incident at Eisenhower when a student who seemed fine to others gave birth to a baby and then threw her away, I became more frightened that I might have information about students that could help save some people. I did mention the names of a few troubled students to a guidance counselor in the school; however, I do not know if the overworked guidance counselor had time to follow up. I also befriended one bright young girl who was very troubled about her relationship with her parents. I bought her a copy of *Brown Girl, Brownstones* by the Barbadian writer Paule Marshall because I hoped it might help let her see that her troubles with her mother were not unusual for a West Indian second-generation youth and also because I hoped it might give her some insight into why her mother behaved as she did. I don't know if it worked.

I was stopped sometimes in the halls by students who wanted to know how to write letters to colleges. I did assist these students. I knew some students were carrying weapons, but I did not tell the teachers or counselors. Thank goodness those weapons did not get used.

Other issues continued to shape how I wrote the book. Do I include sensitive information the teachers told me about helping students to get abortions or about the amount of abuse that goes on in some families? (I included some and suppressed the most controversial.) Do I honor my promise to the Board of Education to protect the identity of the schools where I did the research? (I did.) Do I tell the truth about how out of control the school was, and risk offending or even hurting the reputations of dedicated teachers and administrators who work long and hard in anonymity and are only noticed by the press and the wider city when something goes wrong in their high school? (I did but hope a balanced view came out.) These decisions are all ethical ones in one way or another because they involve making decisions that could hurt or help people by one's actions or inactions.

LOGISTICS AND RECOMMENDATIONS

There are certain recommendations I can make for others who might be doing similar kinds of research. Some are about small issues that nevertheless matter a great deal when you are in the field and trying to figure out the best way to do something. Others are about big issues on which new researchers need some reassurance.

First: Race and gender of the researcher matter a great deal in how you approach your subjects, and they slant to some extent the answers you come up with in your research. But they should not disqualify you from doing research on a particular topic. There are strengths as well as weaknesses in the characteristics people notice about you, which open other doors even as they close some.

Second: Research proposals and funding requirements are guidelines, not ironclad laws, and you must be prepared to creatively change them in the field. To refuse to interview Haitians in the high schools would have been folly on my part; to not use those interviews later would have been wasteful. Use common sense in the field. If the procedures you set up to get a random sample are yielding a biased sample, figure out a new procedure.

Third: Networks matter. Snowball samples work well in in-depth interviewing because the referrals you acquire open doors for you; your previous interviewee or the person recommending someone can vouch that the interview was enjoyable and the interviewer was a good person. When you are doing a case study or many interviews in one institution, you also need to take advantage of networks to get yourself accepted. Having my research assistant hang out with the teenagers worked very well for those purposes.

Fourth: Personal safety is a big issue and an increasing part of what you need to think about in designing your study. If you will pay respondents, you need to think through the safety issues of carrying cash. If you are working in neighborhoods where you do not feel safe, give extra thought to transportation issues. Car rentals and taxis are a legitimate research expense, and one that is increasingly a big proportion of budgets for studies in inner-city neighborhoods. Interviews are now often done in pairs. Two interviewers travel together to provide a feeling of safety, especially if one of the interviewers is a woman and the interviews are not conducted in public spaces. Finally, do not get so involved in the research project that you begin to lose common sense in the rest of your life.

Finally, accept the fact that your presence affects people's lives, and come to terms with how you will affect them. The myth that you can study a group of people or an institution and not change them in the act is a dangerous one. Researchers who are aware that their presence is affecting people are better off than those who deny it.

NOTES

1 INTRODUCTION

1. Jonathan Rieder, "Crown of Thorns," *The New Republic,* October 14, 1991, p. 26.

2. For instance, the lead line in a *New York Times* article on the incident said "Black protesters are demanding the arrest of the *Hasidic* driver of a car that killed a *black* boy in the Crown Heights section of Brooklyn on Monday" (*New York Times,* August 22, 1991; emphasis added); *The New Yorker* reported that "resentment had long simmered between the Orthodox Lubavitcher Hasidic sect and the neighborhood's black majority." Andy Logan, "Around City Hall," *The New Yorker,* September 23, 1991, pp. 106–112. Note that in both cases the ethnic/religious identity of the white driver is deemed important to report but the Guyanese immigrant identity of the young black boy is not.

3. One of the pioneer articles on the experiences of the post-1965 wave of Caribbean immigrants is by Roy S. Bryce-Laporte, "Black Immigrants: The Experience of Invisibility and Inequality," *Journal of Black Studies* 3 (1972): 29–56.

4. In a fascinating paper on the historiography of immigration and assimilation, Gary Gerstle argues that historians such as Oscar Handlin vastly overstated the degree of alienation and separation from the sending country among European immigrants. Gerstle, "European Immigrants, Ethnics, and American Identity, 1880–1950" (Sanibel Island, Fla: Social Science Research Council Conference on International Migration, 1996). The British historian Frank Thistlewaite argued that as many as one-third of the 33 million immigrants who came from Europe between 1820 and 1920 returned home. Thistlewaite, "Migration from Europe Overseas in the Nineteenth and Twentieth Centuries," *A Century of European Migrations, 1830–1930,* ed. Rudolph J. Vecoli and Suzanne M. Sinke (Urbana-Champaign: University of Illinois Press, 1991). See also Rudolph J. Vecoli, "Contadini in Chicago: A Critique of the Uprooted," *Journal of American History* 51 (December 1964): 404–417; Mark

Wyman, *Round Trip America: The Immigrants Return to Europe, 1880–1930* (Ithaca: Cornell University Press, 1993); John Bodnar, *The Transplanted: A History of Immigrants to Urban America* (Bloomington: University of Indiana Press, 1985).

5. Nina Glick Schiller, Linda Basch, and Cristina Blanc-Szanton, "Transnationalism: A New Framework for Understanding Migration," *Annals of the New York Academy of Sciences* 645 (1992); John Lie, "From International Migration to Transnational Diaspora," *Contemporary Sociology* 24, no. 4 (July 1995): 303–306.

6. Robert K. Merton, *Social Theory and Social Structure* (New York: The Free Press, 1967).

7. Also note that many of these characteristics, which were also present in the peasant cultures in the Caribbean countryside, are being undermined by capitalist development and its devastating effects on the Caribbean economy. See Ansley Hamid, "The Political Economy of Crack-related Violence," *Contemporary Drug Problems* (Spring 1990): 31–78; Bonham C. Richardson, *The Caribbean in the Wider World, 1492–1992* (Cambridge: Cambridge University Press, 1992); Orlando Patterson, "Toward a Study of Black America: Notes on the Culture of Racism," *Dissent* (Fall 1989): 476–486; Derek Gordon, Patricia Anderson, and Don Robotham, "Jamaica: Urbanization during the Years of the Crisis," *The Urban Caribbean: Transition to the New Global Economy*, ed. Alejandro Portes, Carlos Dore-Cabral, and Patricia Landolt (Baltimore: Johns Hopkins University Press, 1997), pp. 190–226.

8. Because of logistical problems, the adolescents I interviewed were not the children of the immigrants I interviewed. However, judging from what the worker parents said about their children, and what the teens said about their parents, I suspect that we would have very similar results had we been able to interview the actual children of the adult immigrants we interviewed. See the Appendix for a full discussion of the process of conducting the interviews.

9. We received 374 completed questionnaires, from which we selected the forty-five students with whom we conducted life history interviews.

10. There have been many different claims made about the militancy and political orientations of West Indians in the United States. They are often described as being more conservative than black Americans. For instance, Oscar Glantz found that West Indian college students were much less likely than African Americans to support some of the social protests of the 1960s. Glantz, "Native Sons and Immigrants: Some Beliefs and Values of American Born and West Indian Blacks at Brooklyn College," *Ethnicity* 5 (1978): 189–202. For a discussion of this issue in reference to Colin Powell, see Orlando Patterson, "The Culture of Caution," *The New Republic*, November 27, 1995, pp. 22–26. West Indians are also often described as being more militant than black Americans.

For instance, see Dennis Forsythe, "West Indian Radicalism in America: An Assessment of Ideologies," *Ethnicity in the Americas*, ed. Frances Henry (Paris: Mouton Publishers, 1976), pp. 301–332. I will try to show that both statements are partially true but measure different expectations and actions on the part of the immigrants.

11. My study does not answer the question of what proportion of the second generation is doing well or what proportion is experiencing problems. Rather, the case study of the experiences of young people in the West Indian neighborhood schools describes the kinds of challenges faced by some of the second generation and the range of their responses and adaptations.

2   HISTORICAL LEGACIES

1. Montserrat may have become better known to people in 1997, the year the volcano on the island began erupting.

2. These small islands are also sometimes called the Leeward and Windward Islands from the days of sailing ships. The Leeward are the more northerly of the Lesser Antilles and the Windward are the more easterly and southerly.

3. Bonham C. Richardson, *The Caribbean in the Wider World, 1492–1992* (Cambridge: Cambridge University Press, 1992), p. 56.

4. These linguistic distinctions reflect "official" languages. Most Haitians, for instance, speak Haitian Creole, not French. Aruba has Dutch as one of its official languages but also Papiamento. Jamaican peasants speak a patois language that can be difficult or impossible for English speakers to understand. Franklin Knight, *The Caribbean: The Genesis of a Fragmented Nationalism* (New York: Oxford University Press, 1990), p. 314.

5. David Lowenthal, *West Indian Societies* (London: Oxford University Press, 1972). Lowenthal includes in the West Indies the non-Iberian islands and the countries of South America—French Guiana, Surinam, and Guyana—that are "socially and culturally" West Indian.

6. This includes the foreign-born and those who report that they are of West Indian, non-Hispanic ancestry. There is good reason to believe this number is a very conservative estimate. A sizable number of undocumented West Indians have arrived in recent decades who might be missed by the census. In addition, many people whose parents, grandparents, or great-grandparents came from the Caribbean now identify only as African American and are thus statistically lost to the group. See my discussion of these identity issues in Chapters 3 and 8 of this book. For further discussions of the problems of estimating the West Indian population in the United States, see Orlando Patterson, "The Culture of Caution," *The New Republic*, November 27, 1995, pp. 22–26; Marilyn Halter, "Immigration," *Encyclopedia of African American*

Culture and History, ed. Jack Salzman, David Lionel Smith, and Cornel West (New York: Macmillan Press, 1995), pp. 1344–55.

7. See Lowenthal, *West Indian Societies;* Sidney W. Mintz, *Caribbean Transformations* (Baltimore: Johns Hopkins University Press, 1974); Franklin Knight, *The Caribbean: The Genesis of a Fragmented Nationalism* (New York: Oxford University Press, 1990).

8. Knight, *The Caribbean,* p. 76.

9. Sidney Mintz and Sally Price, *Caribbean Contours* (Baltimore: Johns Hopkins University Press, 1985); Mintz, *Caribbean Transformations,* p. 9.

10. Mintz, *Caribbean Transformations,* p. 257.

11. Lowenthal, *West Indian Societies,* p. 33.

12. Richardson, *Caribbean in the Wider World,* p. 67.

13. Of this total 1,665,000 slaves were brought to the British Caribbean, 1,600,000 to the French, 500,000 to the Dutch, 28,000 to the Danish, and 809,000 to the Spanish. Richardson, *Caribbean in the Wider World,* p. 63. These figures are originally from Phillip Curtin, *The Atlantic Slave Trade: A Census* (Madison: University of Wisconsin Press, 1969).

14. Richardson, *Caribbean in the Wider World,* p. 74.

15. Mintz, *Caribbean Transformations,* p. 313.

16. D. Elliott Parris, "The Contributions of the Caribbean Immigrant to the United States Society," *Journal of Caribbean Studies* 2, no. 1 (1981): 1–13.

17. Dawn Marshall, "Toward an Understanding of Caribbean Migration," *U.S. Immigration and Refugee Policy: Global and Domestic Issues,* ed. Mary M. Kritz (Lexington, Mass.: Lexington Books, 1983), pp. 113–131.

18. Ibid., p. 117.

19. Marshall states that the estimates of the number of West Indians who came to the United States in the first decades of the twentieth century vary, but none are less than 40,000. Ibid., p. 22.

20. The West Indians who found their way eventually to the United States after having lived in Costa Rica, Panama, and other Central American countries had already experienced being a minority in a foreign country, and thus their experiences with U.S. society and race relations were somewhat different than those of immigrants who came straight from the West Indian islands. Roy S. Bryce-Laporte, "Voluntary Immigration and the Continuing Encounters between Blacks: The Post Quincentenary Challenge," *The Annals of the American Academy of Political and Social Science* 530 (November 1993): 28–41.

21. Irma Watkins-Owens, *Blood Relations: Caribbean Immigrants and the Harlem Community, 1900–1930* (Bloomington: Indiana University Press, 1996); Violet Johnson, "Black and Foreign: The Construction and Projection of Racial and Ethnic Identities among Black Immigrants in the United States," *We Are a People: Narrative and Multiplicity in the Construction of Ethnic Identity,* ed.

Paul R. Spickard and Jeffrey Burroughs (Philadelphia: Temple University Press, 1999).

22. Mintz and Price, *Caribbean Contours*, p. 10.

23. Mintz, *Caribbean Transformations*, p. 269.

24. This assumption about the fixity and stability of the identities of European immigrants has been increasingly contested. See the essays in the collection, Virginia Yans-McLaughlin, ed., *Immigration Reconsidered: History, Sociology and Politics* (New York: Oxford University Press, 1990), especially the essay by Charles Tilly, "Transplanted Networks," pp. 79–95.

25. Knight, *The Caribbean*, p. 313.

26. H. Hoetink, *The Two Variants in Caribbean Race Relations: A Contribution to the Sociology of Segmented Societies* (London and New York: Oxford University Press, 1967), p. 59.

27. Orlando Patterson, "Toward a Future That Has No Past: Reflections on the Fate of Blacks in the Americas," *Public Interest* 27 (1972): 30. Patterson points out that in the non-Latin West Indies the white population is nowhere above 3% of the total population and is often less than 1%.

28. Lowenthal, *West Indian Societies*, p. 45.

29. Ibid., p. 64.

30. David J. Hellwig, "Black Meets Black: Afro American Reactions to West Indian Immigrants in the 1920's," *South Atlantic Quarterly* 77 (Spring 1978): 206–224; Dennis Forsythe, "Black Immigrants and the American Ethos: Theories and Observations," *Caribbean Immigration to the United States*, ed. Roy S. Bryce-Laporte and Delores M. Mortimer (Washington, D.C.: Smithsonian Institution, 1976), pp. 55–82.

31. Jack Alexander, "The Culture of Race in Middle Class Kingston, Jamaica," *American Ethnologist* (August 1977): 413–435.

32. Lowenthal, *West Indian Societies*, p. 322.

33. Patterson, "Toward a Future," p. 33.

34. Lowenthal, *West Indian Societies*, p. 71.

35. Ibid., p. 138.

36. For a complete discussion of the development of the one-drop rule in the United States, see F. James Davis, *Who Is Black?: One Nation's Definition* (University Park, Pa.: The Pennsylvania State University Press, 1991); Virginia R. Dominguez, *White by Definition: Social Classification in Creole Louisiana* (New Brunswick, N.J.: Rutgers University Press, 1986).

37. As Dominguez summarizes, anthropologists have found an astounding number of terms in everyday use to distinguish between the categories of black and white. Dominguez "elicited 58 terms from a sample of 50 Cubans, 56 terms from a sample of 43 Puerto Ricans, and 25 terms from a sample of 11 Dominicans in a study of ethnic, racial, and social class identity among

Spanish speaking Caribbean migrants in New York City." *White by Definition,* pp. 273–274.

38. Hoetink, "The Two Variants," p. 178.

39. Alexander, "The Culture of Race," p. 421.

40. Ibid., p. 423.

41. Mintz, *Caribbean Transformations,* p. 299.

42. Lowenthal, *West Indian Societies,* p. 94.

43. Ibid., p. 42.

44. Richardson, *The Caribbean in the Wider World,* pp. 66–67.

45. Lowenthal, *West Indian Societies,* p. 43.

46. Richardson, *The Caribbean in the Wider World,* p. 66.

47. Melville J. Herskovitz, *The Myth of the Negro Past* (New York: Harper and Brothers, 1941).

48. Mintz, *Caribbean Transformations,* p. 325.

49. Ibid., p. 155.

50. Lowenthal, *West Indian Societies,* p. 322.

51. Halter, "Immigration," p. 1353.

52. Watkins-Owens, *Blood Relations;* Halter, "Immigration."

53. Halter, "Immigration," p. 1353.

54. Philip Kasinitz, *Caribbean New York: Black Immigrants and the Politics of Race* (Ithaca: Cornell University Press, 1992).

55. Elizabeth Bogen, *Immigration in New York* (New York: Prager, 1987), p. 21.

56. Kasinitz, *Caribbean New York,* p. 26.

57. For an account of these sweeping changes, see David M. Reimers, "An Unintended Reform: The 1965 Immigration Act and Third World Immigration to the United States," *Journal of American Ethnic History* 3, no. 1 (1983): 9–28.

58. Philip Kasinitz, "The Minority Within: The New Black Immigrants," *New York Affairs* 10, no. 1 (Winter 1987): 44–58, quotation from p. 46.

59. Joseph Salvo and Ronald Ortiz, *The Newest New Yorkers: An Analysis of Immigration into New York City during the 1980's* (New York: Department of City Planning, 1992), p. 40.

60. Ibid., p. 29.

61. Ibid., p. 6.

62. Caribbean immigrants were not the only immigrants to choose New York City, but they chose it in higher proportions than other groups. During the 1950s through the 1970s New York City received just under 20% of the nation's immigrants. During the 1980s about 15% of the nation's immigrants came to New York City.

63. Social remittances are defined by Peggy Levitt as "the ideas, behaviors, identities, and social capital that flow from receiving to sending country communities. They are the north-south equivalent of the social and cultural resources

that migrants carry with them which ease their transition from 'immigrants' to 'ethnics.'" Levitt, "Transnationalizing Civil and Political Change: The Case of Transnational Organizational Ties between Boston and the Dominican Republic," doctoral dissertation, Department of Urban Planning, Massachusetts Institute of Technology, 1996, chap. 3.

64. Lowenthal, *West Indian Societies,* p. 22.

65. Knight, *The Caribbean.*

66. Richardson, *The Caribbean in the Wider World,* p. 131.

67. Ibid., p. 125.

68. Mintz, *Caribbean Transformations.*

69. Richardson, *The Caribbean in the Wider World,* p. 101.

70. William Julius Wilson, *The Truly Disadvantaged: The Inner City, The Underclass and Public Policy* (Chicago: Chicago University Press, 1987). Kasinitz, "The Minority Within"; William Julius Wilson, *The Declining Significance of Race: Blacks and Changing American Institutions* (Chicago: University of Chicago Press, 1978).

71. Joe R. Feagin and Melvin P. Sikes, *Living with Racism: The Black Middle Class Experience* (Boston: Beacon Press, 1994).

72. Elijah Anderson, *Streetwise: Race, Class and Change in an Urban Community* (Chicago: University of Chicago Press, 1990).

73. Roderick Harrison and Claudette Bennett, "Racial and Ethnic Diversity," *State of the Union: America in the 1990's,* vol. 2 of *Social Trends,* ed. Reynolds Farley (New York: Russell Sage Foundation, 1995).

74. Richard Alba, "Assimilation's Quiet Tide," *The Public Interest* 119 (Spring 1995): 3–18.

75. Michael Hughes and Bradley R. Hertel, "The Significance of Color Remains: A Study of Life Chances, Mate Selection, and Ethnic Consciousness among Black Americans," *Social Forces* 68, no. 4 (June 1990): 1105.

76. This distinction is made by Orlando Patterson, "Toward a Study of Black America: Notes on the Culture of Racism," *Dissent* (Fall 1989): 476–486.

77. David R. Roediger, *The Wages of Whiteness: Race and the Making of the American Working Class* (London: Verso Press, 1991).

78. Lawrence Bobo and Camille L. Zubrinsky, "Attitudes on Residential Integration: Perceived Status Differences, Mere In-group Preference, or Racial Prejudice?" *Social Forces* 74, no. 3 (March 1996): 883–910; Stephen Steinberg, *Turning Back: The Retreat from Racial Justice in American Thought and Policy* (Boston: Beacon Press, 1995).

3 RACIAL AND ETHNIC IDENTITY CHOICES

1. Virginia R. Dominguez, *White by Definition: Social Classification in Creole Louisiana* (New Brunswick, N.J.: Rutgers University Press, 1986), p. 266.

2. Henri Tajfel, *Human Groups and Social Categories: Studies in Social Psychology* (Cambridge: Cambridge University Press, 1981) and "Social Psychology of Intergroup Relations," *Annual Review of Psychology* 33 (1982): 1–39; John C. Turner, "Social Comparison and Social Identity: Some Prospects for Intergroup Behavior," *European Journal of Social Psychology* 5 (1975): 5–34 and "Social Categorization and the Self Concept: A Social Cognitive Theory of Group Behavior," *Advances in Group Processes: Theory and Research,* vol. 2, ed. E. J. Lawler (Greenwich, Conn.: JAI Press, 1984).

3. Georg Simmel, *The Sociology of Georg Simmel* (1908; Glencoe, Ill.: The Free Press, 1950).

4. Kian Woon Kwok, "Historical Discontinuity and Cultural Dislocation: The (Non-)Problem of Social Memory in Singapore," paper presented at the Conference on Trauma and Memory (Durham: University of New Hampshire, 1996), p. 4.

5. Alejandro Portes and Dag MacLeod, "What Shall I Call Myself? Hispanic Identity Formation in the Second Generation," *Ethnic and Racial Studies* 19, no. 3 (1996): 527.

6. This research is discussed in Chapter 4.

7. Estimates of the numbers of black immigrants entering the country each year must be based on assumptions about the racial composition of immigrants for whom there is no racial identity information. This has been accomplished in a number of ways. One way is to count all immigrants from a country with a large number of blacks as blacks. Another way is to assume that the racial composition of immigrants is equal to the racial composition of their country of origin or equal to the racial composition of other immigrants already in this country for whom there are census data.

8. Nampeo R. McKenney and Arthur R. Cresce, *Measurement of Ethnicity in the United States: Experiences of the U.S. Census Bureau* (Ottawa, Canada: 1992), p. 184.

9. David Lowenthal, *West Indian Societies* (London: Oxford University Press, 1972).

10. Grenadians also are more likely than others to say they are African American. There is no obvious explanation for these choices in Grenada's demographics or history.

11. 94% of Barbadians and 91% of Haitians said they were black. Among the more diverse Trinidadians and Guyanese, 90% of the Trinidadians said they were black, as did 78% of the Guyanese.

12. McKenney and Cresce, *Measurement of Ethnicity.*

13. We used Haitian as the example since we were not interviewing any first-generation Haitians; thus we would not be priming a particular ethnicity, but

Haitian is a black ethnicity that could call forth the idea of Jamaican or Trinidadian or the like.

14. This woman arrived in the United States when she was 33 years old. She spent eleven years in England before coming to the United States eighteen years prior to this interview.

15. Most Americans do not know very much about Guyana because it is not a tourist destination as many other West Indian nations are. Sadly, Guyana is best known as the site of a bizarre mass suicide led by cult leader Jim Jones in November 1978.

16. "Bajan" is a term that refers to people from Barbados.

17. Of course, we did not speak with first-generation Haitians so I don't know how aware they are of the images other groups hold of them; we did speak to first- and second-generation adolescent Haitians, and they were very aware of these negative stereotypes and described the same attributes as the immigrants quoted here.

18. Mary C. Waters, *Ethnic Options: Choosing Identities in America* (Berkeley: University of California Press, 1990).

19. Everyone we interviewed was either a Christian of some type or not a member of any one religion.

20. Lawrence Bobo and Vincent L. Hutchings, "Perceptions of Racial Group Competition: Extending Blumer's Theory of Group Position to a Multiracial Social Context," *American Sociological Review* 61, no. 6 (December 1996): 951–973.

21. Jennifer L. Hochschild, *Facing Up to the American Dream: Race, Class, and the Soul of the Nation* (Princeton, N.J.: Princeton University Press, 1995).

22. Hochschild notes that "[m]ore poorly educated blacks than any other racial/class group express 'a great deal' of confidence in schools, even though they are not notably more confident about other American institutions . . . It is thus not surprising that more poor black than Latino, Asian or white parents discuss their children's school experiences and plans, restrict television on school nights, set rules about grades, help with homework, and join the parents' association." Ibid., p. 160.

23. Ibid., p. 160.

24. See Chapter 6 for further discussion of the West Indian family form.

25. Waters, *Ethnic Options.*

26. Jennifer Eberhardt and Susan Fiske, eds., *Racism: The Problem and the Response* (Thousand Oaks, Calif.: Sage Publications, 1998); Eberhardt and Fiske, "Motivating Individuals to Change: What's a Target to Do?," *Stereotypes and Stereotyping,* ed. N. Macrae, C. Stangor, and M. Hewstone (New York: Guilford Press, 1996); Eberhardt, "Where the Invisible Meets the Obvious: The

Effects of Stereotyping Biases on the Fundamental Attribution Error," doctoral dissertation, Department of Psychology, Harvard University, 1993.

27. As I have given talks about this study at various colleges and universities around the country, many African-American academics have told me that they are constantly asked by whites whether they are of West Indian ancestry. These professors, who were not West Indian, said they had learned that many whites assumed that a black person with a Ph.D. had to be the descendant of an immigrant.

28. Irma Watkins-Owens, *Blood Relations: Caribbean Immigrants and the Harlem Community, 1900–1930* (Bloomington: Indiana University Press, 1996); Violet Johnson, "Culture, Economic Stability and Entrepreneurship: The Case of British West Indians in Boston," *New Migrants in the Workplace: Boston's Ethnic Entrepeneurs,* ed. Marilyn Halter (Amherst, Mass.: University of Massachusetts Press, 1995), pp. 59–80.

29. This is incorrect. The law allows people to maintain foreign citizenship as well as to adopt American citizenship.

30. Roberto Suro, *Watching America's Door: The Immigration Backlash and the New Policy Debate* (New York: The Twentieth Century Fund Press, 1996); Leon Bouvier, *Peaceful Invasions: Immigration and Changing America* (Lanham, Md.: University Press of America, 1991); Peter Brimelow, *Alien Nation: Common Sense about America's Immigration Disaster* (New York: Random House, 1995).

31. James P. Smith and Barry Edmonston, eds., *The New Americans: Economic, Demographic and Fiscal Effects of Immigration* (Washington, D.C.: National Academy Press, 1997).

32. John Lie, "From International Migration to Transnational Diaspora," *Contemporary Sociology* 24, no. 4 (1995): 303–306.

33. See the following by Nancy Foner: "Sex Roles and Sensibilities: Jamaican Women in New York and London," *International Migration: The Female Experience,* ed. Rita Simon and Caroline Brettell (Totowa, N.J.: Rowman and Allenheld, 1986); "Ideology and Social Practice in the Jamaican Diaspora," Russell Sage Foundation working paper, 1994; *The Caregiving Dilemma: Work in an American Nursing Home* (Berkeley: University of California Press, 1994).

4   WEST INDIANS AT WORK

1. Colin L. Powell and Joseph E. Persico, *My American Journey* (New York: Random House, 1995).

2. Ira De A. Reid, *The Negro Immigrant: His Background Characteristics and Social Adjustment, 1899–1937* (New York: Columbia University Press, 1939); Nathan Glazer and Daniel Patrick Moynihan, *Beyond the Melting Pot* (Cam-

bridge: MIT Press and Harvard University Press, 1963); Thomas Sowell, "Three Black Histories," *Essays and Data on American Ethnic Groups,* ed. Sowell (Washington: The Urban Institute, 1978), pp. 7–64. See also Orde Coombs, "West Indians in New York: Moving beyond the Limbo Pole," *New York Magazine,* July 13, 1970, pp. 28–32; Dennis Forsythe, "Black Immigrants and the American Ethos: Theories and Observations," *Caribbean Immigration to the United States,* ed. Roy S. Bryce-Laporte and Delores M. Mortimer (Washington, D.C.: Smithsonian Institution, 1976), pp. 55–82; Lennox Raphael, "West Indians and Afro Americans," *Freedomways* 4 (1964): 433–445; Owens Smith, "The Politics of Income and Education Differences between Blacks and West Indians," *Journal of Ethnic Studies* 13, no. 3 (1985): 17–30.

3. Sowell, "Three Black Histories."
4. Stephen Steinberg, *The Ethnic Myth: Race, Ethnicity and Class in America* (Boston: Beacon Press, 1989).
5. Suzanne Model, "Caribbean Immigrants: A Black Success Story?," *International Migration Review* 25 (Summer 1991): 248–276, "West Indian Prosperity: Fact or Fiction?," *Social Problems* 42 (November 1995): 535–553, and "An Occupational Tale of Two Cities: Minorities in London and New York," *Demography* 34 (November 1997): 539–550; Matthijs Kalmijn, "The Socioeconomic Assimilation of Caribbean American Blacks," *Social Forces* 74 (March 1996): 911–930; Reynolds Farley and Walter R. Allen, *The Color Line and the Quality of Life in America* (New York: Russell Sage Foundation, 1987).
6. Sowell, "Three Black Histories," p. 43.
7. Ibid., p. 44.
8. Ibid., p. 49. The last year that such a study could be conducted for the second generation was 1970. In 1980 the birthplace-of-parents question was replaced with the ancestry question, which, as we have seen in Chapter 3, is subjective and misses those people who identify as African American or who do not answer the question at all. In 1970 the second generation were also the offspring of immigrants who arrived in the earlier part of the century. They were a select group in terms of their characteristics and behaviors.
9. Glazer and Moynihan, *Beyond the Melting Pot,* p. 35. They also quoted from a novel about Barbadian immigrants in Brooklyn by Paule Marshall. The number of people who use Marshall's fictional story of a Bajan family in Brooklyn as "social science" data about this group is remarkable. Marshall herself describes how this use of her work has startled her. Paule Marshall, "Black Immigrant Women in *Brown Girl, Brownstones,*" *Caribbean Life in New York City: Sociocultural Dimensions,* ed. Constance R. Sutton and Elsa M. Chaney (New York: Center for Migration Studies, 1987).
10. While Reid's book has been the only comprehensive book on black immi-

grants, Kasinitz focused on politics among Caribbean immigrants, and there have been a number of comprehensive books about Haitian immigrants. Philip Kasinitz, *Caribbean New York: Black Immigrants and the Politics of Race* (Ithaca: Cornell University Press, 1992); Tekle Woldemikael, *Becoming Black American: Haitians and American Institutions in Evanston, Illinois* (New York: AMS Press, 1989); Michel S. Laguerre, *American Odyssey: Haitians in New York* (Ithaca: Cornell University Press, 1984); Alejandro Portes and Alex Stepick, *City on the Edge: The Transformation of Miami* (Berkeley: University of California Press, 1993); Flore Zephir, *Haitian Immigrants in Black America: A Sociological and Sociolinguistic Portrait* (Westport, Conn.: Bergin and Garvey, 1996).

11. While these personal accounts gave Reid a rich source of insights into the subjective experience of immigration and assimilation for these immigrants, his sample was also a highly biased one. It would presumably only include highly literate people who enjoyed writing enough to enter such a contest. It also would select for people who either felt strongly enough about positive or negative experiences to want to describe them or for people who felt their life histories were unusual enough that they might win a prize.

12. Reid, *The Negro Immigrant*, p. 121.

13. Kasinitz points out that although Reid is often cited for describing the propensity of West Indians to be employed in business, Reid actually "noted that most West Indian immigrants had menial jobs as waiters, elevator operators, factory hands and unskilled workers, particularly in the garment industry." Kasinitz, *Caribbean New York*, p. 93. In the only study using systematic data to analyze this question, Herbert George Gutman examined the 1925 New York State census to compare West Indians and African Americans. He found that native-born African Americans had a higher proportion of white-collar workers, and West Indians showed a higher proportion of skilled workers. Gutman, *The Black Family in Slavery and Freedom, 1750–1925* (New York: Vintage Books, 1977).

14. Barry R. Chiswick, "The Economic Progress of Immigrants: Some Apparently Universal Patterns," *Contemporary Economic Problems*, ed. William Fellner (Washington, D.C.: American Enterprise Institute for Public Policy Research, 1979).

15. Kristin Butcher, "Black Immigrants in the United States: A Comparison with Native Blacks and Other Immigrants," *Industrial and Labor Relations Review* 47, no. 2 (January 1994): 265–284; Farley and Allen, *The Color Line and the Quality of Life in America;* Model, "Caribbean Immigrants."

16. Kalmijn, "Socioeconomic Assimilation," p. 919.

17. Model, "West Indian Prosperity," p. 543.

18. Ibid.

19. Kasinitz, *Caribbean New York,* p. 108.

20. Roger Waldinger's figures on education among foreign-born and native-born black New Yorkers also show a pattern of declining educational attainment over time for the foreign-born and increasing educational attainment for the native-born. For instance, in 1970 West Indian immigrants were 1.51 times more likely to have graduated from college than all other New Yorkers, while native-born blacks were 70% less likely. By 1990 West Indians were about half as likely as all other New Yorkers to be college graduates (odds 5 0.56), while native blacks were also almost half as likely (odds 5 0.48). In 1970 native-born and foreign-born blacks were about equal in their odds of having less than a high school education (1.23 for native-born and 1.22 for foreign-born). While African Americans increased their educational attainment so that they were almost on a par with all other New Yorkers as measured by the odds that they would be in the lowest education category (odds 5 1.09), West Indians were more concentrated in the least educated group with odds of 2.03 that they were among the least educated. Roger Waldinger, *Still the Promised City? African-Americans and New Immigrants in Postindustrial New York* (Cambridge: Harvard University Press, 1996), p. 76.

21. Virginia R. Dominguez, "From Neighbor to Stranger: The Dilemma of Caribbean Peoples in the United States," Occasional Papers No. 5 (New Haven: Yale University Antilles Research Program, 1975), p. 55. Dominguez found that 73% of the second-generation West Indians had earned their high school diplomas, compared to 48% of African Americans and 43% of first-generation West Indians. Suzanne Model finds that native-born West Indians had higher educational attainment than African Americans in 1970, 1980, and 1990. See "West Indian Prosperity," p. 542.

22. Philip Kasinitz, "From Ghetto Elite to Service Sector: A Comparison of the Role of Two Waves of West Indian Immigration in New York City," *Ethnic Groups* 7 (1988): 173–203, quotation from p. 177.

23. See William Julius Wilson, *The Truly Disadvantaged: The Inner City, The Underclass and Public Policy* (Chicago: Chicago University Press, 1987), for an excellent discussion of how this particular reading of the Moynihan report is extreme and led to decades of liberals shying away from all cultural explanations of poverty.

24. Ibid.; William J. Wilson, *When Work Disappears: The World of the New Urban Poor* (New York: Knopf, 1996).

25. Reid, *The Negro Immigrant,* p. 49.

26. Ibid., p. 84. Smith, "Politics of Income," p. 24, points to the economic vacuum created after slavery was abolished in the Caribbean, which opened opportunities for skilled black craftsmen and artisans. This did not happen in the American South because large numbers of poor whites were available to

take those jobs. The white owners created political and legal barriers to black advancement into those jobs in the form of the black codes—laws restricting skilled jobs in the antebellum South to whites—and the like.

27. Forsythe, "Black Immigrants," p. 65.

28. D. Elliott Parris, "The Contributions of the Caribbean Immigrant to the United States Society," *Journal of Caribbean Studies* 2, no. 1 (1981), p. 10.

29. C. L. R. James, "The Black Scholar Interview," *Black Scholar* (May 1970).

30. One study showed some distinct attitudes of West Indians that fit with cultural stereotypes, but it was based on a very small and nonrandom sample. Oscar Glantz compared the beliefs of West Indian students at Brooklyn College with white Catholics and Jews. He found that "the West Indian group expressed more trust in the responsiveness of the economic reward system, more faith in the value of hard work at school and in the value of hard work generally, and less negativism in their orientation toward the electoral system in the United States." Glantz, "Native Sons and Immigrants: Some Beliefs and Values of American-Born and West Indian Blacks at Brooklyn College," *Ethnicity* 5 (1978): 189–202, quotation from p. 200.

31. Jennifer L. Hochschild, *Facing Up to the American Dream: Race, Class, and the Soul of the Nation* (Princeton, N.J.: Princeton University Press, 1995), p. 160.

32. Model, "West Indian Prosperity," p. 548.

33. For discussions of the 1917 immigration law, see Smith, "Politics of Income." While not every immigrant who entered met literacy criteria after 1917, the law did tend to limit the number of extremely poor and uneducated arrivals. Calvin Holder's analysis of Immigration and Naturalization Service data from 1900 to 1932 found that there was a much higher literacy rate among West Indian immigrants than among those who stayed home. He found that among West Indian immigrants arriving during this period, there was a very small number of professionals—only 3%—but 34% of those arriving were skilled laborers. Quoted in Kasinitz, *Caribbean New York*, p. 94. Smith reported that among those arriving between 1899 and 1910, 46.8% were skilled workers, 8.3% professionals, 35.7% other (presumably mostly women and children), and 6.4% laborers. Smith, p. 27.

34. Evidence to support the importance selectivity plays in explaining differences between West Indians and African Americans comes from Kristin Butcher's analysis. When Butcher compared West Indian immigrants to African Americans who had moved across a state line from where they were born, she found the West Indian advantage evaporated. She concluded that it was the selectivity of movers, whether they be internal migrants or international immigrants, that explained their higher performance. Butcher, "Black Immigrants in the United States." Stanley Lieberson also argued that internal migration among American blacks produced a migrant selectivity advantage. Lieberson, *A Piece*

of the Pie: Blacks and White Immigrants since 1880 (Berkeley: University of California Press, 1980) and "Selective Black Migration from the South: A Historical View," *Demography of Racial and Ethnic Groups,* ed. Frank D. Bean and W. Parker Frisbie (New York: Academic Press, 1978), pp. 119–141.

35. The classic statement of the psychology of the migrant laborer can be found in Michael Piore, *Birds of Passage* (New York: Cambridge University Press, 1979).

36. Alejandro Portes, *The Economic Sociology of Immigration: Essays on Networks, Ethnicity and Entrepreneurship* (New York: Russell Sage Foundation, 1995); Charles Tilly, "Transplanted Networks," *Immigration Reconsidered: History, Sociology and Politics,* ed. Virginia Yans-McLaughlin (New York: Oxford University Press, 1990), pp. 79–95; Douglas Massey, Luis Goldring, and Jorge Durand, "Continuities in Transnational Migration: An Analysis of Nineteen Mexican Communities," *American Journal of Sociology* 99 (1994): 1492–1533.

37. Nancy Foner, "The Jamaicans: Race and Ethnicity among Migrants in New York City," *New Immigrants in New York,* ed. Foner (New York: Columbia University Press, 1987), pp. 195–218; David Lowenthal, *West Indian Societies* (London: Oxford University Press, 1972); Susan Buchanan Stafford, "The Haitians: The Cultural Meaning of Race and Ethnicity," *New Immigrants in New York,* pp. 131–158; Reid, *The Negro Immigrant.*

38. Roy S. Bryce-Laporte, "Black Immigrants: The Experience of Invisibility and Inequality," *Journal of Black Studies* 3 (1972), p. 46.

39. Marilyn Halter, *Between Race and Ethnicity: Cape Verdean American Immigrants* (Urbana-Champaign: University of Illinois Press, 1993).

40. McKay, *A Long Way from Home* (1937; New York: Arno Press, 1969), pp. 8–9, quoted in Irma Watkins-Owens, *Blood Relations: Caribbean Immigrants and the Harlem Community, 1900–1930* (Bloomington: Indiana University Press, 1996), p. 5.

41. Waldinger, *Still the Promised City?* p. 121.

42. American Food Services and United States Financial are pseudonyms. Anonymity was ensured in return for taking part in the study.

43. We asked to interview whites, blacks, and West Indians, but these other workers were referred to us early in the process for interviews, and it would have seemed unfair to refuse to interview them. They provided valuable information from an alternative perspective on ethnic and race relations in the workplace and on working conditions overall.

44. For a more complete discussion of the interviewing process and experiences during the fieldwork, see the Appendix.

45. Joleen Kirschenman and Katherine Neckerman define statistical discrimination as when "employers use group membership as a proxy for aspects of productivity that are relatively expensive or impossible to measure." They go on to note that "those who use the concept disagree about whether employers'

perceptions of group differences in productivity must reflect reality." Kirschenman and Neckerman, "We'd Love to Hire Them but . . .: The Meaning of Race for Employers," *The Urban Underclass,* ed. Christopher Jencks and Paul Peterson (Washington: Brookings Institute, 1991), pp. 203–234, quotation from p. 204. See also Neckerman and Kirschenman, "Hiring Strategies, Racial Bias and Inner City Workers," *Social Problems,* 38 (1991): 433; Harry Holzer, "Informal Job Search and Black Youth Unemployment," *American Economic Review* 77 (1987): 446–552, and "The Spatial Mismatch Hypothesis: What Has the Evidence Shown?" *Urban Studies* 28 (1991): 105–122.

46. Waldinger in *Still the Promised City?,* p. 342, defines West Indians as immigrants from the Anglophobe Caribbean, eliminating immigrants from Haiti, other Francophone countries, and the Dutch West Indies. He defines the native-born African-American niche as industries and occupations in which the concentration of native African Americans was at least 50 percent higher than their share of the economy. Ibid., p. 111.

47. These areas of concentration, however, employ mostly West Indian women—73% of the employees in West Indian niche employment in 1990 were women. Men were more dispersed throughout the economy with only 20% of West Indian men working in the Caribbean niche. Waldinger, *Still the Promised City?,* pp. 120–121.

48. Waldinger notes "28 percent of all employed African-Americans worked in African-American public sector niches; another 9 percent worked in other areas of the public sector where the concentration of black New Yorkers was not quite as high." Ibid, p. 111.

49. Kirschenman and Neckerman, "We'd Love to Hire Them," found in a study of Chicago-area employers that they too placed a high premium on "character" and personal characteristics in hiring entry-level workers.

50. More than a few West Indian immigrant workers mentioned the comedy program *In Living Color.* That show had a Jamaican character who was satirically depicted as having twenty-eight jobs and working constantly. The satire was lost on the immigrants, who talked about the character with pride.

51. This is a well-established fact about immigrants first put forth by Piore, *Birds of Passage.* See also Roger Waldinger, "Changing Ladders and Musical Chairs: Ethnicity and Opportunity in Post Industrial New York," *Politics and Society* 15 (1987): 390.

52. The working-class immigrants earned more in the United States and described a higher standard of material living. The middle-class immigrants generally earned more and could afford more material goods, but many reported that some aspects of their standard of living declined, especially the amount of housing they were able to buy and the fact that they could no longer afford household help.

53. This is similar to statements made by many of the employers interviewed by Kirschenman and Neckerman, "We'd Love to Hire Them."

54. There is a large psychological literature on the genesis and maintenance of stereotypes. One consistent finding is that stereotypes are resistant to change once they are established. When a person holds a stereotype about another person or thing, any violation of stereotypical expectations is not seen as evidence that disconfirms the stereotype but rather as an "exception that proves the rule." These managers therefore retain a stereotype of African Americans as lazy even though they encounter many hard-working African Americans. Jennifer Eberhardt, "Where the Invisible Meets the Obvious: The Effects of Stereotyping Biases on the Fundamental Attribution Error," doctoral dissertation, Department of Psychology, Harvard University, 1993; Jennifer Eberhardt and Susan Fiske, eds., *Racism: The Problem and the Response* (Thousand Oaks, Calif.: Sage Publications, 1998).

55. Susan H. Buchanan, "Language and Identity: Haitians in New York City," *International Migration Review* 13 (1979): 298–313; Woldemikael, *Becoming Black American;* Stafford, "The Haitians"; Foner, "The Jamaicans."

56. Nancy Foner and Richard Napoli contrasted black American and black foreign-born migrant farmworkers. However, they did not study both groups at the same time in the same workplace, and they did not talk to white employers. Foner and Napoli, "Jamaican and Black American Migrant Farm Workers: A Comparative Analysis," *Social Problems* 25, no. 5 (June 1978): 491–503.

57. Robert Blauner has written perceptively about the ways in which whites distinguish between "acting ethnic," which they generally approve of, and "acting racial," which they see as exclusionary. Blauner, "Talking Past Each Other: Black and White Languages of Race," *American Prospect* (Summer 1992): 55–64. These whites would not have responded as favorably to the "clannishness" of the workers if they had described their togetherness as blacks not wanting to be with whites. See also Mary C. Waters, "Optional Ethnicities: For Whites Only?," *Origins and Destinies: Immigration, Race and Ethnicity in America,* ed. Silvia Pedraza and Ruben G. Rumbaut (Belmont, Calif.: Wadsworth Publishing, 1996), pp. 444–454, for a discussion of these dynamics among college students.

58. This white Irish American manager was being interviewed by the author, a third-generation Irish American.

5   ENCOUNTERING AMERICAN RACE RELATIONS

1. Roger Waldinger makes the point that describing something as a cultural trait does not make it permanent. In fact, he argues that immigrants would be very likely to change their culture when the environment changes. "Just as culture is learned through childhood and adult socialization so too are new cultural

patterns learned and devised when the environment changes. Immigrants, after all, are unlikely to be the more traditional members of their original societies; rather they are more likely to stem from those sections of the population already most inclined toward adaptation and change." Waldinger, *Through the Eye of a Needle: Immigrants and Enterprise in New York's Garment Trades* (New York: New York University Press, 1986), p. 9.

2. John Ogbu, "Minority Status and Literacy in Comparative Perspective," *Daedelus* 119, no. 2 (Spring 1990): 141–168 and *Minority Education and Caste: The American System in Cross National Perspective* (New York: Academic Press, 1978).

3. Ogbu, "Minority Status," p. 152.

4. Ibid., p. 153.

5. Ibid.; Signithia Fordham and John Ogbu, "Black Students' School Success: Coping with the Burden of Acting White," *Urban Review* 18, no. 3 (1987): 176–206; Signithia Fordham, "Racelessness as a Factor in Black Students' School Success: Pragmatic Strategy or Pyrrhic Victory?," *Harvard Education Review* 58, no. 1 (1988): 54–84 and *Blacked Out: Dilemmas of Race, Identity and Success at Capital High* (Chicago: University of Chicago Press, 1996).

6. Ogbu, "Minority Status," p. 155.

7. Christopher Jencks, *Rethinking Social Policy: Race, Poverty, and the Underclass* (Cambridge, Mass.: Harvard University Press, 1992), p. 129.

8. Stephen Cornell and Douglas Hartmann, *Ethnicity and Race: Making Identities in a Changing World.* (Thousand Oaks, Calif.: Pine Forge Press, 1998).

9. Many other researchers have noted this tendency to "forget" the discrimination and racism that did exist back home. See, for example, Calvin Holder, "West Indian Immigrants in New York City, 1900–1952: In Conflict with the Promised Land," *West Indians in the United States of America: Some Theoretical and Practical Considerations,* ed. Aubrey W. Bonnett and G. Llewellyn Watson (Lanham, Md.: University Press of America, 1990), p. 59; David Lowenthal, *West Indian Societies* (London: Oxford University Press, 1972), p. 227; Ira De A. Reid, *The Negro Immigrant: His Background Characteristics and Social Adjustment, 1899–1937* (New York: Columbia University Press, 1939). H. Hoetink notes that North American academics make this same mistake; viewing Caribbean society against the backdrop of the American one-drop rule and the starkness of American race relations leads the researcher to conclude race is not a major factor in Caribbean society. Hoetink, *The Two Variants in Caribbean Race Relations: A Contribution to the Sociology of Segmented Societies* (London and New York: Oxford University Press, 1967), p. 52.

10. Some Trinidadian and Guyanese respondents made comparisons between the ways East Indians treated blacks at home and the ways blacks are made to feel

inferior by whites in the United States. But even those few who saw similarities in power dynamics among the groups noted that the problems between blacks and whites in the United States were of a different order of magnitude.

11. Derek Gordon, Patricia Anderson, and Don Robotham, "Jamaica: Urbanization during the Years of the Crisis," *The Urban Caribbean: Transition to the New Global Economy,* ed. Alejandro Portes, Carlos Dore-Cabral, and Patricia Landolt (Baltimore: Johns Hopkins University Press, 1997), pp. 190–226; Ansley Hamid, "The Political Economy of Crack-related Violence," *Contemporary Drug Problems* (Spring 1990): 31–78.

12. Orlando Patterson, "Toward a Study of Black America: Notes on the Culture of Racism," *Dissent* (Fall 1989): 476–486, quotation from p. 478.

13. Ibid.

14. Orlando Patterson, "Toward a Future That Has No Past: Reflections on the Fate of Blacks in the Americas," *Public Interest* 27 (1972): 25–62, quotation from p. 39. Patterson also makes a crucial point about class differences in the West Indies in the development of racial consciousness. West Indians all come from societies in which blacks are disvalued by a powerful white European culture, but the immigrants have a greater sense of personal efficacy because the majority of people in their society are black. Middle-class West Indians have learned to value white European culture over their own and to suffer some assaults on their own personal dignity when they realize (usually in the United States or in the European capitals of London, Paris, or Amsterdam) that their education and class do not earn them full acceptance into white European culture. Yet middle-class West Indians do not see "race" as a barrier to success or ambition and also do not feel a conflict between their race and their success when it is achieved. West Indians from the countryside are also at home in their racial identity. While they might see the higher value placed on white culture than on black culture, they have their own sense of personal dignity and cultural practices, which sustain their sense of personhood and prevent "the ontological wounds and emotional scarring" that white racist culture can perpetrate on black people. The dispossessed urban poor of the West Indies—those who have neither the peasant traditions nor the cultural capital or material well-being of the middle class—are most likely to see a clear tie between their class and racial oppression. Yet all three groups, once they find their way to the United States, bring a less developed sense of personal hurt and personal limitation due to race than is exhibited by many African Americans.

15. Reid, *The Negro Immigrant,* p. 55.

16. See Jennifer L. Hochschild, *Facing Up to the American Dream: Race, Class, and the Soul of the Nation* (Princeton, N.J.: Princeton University Press, 1995), for a review of surveys and anecdotal data on the difficulties faced by blacks. See

also Joe R. Feagin and Melvin P. Sikes, *Living with Racism: The Black Middle Class Experience* (Boston: Beacon Press, 1994); Sam Fulwood, *Waking from the Dream: My Life in the Black Middle Class* (New York: Anchor Books, 1996); Patricia J. Williams, *The Alchemy of Race and Rights: Diary of a Law Professor* (Cambridge: Harvard University Press, 1991).

17. Cornel West, "Nihilism in Black America: A Danger That Corrodes from Within," *Dissent* (Spring 1991): 221–226, quotation from p. 224.

18. D. Elliott Parris wrote about the differences in the psychology of race between African Americans and West Indians in 1981: "The West Indian immigrant is initially shocked by the way in which references to race and its disadvantages dominate the everyday conversations of American blacks. While the American black is more likely to define the white stranger as an enemy until he proves otherwise, the West Indian black is more likely to define the white stranger as a person until he proves enemy." Parris, "The Contributions of the Caribbean Immigrant to the United States Society," *Journal of Caribbean Studies* 2, no. 1 (1981): 1–13.

19. Reid, *The Negro Immigrant*, p. 122.

20. Holder, "West Indian Immigrants," p. 61; David J. Hellwig, "Black Meets Black: Afro American Reactions to West Indian Immigrants in the 1920's," *South Atlantic Quarterly* 77 (Spring 1978): 213; Reid, *The Negro Immigrant*, p. 110.

21. Joyce Roberta Toney argues that historically West Indians used an "exit" strategy at the individual level to deal with racism but a "voice" strategy at the political level, where they felt they could really make a difference in American society. Toney, *A Minority within A Minority: West Indian American Response to Race and Ethnicity in New York City, 1900–1965* (Washington, D.C.: 1990), p. 12. Milton Vickerman notes, for instance, in his current study of Jamaican American men, "[w]ith great frequency the West Indians argued that though there will always be racism, this need not inhibit achievement." Vickerman, "The Responses of West Indians to African Americans: Distancing and Identification," *Research in Race and Ethnic Relations*, vol. 7, ed. Dennis Rutledge (Greenwich, Conn.: JAI Press, 1994), pp. 83–128, quotation from p. 118.

22. Lowenthal notes in *West Indian Societies*, p. 99, that "physiognomy in all its aspects, however, is only one of many ways West Indians perceive and order colour. Ancestry, wealth, education, way of life and associates all play important parts in color ascription as they do in social classification."

23. Sam Fulwood, *Waking from the Dream;* Hochschild, *American Dream*, p. 126; Monique Taylor, "Home to Harlem: Black Identity and the Gentrification of Harlem," doctoral dissertation, Department of Sociology, Harvard University, 1991.

24. Malcolm X and Alex Haley, *The Autobiography of Malcolm X* (New York: Ballentine Books, 1966), p. 204.

25. Jack Miles, "Blacks vs. Browns," *The Atlantic* 270, no. 4 (October 1992): 41–60, quotation from p. 52.

26. Ibid., p. 53.

27. Ibid.

28. Donald P. Kinder and David O. Sears, "Prejudice and Politics: Symbolic Racism versus Racial Threats to the Good Life," *Journal of Personality and Social Psychology* 40, no. 3 (1981): 414–431, quotation from p. 414.

29. Jennifer Eberhardt, "Where the Invisible Meets the Obvious: The Effects of Stereotyping Biases on the Fundamental Attribution Error," doctoral dissertation, Department of Psychology, Harvard University, 1993.

30. Dennis Forsythe argues that West Indians exhibit both a radical streak in opposition to racial subjugation and a conservative base of conformism, legalism, and Anglophonism. Forsythe, "West Indian Radicalism in America: An Assessment of Ideologies," *Ethnicity in the Americas,* ed. Frances Henry (Paris: Mouton Publishers, 1976), p. 305.

31. Hellwig notes that West Indians "readily expressed displeasure with any manifestation of discourtesy from whites. Often they applied for jobs which American custom designated as white." Hellwig, "Black Meets Black," p. 212. Patterson, "Toward a Future," p. 59, discusses the rise of Marcus Garvey and his brand of radical black nationalism as stemming from the heightened racial consciousness of the West Indian peasant with a greater sense of racial and personal dignity being subjected to the starkness of American racial ghettos.

32. Reid, *The Negro Immigrant,* p. 111.

33. Toney notes that "[m]any of the West Indians who came to the United States were among the privileged Afro West Indians at home and so suffered a ruder awakening and underwent more bitterness when faced with American racism, than if they were from the general masses of the society." Toney, *A Minority within a Minority,* p. 3.

34. Reid, *The Negro Immigrant,* p. 107.

35. Vickerman, "Responses of West Indians," p. 94.

36. Ibid., p. 95.

37. Ibid., p. 101.

38. Ibid., p. 111.

39. Tekle Woldemikael, *Becoming Black American: Haitians and American Institutions in Evanston, Illinois* (New York: AMS Press, 1989).

40. Philip Kasinitz suggests that because West Indians are concentrated in the service economy, their interactions with whites are likely to develop these racial overtones. Kasinitz, "From Ghetto Elite to Service Sector: A Compari-

son of the Role of Two Waves of West Indian Immigration in New York City," *Ethnic Groups* 7 (1988): 173–203.

6   INTERGENERATIONAL DYNAMICS

1. Alejandro Portes and Min Zhou, "The New Second Generation: Segmented Assimilation and Its Variants (Interminority Affairs in the U.S.: Pluralism at the Crossroads)," *The Annals of the American Academy of Political and Social Science* 530 (November 1993): 74–97.

2. W. Lloyd Warner and Leo Srole, *The Social Systems of American Ethnic Groups* (New Haven: Yale University Press, 1945).

3. Ibid., p. 72.

4. As Herbert Gans points out, we have learned a great deal about ethnicity since this study. He also points out that Warner and Srole provide a purely cultural theory, which does not address the very important role of the economy in the shaping of ethnic relations and mobility patterns. Gans, "Second Generation Decline: Scenarios for the Economic and Ethnic Futures of the Post 1965 American Immigrants," *Ethnic and Racial Studies* 15 (April 1992): 173–192.

5. Warner and Srole, *The Social Systems*, p. 145.

6. Constance R. Sutton and Susan R. Makiesky have proposed that in some ways assimilation is opposite for blacks than for whites. For whites of the second and third generations, upward social mobility is to move from being an immigrant to being an American. For blacks, they argue, the move from being an immigrant to "merely being American black" is actually downward social mobility. Sutton and Makiesky, "Migration and West Indian Racial and Ethnic Consciousness," *Migration and Development: Implications for Ethnic Identity and Political Conflict*, ed. H. I. Safia and B. M. Du Toit (Paris: Mouton and Company, 1975), p. 142.

7. Gans, "Second Generation Decline."

8. Douglas S. Massey and Mitchell L. Eggers, "The Ecology of Inequality: Minorities and the Concentration of Poverty, 1970–1980," *The American Journal of Sociology*, 95, no. 5 (March 1990): 1153; Stanley Lieberson, *A Piece of the Pie: Blacks and White Immigrants since 1880* (Berkeley: University of California Press, 1980).

9. Portes and Zhou, "Segmented Assimilation"; Alejandro Portes and Julia Sensenbrenner, "Embeddedness and Immigration: Notes on the Social Determinants of Economic Action," *The American Journal of Sociology* 98, no. 6 (May 1993): 1320–51; Alejandro Portes and Min Zhou, "Should Immigrants Assimilate?," *The Public Interest* 16 (Summer 1994): 18–34; Gans, "Second Generation Decline."

10. Gans, "Second Generation Decline," p. 188.

11. Min Zhou, "The Adaptation of the New Second Generation: The Effects of

Race, Family Relations, and the Ethnic Community," paper presented at the conference on Becoming American/America Becoming: International Migration to the United States (Sanibel Island, Fla.: Social Science Research Council, January 1996), p. 26.

12. Portes and Zhou, "Segmented Assimilation."

13. Marcelo M. Suarez-Orozco, "Becoming Somebody: Central American Immigrants in U.S. Inner-City Schools," *Anthropology and Education Quarterly* 18, no. 4 (1987): 287–299.

14. Margaret Gibson, *Accommodation without Assimilation: Sikh Immigrants in an American High School* (Ithaca: Cornell University Press, 1989).

15. Maria Eugenia Matute-Bianchi, "Situational Ethnicity and Patterns of School Performance among Immigrant and Nonimmigrant Mexican-Descent Students," *Minority Status and Schooling: A Comparative Study of Immigrant and Involuntary Minorities,* ed. Margaret Gibson and John U. Ogbu (New York: Garland, 1991), pp. 205–247.

16. John Ogbu, "Minority Status and Literacy in Comparative Perspective," *Daedelus* 119, no. 2 (Spring 1990): 141–168, quotation from p. 148.

17. Douglas Foley, "Reconsidering Anthropological Explanations of Ethnic School Failure," *Anthropology and Education Quarterly* 22 (1991): 60–94.

18. Robert C. Smith, "Doubly Bonded Solidarity: Race and Social Location in the Incorporation of Mexicans in New York City," paper presented at Social Science Research Council Conference of Fellows: Program of Research on the Urban Underclass (Ann Arbor: University of Michigan, June 1994).

19. See, for example, Nina Glick-Schiller, Linda Basch, and Cristina Blanc-Szanton, "Transnationalism: A New Framework for Understanding Migration," *Annals of the New York Academy of Sciences* 645 (1992).

20. Ruben Rumbaut, "The Agony of Exile: A Comparative Study of Indochinese Refugee Adults and Children," *Refugee Children: Theory, Research and Services,* ed. F. L. Ahearn and J. L. Athey (Baltimore: Johns Hopkins University Press, 1991), pp. 53–91; Ruben Rumbaut and K. Ima, "The Adaptation of Southeast Asian Refugee Youth: A Comparative Study," U.S. Office of Refugee Resettlement (1988). These studies have suggested using the term "generation 1.5" for youngsters born abroad but educated in whole or part in the United States. Others have used second generation to include both children of immigrants and the immigrants who come as children. Portes and Zhou, "Segmented Assimilation"; Leif Jensen and Yoshimi Chitose, "Immigrant Generations," *Immigration and the Family: Research and Policy on U.S. Immigrants,* ed. Alan Booth, Ann C. Crouter, and Nancy Landale (New Jersey: Lawrence Erlbaum Publishers, 1997), pp. 47–62. Circular migration makes these categories even more difficult to define, as some youngsters who were born in the United States may have spent more time in their parents' native

country (having returned there often to live for short periods) than other youngsters who were born abroad but do not return often to their native country.

21. Donald J. Hernandez and Evan Charney, eds., *From Generation to Generation: The Health and Well-Being of Children in Immigrant Families* (Washington, D.C.: National Academy Press, 1998).

22. Calculated from the 1990 Census Public Use Microdata (PUM) Sample, 152 PUM areas in tristate metropolitan New York. Because of the problems of identifying West Indians and particularly second-generation West Indians discussed in Chapter 3, I identified West Indian youth using the birthplace-of-parents question. Therefore these numbers do not include second-generation individuals residing outside their parents' households. (There is no way to identify those individuals using census data.)

23. It has long been recognized by sociologists that ethnic voluntary organizations are important in easing the transition into American society for immigrants and their children. Recently Min Zhou has concluded that "the availability of various community based organizations and the intense involvement in them by immigrant parents and children put immigrants into tightly knit ethnic networks, making it possible for the community to reinforce norms and to promote a high level of constancy among standards." Min Zhou and Carl L. Bankston, "Social Capital and the Adaptation of the Second Generation: The Case of Vietnamese Youth in New Orleans," *International Migration Review* 28. (Winter 1994): 821–845, quotation from p. 833.

24. For a very good description of the Labor Day Parade, see Philip Kasinitz and Judith Freidenberg-Herbstein, "The Puerto Rican Parade and West Indian Carnival: Public Celebrations in New York City," *Caribbean Life in New York City: Sociocultural Dimensions,* ed. Constance Sutton and Elsa Chaney (New York: Center for Migration Studies, 1987), pp. 327–350, and Philip Kasinitz, *Caribbean New York: Black Immigrants and the Politics of Race* (Ithaca: Cornell University Press, 1992), Chapter 5.

25. "Visiting unions," common law unions, and children born outside of marriage are prevalent in the West Indies, especially among the lower classes. A common scholarly assessment of the situation in the islands is that the lower classes are characterized by these unstable unions, and the upper and middle classes have more stable unions and marriages. Nancy Foner, "Ideology and Social Practice in the Jamaican Diaspora," Russell Sage Foundation working paper, 1994; Edith Clarke, *My Mother Who Fathered Me: A Study of the Family in Three Selected Communities in Jamaica* (London: George Allen and Unwin Ltd., 1957); Esther Goody, "Delegation of Parental Roles in West Africa and the West Indies," *The Extended Family in Black Societies,* ed. Demitri Shimkin, Edith Shimkin, and Dennis Frate (The Hague: Mouton Publishers, 1978),

pp. 447–484. Given this prevalence of households headed by single parents, it is ironic that West Indian families are described as being superior to African-American families. This difference is often cited as the reason why West Indians do better than African Americans. The fact that West Indians in the United States are more likely to have intact nuclear families than African Americans is due to the selectivity of immigration. Among immigrant groups, Jamaicans have a comparatively high percentage of households headed by single females—34.6% (compared to 15.1% of Filipinos, 14.1% of Mexicans, and 8.2% of Chinese). Only Dominicans have a higher percentage (41.3%). Yet non-Hispanic blacks in the United States have a higher rate than all immigrant groups (43.2%). Ruben Rumbaut, "Origins and Destinies: Immigration to the United States since World War II," *Sociological Forum* 9 (1994): 604.

26. In the case of eight of the youngsters we were unable to find information about their immigration experiences.

27. Goody, "Delegation of Parental Roles," p. 448. Goody notes that Edith Clarke's data from three very different communities in Jamaica found a substantial portion of children living with neither parent (18%). Clarke, *My Mother Who Fathered Me.*

28. Goody, "Delegation of Parental Roles," p. 475.

29. Most students do not finish high schools in the islands where the system does not guarantee an academic high school education for all children.

30. In a study of West Indian adolescent offenders in Toronto, Fay E. Martin and Georgina White speculated that "[i]t may be that the weakness of the connection between parent and child initiated by early and prolonged separation during serial migration, tentatively bridged during post migration years, cannot withstand delinquent behavior." Martin and White, "West Indian Adolescent Offenders," *Canadian Journal of Criminology,* 30, no. 4 (October 1988): 367–380, quotation from p. 370. Shirley Thrasher and Gary Anderson did a study of West Indians in need of family therapy in an area of East Brooklyn. They note that "all of the adult West Indian migrants initially entered the United States alone without their spouse or children. The children were left in the homeland with relatives, especially the grandmother." Thrasher and Anderson, "The West Indian Family: Treatment Challenges," *Social Casework: The Journal of Contemporary Social Work* 69, no. 3 (March 1988): 171–176, quotation from p. 173. Children then rejoin their parents in an uneven process that can take a long time. They argue that this separation is a contributing factor to intergenerational conflict: "The biological parents are forced to reestablish their role as primary caretakers and parental authority figures. These issues increase the potential for conflict. Because these children considered other relatives as their parental figures, it may be difficult

for them to adjust to their biological parents." Ibid. Another study notes that "[m]any parents attempt to discipline their children by threatening to send them back to the West Indies, failing to realize that they might be angrily reacting to the long parent-child separation." Beverly Sewell-Coker, Joyce Hamilton-Collins, and Edith Fein, "Social Work Practice with West Indian Immigrants," *Social Casework* (November 1985): 563–568. In a 1994 study of children left behind in Jamaica by parents who had gone to the United States, C. Crawford-Brown and S. Rattray report that these children experience a high incidence of suicide, suicide attempts, juvenile delinquency, and acting-out behaviors. Crawford-Brown and Rattray, "Barrel Children," unpublished paper, University of the West Indies, 1994.

31. Cynthia Garcia-Coll and Katherine Magnuson, "The Psychological Experi-
ence of Immigration: A Developmental Perspective," *Immigration and the Family*, ed. Booth, Crouter, and Landale, pp. 91–132. The original article is J. P. Graham and C. E. Meadows, "Psychiatric Disorder in the Children of West Indian Immigrants," *Journal of Child Psychology and Psychiatry* 8 (1967): 105–116. A. W. Burke also found problems related to separation of this type among West Indians in Britain. He described mothers who felt very rejected when, after finally reuniting with their children, the children reacted negatively to them as mothers. Burke, "Family Stress and the Precipitation of Psychiatric Disorder: a Comparative Study among Immigrant West Indian Patients in Birmingham," *International Journal of Social Psychiatry* 26, no. 1 (1980): 35–40.

32. This woman was the mother of a teacher I interviewed. She was present for a small part of her daughter's interview and agreed to be interviewed herself.

33. Sheldon Danzinger and Peter Gottschalk show how patterns of income in-
equality have led to the situation where most middle-class and working-class families need two incomes to maintain a standard of living formerly attain-able by just one working member. Danzinger and Gottschalk, *America Un-equal* (New York and Cambridge: Russell Sage Foundation and Harvard University Press, 1995). A number of studies have documented the resulting stresses on families. Crawford-Brown and Rattray, "Barrel Children"; Juliet Schor, *The Overworked American: the Unexpected Decline of Leisure* (New York: Basic Books, 1991); Arlie Russell Hochschild and Anne Machung, *The Second Shift: Working Parents and the Revolution at Home* (London: Piatkus, 1990); Arlie Russell Hochschild, *The Time Bind: When Work Becomes Home and Home Becomes Work* (New York: Metropolitan Books, 1997).

34. Crawford-Brown and Rattray, "Barrel Children."

35. Sharon-Ann Gopaul-McNicol, *Working with West Indian Families* (New York: Guilford Press, 1993); Janet R. Brice-Baker, "Domestic Violence in African American and African Caribbean Families," *Journal of Social Distress*

and the Homeless 3, no. 1 (1994): 23–38; Monica A. Payne and Adrian Furnham, "West Indian Adolescents' Perceptions of Family Functioning," *Journal of Adolescence* 12 (1989): 155–166.

36. Edward Seaga, "Parent-Teacher Relationships in a Jamaican Village," *Social and Economic Studies*, 4, no. 3 (September 1955): 289–302.

37. John Figueroa, "Education for Jamaica's Needs," *CQ* 15, no. 1 (1969): 5–33. Quoted in David Lowenthal, *West Indian Societies* (London: Oxford University Press, 1972).

38. Selma Berrol, *Growing Up American: Immigrant Children in America Then and Now* (New York: Twayne Publishers, 1995), p. 81.

39. Ibid., p. 94.

40. Murray Straus and Denise Donnelly, "Corporal Punishment of Adolescents by American Parents," *Youth and Society* 24, no. 4 (June 1993): 421.

41. Corporal punishment is defined by Murray A. Straus and Anita K. Mathur as "the use of physical force with the intention of causing physical pain, but not injury, for purposes of correction and control. Examples of corporal punishment include slapping, spanking, pinching, and ear twisting." Straus and Mathur, "Social Change and Trends in Approval of Corporal Punishment by Parents from 1968 to 1994," paper presented at the International Symposium on Violence in Childhood and Adolescence (Bielefeld, Germany: Research Center on Prevention and Intervention in Childhood and Adolescence, University of Bielefeld, September 1994), p. 2.

42. For those who experienced it, it was not a rare event; the mean was eight times and the median was five times. Straus and Donnelly, "Corporal Punishment," p. 3.

43. Ibid., p. 439.

44. Murray A. Straus and Anita K. Mathur, "Corporal Punishment of Adolescents and Academic Attainment," paper presented at the annual meeting of the Pacific Sociological Association (San Francisco, Calif.: April 1995), p. 1.

45. See also George K. Hong and Lawrence K. Hong, "Comparative Perspectives on Child Abuse and Neglect: Chinese versus Hispanics and Whites," *Child Welfare* 70, no. 4 (July-August 1991): 463–475, on differences among Chinese, Hispanics, and whites.

46. Lynne Vernon-Feagans, *Children's Talk in Communities and Classrooms* (Cambridge, Mass.: Blackwell, 1996), p. 56.

47. Ibid., pp. 56–57.

48. Straus and Donnelly, "Corporal Punishment," p. 439.

49. Hong and Hong, "Comparative Perspectives," p. 464.

50. Vernon-Feagans, *Children's Talk*, p. 212.

51. Straus and Donnelly argue in "Corporal Punishment," p. 439, that many children who have experienced corporal punishment defend the practice:

"Almost all children defend the use of corporal punishment. However, neither the normality of corporal punishment nor its advocacy by its victims is evidence that it does no harm."

52. Ruben Rumbaut, "Ties That Bind: Immigration and Immigrant Families in the United States," *Immigration and the Family,* ed. Booth, Crouter, and Landale, pp. 3–45 and Rumbaut, "The Crucible Within: Ethnic Identity, Self Esteem, and Segmented Assimilation among Children of Immigrants," *International Migration Review* 28 (Winter 1994): 748–794.

53. Carola Suarez-Orozco and Marcelo M. Suarez-Orozco, *Transformations: Immigration, Family Life, and Achievement Motivation among Latino Adolescents* (Stanford, Calif.: Stanford University Press, 1995).

7   SEGREGATED NEIGHBORHOODS AND SCHOOLS

1. Douglas Massey and Nancy Denton, *American Apartheid: Segregation and the Making of the Underclass* (Cambridge, Mass.: Harvard University Press, 1993), p. 2.

2. Douglas S. Massey, Andrew B. Gross, and Mitchell L. Eggers, "Segregation, the Concentration of Poverty, and the Life Chances of Individuals," *Social Science Research* 20, no. 4 (December 1991): 397; Douglas S. Massey and Mitchell L. Eggers, "The Ecology of Inequality: Minorities and the Concentration of Poverty, 1970–1980," *The American Journal of Sociology* 95, no. 5 (March 1990): 1153; William J. Wilson, *When Work Disappears: The World of the New Urban Poor* (New York: Knopf, 1996); Christopher Jencks, *Rethinking Social Policy: Race, Poverty, and the Underclass* (Cambridge, Mass.: Harvard University Press, 1992); Christopher Jencks and Susan Mayer, "The Social Consequences of Growing Up in a Poor Neighborhood," *Inner City Poverty in the United States,* ed. Laurence Lynn and Michael G. H. McGeary (Washington, D.C.: National Academy of Sciences Press, 1990), pp. 111–186.

3. Massey and Denton, *American Apartheid.*

4. Ibid., p. 13.

5. Ibid., p. 11.

6. Ibid., p. 87.

7. Richard Alba and John R. Logan, "Variations on Two Themes: Racial and Ethnic Patterns in the Attainment of Suburban Residence," *Demography* 28 (1991): 431–453; Richard Alba, John R. Logan, and Kyle Crowder, "White Neighborhoods and Assimilation: The Greater New York Region, 1980–1990," *Social Forces* 75 (1997): 883–909.

8. Massey and Denton, *American Apartheid,* p. 178.

9. Laurie Goodstein, "In Canarsie, Change Cuts on the Bias; Anger Attends Integration of Former White Ethnic Enclave in Brooklyn," *Washington Post,* August 9, 1991, p. A12; Melinda Henneberger, "Sharpton, 400 March in

Canarsie," *Newsday*, August 11, 1991, p. 4; Martin Gottlieb, "Bubble and Trouble in New York's Venerable Melting Pot," *New York Times*, August 29, 1991, pp. B1.

10. Massey and Denton, *American Apartheid*, pp. 131–132.

11. The fact that the neighborhood of Crown Heights is integrated does not mean that the schools are. The Jewish children do not attend public schools; they attend religious schools. The riots show that it is not at all an easy thing for the Hasidic Jews, the West Indians, and the African Americans to share the neighborhood.

12. Barry Bluestone, "The Inequality Express," *American Prospect* 20 (Winter 1995): 81–93, quotation from pp. 82–83.

13. Selma Cantor Berrol, *Growing Up American: Immigrant Children in America Then and Now* (New York: Twayne Publishers, 1995), p. 36.

14. Quoted in ibid., p. 55.

15. Gerald Jaynes and Robin Williams, eds., *A Common Destiny: Blacks and American Society* (Washington, D.C.: National Academy Press, 1989); James P. Smith and Finis R. Welch, "Black Economic Progress after Myrdal," *Journal of Economic Literature* 28, no. 2 (1989): 519–564; Reynolds Farley, ed., *State of the Union: America in the 1990's*, vol. 1, *Economic Trends* (New York: Russell Sage Foundation, 1995).

16. Saskia Sassen, "Economic Restructuring and the American City," *Annual Review of Sociology Annual* 16 (1990): 465–491; Frank Levy, *Dollars and Dreams: The Changing American Income Distribution* (New York: Russell Sage Foundation, 1987); Bennett Harrison and Barry Bluestone, *The Great U-turn: Corporate Restructuring and the Polarizing of America* (New York: Basic Books, 1988).

17. Douglas S. Massey and Deborah S. Hirst, "From Escalator to Hourglass: Changes in the U.S. Occupational Wage Structure, 1949–1989," *Social Science Research* 27 (1998): 51–71.

18. Bluestone, "Inequality Express," p. 83.

19. Ibid.

20. Ibid., p. 85.

21. The historian Joel Perlmann first suggested this image to me in a conversation we had on the topic.

22. Drop-out statistics come from New York City Board of Education, "The Cohort Report: Four Year Results for the Class of 1992 and Followups of the Classes of 1989, 1990 and 1991 and the 1991–1992 Annual Drop Out Rate" (Office of Educational Research, 1993). One of the guidance counselors at Eisenhower describes the process of "cooking the books": "On the books the graduation rate is sixty-five percent, but if you say how many kids who come in as ninth graders graduate as twelfth graders, it's much less than fifty percent. I

have a graduating class; on paper there are 373 students. My usual graduating class is 175; that is much less than fifty percent, and that is not even counting the ninth graders who did not make it into the eleventh grade. The January graduating group and the summer school group would bring in another thirty or forty, but a traditional four-year curriculum graduated 175 of them. So what they do is they play games with them and hold them in a different class, so they do not dampen the statistics. You see most kids take five or six years to graduate. So you don't want these holdovers in the eleventh grade, you don't want them in the senior class because your statistics are going to look bad. So all the schools in the city play the game; it is not just Eisenhower."

23. I was more frightened by the drunk student throwing the chairs than I was by a student who showed me his knife in a threatening way at Truman High. I had tried to scold that young man and asked him to be quiet and to move away from the area where I was interviewing. He obviously felt "disrespected." He did not say a word but slowly showed me a switchblade he had in his pocket. He did move away, but he stared at me the remainder of the period, and at one point, in full view of the librarian, he pulled out his knife and began carving in the wood of the library desk.

24. Susan Chira, "Teen-Agers, in a Poll, Report Worry and Distrust of Adults," *New York Times*, July 10, 1994, p. 16.

25. As Sam Roberts rightly points out, it is difficult to compare the two figures directly since South African students who do not make it to their senior year in high school don't get to take the exams, whereas a larger percentage of students in New York would at least get to take the exams. Nevertheless, the black-white disparities in New York are very disturbing. Roberts, "Low Test Scores Jar South African and US Blacks," *New York Times*, February 12, 1990, p. B1.

26. Thomas Sowell, "Three Black Histories," *Essays and Data on American Ethnic Groups*, ed. Sowell (Washington: The Urban Institute, 1978), pp. 7–64.

27. These perceptions of attitudinal differences will be discussed in the next chapter.

28. For a good discussion of how neighborhoods like Central Brooklyn decline quickly due to redlining, white flight, racial segregation, and the resulting concentration of poverty, see Massey and Denton, *American Apartheid*.

29. Sharon-Ann Gopaul-McNicol notes that in Jamaica only 25% of potential students obtain a free high school education. She estimates that in the other islands the percentage is 30–40%, "except for the very small islands, where the population is so small that all students receive a free high school education." The students who do not gain entrance to the academic high schools can attend programs that are mostly vocational. Gopaul-McNicol, *Working with West Indian Families* (New York: Guilford Press, 1993), p. 13.

8   IDENTITIES OF THE SECOND GENERATION

1. See, for instance, Joyce B. Justus, "West Indians in Los Angeles: Community and Identity," *Caribbean Immigration to the United States,* ed. Roy S. Bryce-Laporte and D. M. Mortimer, RIIES Occasional Papers No. 1 (Washington, D.C.: Smithsonian Institution Research Institute on Immigration and Ethnic Studies, 1976), and Constance R. Sutton and Elsa M. Cheney, *Caribbean Life in New York City: Sociocultural Dimensions* (New York: New York University Press, 1992).

2. Susan Buchanan Stafford, "The Haitians: The Cultural Meaning of Race and Ethnicity," *New Immigrants in New York,* ed. Nancy Foner (New York: Columbia University Press, 1987).

3. Tekle Woldemikael, *Becoming Black American: Haitians and American Institutions in Evanston, Illinois* (New York: AMS Press, 1989), p. 94.

4. Suzanne Michael, "Children of the New Wave Immigration," *West Indians in the United States of America: Some Theoretical and Practical Considerations,* ed. Aubrey W. Bonnett and G. Llewelyn Watson (Lanham, Md.: University Press of America, 1990).

5. Middle class was defined as having at least one parent with a college degree or a professional or business position. Working class was defined as having a parent with a low-skill job. Poor was defined as students whose parents were not currently employed.

6. John Ogbu, "Minority Status and Literacy in Comparative Perspective," *Daedelus* 119, no. 2 (Spring 1990): 141–168; Signithia Fordham, "Racelessness as a Factor in Black Students' School Success: Pragmatic Strategy or Pyrrhic Victory?," *Harvard Education Review* 58, no. 1 (1988): 54–84; Alejandro Portes and Min Zhou, "The New Second Generation: Segmented Assimilation and Its Variants (Interminority Affairs in the U.S.: Pluralism at the Crossroads)," *The Annals of the American Academy of Political and Social Science* 530 (November 1993): 74–97.

7. Fordham, "Racelessness."

8. Ibid., p. 67.

9. Elijah Anderson, *Streetwise: Race, Class and Change in an Urban Community* (Chicago: University of Chicago Press, 1990).

10. W. Lloyd Warner and Leo Srole, *The Social Systems of American Ethnic Groups* (New Haven: Yale University Press, 1945), p. 284.

11. Joe Feagin, "The Continuing Significance of Race—Antiblack Discrimination in Public Places," *American Sociological Review* 56, no. 1 (1991): 101–116.

9   IMMIGRANTS AND AMERICAN RACE RELATIONS

1. Economist George Borjas has argued this position in a number of publications based on empirical research, mostly using U.S. census data. Borjas

argues that more optimistic assessments of the future assimilation of immigrants such as those put forth by economist Barry Chiswick are flawed because they rely on cross-sectional data to make longitudinal arguments. Borjas, *Friends or Strangers: The Impact of Immigrants on the U.S. Economy* (New York: Basic Books, 1990). See also Chiswick, "The Effects of Americanization on the Earnings of Foreign Born Men," *Journal of Political Economy* 86, no. 5 (October 1978): 897–921.

2. Peter Skerry, *Mexican Americans: The Ambivalent Minority* (Cambridge: Harvard University Press, 1993).

3. Nathan Glazer and Daniel Patrick Moynihan, *Beyond the Melting Pot* (Cambridge: MIT Press and Harvard University Press, 1963).

4. Richard D. Alba, *Ethnic Identity: The Transformation of White America* (New Haven: Yale University Press, 1990); Mary C. Waters, *Ethnic Options: Choosing Identities in America* (Berkeley: University of California Press, 1990).

5. Charles Tilly, "Transplanted Networks," *Immigration Reconsidered: History, Sociology and Politics,* ed. Virginia Yans-McLaughlin (New York: Oxford University Press, 1990), pp. 79–95.

6. W. Lloyd Warner and Leo Srole, *The Social Systems of American Ethnic Groups* (New Haven: Yale University Press, 1945).

7. Min Zhou, "Growing Up American: The Challenge Confronting Immigrant Children and the Children of Immigrants," *Annual Review of Sociology* 23 (1997): 63–96; Min Zhou and Carl L. Bankston, "Social Capital and the Adaptation of the Second Generation: The Case of Vietnamese Youth in New Orleans," *International Migration Review* 28 (Winter 1994): 821–845; Alejandro Portes and Min Zhou, "The New Second Generation: Segmented Assimilation and Its variants (Interminority Affairs in the U.S.: Pluralism at the Crossroads)," *The Annals of the American Academy of Political and Social Science* 530 (November 1993): 74–97; Ruben Rumbaut, "Ties That Bind: Immigration and Immigrant Families in the United States," *Immigration and the Family: Research and Policy on U.S. Immigrants,* ed. Alan Booth, Ann C. Crouter, and Nancy Landale (New Jersey: Lawrence Erlbaum Publishers, 1997), 3–45; Rumbaut, "The Crucible Within: Ethnic Identity, Self Esteem, and Segmented Assimilation among Children of Immigrants," *International Migration Review* 28 (Winter 1994): 748–794.

8. Rumbaut, "The Crucible Within"; Carola Suarez-Orozco and Marcelo M. Suarez-Orozco, *Transformations: Immigration, Family Life, and Achievement Motivation among Latino Adolescents* (Stanford, Calif.: Stanford University Press, 1995); Marcelo M. Suarez-Orozco, "Becoming Somebody: Central American Immigrants in U.S. Inner-City Schools," *Anthropology and Education Quarterly* 18, no. 4 (1987): 287–299.

9. Raymond S. Franklin, *Shadows of Race and Class* (Minneapolis: University of Minnesota Press, 1991).

10. Joel Perlmann, "Reflecting the Changing Face of America: Multiracials, Racial Classification and American Intermarriage," Public Policy Brief No. 35 (The Jerome Levy Economics Institute of Bard College, 1997), p. 17.

11. There is a major problem with these Census Bureau projections in that they do not take into account intermarriage and assimilation. They are premised on the idea that ethnic and racial groups do not intermarry. With rising intermarriage among some of these groups, the potential for the group to either increase (if children of intermarried couples identify with the minority group) or decrease (if children identify as white non-Hispanic) is not taken into account in these projections. Indeed, the very meaning of these ethnic and racial groups could change significantly over time so that the ethnic and racial boundaries themselves might look very different. I have explored these issues in other writing. See William Alonso and Mary C. Waters, "The Future Composition of the American Population: An Illustrative Projection," paper presented at the Winter Meetings of the American Statistical Association (Fort Lauderdale, Fla.: January 1993); Mary C. Waters, "Multiple Ethnicities and Identity Choices: Some Implications for Race and Ethnic Relations in the United States," *We Are a People: Narrative in the Construction and Deconstruction of Ethnic Identity*, ed. Paul R. Spickard and W. Jeffrey Burroughs (Philadelphia: Temple University Press, 1999).

12. William A. Henry III, "What Will the United States Be Like When Whites Are No Longer a Majority?," *Time*, April 9, 1990.

13. Noel Ignatiev, *How the Irish Became White* (New York: Routledge, 1995), p. 41.

14. James Loewen, *The Mississippi Chinese: Between Black and White* (Prospect Heights, Ill.: Waveland Press, 1988), quotation appears in the frontmatter of the book.

15. Gary Gerstle, "European Immigrants, Ethnics, and American Identity, 1880–1950," paper presented at the conference on Becoming American/American Becoming (Sanibel Island, Fla.: Social Science Research Council, January 1996), p. 54.

16. Reynolds Farley, *The New American Reality: Who We Are, How We Got There, Where We Are Going* (New York: Russell Sage Foundation, 1996), pp. 264–265.

17. Paul Gilroy, "One Nation under a Groove: The Cultural Politics of Race and Racism in Britain," *Anatomy of Racism*, ed. David Theo Goldberg (Minneapolis: University of Minnesota Press, 1990), pp. 265–266. See also Anthony Appiah, "Race, Culture and Identity—Misunderstood Connections," in Anthony Appiah and Amy Gutmann, *Color Conscious: The Political Morality of Race* (Princeton: Princeton University Press, 1996), pp. 30–105.

18. Reuel Rogers, "Somewhere between Race and Ethnicity: Afro Caribbean Immigrants, African Americans, and the Politics of Group Identity," dissertation prospectus, Princeton University, 1996.

19. Gilroy notes that when culture is used to explain the place of groups in the social structure, the concept of culture is used in a very specific way: "not as something intrinsically fluid, changing, unstable and dynamic, but as a fixed property of social groups." Gilroy, "One Nation," p. 266.

20. Waters, *Ethnic Options.*

21. W. E. B. Du Bois, *The Souls of Black Folk* (1903; New York: Vintage Books, 1990).

APPENDIX

1. Mary C. Waters, *Ethnic Options: Choosing Identities in America* (Berkeley: University of California Press, 1990).

2. The best sources for advice about how to do field research are not "how to" books but the methodological sections of actual studies. These are much more common and, I believe, more truthful in ethnographic studies rather than in interview studies. Some excellent discussions of the dilemmas of fieldwork include Herbert J. Gans, *The Urban Villagers: Group and Class in the Life of Italian-Americans,* rev. ed. (New York: Free Press, 1982); Elliot Liebow, *Tally's Corner; a Study of Negro Streetcorner Men,* (Boston: Little, Brown, 1967) and *Tell Them Who I Am: The Lives of Homeless Women* (New York: Free Press, 1993); Jay MacLeod, *Ain't No Makin' It: Aspirations and Attainment in a Low-Income Neighborhood,* (Boulder: Westview Press, 1995); Judith Stacey, *Brave New Families: Stories of Domestic Upheaval in Late Twentieth Century America* (New York: Basic Books, 1990).

3. For a discussion of the ways in which the interests of "ethnic community" leaders diverge from the individuals in the group, see Mary C. Waters, "Ethnic and Racial Groups in the USA: Conflict and Cooperation," *Ethnicity and Power in the Contemporary World,* ed. Kumar Rupesinghe and Valery A. Tishkov (Tokyo: United Nations University Press, 1996), pp. 236–262.

4. I suspect most people who suggested taxi drivers also had the TV sitcom *Taxi* in mind. In that show there was a great deal of interaction among the drivers as they sat with the dispatcher waiting to go out in their cars. I have been assured by many taxi drivers that this is not the situation in real life.

5. The segregation of workplaces by gender was also a problem as I wanted equal numbers of men and women. Taxi drivers were all men. The hospital workers were disproportionately women. The sample I finally pulled from the food-service workers and the teachers did include more females than males. Since more West Indian women than men are employed, and since the immigrant flow is disproportionately female, I did not worry too much about this out-

come. It also seemed fitting to me that if there were to be a bias it be toward women, since we have had scores of studies of "immigrants" that have been based totally on the experiences of men.

6. The names of all of the companies I studied have been changed. I promised the managers who gave me permission to study them that I would not identify their companies.

7. I have since heard of ethnographers paying up to $100 to people to make themselves available for a series of life history interviews.

8. Liebow, *Tally's Corner;* Carol B. Stack, *All Our Kin* (New York: Basic Books, 1997).

9. Robert Merton has written the most sensible and well reasoned analysis of these issues that I have seen. Merton, "Insiders and Outsiders: A Chapter in the Sociology of Knowledge," *American Journal of Sociology* 28, no. 1 (July 1972): 9–47.

10. I am quite aware that this may change with publication of the book.

INDEX